Cross-Examination Handbook

ASPEN COURSEBOOK SERIES

CROSS-EXAMINATION HANDBOOK
Persuasion, Strategies, and Techniques

Second Edition

RONALD H. CLARK
Distinguished Practitioner in Residence
Seattle University School of Law

GEORGE R. (BOB) DEKLE, SR.
Legal Skills Professor
University of Florida School of Law

WILLIAM S. BAILEY
Professor from Practice
University of Washington School of Law

Wolters Kluwer

Published by Wolters Kluwer in New York.

Wolters Kluwer serves customers worldwide with CCH, Aspen Publishers, and Kluwer Law International products. (www.wolterskluwerlb.com)

To contact Customer Service, e-mail customer.service@wolterskluwer.com, call 1-800-234-1660, fax 1-800-901-9075, or mail correspondence to:

Wolters Kluwer
Attn: Order Department
PO Box 990
Frederick, MD 21705

Printed in the United States of America.

1 2 3 4 5 6 7 8 9 0

ISBN 978-1-4548-5200-1

Cross-examination handbook : persuasion, strategies, and techniques / Ronald H. Clark, Distinguished Practitioner in Residence, Seattle University School of Law; George R. (Bob) Dekle, Sr., Legal Skills Professor, University of Florida School of Law; William S. Bailey, Professor from Practice, University of Washington School of Law. -- Second Edition.
    pages cm
 Includes bibliographical references and index.
 ISBN 978-1-4548-5200-1 (alk. paper)
 1. Cross-examination--United States. I. Dekle, George R., 1948- author. II. Bailey, William S. (William Scherer), author. III. Title.
 KF8920.C57 2015
 347.73'75--dc23

                                                        2014042654

Cover: Dana Verkouteren was the courtroom artist in Senator Ted Stevens' trial.

ABOUT WOLTERS KLUWER LAW & BUSINESS

Wolters Kluwer Law & Business is a leading global provider of intelligent information and digital solutions for legal and business professionals in key specialty areas, and respected educational resources for professors and law students. Wolters Kluwer Law & Business connects legal and business professionals as well as those in the education market with timely, specialized authoritative content and information-enabled solutions to support success through productivity, accuracy and mobility.

Serving customers worldwide, Wolters Kluwer Law & Business products include those under the Aspen Publishers, CCH, Kluwer Law International, Loislaw, ftwilliam.com and MediRegs family of products.

CCH products have been a trusted resource since 1913, and are highly regarded resources for legal, securities, antitrust and trade regulation, government contracting, banking, pension, payroll, employment and labor, and healthcare reimbursement and compliance professionals.

Aspen Publishers products provide essential information to attorneys, business professionals and law students. Written by preeminent authorities, the product line offers analytical and practical information in a range of specialty practice areas from securities law and intellectual property to mergers and acquisitions and pension/benefits. Aspen's trusted legal education resources provide professors and students with high-quality, up-to-date and effective resources for successful instruction and study in all areas of the law.

Kluwer Law International products provide the global business community with reliable international legal information in English. Legal practitioners, corporate counsel and business executives around the world rely on Kluwer Law journals, looseleafs, books, and electronic products for comprehensive information in many areas of international legal practice.

Loislaw is a comprehensive online legal research product providing legal content to law firm practitioners of various specializations. Loislaw provides attorneys with the ability to quickly and efficiently find the necessary legal information they need, when and where they need it, by facilitating access to primary law as well as state-specific law, records, forms and treatises.

ftwilliam.com offers employee benefits professionals the highest quality plan documents (retirement, welfare and non-qualified) and government forms (5500/PBGC, 1099 and IRS) software at highly competitive prices.

MediRegs products provide integrated health care compliance content and software solutions for professionals in healthcare, higher education and life sciences, including professionals in accounting, law and consulting.

Wolters Kluwer Law & Business, a division of Wolters Kluwer, is headquartered in New York. Wolters Kluwer is a market-leading global information services company focused on professionals.

This ongoing labor of love is rededicated to our loved ones.

To Nancy, Brady, Soojin, Malachi, Riley, Clancy, Kara, Beatrice,
Samuel Colby, and Darren
Ronald H. Clark

To Lane, Laura, George, John, Jamie, John Jr., Jewel, and Star
George R. (Bob) Dekle, Sr.

To Sylvia, Rob, Mimy, and Lillian
William S. Bailey

Summary of Contents

Contents

CHAPTER 10
WITNESS CONTROL

CHAPTER 11
PREPARING THE WINNING CROSS

Acknowledgments

We express our gratitude to Professor Marilyn J. Berger and Professor John B. Mitchell, and we acknowledge their talent, scholarship, and most of all their contributions to this *Cross-Examination Handbook.* A significant share of what appears in this book is derived from the collaborative authorship of Marilyn J. Berger, John B. Mitchell, and Ronald H. Clark on pretrial and trial advocacy books.

Many thanks for the support and assistance provided through Seattle University School of Law: Dean Annette C. Clark; Dean for Finance and Administration Richard Bird; and law clerks Christopher J. Lewis and Erica M. Stirling.

We are thankful to the following individuals who provided their insights and editorial assistance to improve the book: Karen Townsend, District Court Judge and Director of Montana Law School's Advanced Trial Advocacy Program; Stewart P. Riley, attorney, Seattle, Washington; Michael J. Flaherty, First Assistant District Attorney in Erie County, New York; D. Shane Read, author of *Winning at Trial* and *Winning at Deposition;* and the Hills.

And, we want to express our appreciation to our friends and colleagues at Aspen Publishers: Vikram A. Savkar, Vice President and General Manager; Kris Clerkin, former Vice President and General Manager; Carol McGeehan, Publisher; Steve Errick, former Managing Director; Dana Wilson, our Managing Editor; John Devins, former Managing Editor; Christine Hannan, Managing Editor; Carmen Corral-Reid, Assistant Editorial Director; Michael A. Gregory, Director of New Markets; Renee Cote, Manuscript Editor; and Lisa Wehrle, Manuscript Editor for the first edition.

Cross-Examination Handbook

CHAPTER 1

INTRODUCTION TO BOOK & COMPANION WEBSITE

"In all criminal prosecutions, the accused shall enjoy the right . . . to be confronted with the witnesses against him."

— Sixth Amendment to the Constitution
of the United States

"It may be that in more than one sense [cross-examination] takes the place in our system which torture occupied in the medieval system of the civilians. Nevertheless, it is beyond any doubt the greatest legal engine ever invented for the discovery of truth. However difficult it may be for the layman, the scientist, or the foreign jurist to appreciate its wonderful power, . . . cross-examination, not trial by jury, is the great and permanent contribution of the Anglo-American system of law to improved methods of trial-procedure."

— 5 J. Wigmore, Evidence § 1367, p. 32
(J. Chadbourn rev. 1974)

I. INTRODUCTION

A. Overview

How important is cross-examination to trial work, and indeed, to justice itself? Our founding fathers felt strongly enough about cross-examination to imbed it into our Constitution in the confrontation clause. John Henry Wigmore, author of the enduring treatise *Wigmore on Evidence,* described cross as the "greatest legal engine ever invented for the discovery of the truth." More recently, Justice Stevens of the United States Supreme Court wrote:

> Even if one does not completely agree with Wigmore's assertion . . . in the Anglo-American legal system cross-examination is the principal means of undermining the credibility of a witness whose testimony is false or inaccurate.

United States v. Aslerno, 505 U.S. 317, 328, 112 S. Ct. 2503, 2511, 120 L. Ed. 2d 255, 266 (1992) (Stevens, J., dissenting).

Just as the importance of cross-examination to our system of justice is irrefutable, so is the difficulty of performing it well. Constructing a winning cross-examination, both an art and a science, has always been one of the most formidable challenges faced by any trial lawyer. In his seminal book on the subject over 100 years ago, Francis L. Wellman put it this way:

> Cross-examination . . . requires the greatest ingenuity; a habit of logical thought; clearness of perception in general; infinite patience and self control; power to read men's minds intuitively, to judge of their motives; ability to act with force and precision; a masterful knowledge of the subject matter itself; an extreme caution, and above all, the instinct to discover the weak point in the witness under examination.

The Art of Cross-Examination 28 (new ed. Book Jungle 2007; original ed. Simon & Schuster 1903).

While many things have changed over the intervening century since Wellman's time, the difficulty and importance of cross-examination remain constant. The stakes in many modern trials are considerably higher, putting trial advocates in both criminal and civil cases under great pressure to construct skillful cross-examinations. An essential purpose of this book is to look closely at both the art and science of cross-examination, translating the necessary elements into an easy-to-understand, user-friendly approach.

This book is designed for law students and for both inexperienced and experienced trial lawyers. It provides the building blocks for preparing and conducting winning cross-examinations. Too few trial lawyers are good at cross-examination because, in part, they do not fully prepare. This book is all about preparing for cross-examination. Like everything else in trial work, it is preparation that counts most, and this book will show you how. Any hard-working lawyer can master the winning cross-examination concepts, strategies, and techniques presented here.

Besides providing law, practical strategies, and skills in every chapter, *Cross-Examination Handbook: Persuasion, Strategies, and Techniques, Second Edition,* illustrates through cross-examination transcripts, closing arguments, and case examples. Some of these are famous cases, such as the *Scopes Trial, George Zimmerman* (acquitted of the murder of Trayvon Martin), *Dr. Conrad Murray* (convicted of the manslaughter of Michael Jackson), *O. J. Simpson, Enron, Senator Stevens,* and *Bruno Hauptmann* (convicted of murdering the Lindbergh baby) trials. Others are not. All our editorial choices have been motivated by the same goal—to make cross-examination come alive. We want you to feel the same sense of excitement and creative challenge in constructing winning cross-examinations in your own cases that we have in ours. This book also covers the necessary foundation of ethical, legal, and courtroom custom boundaries of a proper cross-examination.

B. The Book

Cross-Examination Handbook begins with three chapters devoted to planning and constructing a winning cross-examination: Chapter 2 explains the purposes of cross and building a case theory; Chapter 3 covers concession-seeking cross and introduces basic impeachment concepts; and Chapter 4 discusses how to translate facts and ideas into persuasive questioning strategies. Chapter 5 shows you how to bring the cross-examination alive in the courtroom and make it memorable with visuals. Chapters 6 through 8 further explore impeachment, one of the most critical components of a successful cross-examination. Chapter 9 concentrates on the cross-examiner's character and conduct in trial. Chapter 10 focuses on controlling the unruly witness. Chapter 11 starts with further general witness preparation advice and then moves on to expert witnesses. Chapter 12 is dedicated to strategies, methods, and skills needed for cross-examining experts. Chapter 13 discusses the problems presented by adverse witnesses, deponents, forgetters, interview refusers, and more. Chapter 14 defines the ethical and legal bounds of cross and explains how to avoid and meet objections to cross-examination questions. Finally, Chapter 15 introduces the cases and assignments that are designed to give you experience in planning and performing cross-examinations.

Accompanying these chapters are checklists that provide quick reminders of the suggested approaches to the various strategies and skills.

II. WEBSITE — ASSIGNMENTS, CASE FILES, ACTORS' GUIDE, AND SUPPLEMENTARY MATERIAL

A. Assignments

Cross-Examination Handbook comes with a companion website, www.aspen lawschool.com/books/clark_crossexam2e, containing all the materials necessary for role-play performance exercises with cross-examination strategies and skills. The website contains both assignments and four case files. They can be used by students in law school trial advocacy classes and clinics as well as by practicing lawyers and in continuing legal education workshops that involve the attendees in role-playing exercises.

To access the materials on the website go to www.aspenlawschool.com/ books/clark_crossexam2e and enter the access code that's on the card that came with this book.

Chapter 15 provides summaries of two civil and two criminal cases along with a sample of the assignments. For each of the four cases, there are ten or more assignments. The assignments correspond to chapters of this book and provide practical experience in the areas covered by the chapters. For example, Chapter 7 covers how to impeach a witness with a deposition; assignments and Case File materials are provided so that law students and practicing lawyers can perform such an impeachment. The versatility of the materials allows the teacher to select as many or as few of the assignments for the students to perform as the instructor wishes to cover.

Each assignment comes with suggested reading, which the instructor may assign. For instance, if *Cross-Examination Handbook* is adopted as a supplement in a trial advocacy class, the instructor may assign readings in *Cross-Examination Handbook* to which the assignment is cross-referenced with suggested and selected readings for each assignment.

B. Case Files

The assignments are performed using the Case Files on the website. The Case Files contain exhibits, witness statements, legal documents, photographs, diagrams, and other materials necessary to carry out the assignments. The cases involve both criminal and civil cases, including an Internet predator case, an automobile accident case, an employment discrimination and retaliation case, and a murder case.

C. Actors' Guide

To make the skills development assignments as realistic as possible, the Actors' Guide provided to your instructor on the website, www.aspenlawschool .com/books/clark_crossexam2e, contains information for those in the class playing witness roles. The background materials will provide personal history and instructions on how each witness is to behave and respond.

D. Supplementary Materials

The website for the *Cross-Examination Handbook* contains a wide variety of supplementary material. See www.aspenlawschool.com/books/clark _crossexam2e.

PURPOSES OF CROSS & THE TOTAL TRIAL APPROACH

". . . But this wasn't going to be an easy case. We had to show egregious monopolistic practices and undercut the credibility of their witnesses. I was thinking about what we were going to do when their witnesses came on. That was going to be the challenge of the cross-examination: to get somebody who has every incentive to tell a story that is not helpful to you to reveal the truth."

> —**David Boies** commenting on the
> Microsoft Antitrust case,
> *Wired,* August 2005

I. PURPOSES OF CROSS-EXAMINATION

Cross-examinations are not conducted in isolation. They are part of the total trial plan, the ultimate goal of which is a favorable verdict. You want the judge and the jury to adopt your case theory and reject that of the other side. Your cross always must keep that objective in mind, calculating the persuasive effect of any strategic move on the target audience. We use the phrase "winning cross-examination" throughout this book as a reminder that the goal is to win the desired verdict, and a winning cross is one that is designed and conducted to produce that result.

Without a workable case theory, cross-examination is as worthless as a car without an engine. A case theory is the story you tell the jury. It guides every aspect of trial planning and performance. The case theory is critical to a winning cross, which provides a powerful opportunity to communicate it to the jury as part of the total trial approach.

The purposes of cross are to preserve and build upon your case theory or demolish the other side's, and in this way persuade the jury. The seminal book on cross-examination is *The Art of Cross-Examination* by Francis Wellman (new ed. Book Jungle 2007, original ed. Simon & Schuster 1903). Contributing author and renowned trial lawyer Emory R. Buckner observed in it that "more cross-examinations are suicidal than homicidal." Buckner's explanation for the frequency of disastrous results is the basic failure to understand that the purpose of cross is "to catch truth, ever an elusive fugitive."

This chapter offers a blueprint for constructing a sound case theory based on the cross-examiner's truth. Also, we will show you how to attack the flaws and vulnerabilities in your opponent's case theory. In the next chapter, we will explain how the case theory guides the identification and selection of the content of your cross.

II. CASE THEORY AS A BLUEPRINT

Developing a case theory is like building a house. The attorney is both the architect who designs it and the contractor who constructs it. The case theory has two interrelated components: the *legal theory* and the *factual theory*.

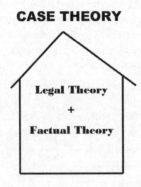

CASE THEORY

Legal Theory
+
Factual Theory

The best way to understand the construction and use of a case theory is to present it in the context of a case. While there are slight differences in application of the case theory development approach between criminal and civil trials, we will explore the differences as we go along. We start with the civil *Samba Sports Drowning* wrongful death case. In the next chapter we introduce the criminal *Convenience Store* robbery case. These two cases are not purely hypothetical; rather they are derived from actual cases.

Like two threads, these same two cases are woven through Chapter 3, The Content & Concession-Seeking Cross, and Chapter 4, Constructing the Cross. This continuity should give you a full understanding of the three stages of creating a winning cross-examination: (1) developing the case theory; (2) using the case theories of all parties to identify content; and (3) structuring that content of cross to be effective in telling that story.

III. PLAINTIFF'S COUNSEL AS A BUILDER: CIVIL CASE ILLUSTRATION—*SAMBA SPORTS DROWNING*

Imagine you are the lawyer representing plaintiff James Young in the *Samba Sports Drowning* wrongful death civil case, which we use as an illustration of how to formulate a case theory that will serve as a guide in planning a winning cross-examination. The case is a wrongful death action against the boat manufacturer, based on product liability. Besides damages claims for the loss of value to Lindsay Young's estate, the complaint also alleges negligent infliction of emotional distress on behalf of her father. Your legal theory for James Young is that he was a foreseeable plaintiff—a family member who was present at the scene at the time of the incident or arrived shortly thereafter—and experienced emotional distress with objective symptoms. The facts of the case are as follows:

Samba Sports Drowning Wrongful Death Case

On a summer's night, James Young's 21-year-old daughter, Lindsay, drowned in Diamond Lake after inhaling carbon monoxide fumes around the swimmer's platform on a Samba in-board ski boat. Lindsay disappeared from the surface of the water after pushing off to swim to shore. Her friends frantically began searching for her when she didn't resurface.

An excellent athlete and swimmer, Lindsay was not wearing a life jacket on the boat that night. Lindsay's friends promptly called the authorities to assist in their search for her, as well as her father. James Young was there in five minutes, arriving at approximately 3:00 a.m. Police cars, an ambulance, and the fire department were already at the scene. At approximately 6:00 a.m., rescuers located Lindsay's body beneath the surface and attached a buoy to it. On a dock 100 yards away, Mr. Young

---

continued ▶

could see his daughter's lifeless body pulled into the search and rescue boat and then loaded into an ambulance by the shore.

The cause of Lindsay's death was attributed to drowning from a lethal dose of carbon monoxide. In the years prior this event, the ski boat industry had learned of the dangers of carbon monoxide for riders in the back of the boat. While industry members made no specific mention of carbon monoxide risks to the public, most manufacturers put a small decal by the stern of their boats, making a general warning against being on or swimming near the platform when the engine was running.

Aaron Weholt of Legal Media, Seattle, Washington

The plaintiff's lawyer in a civil case and the prosecutor in a criminal case are similar in that both have the burden of proof, which requires them to build a case with the evidence necessary to convince a judge or jury. They are builders by trade. They start with the law and the facts, building these into a persuasive story with which their burden of proof can be met and their client wins.

The formal process starts when counsel reveals their legal theory in the civil complaint or criminal charging document. If the case later goes to trial, the opening statement of the prosecutor or plaintiff's counsel demonstrates the trial factual story supporting the legal theory. During the case in chief, counsel builds the case with the witnesses' direct testimony and exhibits. During the defense's case, the prosecutor or plaintiff's counsel can build and support the plaintiff's case by gaining concessions during cross-examinations. Finally, in closing, counsel can close the circle begun during cross by arguing that the concessions by defense witnesses support the plaintiff's case and how the cross-examinations discredit the defense's case.

A. Legal Theory

The civil plaintiff's burden of proof is the preponderance of the evidence standard, as opposed to the prosecution's higher beyond-a-reasonable-doubt burden. The actual legal elements of proof for civil matters often are in the same generic locations as for criminal cases: court decisions, statutes, and regulations. However, the actual elements of proof are different. Proving murder against a criminal defendant is very different than wrongful death against a civil one. There are no common law crimes, only statute-based ones. A prosecutor is limited to the legal theories found in statutes. Negligence in civil cases may well be defined by common law elements of proof set forth in court decisions, as well as legislative statutory enactments.

For civil plaintiffs, a legal theory must support the claim for relief, which can take the form of damages for negligence in the *Samba Sports Drowning* case. The negligence claim for wrongful death places the burden on the plaintiff to prove these elements of negligence: (1) duty of care; (2) breach; (3) proximate cause of injury; and (4) compensable harm.

B. Factual Theory

The factual theory is constructed from the mass of evidence that either already exists or is likely to be available with further investigation. The factual theory has two subparts: (1) *sufficient* to support the legal theory and (2) *persuasive*. It can be viewed as follows:

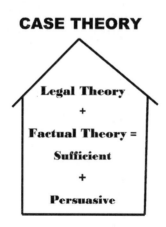

CASE THEORY

Legal Theory

+

Factual Theory =

Sufficient

+

Persuasive

Factually Sufficient

In order to be able to survive a motion for summary judgment and try the *Samba Sports Drowning* case to a jury, as plaintiff's counsel, you must demonstrate facts that prove a prima facie case of negligence. As to the products liability claim on behalf of Lindsay Young's estate, you will need facts that show that the defendant manufacturer knew or had reason to know of the carbon monoxide harm, but did not warn consumers or take engineering measures to fix the problem. Proof in the plaintiff's liability case can take the form of corporate or industry documents, expert testimony, or fact witnesses. Mr. Young's negligent infliction of emotional distress claim will be based on how he has been affected by Lindsay's drowning, coupled with the testimony of a psychologist that he suffers from anxiety and depression stemming from the event.

Persuasive

Plaintiff's counsel starts with a factually sufficient story, but it is not enough to mechanically introduce evidence that is sufficient in supporting the legal theory. A jury cannot be predicted to decide in a purely logical way because it is filled with human emotions and beliefs shaped by families of origin, communities, and life experiences. The group dynamic makes a logic-prediction model even more difficult, as the whole is greater than the sum of its parts. Jury deliberation is a process of exchange and compromise between the competing perspectives of the jurors.

You must convince the jury to render the verdict that you are seeking by reaching both their hearts and their minds. As plaintiff's counsel, your goal in the *Samba Sports Drowning* case is to develop a persuasive factual presentation that will convince a jury to find for your client. The same five components that we discussed with regard to criminal prosecutions apply here: (1) a narrative; (2) about human values and needs; (3) with a powerful human interest theme; (4) that is credible; and (5) supported by a sufficient quantity of evidence.

1. A Narrative Story

Behavioral scientists have determined that the human brain has a preference for absorbing information in narrative form. Professor Dan P. McAdams of Northwestern University has spent his career studying stories and their effect on human beings and has concluded, "We find that these narratives guide behavior in every moment, and frame not only how we see the past but how we see ourselves in the future. Benedict Carey, *This Is Your Life,* N.Y. Times, May 22, 2007. Jury research has refined this principle even further, demonstrating that evidence presented in story form is more persuasive than reciting facts outside of a narrative construct. Nancy Pennington & Reid Hastie, *Cognitive Theory of Juror Decision-Making: The Story Model,* 13 Cardozo L. Rev. 519, 542-43 (1991).

Even mathematicians recognize that storytelling is important to winning a case at trial. Leonard Mlodinow, in *The Drunkard's Walk—How Randomness Rules Our Lives* 29 (Penguin Books 2008), tells of an experiment where different juries were given identical facts, but with different sides telling a more vivid story. In each case the jury voted with the side that told the more vivid story.

In that cross-examination has the potential to sway a jury more than any other source of information in a trial, thinking of cross in story form increases its persuasive effect. As the trial lawyer, you need to ask yourself, "What is my case story, what is the story's moral, and how do I present this story to a jury most effectively in my cross-examination?"

What is a story? It is defined as the telling of an event or events in narrative form, which communicates some information about the human condition. Every good story has a dialectic, a struggle between two or more opposing forces. Just as people need to root for one side or the other in an athletic contest, so do they with the characters in a story. Usually people identify with the hero, who struggles against the villain, with the odds stacked against her. The hero must be a symbolic representation of the audience in some way.

Human values are an integral part of the story. There is always a good versus evil component in a persuasive trial story, the forces of dark against the forces of light. Some of the best known experiments in psychology attempt to establish just how moral human beings really are. While the academic debate continues, certain things are clear:

> . . . People's ethical decision making is strongly driven by gut emotions rather than by rational, analytic thought . . . We have gut feelings of what is right and what is wrong.

Sharon Begley, *Adventures in Good and Evil,* Newsweek, April 25, 2009, at 32-33, 40-41.

The essential purpose of cross-examination is to tell your persuasive story to the jury. You want to polarize the jury, compel it to take sides in the story, to identify with your side of the case. The best way to accomplish this is by taking the moral high ground, structuring the cross-examination story in such a way that the divide between good and evil in the story is clearly identified.

However, ABA Rule of Professional Conduct 3.4 and case law impose limitations on this good-versus-evil storytelling approach. RPC 3.4 states:

> A lawyer shall not: . . .

> (e) In trial . . . state a personal opinion as to the justness of a cause, the credibility of a witness, the culpability of a civil litigant or the guilt or innocence of an accused.

Therefore, counsel must guard against ever expressing a personal opinion that could be interpreted as violating this Rule.

Further, under case law, name-calling or making pejorative remarks about a party can result in reversal as is shown in *Negative Characterization or Description of Defendant, by Prosecutor During Summation of Criminal Trial, as Ground for Reversal, New Trial, or Mistrial—Modern Cases,* Thomas M. Fleming, 88 A.L.R. 4th 8. Name calling a defendant in a criminal case has been held as reversible error because it is intended to inflame the passion and prejudice of the jury. While counsel must be mindful of these ethical boundaries, no prohibition exists against crafting a case-theory story of good versus evil and then telling that story through cross because that story is the truth as you contend the facts reveal.

There is a reason why fairy tales such as Sleeping Beauty or Little Red Riding Hood have survived for centuries. In every one, there is a struggle between good and evil, with the innocent put in harm's way, creating suspense and dramatic tension in the story. We, the audience, identify with Sleeping Beauty, not the evil fairy who puts her under a spell. The villains in each fairy tale are carefully drawn, with evident cruelty.

While this may sound simplistic at first, the fairy tale structure is helpful in coming up with a narrative story in both criminal and civil cases. The main objective of the narrative story is for the jury to think of your client as the princess or prince and the opposing party as the wicked witch. Although you won't actually address the jury using these terms, the fairy tale analysis gives a lawyer guidance in how to draw the basic story lines, as well as the underlying tone.

In the wrongful death case of Lindsay Young, you, as plaintiff's counsel, could start the process of brainstorming to develop the narrative story by thinking of the facts of her death as a moral, imperative-filled fairy tale. If you were to reduce the moral dynamics of the story to a classic fairy tale format, it might read something like this:

Narrative Story

Fairy Tale

Once upon a time, in a faraway land, there was a kind, virtuous, and lovely young woman. She was close to her family, had many friends, and dreams of a bright future.

There was a powerful prince in that same land who thought only of himself, preoccupied with his wealth and privilege.

The prince loved to go places in a hurry, ordering his servants to drive his carriage through the streets at full speed. Though he knew this could be dangerous to people on the road, he expected them to hear him coming and get out of the way.

One spring day, the virtuous young woman walked along the road in the sunshine. She didn't see or hear the prince's carriage coming up behind her until it was too late. She was run over and killed. The prince told the gathering crowd, "It was not my fault. She should have gotten out of the way."

This adaptation of the fairy tale structure has all the ingredients of the familiar good-versus-evil story. As the plaintiff's lawyer, this tale of the arrogant, greedy prince generates the kind of feelings you want the jury to end up having about the defendant manufacturer at the end of the case.

You could break the *Samba Sports Drowning* wrongful death story down into two parts reflecting the company's moral failure: (1) a lack of caring about the lives of others and (2) a preoccupation with money and power. Like the fairy tale, this narrative structure is designed to lead to the ultimate moral of the story: the defendant company had reason to know that product users like Lindsay might die, but, like the prince in our fairy tale, left it to them to get out of the way.

2. About Human Values and Needs

As mentioned previously, a persuasive factual story must be about human values that the jurors share, such as honesty, fair treatment, safety, and family. These values are critical to swaying a jury. The plaintiff's story in this case is about a tragic loss. Unlike Sleeping Beauty, Lindsay Young cannot be brought back to life. Numerous behavioral science studies have proven how parents of children who are killed, at any age, suffer for the rest of their lives. Mr. Young's loss fits right into the general spectrum of values in Maslow's pyramid. We can recognize the importance of losing a family member or loved one through our own connections to the people in our lives.

The real challenge in the telling of this story is to set up the defendant manufacturer so that the jury thinks of it in the same terms as the reckless prince in the fairy tale. The fact that Lindsay Young died is not enough. There has to be moral culpability on the part of the defendant.

3. Human Interest Theme

Trial work is storytelling. To bring the story to life, counsel will want to tell a story about a real human being, someone that the jury can care about. In a civil case, the person is usually the lawyer's client; in a criminal case, the prosecutor's story ordinarily is about the victim and the defense's story is about the defendant.

Over 2,300 years after it was written, Aristotle's *The Poetics* remains one of the defining works of the elements of a story. Aristotle (with our annotations) broke down the structure of dramatic storytelling into six parts:

1. Plot ....The Sequence of Events
2. Character ....Protagonist (your client); Antagonist (the opposing party); Supporting Cast (witnesses); Audience (the jury)
3. Thought.................Theme of the Story
4. Diction ....Words Used to Tell the Story
5. Spectacle...............The Visuals That Accompany the Words
6. Song ....The Music or Orchestration

With the exception of song, which is more appropriate to a play or a movie, the other five elements of *The Poetics* help a lawyer to craft the trial story. With each new case, a lawyer must ask: What is the plot? Who are the characters? What is the theme? What words or phrases best tell the story? What visuals will enhance the words as the story unfolds in the courtroom?

While both prosecutors and civil plaintiff's lawyers must establish points of identification between alleged victims and the jury members, civil trials give lawyers much greater latitude in the crafting and telling of the trial stories. The success of the plaintiff's wrongful death case against Samba Sports depends heavily on making Lindsay Young a likeable, sympathetic, and worthy person, bringing her hopes and dreams for her life into the courtroom. The jurors will have to know her as well as they would their own daughter or sister, valuing her life in the same way. This cannot be done by appeals for sympathy, but rather, by bringing Lindsay's humanity into the trial story. Part of this powerful human interest theme can be developed from the people that knew Lindsay: family, teachers, friends, employers, and her pastor. Photos and videos that show her doing the same kinds of things as the jurors do also build the human interest.

The most compelling human interest theme in the *Samba Sports Drowning* case is that of a promising young life ended before she had a chance to fulfill her dreams. As the family's lawyer, you look for ways to make this real. Lindsay Young kept a diary over the years, with a number of passages that communicate who she was as a person:

> I have thought many times about the things I want my life to be, the "might" and the "could" in my future. I am lucky to have a family that supports and encourages me to reach for my dreams, in a world where others starve and suffer every day.
>
> Memories of my family and friends are deep within me, they always will be there. Many times the memories make me want to laugh or smile, but sometimes they are hard ones I'd rather forget. It is important to me to be a leader, trying to do something good.
>
> While I want to be successful, it has to be in a way that helps others and contributes to making the world a better place.

In any civil personal injury or wrongful death case, evidence about the nature and quality of the plaintiff's life is relevant to damages, giving plaintiff's counsel wide latitude. This requires evidence about the plaintiff's life. Besides offering evidence about decedent Lindsay Young in this case, plaintiff's counsel also has to describe the nature of the parent-child relationship here and the effects on Mr. Young from what he saw the night that his daughter died. By contrast, in a murder trial, evidence about the impact on family members of the death of the victim would be inadmissible as irrelevant to the charge.

4. Credible Story

The trial story must be believable to be persuasive. Jurors take their job in the courtroom very seriously and will not engage in the same kind of suspension of disbelief as when they go to see a movie. They expect a lawyer to present a believable trial story that comports with their common sense, cultural values, and experiences in everyday life.

Not only does the story itself have to be credible, but the witnesses who tell it in court have to be believable, backed up by exhibits and demonstrative evidence. Much of the evidence supporting plaintiff's story in the *Samba Sports Drowning* case is credible and beyond dispute, such as the circumstances of Lindsay's drowning, the cause of her death, the effect upon her family as well as the design and manufacture of the boat, the marketing, and a failure to adequately warn customers. Plaintiff's counsel will want to prove that Simon Howell, the CEO of Samba Sports, Inc., was so callous as to ignore his obligation to warn customers and users about the risks of potential carbon monoxide poisoning, becoming a real-life version of the arrogant prince in the hypothetical fairy tale based on the facts of this case. Plaintiff's counsel, as you shall see in the next two chapters, can use cross-examination of Mr. Howell to tell the story of his failure to warn the public of the dangers from carbon monoxide of which he and other members of his industry were aware.

5. Sufficient Quantity of Evidence

Because this is a civil case, plaintiff must prove each of the elements of the claims by a preponderance of the evidence. Even before this case goes to trial, the defense will bring a motion asking for summary judgment as a matter of law. For example, to qualify for a claim of negligent infliction of emotional distress against the defendant manufacturer, James Young will have to show that the risk to him was foreseeable and should have been known to the manufacturer. Also, he must prove that he suffers from an emotional condition manifested by objective symptoms.

IV. DEFENSE COUNSEL AS A BUILDER: CIVIL CASE ILLUSTRATION—*SAMBA SPORTS DROWNING*

Criminal and civil defense lawyers do not have to prove anything, unless they take on the burden of an affirmative defense. But not having the burden of proof does not mean that criminal and civil defense lawyers can just sit back and say, "My client didn't do it." A simple denial is not enough, particularly if the prosecutor or civil plaintiff lawyer puts on a persuasive case. Once this happens, the balance tips, with the jury looking to the defense to explain why things are not as they appear to be. What then?

Effective defense counsel does not wait and then scramble at the last minute to piece together an ad hoc story. From the beginning, defense carefully builds its own story to explain what happened, with a very different spin than the opposition.

Besides poking holes in the proof of the other side, the defense tends to focus on different aspects of the events at issue. In the *Samba Sports Drowning* wrongful death case, the background setting of 20 year olds at a late-night summer party, with no life preservers on the boat and twice the number of passengers for the boat's rated capacity raises questions about what caused the drowning.

The defense story has to expose the prosecution's or plaintiff's legal and factual theories as simplistic, misguided, and full of holes, despite a surface plausibility. The specter of alternative explanations and missing parties is raised throughout the defense case.

1. A Narrative Story

In the *Samba Sports Drowning* case, the defense cannot appear to be callous or unsympathetic, as the death of a likeable, promising young woman is a truly tragic event. However, this cannot be allowed to prevent the defense from raising the tough questions about who was to blame for what happened.

In the first instance, the defense has to humanize their corporate client, Samba Sports, Inc., the manufacturer of the boat that Lindsay Young was on that night. This is somewhat difficult, in that a corporation is an artificial business entity created for the purpose of limited liability. Many jurors are inclined to think, "Corporations don't really care about people; all they look at is the bottom line."

The best way to present a corporation in a positive light is to develop the story of how it came to be, telling of the people who brought the company to life and their vision for the product or service. This requires picking out a member or members of the defendant company who can put a positive face on it for the jury. In the *Samba Sports Drowning* case, this message can be delivered through CEO Simon Howell and his brother-in-law Paul Simmons, who co-founded the company. They will testify that the company was founded upon a dedication to quality, value, safety, and constant improvement.

2. About Human Needs and Values

The defense approach to the human-needs-and-values part of the story emphasizes a very different aspect: personal responsibility for one's own actions. From our earliest beginnings, we human beings have banded together into groups and societies, cooperating with one another for the common good, realizing the greater security and safety that comes in numbers. For our cave dwelling ancestors, this included hunting animals for food and defending against enemies. In later agrarian societies, working together to grow crops for the community food supply became the main focus. Whatever form a society might take, hunter-gatherer or agrarian, the bottom line has been that everybody must do their part.

In modern life, it is no longer necessary to band together to fend off saber-toothed tigers, and most of us don't work the land beyond mowing our lawns. But the personal responsibility aspect of society that has been with us since the beginning remains. It is this human need and value that the defense in a civil case often will organize their story around. In the *Samba Sports Drowning* case, through the defense presentation and cross-examinations, defense counsel will elicit testimony that Robert Gilligan, Lindsay Young's high school friend, owned and operated the boat and made a number of errors of judgment. First, he loaded twice the number of people on board that Samba Sports Inc. posted as the maximum capacity. Second, he had no life jackets or running lights. Third, he operated the engine when people were in the back, despite a warning not to do so. The defense theme highlighted in cross is that a party boat full of young people is a recipe for disaster.

3. Human Interest Theme

Having injected the societal value of personal responsibility into the story, with the objective of educating the jury about another explanation for what really caused Lindsay Young's death, the defense in the *Samba Sports Drowning* case now can take this one step further, raising the powerful human interest theme of personal choices. While it is a somewhat delicate matter to blame the victim for her own demise, particularly one as appealing as Lindsay Young, jurors try to scrupulously follow the judge's instructions that they are not to let sympathy or prejudice enter into their verdict.

A powerful human interest theme for the defense in the *Samba Sports Drowning* case is that the defendant made personal choices that led to the tragedy. During cross-examination of the witnesses, defense counsel can emphasize the bad choices she made. Through a concession-seeking cross, counsel can tell the story of Lindsay's choices which consist of: not wearing a life jacket; being out late at night on an overcrowded boat; and staying at the back of the boat for almost two hours even though a warning was posted right in front of her on the swim platform not to be there when the engine was running. Additional bad-choice concessions include that after swimming for an extended period, cold and tired, Lindsay made the bad decision to push off from the boat and swim alone to the dock.

4. Credible Story

Defense counsel in the *Samba Sports Drowning* case will do a careful fact investigation, taking statements and/or depositions from everyone who was present on the night Lindsay Young died. From this, counsel will be able to build a credible story in support of its themes of personal responsibility and poor choices. While the plaintiff will argue that the overloaded boat was not a proximate cause of the harm to Lindsay, this undisputed fact tends to back up the defense story to some degree, that the group that night were not responsible boat users.

The defense also will bring credibility to its story by carefully selecting experts to discuss the engineering aspects of the case. This ski boat complied with all Coast Guard safety requirements and industry standards, which supports the defense narrative story that Samba Sports, Inc. put pride and professionalism into its products. The defense engineering experts will describe how it is impossible to add a catalytic converter to the inboard engine, leaving the warning by the stern as the only reasonable alternative, which the company did.

5. Sufficient Quantity of Evidence

In any civil case involving the death of a human being, given the large potential exposure, the defense puts enormous time and effort into identifying and developing evidence, then combining it into the story. Expert witnesses are a critical part of this process, adding a technical dimension to the defense evidence presented to the lay jury. Scientific or industry studies are commonly discussed, with the use of charts, graphs, and blow-ups containing this information used in conjunction with the experts. While the defense must be selective, it knows that the more quality information it presents, the more difficulty the opposition will have in getting the jury to hold against their client.

V. DEMOLISHER—POINTS OF VULNERABILITY AS GUIDES

A. Points of Vulnerability

Wrecking-ball assaults on the opposing party's case theory concentrate on one or two points of vulnerability:

1. *Persuasive insufficiency.* Impeachment of a witness's credibility is a primary source of opposition attack. Could she see what she claims from where she was standing? Does he have any physical or emotional incapacity affecting his credibility? Is there any bias that caused him to shade his testimony one way or the other?
2. *Factual insufficiency.* Are the facts sufficient to support the legal theory as a matter of law? For example, in the *Samba Sports Drowning* case, is the plaintiff unable to produce objective evidence that James Young is suffering a diagnosable emotional condition?

B. Defense Counsel as a Demolisher

In contrast to the prosecutor's or plaintiff's counsel's role as a builder, defense counsel's trade, by necessity, is to be a demolisher. While the prosecutor or plaintiff's counsel attempts to build a case with testimony and exhibits, defense counsel strives to destroy it. Building upon diligent investigation and careful strategic thought, where potentially successful angles of attack are identified, cross-examination is a major piece of equipment that can inflict the damage on the opponent's case. Here, we offer two examples of how defense cross-examinations can attack case theory on persuasion and factual insufficiency grounds.

Persuasive Insufficiency

This type of attack focuses on the prosecutor's or civil plaintiff's inability to convince a jury of its legal theory. Even if technically sufficient to be a prima facie case, the jury should find that the prosecution or civil plaintiff has failed to prove one or more elements by the applicable burden of proof. For instance, in a civil case, unpersuasive expert testimony might cross over the line into junk science. The failure of this proof could, in turn, lead to the collapse of the proximate cause between a car accident and the claimed physical injuries.

One attack is intended to expose the unbelievable nature of the plaintiff's/ prosecution's story. Jurors use common sense and common experience to filter and sort information, comparing the stories they hear in a trial with real life. They will reject stories that don't make sense to them.

Jurors are also receptive to arguments regarding the credibility of the prosecution's or civil plaintiff's proof. They fully understand that their job includes determining whether the burden of proof has been met, evaluating the credibility of the witnesses. Therefore, defense counsel will scrutinize the plaintiff's story to detect flaws in it and seek any concessions based on those flaws.

One possible approach to detecting these deficiencies is first to imagine the perfect prosecution or civil plaintiff's case. Then, defense counsel can compare and contrast the perfect case with the actual facts. With this analysis, any deficiencies in the prosecution's or civil plaintiff's case are revealed, with a defense story and argument built upon them.

Assume you are defense counsel in a convenience store robbery case. The perfect prosecution case on identity would be where the robber's face was fully visible, under a bright light with enough time for the witness to memorize his face. On cross, as defense counsel, you could seek concessions from the victim that these ideal conditions did not exist at the time of the robbery. In closing you could compare these facts with those of the prosecution's case and argue that the prosecution has not proven the defendant guilty beyond a reasonable doubt as follows:

Defense Summation—Credibility of the Story

A Robbery Case

We've talked about the fallibility of eyewitness identification. Was the robber's face fully visible? No. The victim told you that the robber had his hat pulled down over part of his face. Was the robber standing in a well-lighted place so the victim got a good look at his face? No. The victim told you, quite candidly, that the light bulb nearest the counter was burnt out. Was the victim able to get a good look at the robber? No. As he conceded, the robbery took a matter of moments and most of that time he was concentrating on the gun barrel pointed at his face.

Factual Insufficiency

Attacks on the factual sufficiency of the plaintiff's legal theory center on the failure to prove all the required elements of a prima facie case. For example, due to a successful motion suppressing the victim's identification of the defendant, the only evidence in the convenience store robbery case is that the defendant was seen within a block of the store.

In the *Samba Sports Drowning* wrongful death case, defense counsel could attack Mr. Young's claim for negligent infliction of emotional distress because of when he arrived at the scene on the night of his daughter's death.

Factual Insufficiency

The Samba Sports Drowning
Wrongful Death Case

Diamond Lake, where Lindsay Young drowned, is in the state of Major. The tort of negligent infliction of emotional distress only permits a family member to recover damages for foreseeable intangible injuries caused by seeing a loved one injured or "shortly after the traumatic event and before a material change has been made." This limits the scope of liability for bystanders who suffer emotional distress from seeing the victim. Mr. Young conceded in his deposition that he did not see his daughter in pain or hear her cry out. She had disappeared from the surface of the water long before he got there. As defense counsel, you could move for summary judgment on the grounds that this "arrived shortly after" element is missing, entitling you to summary judgment as a matter of law.

C. Plaintiff's Counsel and Prosecutor as Demolishers

Plaintiffs and prosecutors also can assume the role of the wrecking crew when the civil defendant raises a counterclaim or defense, or when the criminal defendant raises a defense or relies upon reasonable doubt alone. In the next chapter at pages 41-42, we provide an illustration involving the prosecution's attack upon the alibi witness.

VI. OTHER PURPOSES FOR AND MISUSES OF CROSS-EXAMINATION

In the interests of reality and completeness, we now discuss other purposes to which cross-examination can be put. The vast majority of these methods do not serve the purposes of building, preserving, or demolishing as we have explained them. Paradoxically, these methods actually can damage the cross-examiner's case.

A. Discovery

In his monumental study of the law of evidence, Professor John T. Wigmore called cross-examination "the greatest legal engine ever invented for the discovery of the truth." 5 Wigmore § 1367. Numerous legal opinions, such as *California v. Green*, 399 U.S. 149, 158, 90 S. Ct. 1930, 1935, 26 L. Ed. 2d 489 (1970), and *Fox ex rel. Fox v. Elk Run Coal Co., Inc.*, 739 F.3d 131, 137 (2014), have parroted that maxim. However, while cross-examination can expose falsehoods and disclose truth, it is not a good machine for discovering it. A lawyer should have already discovered the truth before the trial begins, with an interpretation of it entitling the lawyer's client to win. A trial should be an exercise in revealing competing interpretations of the truth to the jury, which then chooses between them or fashions its own version during deliberation.

Occasionally, however, cross can discover new witnesses or evidence. Every now and then a witness will give totally unexpected testimony involving unknown witnesses or evidence. For example, the defendant in a driving under the influence case may testify that a bystander tried to intercede with the officer on his behalf. If the arresting officer denies this, a potential credibility issue is raised. If the prosecutor's cross-examination of the defendant can identify enough detail to locate the bystander, who then refutes the defendant's claims, the prosecution can call the bystander in rebuttal to confirm the officer's testimony.

B. Placate Kibitzers, Clients, and Others

A trial lawyer is bound to get advice on cross-examination from a variety of sources, including the client. Remember the story of the English solicitor who successfully hounded his barrister to ask a certain question on cross-examination. When the question was asked, the answer devastated the barrister's case. The barrister turned to the solicitor and said, "Go home, cut your throat, and when you meet your client in Hell, beg his pardon!" Nobody knows the case better than the lawyer who is trying it. Trust your own instincts first and foremost.

C. Avoid Criticism

Lawyers sometimes do cross-examination for motives unrelated to the case itself, including to avoid bar complaints, malpractice suits, and in criminal cases, post-conviction motions alleging incompetence of counsel. A vociferous and tedious cross-examination done for show is like a tale told by an idiot. Avoid it at all costs.

D. Ego Gratification

Cross-examination is neither the time nor the place for ego gratification. The cross-examiner who self-consciously sets out to impress the jury is heading for a fall. What useful purpose does it serve to discredit and embarrass a witness whose testimony has not hurt the examiner's case theory? The jury has a long memory for any unnecessary cruelty shown to witnesses.

Television cameras in the courtroom can induce a particular loss of impulse control, much to the detriment of a lawyer's credibility. Avoid the temptation to engage in a Hollywood arm-waving cross-examination for the viewing audience. Favorable verdicts come in spite of, not because of, such efforts.

Some attorneys insist that the primary purpose of cross-examination should be "to look good," to dazzle the jury. The reality is that facts win cases and unprofessional lawyers lose them. Histrionics are contraindicated. The lawyer who has the facts and presents them well is going to win.

CHECKLIST: PURPOSE OF CROSS

Purpose of Cross-Examination

❑ Winning a favorable verdict is the ultimate goal of cross-examination.
❑ A winning cross-examination is one that builds up and preserves the examiner's case theory and/or demolishes the other side's case theory.

Building a Case Theory

❑ Counsel's *case theory* is a combination of a legal theory, such as the plaintiff's *legal theory* of negligence or the defense's legal theory of assumption of risk and a *factual theory.*
❑ The *factual theory* must be not only legally sufficient (i.e., produce enough evidence to support the party's legal theory), but also tell a persuasive story—one that will compel the jury to render a favorable verdict.
❑ The persuasive story is composed of these five elements:
   1. A *narrative story,* which is the telling of an event or events in narrative form;
   2. *About human values and needs* that the jurors care about, for example freedom, belonging, or safety;
   3. With a powerful *human interest theme,* such as a story about a human being that the jury can relate to;
   4. Supported by *credible evidence;* and
   5. A *sufficient quantity of evidence.*

Demolishing the Opponent's Case

❑ A demolition cross finds the areas of vulnerability in the opponent's case and attacks them.
❑ Points of vulnerability are:
   1. *Persuasive insufficiency,* such as when a key witness is impeachable;
   2. *Factual insufficiency,* for example, evidence is missing on an essential element of the other side's legal theory.

CHAPTER 3

THE CONTENT & CONCESSION-SEEKING CROSS

"Never, never, never, on cross-examination ask a witness a question you don't already know the answer to, was a tenet that I absorbed with my baby food. Do it, and you'll often get an answer you don't want, an answer that might wreck your case."

— Spoken by **Atticus Finch**, in Harper Lee's
To Kill a Mockingbird
188 (J. B. Lippincott & Co. 1960)

I. THE CONTENT OF CROSS

What are you going to ask about during your cross-examination? What is the content going to be and how do you go about identifying and selecting it? This chapter explores these two questions and offers methodologies and tools for answering them.

The essential purpose of cross-examination is to help convince the jury to render a verdict in your client's or, in the prosecutor's situation, the people's favor. You want the jury to adopt your case theory and reject your opponent's. To accomplish these goals, you can elicit two types of information. First, you can gather concessions that either build upon or protect your own case theory or damage the other side. Second, you can impeach the witness's credibility as unworthy of belief thereby damaging your opponent's case. Cross can be crafted to produce one or both results. A concession can result in the impeachment of a witness who refuses to admit the truth as you see it.

Although the main focus in this chapter is on identifying and selecting concessions, it also covers how to identify material for impeachment. More in-depth discourses on impeachment cross-examinations are reserved for Chapters 6 through 8.

Why favor a concession-seeking cross over an impeachment one? First, almost every witness called by your opponent can offer you some concession that helps build or reinforce your case. Second, if a concession turns a witness to your advantage, you may not need to pursue impeachment. Third, it is usually easier to garner concessions than to impeach. Fourth, it is only natural for jurors to give more weight to any testimony by a witness that is contrary to the interests of the side who endorsed that witness. Behavioral science has proven that people give far more credibility to any such admissions against interest. *See generally* Robert H. Klonoff & Paul L. Colby, *Sponsorship Strategy: Evidentiary Tactics for Winning Jury Trials* (1990). Fifth, if the fact is established through the other side's witness, it is unlikely that the other side will contest it. If challenged, the rebuttal is that the opponent's witness testified to it.

II. METHODOLOGY FOR SELECTING THE CONTENT

The methodology for identifying and selecting the content for a successful cross-examination involves a four-step process:

- Step 1: *Formulate your case theory* to guide the concessions that you will seek.
- Step 2: *Analyze the opposing party's case theory* to understand what information it admits.

- Step 3: *Brainstorm* the law and facts of the case for a working list of *concessions points.*
- Step 4: *Brainstorm* the facts for *impeachment material.*

These steps are interactive, leading you to ideas for factual concessions and impeachment, which in turn help build your closing. In Chapter 4, Constructing the Cross: Your Chance to Testify, we cover how to take the results of the brainstorming process and mold them into a persuasive cross-examination.

III. STEP 1: CASE THEORY AS GUIDE

The search for the content of cross-examination begins with both your case theory and that of your opponent. In the previous chapter we covered how to formulate that case theory.

IV. STEP 2: YOUR ADVERSARY'S CASE THEORY

Analyzing your opponent's case theory will point to concessions and admissions that enhance your case theory and diminish the credibility of the other side's. To illustrate how this process works, consider these common defenses that arise in diverse criminal cases:

Cross-Examination

Analysis of Your Adversary's Case Theory

- Alibi — Defense Argument: "My client was across town celebrating his birthday at the time of the robbery."
- Consent in a Sexual Assault Case — Defense Argument: "Yes, he had sex with her, but she consented."
- Self-Defense — Defense Argument: "Sure she stabbed her husband. If she hadn't, he would have killed her."
- Insanity — Defense Argument: "Yes, she killed her sister; but she was insane at the time. She didn't know the difference between right and wrong."

These potential defense case theories employ a confession and avoidance strategy. They concede some facts crucial to proving the elements of the charged crime but provide a viable defense. This is potentially effective because it removes much of the taint from the defendant: "Yes, the death happened, but the defendant was not responsible." For example, in a self-defense stabbing case, the defendant will concede to having stabbed the victim. The prosecutor can turn this around, taking advantage of the inherent concession of helpful facts in constructing the cross-examination.

V. STEP 3: BRAINSTORMING FOR CONCESSIONS

A. The Key Question

The third step is to brainstorm in order to identify concessions that build or preserve your case theory or demolish the other side's case theory. During the brainstorming process, you write down short factual statements that answer this key concession-seeking question:

> "What must the witness concede or face having her answer labeled a lie, mistaken, or preposterous?"

A tentative closing argument that embraces your case theory and refutes your opponent's is a valuable planning and design tool for answering the key question. Look forward to closing argument, and then backward to the witness and potential cross-examination. Think about the points you want to make in your tentative closing argument and what you can get from the witness that will be usable in closing. This will provide a guide to the factual points sought in cross-examination.

In reality, this will be an interactive process where your list of concession points triggers how those points can be used in closing. Your ideas for closing will lead you to concession factual points. Now think about cross-examination. What witness information would you be able to elicit on cross that could support the argument? You want to identify specific facts that you can use in argument. For example, in a case in which your client is suing for breach of contract, a concession you might obtain from the other side's witness is the fact that a signed contract exists.

The goal of your brainstorming session is to formulate and write single-fact statements that will support your argument, rather than writing conclusions. For example, rather than writing "the witness is biased," which is the argument you want to make at the end of the case, you would note facts that would lead the jury to that conclusion, such as, "the witness has known the opposing party for ten years," "the witness eats lunch with opposing party twice a week," "the witness was the party's bridesmaid at her wedding," and so on.

The operational word in the key question—*"must"*—needs further elaboration. The witness must make the concession because the cross-examiner can prove it or because to not make the admission defies common sense. The significance of the key question is that it both illuminates how concession-seeking cross-examination works and provides a device for identifying the type of concessions you want. The concession being sought is the truth, and the cross-examiner can prove the proposition. The witness will either grant the concession or deny the provable truth and be impeached. In other words, to plan a concession-seeking cross is to also plan an impeachment cross-exam.

In Chapters 6 through 8 on impeachment cross we explain and illustrate the ways in which the cross-examiner can discredit a witness's refusal to give the concession. Here is a checklist of some of those ways along with summaries of illustrations and page numbers for the areas of impeachment:

CHECKLIST
Discrediting the Witness's Refusal to Concede the Point

- ❑ • *Lack of Personal Knowledge*—The provable facts establish that the witness could not know what the witness claims to know. For example, see Lincoln's cross-examination of a witness who claimed to have seen a shooting at night by moonlight when the almanac showed the moon was not on the horizon at the time of the shooting (pages 120-122).
- ❑ • *Contradiction*—The witness's testimony is contradicted by extending the premise propounded by the witness out to an absurd result. For instance, in cross-examining William Jennings Bryan on his literal interpretation of the Bible, Clarence Darrow showed that they led to results that would be contrary to common sense (pages 136-139). Or, the witness's testimony could be contradicted in other ways, such as when F. Lee Bailey had Mark Fuhrman deny that he ever used a racial slur during the ten years before he testified and later produced an audiotaped interview in which Fuhrman uttered a racial slur (pages 166-168).
- ❑ • *Common Sense*—The witness's testimony is contrary to common sense. For example, Senator Ted Steven's claim that an expensive vibrating chair that he kept in his home was merely on loan (pages 139-141).
- ❑ • *Prior Inconsistent Statement*—The witness's testimony contradicts her prior statement in a deposition, statement, or other form (pages 143-147).

Shana Alexander's *The Pizza Connection: Lawyers, Money, Drugs, Mafia* 318-320 (Weidenfeld & Nicholson) (1988) recounts the story of a $1.65 billion heroin and money laundering conspiracy trial that lasted 18 months, resulting in 18 men being convicted. The following account from *The Pizza Connection* provides an excellent illustration of not only how this key-question technique can work to formulate a concession-seeking line of cross-examination but also how a witness can be impeached when he or she does not grant the concession:

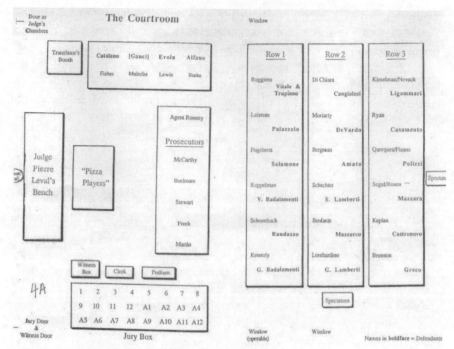

Courtroom layout and players in the Pizza Connection trial

CROSS-EXAMINATION

Concession-Seeking Cross
The Pizza Connection Case
Place: Courtroom in New York   When: January 1987

(Defense counsel) Larry Bronson's defense of (defendant) Sal Greco is focused on his client's need to prove that he was not in a Bagheria farmhouse in early March 1980 watching a heroin quality-control test. Bronson will show he [Greco] was quietly, busily at home in New Jersey. He calls Greco's good friend and tax accountant, Justin Pisano, a man who keeps detailed date books.

Under patient examination by Bronson, the witness goes through a precise account of driving to the Jersey Shore three Sundays in March to go over Greco's accounts and to visit nearby pizzerias with his client in order to compare their business with that of the Greco pizzeria in Neptune City.

Stewart's cross-examination of Pisano becomes this prosecutor's finest hour. He concentrates on the March date-book entries.

"On March 2, yes, I drove down to see Greco," Pisano says, "and we had a leisurely dinner."

"You told us yesterday you were in no rush, right?"

"Yes."

"And that's the truth, the whole truth, and nothing but the truth?"

"Yes."

"Then what is this appointment for 7:00 p.m., with Troviatta?"

"Just a tax appointment. Early March is income tax time, and I made many Sunday and night appointments to service all my tax clients."

"What is Troviatta's first name? Where does he live?"

"I don't remember. I don't even think I do their taxes anymore."

Stewart remembers. He says Pisano was thirty-five miles away from Greco's pizzeria that night, in the heart of Manhattan, at Lincoln Center, at the opera.

Pisano emphatically denies this. He has only been to Lincoln Center once in his life, to hear Pavarotti.

"Are you an opera fan?"

"Nope. Only been to one opera in my life, when I was in high school."

Stewart shows the witness, and the jury, the Sunday-evening newspaper opera listing for March 2, 1980, at the New York State Theater at Lincoln Center: *La Traviata*.

Bronson objects. "Misleading the witness, your Honor. His witness's tax client is named Troviatta—with two t's."

"And the advertisement for the opera is spelled *T-R-A-V-I-A-T-A*, right?" Stewart asks.

"No. It's *La* Traviata," says Pisano gamely.

"La Traviata?"

"Right. I don't see the comparison to Troviatta."

"Except for the time. *That's* a coincidence. Isn't it?"

Pisano agrees, and Stewart directs him to look at the entry for two Sundays ahead, March 16, at one in the afternoon.

"Are you referring to Carmen? Carmen Sangari, who I no longer do?"

"Carmen Sangari?" Stewart produces the *New York Times*, and asks him to read aloud the opera listing for that Sunday afternoon. Pisano looks, and agrees that this is truly an amazing coincidence.

Spectators have begun to giggle. But Stewart is not finished. He directs the witness's attention to his diary entry for the following Sunday at 7:00 p.m. "Is that a tax client of yours?"

The giggling turns to guffaws. The notebook says, "Barber of Seville."

Alexander, *supra*, at 318-20.

Assistant U.S. Attorney Robert Stewart, the cross-examiner, started with the truth—the alibi witness Pisano was at the opera at the time that defendant Sal Greco was witnessing the heroin quality-control test. Stewart could prove it with Pisano's diary and the *New York Times* opera listings. The alibi witness's truthful answer to the question, "What must this witness concede to stamp the answer a lie, mistaken, or preposterous?" would have been that he was at the opera and not with Greco. If he had made the admission, he would have conceded that he could not provide an alibi for Greco. When Pisano did not give the concession, his answer was not credible.

Next, we provide illustrations of successful concession-seeking cross-examinations.

B. The Ted Bundy Illustration — Concession-Seeking Cross

The Theodore Robert (Ted) Bundy trials in Florida provide examples of concession-seeking cross-examinations.

Ted Bundy on February 12, 1980,
the day after he was sentenced
to death for murdering Kimberly
Diane Leach Florida State Archives

Ted Bundy seemed to be a promising young man in the 1960s and early 1970s, attending the University of Washington in Seattle, working as the office manager for Nelson Rockefeller's Presidential campaign and later on a Washington state gubernatorial race, carrying on what for a time seemed to be a normal relationship with another university student and volunteering for a suicide hotline. During that volunteer work he met young Seattle police officer Ann Rule, who would later chronicle Bundy's crimes in her true crime book, *The Stranger Beside Me*. Bundy graduated with a degree in psychology in 1972, entered law school at the University of Puget Sound (but did poorly), and eventually dropped out.

Although it cannot be ascertained how early Bundy began killing, his known killing spree started in 1974. In that year, University of Washington, Central Washington State College, and Evergreen State College women students began disappearing. In a park and in broad daylight, Bundy lured two women to his Volkswagen Beetle by wearing his arm in a sling and asking them for help. The women's bodies were later recovered. In the fall of 1974, Bundy had moved to Salt Lake City and enrolled in the University of Utah Law School, where he continued to murder women in both Utah and Colorado. In 1975, Bundy was convicted in Utah of kidnapping and sentenced to prison. While in Aspen, Colorado awaiting a hearing on a murder charge there, he escaped by jumping from a law library window. He was recaptured, but later escaped from the jail.

Bundy traveled east and south, arriving in Tallahassee, Florida. On January 15, 1978, Bundy snuck into the Chi Omega sorority house in the middle of the night. He killed two sorority women, sexually assaulting one of them and beating two other women before fleeing. Bundy then went to Lake City, Florida where he kidnapped, sexually assaulted, and murdered a 12-year-old girl named Kimberly Diane Leach.

A few days later, Bundy was arrested driving a stolen car and was transported to Tallahassee to be prosecuted and convicted for the Chi Omega murders. A key piece of evidence was the bite mark left on one of his victims, which the forensic odontologist was able to match to a cast of Bundy's teeth. The court sentenced Bundy to death.

Next, Bundy was prosecuted for the murder of Kimberly Diane Leach. The evidence included testimony of an eyewitness who saw Bundy with the girl, fibers in Bundy's van that matched the victim's clothing, and fibers on the victim's clothing that matched Bundy's clothing. Again, the court sentenced Bundy to death. While in prison, Bundy confessed to many of his murders and tried to delay his execution by offering to discuss more of his slayings. This was to no avail and Bundy was electrocuted on January 24, 1989.

Factually Sufficient

In the trial of Ted Bundy for the murder of Kimberly Diane Leach, the State's medical examiner opined that the victim died of "homicidal violence to the neck area, type undetermined." The defense called a counter expert who testified persuasively there was no evidence of homicidal violence to the neck area. In case theory terms, the doctor attacked the factual sufficiency of the prosecution's case. Cross-examination of the doctor aimed at obtaining a concession that the death was a homicide—factually sufficient to support the legal theory of murder. The cross-examination, as remembered by one of the prosecutors, George "Bob" Dekle went as follows:

CROSS-EXAMINATION

Concession-Seeking Cross
Ted Bundy Murder Case

Q. I am going to ask you to assume certain facts to be true for the purpose of asking you a hypothetical question. I would like for you to assume the facts in your knowledge at this point in time, based upon the autopsy photographs, I want you further to assume. *[Here the circumstances of the victim's disappearance and subsequent discovery were given in detail.]* Assuming only what has been represented to you, at this point, you can rule out suicide?

A. Suicide in this age group is rare. The circumstances would make suicide far down on the list of probabilities

Q. And you have already ruled out natural causes?

continued ▶

A. As a probability, yes.

Q. Can you rule out accident?

A. Accident would be a little more difficult, but it would not be the first thing that would come to one's mind.

Q. And the first thing is?

A. Given the situation as you depicted it, the first thing that would come to mind would be that of a homicide.

Q. Doctor Lipkovic determined that the victim died as the result of a homicide. Do you have any disagreement with that as a cause of death?

A. Just homicidal violence?

Q. Yes, sir.

A. And no other specifics?

Q. Yes sir.

A. As a specific diagnosis I would not use that terminology. Having a feeling for what he was saying, I would probably not disagree with it, no sir.

Q. You would agree with the diagnosis of homicide?

A. I would disagree with it as a diagnosis, *but not as an opinion based on his experience.*

The indictment alleged that Bundy killed his victim "in some manner and by some means to the grand jury unknown, thereby inflicting in and upon the said Kimberly Diane Leach mortal wounds and injuries or mortal sicknesses, of and from which said mortal wounds and injuries or mortal sicknesses the said Kimberly Diane Leach died." The jury didn't need to believe the killing was by homicidal violence to the neck area. Homicidal violence to any area was good enough.

Persuasive—Credible Story

Sometimes a cross-examiner can wring admissions from a witness that reflect favorably on the credibility of an examiner's witnesses (and thereby the credibility of the cross-examiner's story). A striking example of this type of cross took place when Bundy stood trial for the Chi Omega Murders in Tallahassee. His defense team filed pleadings questioning Bundy's competence to stand trial. The defense hired a prominent local psychologist to examine Bundy, and he concluded that Bundy was not competent to stand trial because he was a sociopath. The expert opined that Bundy's sociopathic personality disorder was so severe it prevented him from assisting in his defense. One of the investigators for the prosecution team had an old fishing buddy from Georgia by the name of Hervey Cleckley, who happened to be a psychiatrist. The Chi Omega prosecution team retained Dr. Cleckley, and he opined that while Bundy had certain capacity issues, he was competent to stand trial. There was reason to suspect, however, that Dr. Cleckley might not be up on the latest developments in his field because he used the antiquated term "psychopath" instead of the then more modern and trendy "sociopath" (today it is called "antisocial personality disorder"). At the hearing the defense expert testified quite convincingly that Bundy was not competent due to his sociopathic personality disorder.

On cross-examination, the prosecutor asked about any authorities the doctor might rely upon in diagnosing sociopathic personality disorder. The doctor said that probably the most influential work on the sociopathic personality was a book entitled *Mask of Sanity*, written by a Dr. Hervey Cleckley. A few more questions revealed that the defense expert stood in awe of Cleckley and his work, and would readily admit that Cleckley was the premier expert in the field of sociopathy. Needless to say, after Dr. Cleckley testified for the prosecution, the judge had no problem finding Bundy competent to stand trial. When Bundy later stood trial for the murder of Kimberly Diane Leach, the defense did not even raise the issue of competence.

C. The Zacarias Moussaoui Illustration— Concession-Seeking Cross

It sometimes happens that a party will concede everything. The *Zacarias Moussaoui* case serves as another example of a cross-examination designed to produce sufficient facts that support the examiner's case theory.

Zacarias Moussaoui was an al Qaeda operative arrested in August 2001 with a 747 flight manual and other incriminating evidence. He is the only defendant ever prosecuted for involvement in the 9/11 terrorist attack. Moussaoui was indicted on charges including conspiracy to commit acts of terrorism and conspiracy to commit aircraft piracy. In April 2005, he pled guilty to the charges and on February 6, 2006, jury selection began for the penalty phase to determine whether Moussaoui would be sentenced to death or life imprisonment.

Zacarias Moussaoui

United States Attorney Robert Spencer's questioning of Moussaoui is an example of a pure concession-seeking cross-examination, which produced chilling and damaging admissions.

CROSS-EXAMINATION

Concession-Seeking Cross
Moussaoui Penalty Phase

U.S. Attorney Robert Spencer: You told the jury that you have no regret for your part in any of this?

Moussaoui: I just wish it will happen on the 12th, the 13th, the 14th, the 15th, the 16th, the 17th, and I can go on and on.

Q.   No remorse?

A.   There is no remorse for justice.

Q.   You also enjoyed the testimony about the attack on the Pentagon?

A.   Definitely.

Q.   You smiled at times during that testimony, didn't you?

A.   That's for sure. I would have even laughed if I didn't know that I would be kicked out of the court.

Q.   Right. You enjoyed seeing the Pentagon on fire?

A.   My pleasure.

Q.   And you remember hearing Lt. Col. John Thurman describe he had to crawl out with his face against the floor to save his life?

A.   He was pathetic.

Q.   You enjoyed that, didn't you?

A.   I was regretful he didn't die.

Q.   Well, here is somebody who did die. [A victim's picture is shown on the courtroom's screens.] Do you remember that gentleman?

A.   I remember his wife, the blond-haired girl.

Q.   That's Vince Tolbert, who worked for the United States Navy, right? He was killed on 9/11 in the Pentagon.

A.   Yes, the one that said to her children that some bad people have killed her husband. And she forgot to tell to her children that her husband was working classified, something about targeting.

Q.   And it made you particularly happy that he was killed that day, correct?

A.   Make my day.

Q.   Do you remember the testimony of Lt. McKeown?

A.   The woman like was talking about: Where are my boy, where are my boy?

Q.   Right. Sobbing in that very chair because the people under her command were killed. Do you remember that?

A.   I think it was disgusting for a military person to pretend that they should not be killed as an act of war. She is military. She should expect that people who are at war with her will try to kill her. I will never, I will never cry because an American bombed my camp.

Q.   And you were happy that her two men were killed that day?

A.   Make my day.

Q.   All right. You were happy that every single person who came in here sad, telling about the effect that you and your brothers [had], you were happy about all that, weren't you? No regret, no remorse—right, Mr. Moussaoui?

> *A.* No regret, no remorse.
> *Q.* Like it to all happen again, right?
> *A.* Every day, until we get here to you.

The jury was unable to unanimously agree that Moussaoui should be put to death with one juror holding out and never explaining why. Consequently, Moussaoui was sentenced to six consecutive life imprisonment terms. Timothy Dwyer, *One Juror Between Terrorist and Death,* The Washington Post, May 12, 2006.

VI. STEP 4: BRAINSTORMING FOR IMPEACHMENT MATERIAL

You will also brainstorm to determine how you could impeach the witness. You list areas of impeachment that apply to the witness. The following is a list of areas of impeachment that you can review during your brainstorming process.

CHECKLIST
Areas of Impeachment for Cross-Examination

All Witnesses
- ☐ I. Reliability — Chapter 5
  1. Lack of Personal Knowledge
  2. Mental and Sensory Deficiencies
  3. Bias and Interest
- ☐ II. Report — Chapter 6
  4. Improbability
  5. Prior Inconsistent Statement
  6. Contradiction
- ☐ III. Reporter — Chapter 7
  7. Prior Convictions
  8. Prior Misconduct Probative on Untruthfulness
  9. Character Witness

Expert Witnesses
- ☐ All of the above
  10. Qualifications
  11. Reliability of the Field
  12. Basis for Opinion
  13. Opinion
  14. Learned Treatises

VII. BRAINSTORMING FOR CONTENT:
CONVENIENCE STORE ROBBERY
CRIMINAL CASE ILLUSTRATION

Now, let's apply this methodology to the *Convenience Store Robbery* case.

Blue Moon News convenience store

Convenience Store Robbery Case

Blue Moon News is a popular newspaper and magazine shop. It is open 24 hours a day. At about 11:30 p.m. on January 15 of this year, the elderly clerk, Mr. Gardner Newman, noticed a man, about 5 feet 7 inches tall, who had been browsing at the magazine rack, approach the counter. The convenience store was dimly lit and no one else was in the store. The man, who had his baseball hat pulled down, laid the magazine he was carrying on the counter, put his hand into his coat pocket, pulled out what appeared to be a revolver, and demanded cash from the register. Newman handed over the money, and the man fled on foot. A partial print on the magazine matched the fingerprint of the 23-year-old defendant, Mike Ryan, who has a lengthy juvenile criminal history for shoplifts and a robbery. The defendant is from a low-income background and used to work at a tire dealership. Newman identified the defendant's picture in a photo montage as that of the robber. He initially described the robber to the police as six feet tall.

The defense filed a notice that witness Greg Lewis Delaney would be called to testify in support of an alibi. Delaney and the defendant worked together at the Tire Universe dealership for two years, until the defendant's layoff on December 15 of last year. Detective Malcomb interviewed Delaney, who told him about a party at Delaney's apartment complex on January 15, approximately four miles from the convenience store. This witness stated that "Mike was at my party from 10:00 p.m.

until the end at 3:00 a.m., at least I think so." Delaney estimated that 40 to 50 people attended the party, and "most everybody was drinking." After the party, Delaney had not heard from the defendant for about two months, when he called to ask for Delaney's alibi testimony.

Assume you are the prosecutor. You are planning the cross-examination of a defense alibi witness, Greg Lewis Delaney. Your case theory is that Mike Ryan committed the robbery. The defense theory is reasonable doubt based upon misidentification and alibi. With the case theories in mind, you brainstorm for concessions that Delaney, the alibi witness, must make. You look for facts that Delaney must admit or be contradicted by witness testimony, evidentiary inferences, or common sense.

The process of brainstorming involves a constant interactive search for possible factual concessions, considering how they might sound in closing argument. Keeping constant focus on your tentative closing will lead you to other concessions to pursue in cross. For clarity, we present first the tentative closing arguments followed by the list of factual concessions, realizing that your brainstorming might well develop these in the reverse order.

Facts Bolstering the Prosecution's Case Theory

The following arguments come from an inherent concession in an alibi defense: that the robbery took place. The motive and opportunity points build off of this, strengthening the prosecution's case theory.

Prosecutor's Tentative Closing Argument

Facts Bolstering the Prosecution's Case Theory in the *Convenience Store Robbery* Case

The state must prove beyond a reasonable doubt the elements of robbery in the first degree listed here on the chart. All but one of these elements are uncontested. The Blue Moon News was robbed on the night of January 15. Neither the defendant nor his alibi witness disputes this. The single element at issue is whether the defendant committed that robbery.

The defendant had both a motive and opportunity to commit the robbery. The defendant himself admits that he was laid off in mid-December of last year. He needed money. Also, as you heard from Mr. Delaney, he is familiar with the Blue Moon News convenience store, located just four miles away from his apartment. The defendant could have easily left the party, driven to the store, robbed it, and returned to the party without anyone noticing that he'd left. Standing alone, the fact that the defendant was at a place near the Blue Moon News on the night of robbery is not enough to convict him but, when taken with the other evidence, it is another piece pointing to him as the robber.

A list of factual statements that may be employed in the cross-examination of Greg Lewis Delaney stems from this ends-means thinking:

List of Factual Statements

Facts Bolstering the Prosecution's Case Theory
in the *Convenience Store Robbery* Case

The Convenience Store Was Robbed
- The witness doesn't dispute that the Blue Moon News was robbed on January 15 of this year.

Motive
- The witness worked at Tire Universe with the defendant.
- The defendant was laid off in mid-December of last year.
- He hasn't returned to work.

Non-Alibi—Defendant Could Have Snuck Out and Robbed the Blue Moon News
- The witness is familiar with the Blue Moon News convenience store.
- Blue Moon News is four miles from the witness's apartment complex.

Facts Showing Mistake or Lack of Perception

Now we turn to the prosecution's attack on the defense alibi witness by showing that his testimony is not persuasive because he could not have known of the defendant's whereabouts at all times between 10:00 p.m. on January 15 and 3:00 a.m. the next day. Another view of this line of cross-examination is to see it as an impeachment cross-examination showing lack of personal knowledge. Either way the examination is viewed, the tentative closing could be as follows:

Prosecutor's Tentative Closing Argument

Facts Showing Mistake or Lack of Perception
That the Defendant Was at the Party from 10:00 p.m. to 3:00 a.m.
in the *Convenience Store Robbery* Case

Mr. Delaney so desperately wants to believe that his friend never left the party because anyone would feel the same way if they were in his situation. However, the circumstances of the party made it all but impossible for Delaney to vouch for the defendant's every moment from 10:00 p.m. to 3:00 a.m.

Look at the diagram Delaney drew of his apartment; look at the photos on the screen of Delaney's living room, dining area, family room area, kitchen, and patio and backyard with a walkway leading around the complex to the street. This was not a sit-down dinner for eight. Between 40 and 50 people were mingling around

---

> throughout the space, talking, and drinking. And Delaney wasn't just another guest; he was the host.
>
> Delaney was busy making sure that his guests got enough food and drink, mingling around, talking to everyone. He did not have the defendant on a leash and couldn't see his entire apartment from any one spot. Most important, you can walk out on the patio and right out onto the street. There is simply no way that Delaney would have noticed if the defendant slipped out for a while, particularly if the defendant did not wish to be noticed.

This closing is based on the central idea that Delaney was mistaken, unable to account for the defendant during the entire time at a big party. The prosecutor brainstorms from this in search of the facts that support the argument.

List of Factual Statements

Facts Showing Mistake or Lack of Perception
That the Defendant Was at the Party from 10:00 p.m. to 3:00 a.m.
in the *Convenience Store Robbery* Case

- The party was at Delaney's apartment complex.
- At the party, people were in several rooms.
- People were milling around.
- Between 40 and 50 people attended the party.
- Delaney was the host.
- Delaney moved around and mingled.
- People were drinking.
- Delaney was drinking.
- Delaney did not keep track of when people arrived or left the party.

Brainstorming for Impeachment Material

Now it is time to turn to the nine potential categories where Delaney might be vulnerable to being impeached, as a lay witness. As before, you brainstorm and make a list.

Bias or Interest

Bias or interest of the witness seems to apply in this case. Delaney worked with the defendant and saw him socially. Closing on the theme of witness bias could go this way:

Tentative Closing Argument

Witness Bias and Interest in the *Convenience Store Robbery* Case

Some people work in the same place and barely even pass each other. So it wouldn't mean all that much to say they worked together. But that wasn't the case with the defendant and his alibi witness, Delaney.

For over two years, they worked together with only four other people in the showroom of Tire Universe. They ate lunch together and talked about their lives almost every day. And they saw each other socially outside of work. So when Delaney threw a party on January 15, it's no surprise he invited his good friend, the defendant. And it is no surprise that when defendant arrived at the party, Delaney was happy to see him. So it's no surprise that last week, when he testified sitting in that seat on the witness stand (counsel points to the witness chair), Delaney would want to help his good friend out of a jam.

Delaney did not want to believe that his friend stuck a gun in another man's face and robbed him. This is not a criticism of Delaney. It's only human. Delaney would want to believe that his close friend was at that party every moment from start to finish.

The tentative closing above all comes from the evidence in the case, gained through discovery and investigation. Delaney had to admit these facts or be impeached.

List of Factual Statements

Witness Bias and Interest in the *Convenience Store Robbery* Case

- They both worked at Tire Universe.
- Until December 15 of last year, defendant Mike Ryan also worked there.
- Delaney and the defendant worked there for two years together.
- Tire Universe is a small business.
- There are few employees.
- Delaney worked in the same room as the defendant.
- For two years they saw each other almost every day at work.
- They ate lunch together.
- They talked daily.
- The two socialized when they worked at Tire Universe.
- On January 15, the witness threw a party.
- The defendant attended the party.
- The witness and defendant spoke at the party.
- The witness was happy the defendant attended the party.

- The witness invited the defendant to the party.
- The witness considered the defendant a friend.
- The witness wants to help the defendant.

Prior Inconsistent Statement

When detective Malcomb interviewed Greg Lewis Delaney on April 15, four months after the robbery, Delaney expressed some doubt about whether the defendant had been at his party for the full extent of it, saying: "Mike was at my party from 10:00 p.m. until the end at 3:00 a.m., at least I think so." If Delaney were to testify at trial consistent with his prior statement to the detective, the prosecutor could argue that the alibi is less than convincing. Even the alibi witness is not sure that the defendant was in attendance for the entire party. However, even if Delaney testifies on direct that he is sure Ryan stayed, the prosecutor can effectively use the prior inconsistent statement in closing:

Prosecutor's Tentative Closing Argument

Prior Inconsistent Statement in the *Convenience Store Robbery* Case

Delaney is *positive* today that the defendant never, ever left his party. But when he talked to Detective Malcomb on April 15, in the familiar surroundings of his own apartment, he was anything but positive. Delaney told you on the stand that he wanted to be as accurate as possible with what he told the detective and certainly would never have lied to the detective. So that night, when Delaney wanted to be as honest and accurate as could be, he did not tell the detective he was "positive" the defendant had been with him all evening; he did not say he was "certain." When indicating that the defendant had been at the party all evening, Delaney qualified his statement, "At least I *think* so." In that single phrase, he really said, "I think he was there, but I could be wrong."

List of Factual Statements

Prior Inconsistent Statement in the *Convenience Store Robbery* Case

Delaney must concede certain facts concerning his statement to the detective.

- The detective came to Delaney's house.
- Delaney spoke to the detective on April 15.
- Delaney was aware that the detective was seeking the truth from witnesses during the investigation.

continued ▶

- Delaney knew it was important to tell the truth to the detective.
- The detective asked Delaney about the January 15 party.
- Delaney said to the detective, "Mike was at my party from 10:00 p.m. until the end at 3:00 a.m., at least I think so."

VIII. BRAINSTORMING FOR CONTENT: *SAMBA SPORTS DROWNING* CIVIL CASE ILLUSTRATION

The four-step approach works equally well for civil cases, as we will demonstrate by turning to the *Samba Sports Drowning* wrongful death case. Here we concentrate on brainstorming for content in this case as another illustration of how to apply the method. See pages 7-8 to review the facts of the *Samba Sports Drowning* case.

Imagine you are plaintiff's counsel. Your case theory is that Samba Sports, Inc. was negligent in failing to warn about risks and in designing, manufacturing, and marketing the ski boat. Your narrative story is that the CEO of Samba callously failed to inform boat users of the danger of carbon monoxide poisoning and blames the victim for failing to protect herself. Defendant Samba claims that adequate warning was given to its customers and that Lindsay Young was at fault in not heeding the warning.

To brainstorm for the content of the cross-examination of Samba's CEO Simon Howell, you utilize ends-means thinking. You envision what you want to argue in closing and ask yourself, "What truths must Simon Howell concede on cross that I can use that closing?" You are trying to identify the truths that must be conceded; those concessions he must make or show the answer to be a lie, mistaken, or preposterous.

For example, you focus on what Samba's defense case theory concedes and arguments that flow from the defense's story that the corporation is blameless.

> ### Plaintiff's Counsel's Tentative Closing Argument
>
> ### Facts Bolstering the Plaintiff's Case Theory in the *Samba Sports Drowning* Wrongful Death Case
>
> Her Honor just read jury instruction 5 defining negligence to you. The defense doesn't dispute that the evidence supports almost all of the elements of negligence. As the instruction states, the plaintiff must prove that the defendant owes a duty to the plaintiff. No question about this. You heard Mr. Howell, the CEO of Samba Sports, Inc. admit to the first element—that the corporation and he had the duty to warn people who use their ski boats that they may be killed by carbon monoxide if

they were on or near the swim platform at the back of the boat when the engine was running. Howell also admitted this third element—a causal connection between the boat's emission of carbon monoxide and Lindsay's death. You heard Mr. Howell testify that he doesn't quarrel with the fact that Lindsay was hanging on to and swimming near the swim platform just before she died and he doesn't dispute that she died from carbon monoxide emitted from the boat's engine. And what did he say about the fourth element—breaching that duty? Did he fulfill his obligation to warn customers? Howell, on cross-examination, admitted that he didn't send letters to customers warning them in any way of carbon monoxide poisoning.

Brainstorming ahead to the end result of the plaintiff's closing on each of the elements of the cause of action leads directly to thinking about the facts that the CEO must admit—the means to the end. The back-and-forth process of building this tentative closing enables plaintiff's counsel to flesh out not only the points to discuss in closing, but also the facts that need to be established in cross. The following is a list of the factual points for plaintiff's cross of Howell. There is much more to cover during the cross-examination of Mr. Howell as you will learn in Chapter 4, Constructing Cross: Your Chance to Testify (see pages 74-79).

List of Factual Statements

Facts Bolstering the Plaintiff's Case Theory in the *Samba Sports Drowning* Wrongful Death Case

- Howell is the President and Chief Executive Officer of Samba Sports, Inc.
- Samba owed a duty to warn users of the boat about the risk of carbon monoxide poisoning.
- Howell, as President and CEO, is accountable for warning customers about the risks of carbon monoxide poisoning.
- Howell doesn't question the fact that Lindsay Young died of carbon monoxide poisoning.
- Howell doesn't quarrel with the fact that just before her death, Lindsay was swimming near the swimming platform while the engine was running.
- He doesn't contest that Lindsay drowned as a result of inhaling a lethal dose of carbon monoxide from the boat's engine.

IX. FILTERING OUT

Just as important as identifying potential content for cross-examination is the act of filtering out that which is not helpful to your case.

A. Avoid Minutiae

Avoid spending too little time on the issues that matter and too much time on issues that don't. If jurors see a cross-examiner devote inordinate time to an inconsequential detail, they may distort the importance of that detail in the elements of proof.

For example, in a home-invasion robbery case, the defendant called an alibi witness. Speaking through an interpreter, the witness testified the defendant was hundreds of miles away in another city at the time of the robbery. Furthermore, "No tiene carro." The defendant did not have a car. The prosecutor knew the defendant did have a car and made this the centerpiece of cross-examination, building slowly to the climactic point of car ownership. However, the witness explained that "no tiene carro" simply meant the defendant had no car available. The car had been temporarily given as security for a loan, which was quickly verified by a call to the pawn shop. The cross-examination collapsed and the defendant later was acquitted, all due to the prosecutor belaboring an inconsequential point.

B. Know the Answer

In *To Kill a Mockingbird,* Atticus Finch recites the most often quoted maxim of cross-examination technique: *"Never, never, never, on cross-examination ask a witness a question you don't already know the answer to . . ."* A good illustration of the adage came during trial of Ted Bundy for the murder of Kimberly Diane Leach. It was important for the prosecution to prove that the victim had been in Bundy's stolen van. Part of the evidence placing her there was a bloodstain found on the carpet inside the van. During the days before DNA evidence, all that crime labs could test for was ABO type and a few enzymes. The serologist was able to identify the ABO type as being consistent with the victim's, but because of advanced decomposition, he could do nothing with the enzymes. When pre-trying the serologist, the prosecutor asked if there was any indication whatsoever about the enzymes in the bloodstain. The serologist said they were probably consistent with the victim's, but the findings were not sufficiently certain for him to testify to them. The prosecution presented only evidence as to the ABO type at trial.

On cross-examination, the defense attorney asked the serologist if he had any inkling as to what the enzymes were. The serologist said he had some indications, but not sufficient for him testify to an opinion. The defense attorney asked the serologist to reveal his findings as to the enzymes. The serologist refused. The defense attorney insisted to the point of asking the judge to order the serologist to answer. Finally, reluctantly, the serologist testified that his indications were that the enzymes in the bloodstain probably matched the enzymes in the victim's blood. Needless to say the prosecution mentioned this fact on redirect examination and in final argument.

As wise as Atticus Finch's advice may seem, slavish adherence to it can lead to some incredibly brief cross-examinations. In fact, whenever counsel asks any question, it is impossible to know with certainty what the witness is going to say. Sometimes even the friendliest witnesses can disappoint us. If your own witnesses can disappoint you, how can a trial lawyer ever know the answer that a hostile witness will give? If counsel can never know for sure what the answer will be, what could Finch mean? It means that for most questions the cross-examiner asks, the examiner should be relatively sure that if the witness fails to answer as expected, the witness will look like a liar, mistaken, or ridiculous. Put another way: if the witness does not answer as expected, the cross-examiner can impeach the witness.

Exceptions

You will occasionally ask questions when you do not know for sure what the witness will say. This can be safely done in five different situations:

1. Low Risk and Likely Good Return

Counsel can ask exploratory questions when a high degree of certainty exists that, no matter what the witness says, the answer will not hurt and is likely to help. It is like prudent investing, where the risk is low and it is likely to produce a good return.

For instance, in a murder case, the defendant shot a man to death as the victim sat down in his pickup truck to drive home. The crime took place in a small Southern town where every pickup had a gun rack in the rear window. Without any idea what the eyewitness would say, the defense attorney asked him which way the gun in the gun rack was pointing. The witness said the gun was pointing toward the defendant. This testimony gave the defender a jury argument that because the gun was pointed at the defendant coupled with the fact that the victim was backing into the seat, the victim presented an immediate threat to him, and the defendant acted in justifiable self-defense. The defense attorney did not know the answer, but the great benefit of the hoped-for payoff was worth risking the potential slight harm that might have come from the witness saying the gun was pointed in the other direction.

2. Win Either Way

You can ask interrogatory questions when, no matter what the witness says, the cross-examiner benefits. For example, consider the cross-examination of the defendant who stood trial for burglary, robbery, and the sexual battery of a ten-year-old girl. The defense claimed that the defendant could not have committed the crimes because at the time of the burglary, he was sodomizing a 14-year-old boy. One touching scene occurred when the defendant was to be sworn as a witness, and he announced that his religious scruples prevented him from swearing. Instead, he affirmed "under pains and penalties of perjury."

The prosecutor resisted the temptation to ask him what denomination forbade swearing but condoned pederasty. The prosecutor agonized over whether to ask the defendant a provocative question: Did the defendant have an orgasm while sodomizing the boy? Although the prosecutor risked offending the judge and jury, he reasoned that no answer the defendant could give would hurt. If he answered "Yes," he would give the jury even more reason to dislike him than he gave them on direct examination. The prosecutor asked the question. The defendant denied having an orgasm. Because the boy only lived a few blocks from the victim, that opened up the argument that the defendant, aroused and unsatisfied from his sexual encounter with him, walked the few blocks to the victim's home, broke in, and satisfied his lust by sexually battering her.

3. Honest Witness

If you are convinced that the witness is honest or honest-but-partisan and on the side of the case that would benefit from an honest answer, you may feel safe in asking the exploratory question. If the answer is disagreeable, you can console yourself with the thought that the answer is likely true. If you distrust the witness but discern that he does not realize the importance or implications of the question, you may feel secure in asking it. When you distrust the witness and believe the witness knows the importance of the question, almost never ask the interrogatory question.

4. Need to Know

Sometimes the need to know the answer outweighs the danger of a harmful answer. In the dynamics of a witness's examination, sometimes points arise that cry out for an answer. When counsel avoids asking a burning question because she fears the answer, she can expect the jury to get hung up on that very point. It is far better to deal with an unfavorable answer than have a jury return a verdict against you because the question was never asked.

Rarely will a case rise or fall on the failure to ask a single question or line of questions. In most cases, the stakes will be lower, but counsel should still take the chance if the situation calls for it. For example, in a conspiracy and murder case, the defense was alibi. Several witnesses testified that the defendant was in another state the week of the shooting. However, no one could specifically account for his whereabouts on the day of the shooting. When the defendant testified, he did not say a single word about where he was or what he did the day of the shooting. The prosecutor had an almost overpowering urge to ask him where he was the day of the shooting but knew that to ask would fly in the face of the time-honored maxim. What if the defense attorney had laid a trap? The defendant was never asked where he was the day of the killing. He should have been. The not guilty verdict could not have been any worse if the subject had been thoroughly explored on cross-examination.

5. Doesn't Matter

Often there is no risk in asking a question because the specific answer given just doesn't matter. For example, in the *Convenience Store Robbery* case, when the prosecutor asks Delaney about the number of the people at the party and has him describe and draw his apartment and patio, the prosecutor may not know the answers to these questions, but the specific answers do not matter. The likelihood of getting damaging answers is nil. However, the line of questions is likely to elicit information that will enable the prosecutor to later argue in closing that several people were there, they were milling around, and therefore, Delaney would not have been able to keep track of the defendant.

CHECKLIST: CONTENT & CONCESSION-SEEKING CROSS-EXAMINATION

Step 1. Formulate a Case Theory

❏ The case theory is what the cross will build, reinforce, and protect with concessions from the witness.

Step 2. Analyze the Opposing Party's Case Theory

❏ By its very nature, the other side's case theory may concede aspects of your case.
❏ A thorough understanding of the opposing party's case theory can reveal concessions that may be sought on cross to undercut that case theory.

Step 3. Brainstorming for Concessions

❏ A tentative closing argument is an excellent tool for planning cross because it embodies both your case theory and your refutations of the other side's case theories
❏ Ask yourself: "What information might I obtain through cross-examination of this witness to argue these points in closing argument?"
❏ It is a back-and-forth process. Think ahead to points to argue in closing and then back to the facts that may be elicited on cross to make the point in closing.
❏ Ask yourself the concession-seeking question: "What must the witness concede or face having the answer labeled a lie, mistaken, or preposterous?"
❏ The witness must grant the concession or be impeached because you can prove the fact sought or because failure to make the admission defies common sense.
❏ Concessions identified through this process are those that build, reinforce, or protect the case theory or damage the opponent's.

Step 4. Brainstorm for Impeachment Material

❏ Brainstorm for *impeachment material* using this list of impeachment areas for all witnesses:
   1. Lack of personal knowledge;
   2. Mental and sensory deficiencies;

3. Bias and interest;

4. Improbability;

5. Prior inconsistent statements;

6. Contradiction;

7. Prior convictions;

8. Prior misconduct probative on untruthfulness; and

9. Character witness.

❑ Brainstorm for impeachment material for an expert, which includes the nine areas mentioned above and the following additional five:

1. Qualifications;

2. Reliability of the field;

3. Basis for opinion;

4. Opinion; and

5. Learned treatises.

Filter Out

❑ Filter out content that is not helpful to your case.

❑ During cross, avoid asking about minutiae and spend time on things that matter.

❑ Never ask a question on cross that you don't already know the answer to, except:

1. When it is almost certain that the answer won't hurt and it most likely will help;

2. When no matter what the answer is the examiner benefits;

3. When the witness is honest and you are on the side of the honest answer;

4. When your need to know the answer outweighs any danger in asking for it; and

5. When you don't care what the specific answer is.

CHAPTER 4

CONSTRUCTING THE CROSS
Your Chance to Testify

"The formula for successful cross-examination is simply stated: Use plain declarative sentences, add only one new fact per question, and lock in an answer before administering the coup de grace. Think of cross-examination as a series of statements by the lawyer, only occasionally interrupted by a yes from the witness."

— **Roy Black**, *Black's Law* 43 (Simon & Schuster 1999)

I. YOUR TIME TO TESTIFY

Cross-examination is your opportunity to testify. That's right; it's your opportunity to testify. While you are not really testifying in the strictest sense, ideally cross consists of you making substantive statements, and the witness affirming them. You decide the content, wording, exhibits, pace, duration, and factual sequence in which your story is told to the jury. You also determine the amount and type of movement for yourself and the witness, except when courtroom practice, such as that in federal court, restricts you to a podium. Cross is your best chance to relate your factual story and theme at trial.

Once you have adopted a your-time-to-testify approach, you may no longer see cross as a battle with the witness. Rather, it is a challenging and rewarding opportunity to teach the jury your case theory.

You have brainstormed and identified the witness's factual and opinion concessions and the impeachment points that you want to communicate to the jury. During cross-examination itself, your questions will be predominantly leading and designed to make those points. You will know what the answer will be, except for rare occasions when you give the witness a chance to contribute some testimony. But, those occasions are only in limited situations when the answer cannot harm your case.

A well-constructed cross-examination does not reinforce points made on direct or allow witnesses wide latitude in their responses. Do not merely repeat the same information from the direct. That is not cross-examination; that is supplemental direct examination, from which you will gain little. First, it merely reemphasizes the points already made by your opponent. Second, it may bring out additional harmful details omitted by your opponent. Third, it is rare to catch a witness off guard. Fourth, repetition is dreadfully dull and inevitably unsuccessful.

Instead, to maximize persuasion, you want to divide your cross-examination into topical units, arranged in a logical, but not necessarily chronological order. The main objective is to make your case theme and theory clear to the jury, telling a persuasive narrative story.

In the previous two chapters, we discussed how to identify the factual concessions and impeachment points for your cross. This chapter covers how to organize that material into a usable format for trial. Also, this chapter examines how to transition between subjects; the order of cross-examination; the four types of questions; and how to finish your cross.

II. CROSS NOTES

A. Write the Cross-Examination

The best preparation sequence is to start by writing out your cross-examination questions. This is a planning tool, recognizing that all of us do some of our best thinking when turning strategy into written form. Putting the cross-examination on paper will help you to think more clearly about the material, shaping it to maximize the jury's understanding. The inadvisability of open-ended questions will seem clearer when they are right in front of you. So will questions that fail to gain favorable concessions or discredit the witness. Additionally, when the cross is written, possible flow-breaking objections by your opponent are more readily identified. Then you can either rephrase the objectionable questions or develop a strategy to meet the objection at trial.

We are aware that the conventional wisdom on planning a cross-examination is different from what we have just told you. But an effective cross-examination is very much like a scene from a play, where careful consideration is given to every line, with multiple revisions by the playwright until the scene advances the story and its themes. You should plan your cross-examinations the same way. We have watched experienced lawyers who did not write out their cross-examinations in the strategic pretrial planning phase. They should have.

B. Cross-Notes Format and Topical Units

We have found the cross-notes format below to be effective in writing out cross-examinations:

CROSS-NOTES FORMAT FOR CROSS-EXAMINATION

TOPIC: Witness is biased

FACTS	REFERENCES & NOTES

At the top or side of the page, put a topical label of the potential closing argument that you may make at the end of the case, such as, "Witness is biased." All of the notes on that topic are written in a self-contained topical unit. Like a scene in a movie, it can be viewed on its own and also as part of the movie's overarching story.

The pages of each new topical unit are numbered sequentially through the end of that unit. Each unit concentrates on a single topic, which is summarized in the label. This format will keep you on point, curbing any tendency to wander during the cross. Limiting each unit to a single-subject also will keep things clear for the jury.

On the left side of the cross-notes page, write short statements of fact. These are what you have settled on after all the brainstorming for content and organizing the resulting information. While full statements may help your trial preparation, these are not appropriate for cross notes. For instance, in preparation for the *Convenience Store Robbery* case, the prosecutor may write out the question: "Once the party got going, there were 40 or 50 people at your apartment?" The words of a lengthy statement like this acts as an eye magnet. You will read the words and lose eye contact with the witness. During cross, you want to look the witness in the eye, watching for reactions, listening intently to the answers. To facilitate this, your cross notes should be a list of key words and short phrases, similar to cue cards. These mainly serve as reminders. A good prompt in the *Convenience Store Robbery* case would be something like: "40-50 people there." Make the words on the page to large enough so they are easy to read. Otherwise, the cross notes will slow you down, putting more focus on the page, when it belongs on the witness.

The right column is available for three things. First it is where you write references to the file, such as deposition statements, with page and line notations. If the witness does not provide the desired answer, you are ready to pounce on the inconsistency. Confronting a witness with a prior statement normally will give you the concessions you are seeking. Indeed, if you successfully deposed the witness, your questions at trial likely will mirror the deposition, producing the same results. Second, the right column can be used to take notes of any of the witness's responses that you find remarkable or noteworthy enough to quote later in closing argument. Third, the right column contains references to the law that you may need to respond to an objection to your cross.

This approach will give you four advantages:

Advantages of the Cross-Notes Format

- First, short written factual statements reinforce the information flow concept that *you are testifying*, not trying to discover something from the witness.
- Second, making statements nudges you toward only *leading questions* rather than open-ended ones, such as "Why did you do that?"
- Third, the one-fact-per-question method *avoids asking the witness for conclusions*, such as "You are biased, correct?" This approach will lead the jury to the desired conclusion independently, with a vested proprietary interest.
- Fourth, it compels *ends-means thinking* with statements (questions) designed to advance your case theory and discredit the other side's.

C. The Words

The ultimate success of a cross-examination depends on the words, sentences, and sequencing that the lawyer chooses. Great care must be given to make these points in a clear and convincing manner.

Cross-examination is composed of spoken words, which are different than written words. Even a brilliant speech to the ear can seem inarticulate to the eye. Anyone who has read their own trial transcript knows this. The reverse is also true, where well-written words on the page do not seem so when spoken aloud.

While effective courtroom communication requires plain spoken English, the legal profession as a whole has trouble with this. There are a number of reasons why. Lawyers spend years in college and law school speaking written English. The habit of using legal jargon only adds to the problem. Further, in criminal cases, lawyers on both sides draw on the argot of the police and the underworld, resulting in a mutant combination of stilted written English, legalese, cop talk, and crook talk: "He subsequently exited his vehicle and terminated the altercation."

Trial lawyers need to speak clearly and simply. Use powerful verbs and nouns. Drop unnecessary adjectives and adverbs, which only allow the witness an opportunity to explain away and dodge. For instance, asking, "He fully complied with your request?" would permit an evasive, "That depends on how you define 'fully.'" Alternatively, the witness can give a speech, explaining, "No, he didn't. While he did provide the invoice, he didn't turn over the supporting documentation. He also didn't tell me . . ." Control is maintained by omitting the adverb "fully" and substituting nouns: "He complied with your request to turn over the invoice?"

English has a rich vocabulary drawn from many sources. Legalese tends to come from Latin and Norman French. The most powerful words in English are Anglo-Saxon. Almost every curse word in English has an Anglo-Saxon origin. Anglo-Saxon words are simple. They are explosive. They are satisfying to speak and to hear. Compare the following:

Latin/Norman French	Anglo-Saxon	Latin/Norman French	Anglo-Saxon
Bovine	Cow	Feline	Cat
Canine	Dog	Rodent	Rat
Repair	Fix	Excavate	Dig
Implement	Tool	Aviator	Flyer
Insect	Bug	Celerity	Speed

Avoid words from Latin and Norman French. Instead, use the Anglo-Saxon. Try to screen out any legalese. And, avoid cop-talk, which can infect the vocabulary of any lawyer working in the criminal justice system. Substitute plain English, such as replacing "exited her vehicle" with "got out of her car," "altercation" with "fist fight," and "subsequent to" with "after." While it goes against legal training and communication with law enforcement officers and requires self-conscious effort, it results in greater persuasion. The bottom line solution is to avoid jargon and big and refined words.

A trial lawyer is off to a good start by speaking plainly, using simple words. But this is only the beginning of effective communication. String those simple words together into simple sentences with one noun, one verb, and, if necessary, one predicate nominative or direct object. Avoid compound complex sentences with dependent clauses and participial phrases.

D. Statements, Not Questions

Never forget that the essential purpose of cross-examination is to put your trial story before the jury. The witness is only a medium to deliver the message. That is why the left column of the cross-notes format is filled with statements, not questions. People ask questions because they do not know the answer. This is not your situation as a cross-examiner.

Questions seeking information are inappropriate and even dangerous in cross-examination. They can make a witness seem the fount of information for the jury, giving up a lawyer's power and control. Questions cede power to the witness while statements retain control by the lawyer.

In the context of obtaining concessions, the maxim: "Never ask a question you don't know the answer to," has three corollaries:

1. Display your knowledge of the answer to the witness;
2. The jury; and
3. Before the witness speaks.

A witness who understands that the lawyer knows the answer will be less likely to try to evade. Jurors who know the right answer before a witness speaks will be disappointed when the witness fails to provide it. How can the examiner accomplish all this? With statements, not questions. Just state the facts and anticipate that the witness will agree. Example:

Q. You saw a car.

Say it with a period. Do not say it with a question mark. The court reporter will supply the question mark in the transcript.

Opposing counsel might say, "Your Honor, I object. Counsel isn't asking questions, she's making statements. She's testifying." This objection might have some merit if counsel makes long, complex statements. But if you stick to short statements, this objection is easily defeated. How? Give the court and counsel a grammar lesson. The "statement" is really a question. It is an elliptical question in which the phrase ". . . didn't you?" or ". . . isn't that right?" is understood. It just sounds like a statement because of the period at the end.

If the judge sustains the objection, you only need add "true," "correct," or "isn't that right" to convert the statement into a question. Alternatively, raise the tone of your voice at the end of the statement. Tonal inflection can transform a statement into a question. After making a few statements followed by "true" or another suffix, go back to making unadorned statements. Counsel should not object again.

E. The "Yes" Effect and the Stacking Technique

A short, plain English statement demands a "yes" answer. By contrast, long, leading questions that suggest the desired answer carry the seeds of their own demise. For example:

> Q. It's a fact that you saw a blue automobile driven by the defendant speed down the road, veer into the left lane, and strike the plaintiff, knocking him off his bicycle, isn't it?

Long, leading questions invite disagreement. The witness can pick any of at least six facts in this question for selective denial.

> A. No, I didn't see a blue automobile driven by the defendant speed down the road, veer into the left lane, and strike the plaintiff, knocking him off his bicycle.

Now the questioner must sift through the facts with a series of questions trying to find out why the witness did not give the "yes" concession. The jury will enjoy the cross-examiner's discomfiture so much that they may miss any helpful admission obtained.

Short leading questions have the same objective as long leading questions, but they don't give the witness nearly as much wiggle room. This is the "yes" effect. Example:

> Q. You saw a car, true?

The statement has only one fact. The witness does not have as many options, either admitting the fact or denying it. Selective denial does not work here. Short questions demand short answers.

In Chapter 10, Witness Control Strategies & Techniques, we discuss evasion tactics that witnesses employ and how the examiner can defeat them. The most powerful countermeasure is the short, plain English leading question. The fewer words, the more forceful the statement, giving the witness a hard time deflecting, avoiding, or selectively answering.

Short statements can be stacked upon one another like laying bricks until they build a wall. With this stacking technique, you can compound multiple concessions and help the jury retain the information. For example:

Stacking Technique

Q. You saw a car.

Q. The car was blue.

Q. The blue car was going west.

Q. The defendant was in the blue car going west.

Q. The defendant was driving the blue car going west.

Q. The defendant was speeding as he drove the blue car west.

Q. As the defendant sped west in the blue car, he crossed the center line.

Q. As the defendant sped west in the blue car, he crossed the center line and struck the plaintiff.

Q. When the defendant sped west in the blue car, crossed the center line, and struck the plaintiff, he knocked him down.

Q. When the plaintiff hit the pavement of the left lane, the defendant continued speeding west in the blue car and ran over him.

Q. After the defendant in the blue car speeding west ran over the plaintiff in the left lane, he didn't stop.

Q. After the defendant in the blue car speeding west ran over the plaintiff in the left lane, he drove on down the street until you could no longer see him.

The last question of this series may look long, but it is based on facts that were introduced one at a time in the series. The concessions are sequenced, building upon one another until they provide a complete picture of the defendant's negligent driving.

F. *The Convenience Store Robbery* Criminal Case Illustration

Let's apply the cross-notes format to the *Convenience Store* robbery case introduced at pages 36-37, and the cross-examination of the defendant's alibi witness, Greg Lewis Delaney. First, we list the factual bullets from our brainstorming on what the witness must either admit or answer to seem evasive or not credible to the jury. Second, those points are put into the compact cross-notes format. Third is the likely result of this exchange between lawyer and witness in trial.

Facts Showing Mistake or Lack of Perception

There are a number of factual statements that expose the weakness of the alibi witness in this case. For the full list of points, see either pages 38-39 or the transcript that follows the list of factual statements.

List of Factual Statements

Facts Showing Mistake or Lack of Perception That the Defendant Was at the Party from 10:00 p.m. to 3:00 a.m. in the *Convenience Store Robbery* Case

- The party was at Delaney's apartment complex.
- At the party, people were in several rooms.
- People were milling around.
- Between 40 and 50 people attended.
- Delaney was the host.
- Delaney moved around and mingled.
- People were drinking.
- Delaney was drinking.
- Delaney did not keep track of when people arrived or left the party.

These cross notes are available for the prosecutor to use as a reference during the examination of this witness. They are in statements, not questions, consistent with the essential purpose of cross-examination — to deliver your message to the jury.

CROSS-NOTES FORMAT
The *Convenience Store Robbery* Case

TOPIC: Mistake-Perception Problem

FACTS	REFERENCES & NOTES
- Party was at your apartment complex	
- People weren't only in one place — say the living room	Diagram it
- People milling around	
- 40-50 people there	Delaney's witness statement, p. 4
- You were host	
- You moved around and mingled	
- People were drinking	
- You were drinking	
- You were drinking throughout the evening	
- You did not know when each person arrived or left the party	
- You did not check watch or write the times — no reason to	
- When in one room cannot see into other rooms	
- Can walk out back and around front to street	

The prosecutor's objective is to demolish the defendant's alibi while supporting the prosecutor's case theory that the defendant robbed Blue Moon News.
These cross notes will help the prosecutor focus on the inability of the alibi witness to have observed the defendant at the party for the entire time.

The prosecutor's cross-examination questions now are placed in a full transcript, giving you a feel for the rhythm, buildup, and structure of how this alibi
witness is attacked. When the prosecutor testifies through leading questions, the
witness almost always answers them as the cross-examiner wishes.

TRANSCRIPT

Facts Showing Mistake or Lack of Perception That the Defendant Was at the Party from 10:00 p.m. to 3:00 a.m. in the *Convenience Store Robbery* Case

Prosecutor: *Q.* Now, this party went on from 10:00 p.m. to 3:00 a.m.?

Delaney: *A.* Uh huh.

Q. And once it got going, there were 40 to 50 people there?

A. I guess.

Q. This was at your apartment on 116 Bay Street?

A. Yes.

Q. Your Honor, may Mr. Delaney step down to the easel?

Judge: You may step down, Mr. Delaney.

Q. The blank page has been marked State's Exhibit #6 for identification. I'm handing you a blue marker. Mr. Delaney, could you please give us a rough diagram of
your apartment?

A. I can't really draw very well.

Q. No problem. Nothing artistic or to scale. Just give us a rough sketch.

A. Okay. *[Proceeds to draw.]*

Q. Could you label each room?

A. Sure.

Prosecutor: Let the record reflect that the witness has used a blue pen to draw the
apartment and has labeled each room.

Q. Okay, take us through your apartment.

A. Well, here's a small entry hall. To the left is the living room . . . *[Witness goes on to
explain all the rooms in his apartment.]*

Q. Thank you. Please return to your seat on the witness stand. Now, your apartment
is on the first floor?

Prosecutor: Your Honor, I offer State's Exhibit #6.

Defense Counsel: No objection.

Judge: Exhibit 6 is admitted.

A. Yes.

Q. So, in addition to the rooms you've shown us on the diagram, you've got a patio
off the family room?

A. Yes.

Q. And from there you can step right into the backyard of the apartment complex?

A. Yes.

Q. May I approach the witness, Your Honor?

Judge: You may.

Q. Mr. Delaney, I'm showing you what has been marked as State's Exhibit #7 for identification. That's a photo of your patio and the backyard?

A. Yes.

Q. That fairly and accurately represents what the patio and backyard look like on January 15?

A. Sure.

Q. I offer State's Exhibit #7 into evidence.

Judge: Any objection?

Defense Counsel: No.

Judge: So admitted.

Prosecutor: I'm placing the photograph on the document camera so everyone can see it. There's this walkway here across the backyard?

A. Uh huh.

Q. That goes all the way around the complex to the street?

A. Yes.

Q. So, if you wanted to, you could walk out the family room onto the patio and then go on that walkway around the building to the street in front of the apartment complex?

A. I guess.

Q. Thank you, Your Honor. Now, Mr. Delaney, this was not a sit-down dinner, was it?

A. No.

Q. Those 40 to 50 people were going all through your apartment?

A. Not my bedroom.

Q. But the living room?

A. Yes.

Q. They went in the kitchen?

A. Some.

Q. The family room?

A. Yeah.

Q. Dining room?

A. Yes.

Q. Out on the patio?

A. Uh huh.

Q. You're a good host?

A. I try.

Q. So, as they say, you mingled among your guests?

A. Yes.

Q. Made people feel welcome?

A. I guess.

Q. Introduced people?

A. Most of these people knew each other.

Q. You were talking to people?

continued ▶

A. Yes.

Q. Making sure they had drinks?

A. Yes.

Q. And food?

A. Sure.

Q. You had a few drinks yourself?

A. Sure.

Q. You were in different rooms over the course of the evening?

A. Yes.

Q. And when you're in the kitchen, you can't see the family room?

A. No.

Q. Or the living room?

A. No.

Q. And from the living room, you can't see the family room?

A. No.

Q. Or the dining room?

A. No.

Q. Now let's talk about other people who attended your party. Name a couple other people who were in attendance.

A. Randy and Karen Erickson and Burke Robinson.

Q. When did Randy Erickson arrive?

A. Early in the party. Maybe around 10:30 p.m.

Q. What did you talk to Karen Erickson about?

A. The Super Bowl, I think.

Q. When did Burke Robinson arrive?

A. I'm not sure.

Q. What did Burke Robinson have to drink?

A. He likes Scotch.

Q. You testified that the defendant was at your party from 10:00 p.m. on January 15 until 3:00 a.m. the following morning, correct?

A. Yes.

Q. You didn't check your watch when he arrived, did you?

A. No.

Q. You didn't write down the time he arrived, correct?

A. No.

Q. The defendant wasn't the first to arrive, was he?

A. No.

Q. You had no reason to note the time of his arrival?

A. No.

Q. You didn't keep track of when the 40 to 50 people arrived, did you?

A. No.

Q. You had no reason to?

A. No.

Q. The first time you were asked to remember when you saw the defendant at your party was when the defendant called you?

A. I guess.

> *Q.* He called you two months after your party?
> *A.* Yes.
> *Q.* With all the people there and the drinking, you're not sure when you saw the defendant at your party, are you?
> *A.* Not every second. But, I know he was there the entire time.

If Delaney had conceded that he was unsure when he saw the defendant at the party, the cross-examination should have stopped, ending with a triumphant, "No further questions." Such a concession would have taken out the defendant's alibi witness completely. As it is, Delaney's certainty that the defendant never left the party will seem implausible to the jurors, based on their experience and common sense.

Witness Bias and Interest

Brainstorming also has produced factual statements regarding the witness's bias. These will play an important role in the content of the cross. For the full list of points, see either page 40 or the transcript that follows the list of factual statements.

List of Factual Statements

Witness Bias and Interest
in the *Convenience Store Robbery* Case

- They both worked at Tire Universe.
- Until December 15 of last year, defendant Mike Ryan also worked there.
- Delaney and the defendant worked there for two years together.
- Tire Universe is a small business.
- There are few employees.
- Delaney worked in the same room as the defendant.
- For two years they saw each other almost every day at work.
- They ate lunch together.
- They talked daily.
- The two socialized when they worked at Tire Universe.
- On January 15, the witness threw a party.
- The defendant attended the party.
- The witness and defendant spoke at the party.
- The witness was happy the defendant attended the party.
- The witness invited the defendant to the party.
- The witness considered the defendant a friend.
- The witness wants to help the defendant.

CROSS-NOTES FORMAT
Convenience Store Robbery Case

TOPIC: Bias

FACTS	REFERENCES & NOTES
• You work at Tire Universe	
• Until December 15 of last year the Def., Mike Ryan, also worked there	
• You and the Def. worked there for two years together	
• Small business	
• Few employees	
• You worked in same room as the Def.	Delaney's witness statement, p. 3, l.4
• For two years saw each other almost every day at work	
• Ate lunch together	
• Talked daily	Delaney's witness statement, p. 3, l.7
• You socialized with the Def. When both worked at Tire Universe	
• January 15, you threw a party	
• Def. was there	
• You and he spoke	
• He seemed happy at the party	
• You invited him	
• Considered him a friend	
• Want to help him here	

TRANSCRIPT

Witness Bias and Interest
The *Convenience Store Robbery* Case

Prosecutor: *Q.* Mr. Delaney, you work at Tire Universe?

Delaney: *A.* Yes.

Q. You work in the showroom?

A. Yes.

Q. The defendant also worked in the showroom?

A. For a while.

Q. In fact, you and Ryan worked together in that showroom for two years, until he left on December 15?

A. I'm not sure about the date he left.

Q. But, it was around mid-December?

A. Seems about right.

Q. You worked together for two years?

A. Yes.

Q. Besides you and the defendant, there were only four other employees who also worked on the floor?

A. Yes.

Q. So, for two years, you and the defendant saw each other almost every weekday?

A. Pretty much.

Q. You ate your lunch together most days?

A. I guess.

Q. You talked together?

A. Well, sure . . . we were working together; you have to talk.

Q. But you also talked about personal things?

A. Yeah.

Q. You talked about what was going on in your lives?

A. Sometimes.

Q. You went out with defendant after work sometimes?

A. Yes.

Q. You socialized together on some weekends?

A. Sometimes.

Q. You became friends?

A. Yes.

Q. So when you threw a party on January 15, you invited your friend, the defendant?

A. Sure.

Q. And he came?

A. Yes.

Q. You were happy he was there?

A. I guess.

Q. You took time to talk to him?

A. Yeah.

While Delaney is vulnerable to being impeached as the defendant's friend, biased in his favor, all is not so simple. The tactical choices here illustrate the need to remain focused on and consistent with your case theory. Just because you can do something on cross does not mean that you should. The mere fact that bias is on the list of possible impeachment areas does not mean that it should be routinely explored. Perhaps the witness will not appear as biased to the jury as you think.

Even more important, a bias contention may be inconsistent with the purpose of your cross. Here, the prosecutor's theory is that the defendant robbed the convenience store. The purpose of cross of the alibi witness is to demolish the claim that the defendant and the witness were together throughout the party. But this could blow up in the prosecutor's face under certain conditions. For example, if the witness is a close friend of the defendant, it is more likely that they would have spent significant time together at the party, with Delaney tracking his whereabouts. But, if they are simply work acquaintances, this proposition is far less likely. The message here is to look at your facts critically prior to a cross-examination, being very sure of what the implications will be to a reasonable jury.

Inconsistent Statement

List of Factual Statements

**Prior Inconsistent Statement
in the *Convenience Store Robbery* Case**

Delaney must concede certain facts concerning his statement to the detective.

- The detective came to Delaney's house.
- Delaney spoke to the detective on April 15.
- Delaney was aware that the detective was seeking the truth from witnesses during the investigation.
- Delaney knew it was important to tell the truth to the detective.
- The detective asked Delaney about the January 15 party.
- Delaney said to the detective, "Mike was at my party from 10:00 p.m. until the end at 3:00 a.m., at least I think so."

**CROSS-NOTES
Prior Statement—Unsure
Convenience Store Robbery Case**

TOPIC: Prior Inconsistent Statement

FACTS	REFERENCES & NOTES
<ul><li>Ever make a statement to anyone indicating that you were not sure about the time?</li><li>Sure about that too</li><li>You spoke to detective on April 15</li><li>Det. was at your home</li><li>It was 7:00 p.m.</li><li>He asked you about the January 15 party</li><li>You said to the Det.: "Mike was at my party from 10:00 p.m. until the end at 3:00 a.m., at least I think so."</li></ul>	Delaney's witness statement, p. 5

The prosecutor's cross notes now form the basis of the questioning of Delaney on the prior inconsistent statement.

TRANSCRIPT

Prior Statement—Unsure
The *Convenience Store Robbery* Case

Prosecutor: *Q.* So, you're telling the jury that you have no doubt the defendant was at your party for every moment from 10:00 p.m. to 3:00 a.m.?

Delaney: *A.* None. He was there!

Q. *[Prosecutor focuses witness on prior conversation with detective.]* On April 15, you had a conversation with Detective Malcomb?

A. April 15? I'm not sure about that date.

Q. But you did talk to the detective around mid-April?

A. Yeah.

Q. He came over to your apartment?

A. Yes.

Q. Around 7:00 p.m., after dinner?

A. I guess.

Q. The detective wanted to talk about the defendant and defendant's alibi that he was at your party?

A. Yes.

Q. *[Now Prosecutor does buildup, bringing out commonsense reasons why Delaney's statements to the detective would be accurate.]* When you talked to the detective, you knew this was a serious matter?

A. Yes.

Q. A serious crime was charged, armed robbery?

A. Yes.

Q. So, you were not going to lie to a member of law enforcement, were you?

A. Of course not.

Q. You were going to try to be as accurate as possible?

A. Of course.

Q. The detective asked you the time during which the defendant had been at your party?

A. Uh huh.

Q. You told him, "Mike was at my party from 10:00 p.m. until the end at 3:00 a.m., at least I think so."?

A. *[If Delaney answers "Yes," undoubtedly accompanied by some explanation, the impeachment is complete. If he denies making the statement, the prosecutor will have to recall the detective in rebuttal to get out Delaney's statement and thereby complete the impeachment.]*

Note that with the concessions obtained, the prosecutor's closing argument can now refer to Delaney's uncertainty about how long the defendant had been at the party: "At least I think so."

III. TYPES OF QUESTIONS

Two types of questions may be asked during trial: (1) interrogatory and (2) leading. As a rule for cross-examination, avoid the first type and stick to the second.

A. Interrogatory

Never Ask "How" or "Why" Questions

"Why . . .?" and "How . . .?" are interrogatory or exploratory questions, non-leading in nature. Stay away from them in your cross-examination, as they almost always turn control over to the witness. Open-ended "why" questions allow a witness to expound. More likely than not, the answer will damage your case.

For example, in a burglary trial, the investigating officer on direct examination identified a screwdriver found at the scene as belonging to the defendant. When the screwdriver was offered into evidence, defense counsel crossed the witness. Defense counsel's first, last, and only question was "How do you know that the screwdriver belongs to my client?" The witness smiled and said, "Because, counselor, he told me it was his screwdriver."

"Why" questions present even more pitfalls than "how" questions. When anyone takes any action, it can be explained on three levels:

1. *Reason* — the actual reason he did whatever was done;
2. *Rationale* — how he explains the actions to himself; and
3. *Rationalization* — how he explains his actions to others.

The *reason* a person scratches is an itch, which explains the action to himself and others. More complex activities are less easily explained. A person might shoot another in a bar fight because he was drunk and angry. His *rationale* justifying this could be that the victim was asking for it. Neither his reason nor his rationale provides a legal defense. Therefore, he *rationalizes* it to others by claiming the victim was attacking him.

The different levels of explanation are illustrated in the seemingly hopeless defense of two men in a robbery case. While seven eyewitnesses identified the defendants as the robbers, the defense was mistaken identity. The jury stunned the courtroom by returning a verdict for grand larceny, which carried a five-year sentence, not for robbery, which carried a life sentence. The defendants, professional robbers, were ecstatic.

As defense counsel walked out of the courtroom, he passed two jurors, who were talking about their verdict. He overheard a juror say, "They just didn't prove it." "They just didn't prove it" was their rationale for the not guilty verdict on the robbery charge. If "they just didn't prove it," the verdict should have been not guilty on the lesser grand larceny charge as well.

The next day the local paper editorialized about how the defense attorney hoodwinked the gullible jury. The jurors then called the sheriff, saying they had made a mistake. The prosecution filed a motion for a new trial, and the judge reconvened the jury to get their explanation for their verdict.

The jurors had been instructed on robbery and the grand larceny lesser offense. Each juror testified that they had been confused by the number of verdict forms, and they had chosen grand larceny because it must be the biggest crime. After all, it was "grand," wasn't it?

Their rationalization didn't match the rationale the defense attorney had heard the day of the verdict. Their rationale also didn't match the verdict forms. The robbery verdict said, "Guilty of robbery as charged in the information," but the grand larceny verdict said, "Guilty of the lesser offense of grand larceny." The trial judge ordered a new trial.

Ultimately, the appellate court reinstated the grand larceny verdict because reconvening a discharged jury to reconsider their announced verdict violates the constitutional proscription against double jeopardy. The reason for the verdict was stupidity. The rationale for the verdict was insufficient evidence. The rationalization for the verdict was confusion.

The three levels we just have discussed help explain the conventional wisdom that "why" questions are not part of an effective cross-examination. Whenever counsel asks "why," the question invites the witness to rationalize. If your questions invite a self-serving monologue, you are stuck listening to the unwanted answer.

Exceptions to the Rule

Never say never. In a well-planned and executed cross-examination, a "why" question can be effective. This requires the questioner to lock all doors through properly sequenced preliminary questions, leaving the witness no avenue of escape.

Counsel should never ask a "why" question unless it has been carefully considered with an expected payoff worth the risk. In most instances, you will end up saving the "why" question for final argument. That way, you can answer it yourself, certain of an explanation you like. Letting a witness answer the "why" question is always a gamble.

Take the example of Horace Morgan, who gave his friend Red White a ride to the home of White's estranged wife. Morgan sat in his car and watched White enter the home, armed with a .45 caliber automatic. A few minutes later, Morgan heard a fusillade of shots, and then White returned to the car. White handed the gun to Morgan and said, "I killed the bitch. Will you hide my gun for me?" Morgan took the gun and gave it to his girlfriend to keep.

When White got arrested, the girlfriend turned the gun over to law enforcement and Morgan was charged with accessory after the fact to first degree murder. At trial Morgan insisted that he had no intention of hiding the gun or helping White evade arrest. The cross-examination went like this:

Asking the "Why" Question

Q. Now, the officers asked you if Mr. White had any guns, didn't they?

A. Yes, sir.

Q. And you told them about him having a .410 shotgun?

A. Yes, sir.

Q. And you knew at that time that he had more than a .410, didn't you?

A. I didn't have a lawyer present to be answering that type of a question.

Q. You have a lawyer present now?

A. Yes, sir.

Q. And I'm asking you, at the time that you told them that he had a .410, you knew he had another gun?

A. For just a few hours.

Q. You knew that he had another gun, didn't you?

A. I guess, yes, sir.

Q. And that gun was a .45?

A. Yes, sir.

Q. The same caliber as the one that the police said had killed White's wife?

A. Yes, sir.

Q. And you didn't want them to know about that gun, did you?

A. I had full intentions of giving the gun up to them.

Q. So you figured just telling them about the .410 was going to help them find the .45 at your girlfriend's house?

A. No, sir. I don't see how that works.

Q. As a matter of fact, when you told them about the .410 and didn't tell them about the .45 you were hiding that .45 from them, weren't you?

A. No, sir. I wasn't hiding it from nobody.

Q. Then why didn't you tell the police about the .45 at your girlfriend's house?

A. I just had it put up until I knew for a fact whether he was telling me the truth or lying about killing his wife.

Q. The police had just told you that he'd killed his wife with a .45, hadn't they?

A. Yes, sir, but I didn't know if I could believe them, either.

In the previous example, the prosecutor felt safe in asking the "why" question for two reasons: (1) lack of any credible exculpatory answer, and (2) a defendant without the brain power to invent one. If the prosecutor had held the defendant's intellect in higher regard, the "why" question might not have been asked.

B. Leading

Only Leading Questions

Leading questions are authorized for cross-examination by Federal Evidence Rule 611(c) and similar state evidence rules. A leading question is one that suggests the answer. Most of your cross-examination questions should be leading. Leading questions keep the control of the examination with the questioner. Embedding the desired answers best safeguards against harmful ones. Further, leading questions enable the cross-examiner to tell the case story as the examiner wants it told.

The statements in your cross-notes format ("Tire Universe is a small business") drive the leading form. The cross-examiner can either add a word or two ("Tire Universe is a small business, true?") or raise the tone of voice at the end of the sentence in order to make the statement sound more like a question.

Exceptions to the Rule

Although some contend that a cross-examiner should only ask leading questions, we do not agree with this as an absolute rule. When it is safe to do so, you should ask interrogatory, rather than leading, questions. Otherwise, jurors may conclude that you alone are testifying. Also, persistent statements by counsel compelling a "yes" or "no" answer tend to become tedious.

The only-leading-questions rule can safely be broken in three situations. First, open-ended questions can be asked of honest, nonpartisan witnesses, provided you are on the side of the truth, which we hope you always will be. The more partisan the witness, the riskier it is to ask open-ended questions. The other side's expert falls into this category. The interrogatory question likely will be taken as an opening to give a speech to the jury.

Second, if the witness tells an ill-conceived lie, open-ended questions can provide the witness with the means of self-destruction. A cross-examiner can invent questions far faster than a lying witness can invent details. Sir Walter Scott's admonition, "Oh, what a tangled web we weave, when first we practice to deceive," applies to the liar in this situation.

Third, the cross-examiner can ask a non-leading question when the risk of a damaging answer is low or nonexistent. For example, in the *Convenience Store Robbery* case, the prosecutor can ask the alibi witness open-ended questions about the party, such as, "Where were the other people at 11:00 p.m.?" because the response carries little or no danger of a bad answer.

Anticipatory Question

The anticipatory question is a reverse psychology kind of leading question, setting up the witness to give an answer contrary to what would be expected. The anticipatory question serves to highlight the answer. In the *Convenience Store Robbery* case, the prosecutor's question to the alibi witness is a classic form of this subtype: "So, Mr. Delaney when you learned that your friend Mike Ryan had been arrested for robbery committed at the time when he was at your party, you immediately went to the police and told them?" It is basic human nature to try and save an innocent friend from being wrongfully accused. When the alibi witness answers "No," as the prosecutor knows he will, it discredits the defendant's claim of being at the party at the time of the robbery.

Accusatory Question

The accusatory form is another subtype of the leading question; it accuses the witness of something that you want the jurors to deduce on their own. For instance, the prosecutor could accusatorily ask alibi witness Delaney, "The fact of the matter is you have no idea where the defendant was during most of the time of the party, do you?" Or, "The defendant is your friend and you would say anything for him, right?"

There are four reasons for asking the accusatory question. First, by making a closing argument point, which is what the accusatory question does, you highlight the conclusion for the jury and stamp the witness's denial as patently false. Second, the accusatory question serves as a signpost for any juror who may have missed the thrust of the line of questions. Third, in the interest of fair play, the accusatory question provides the witness with an opportunity to deny the accusation. Fourth and finally, if you reserve the accusation for closing, wise opposing counsel will ask the unasked accusatory question on redirect and have the witness explain or otherwise defuse the impeachment.

However, when you ask the accusatory question it is probable that the witness will disagree with your accusation. And, if given a chance, the response with contain either an explanation or evasion. Also, you may draw a sustained objection that the accusatory question is argumentative. For these reasons, you may decide to reserve the accusation for closing argument.

Agreement Question

The agreement question is another form of leading the witness. It phrases questions amicably in order to elicit concessions. The cross-examiner can begin by asking, "Let's see what we can agree about. Is that all right with you?" The technique is to just add the phrase "Can we agree" at the beginning of each concession-seeking statement on the cross-notes format. An example in the *Convenience Store Robbery* case for the alibi witness is when the prosecutor asks, "Mr. Delaney, can we agree that 40 to 50 people attended your party?" Naturally, there are other phrasings of the agreement question, such as, "Wouldn't it be fair to say . . . ?" or, "You would agree that . . . ?"

IV. ORGANIZATION OF CROSS-EXAMINATION

A. Persuasive Order

The cross-notes format assembles your ideas into topical units, such as "bias." Like a movie scene, each topical unit has a beginning, middle, and end. Next, just like individual scenes are edited into a movie, you must organize these topical units into a unified story for the cross. Because the units usually are self-contained, you can move them around. You can tab the sections and arrange them either in a notebook, file, or other organizer until you are satisfied. Your fundamental goal throughout this process is to end up with the most persuasive presentation possible.

Cross-examination can be organized in at least three ways: chronological, topical, or a mixture of the two. In the *Convenience Store Robbery* case, an example of a combined chronological and topical cross on witness bias would be to focus questions on the relationship between the alibi witness and the defendant and then trace their relationship forward from when they first met.

B. Primacy

Knockout First

When you first rise to cross-examine a witness, the jury is paying close attention. Like any good movie, the opening scene—topical unit—should grab the audience's attention and draw the audience into the story. Because you are the director, you can start the storytelling anywhere you wish.

For these reasons, if you are extremely confident, and we mean absolutely sure, that you can immediately decimate either opposing counsel's case theory or the witness with a few well-phrased questions, you probably should do so. It is like going for knockout in the first round of a boxing match. You may be able to achieve it or, at least, put the witness on the defensive and backpedaling. A horrendous inconsistency between the witness's present testimony and prior testimony in a deposition can be a good starting place. This strategy incorporates the doctrine of primacy: the jury remembers best what it hears first.

For example, assume that in a negligence case, the passenger in the defendant-driver's car testifies at trial that the driver was "not distracted in any way" prior to the collision. She had testified to the contrary in her deposition, stating that the defendant was talking on her cell phone. The plaintiff's lawyer's cross-examination begins by firmly fixing the not-distracted-in-any-way version and then proceeds to deliver the knockout.

PRIMACY — THE KNOCKOUT

Driver Negligence Case

Q. Do you recall having your deposition taken in my office on June 23 of last year?

A. Yes.

Q. Do you remember raising your right hand and swearing to tell the truth?

A. Yes.

Q. Do you remember testifying as follows; I'm starting on page 23, line 12, do you see it here in the transcript of your deposition?

A. Yes.

Plaintiff's Counsel: Please listen as I read your deposition. Q. What was the defendant doing just prior to the collision? A. She was on her cell phone arguing with her mother.

A. Yes.

Q. Did I read that correctly?

A. Yes.

---

continued ▶

> *Q.* Now today you just raised your right hand and swore to tell the truth and testified that the defendant was not distracted in any way just prior to the collision, correct?
>
> *A.* Yes.
>
> *Q.* Which version would you like this jury to believe: what you testified to here or what you testified to during your deposition?

Concessions First

It would be great to flatten a witness at the outset of cross-examination, but you seldom can. As a general principle, cross-examination should normally begin with questions designed to obtain concessions. You can begin in a pleasant, non-confrontational manner that is likely to elicit "yes" answers. We discuss the character and manner of the cross-examiner in greater detail in Chapter 9.

You could employ the can-we-agree questioning technique. This approach is sometimes referred to as "pet-the-dog." Ideally, your initial questions will be ones that the witness will want to answer with "yes." In the *Convenience Store Robbery* case, defense counsel might begin to attack the identification of the defendant with questions such as, "That must have been really scary when you saw the gun? You must have been thinking that this person might panic or be crazy and shoot you?" Pet the dog first and a tail wags, but abuse the dog and you risk getting bitten. If you appear friendly when you begin to cross-examine the witness, it is more likely that you will get the responses you want.

Factors to Consider

The objectives set for cross and the psychology of the witness dictate how to sequence a cross-examination. For example, if the objectives are to elicit both concessions that bolster the examiner's case theory and impeachment material, the cross-examiner may begin by harvesting those concessions and once that has been achieved, then turn to impeachment. On the other hand, the cross-examiner may begin by gaining concessions, and if that is accomplished—if the witness has been turned to the examiner's advantage—the examiner may forgo impeaching the witness. If the witness is unlikely to give concessions, the cross may be devoted to discrediting the witness and the witness's testimony.

The evasive witness serves as an example of how a witness's psychology determines the order of the cross-examination. Assume that the objective of the cross is to gain concessions but that the witness deflects the questions and then bridges to information that the witness wishes to testify to. Here, the cross-examiner may shift to impeachment with the witness's prior inconsistent statements in the witness's deposition in order to get control over the witness. When the witness attempts to evade, the examiner turns to the deposition in which the witness was asked the same question and gave a different answer. The examiner continues asking questions directly from the deposition in order to reign in the witness whenever the witness attempts to depart from the answer given in the deposition. Having gained control over the witness, the examination returns to the original objective of gaining concessions supportive of the examiner's case theory.

C. Recency

Strong, Memorable Ending

Like a good movie, an effective cross-examination should have a strong, memorable ending. This approach incorporates the doctrine of recency, which is related to primacy, covered earlier in this chapter. Primacy refers to what is heard first, recency to what is heard last. People remember best what they hear first and second best what they hear last. According to some schools of thought, as a cross-examiner goes through the cross, if the examiner scores a major point, she should not be afraid to sit down without covering all the other points the examiner planned to cover. Ordinarily, this strategy is a good one. However, we believe that stopping early also can reflect a lack of preparation, skill, or confidence. If you have thoroughly prepared your cross, you will finish with a strong, invulnerable point based on admissible evidence that the witness must concede or be impeached. However, on those rare occasions where this falls flat, loop back to a previous topic that was productive and then return to your seat victorious.

Ending with a bang and adhering to the doctrine of recency should not just be reserved for the very end of a cross-examination. Watch the clock and try to end each court session of cross this way, particularly at the end of the day. This leaves the jurors with something favorable to the cross-examiner to take away.

Recross

Also, consider holding something in reserve for recross-examination in order to have the last word. However, you may not be able to recross because recross is "normally confined to questions directed to the explanation or avoidance of new matter brought out on redirect." C. McCormick, *Evidence* § 32 (E. Cleary 2d ed. 1972), 64, and the redirect may not provide the basis for a recross.

As an example of reserving material for recross, in the *Convenience Store Robbery* case, during cross of Delaney, the prosecutor could omit any mention of the witness's prior statement to the detective that was equivocal on whether the defendant was at the party the entire time. It is likely that defense counsel will come back on redirect and have Delaney declare that the defendant was present for the party in its entirety. Then, on recross, the prosecutor can bring out Delaney's prior inconsistent statement. This will leave the jury with a powerful impression that the witness was, at a minimum, mistaken. The only risk here is that the defense redirect will not go into the subject you have saved for recross. If so, the court likely will sustain an objection that the prosecutor's line of questions is outside the scope of the redirect.

V. TRANSITIONS

As you move from topical unit to topical unit or event to event within a unit, use transitional language. These statements are like signposts that tell the jury where you are going. For example, in cross-examining Delaney, the prosecutor could say, "Now, Mr. Delaney, let's discuss your relationship with the defendant."

VI. STORYTELLING THROUGH CROSS—THE *SAMBA SPORTS DROWNING* CIVIL CASE ILLUSTRATION

In Chapter 2, Purposes of Cross & the Total Trial Approach, we discussed the importance of telling a narrative story at trial because that is a key to persuasion. See pages 10-12. The cross of the CEO in the *Samba Sports Drowning* wrongful death case serves as an illustration of how the narrative can be told through cross-examination. On page 12, an analogous fairy tale was told about an arrogant prince who ran down a young woman with his carriage and blamed her for not getting out of the way. This tale serves as the theme for the narrative story unveiled during cross of the CEO. As you will see, this story is a composite of units, just like a movie is a collection of scenes organized into a narrative story. In the *Samba Sports Drowning* case, the scenes are arranged as follows:

- The Core Moral Issue;
- They Should Have Known;
- Causation;
- Duty to Warn;
- Failure to Warn About the Risks to Users;
- The Buck Stops with the CEO; and
- Failure to Conduct an Easy Test.

Counsel starts out his cross-examination of Mr. Howell in the *Samba Sports Drowning* case by focusing on the core moral responsibility in this story: No manufacturer would want to see the product user suffer serious injury or death.

TRANSCRIPT

The Core Moral Issue
***Samba Sports Drowning* Wrongful Death Case**

Q. Do you consider yourself a responsible boating manufacturer?
A. Yes, sir, I do. . . .
Q. You don't want to see customers die using your products?
A. No sir.

Blaming the victim is often an industry defense in product liability cases. Accordingly, it is important to the jury's moral fault determination that cross reveals that the manufacturer has superior knowledge about the potential harm from a product. As a starting point, the defendant's CEO must admit that his company was the boat expert, not consumers like the victim.

With the superior knowledge of this manufacturer admitted, counsel's next step is to establish the causal connection between the product defect and the victim's death.

TRANSCRIPT

They Should Have Known
Samba Sports Drowning Wrongful Death Case

Q. You have a greater knowledge base than the people who buy your boats?

A. We would have, I would feel, a greater knowledge. . . .

Q. Yes. You are the experts in the field of manufacturing ski boats?

A. We believe we are, yes.

Q. And you would agree with me that the greater the risk to health is involved with the use of a product, the more you want to warn the customer and at least tell them what that risk is?

A. Yeah. If it's a risk we know of, yes.

Q. You have no quarrel with the proposition that a reasonable manufacturer must warn a customer of the dangers it knows about?

A. No, I don't.

TRANSCRIPT

Causation
Samba Sports Drowning Wrongful Death Case

Q. You don't have any quarrel with the fact that Ms. Lindsay Young was a passenger on your boat just prior to her death?

A. That seems to be the case.

Q. You don't dispute that she was swimming near the swimming platform at the back of the boat when she disappeared from the surface of the water?

A. I don't know.

Q. Likewise, you don't quarrel with the fact that the engine was running when she was swimming by the platform?

A. I don't.

Ski boat manufacturers have standing technical committees that promulgate written standards and advise manufacturers on safety issues concerning products of interest. In applying these industry publications to the facts of this case, plaintiff's counsel develops the cause and effect relationship between the carbon monoxide exposure and the victim's death.

TRANSCRIPT

Causation—Continued
***Samba Sports Drowning* Wrongful Death Case**

Q. A few questions back, I asked you about the toxicology report that said Lindsay Young had a 52 percent blood saturation of carbon monoxide?

A. Okay.

Q. Do you remember that it was 52 percent?

A. Yes.

Q. You are aware that boating industry standards state that 50 percent saturation of carbon monoxide or greater leads to permanent brain damage or death?

A. Yes. I mean, it's on a chart.

Q. You're a financial guy, you know numbers?

A. Yes, sir.

Q. And we know that the coroner said that she had 52 percent saturation of carbon monoxide and that the industry standards say 50 percent or greater leads to permanent brain damage or death?

A. It says that, yes. It has a chart dealing with times and exposures.

Like the reckless prince in his carriage, the manufacturer just didn't care.

Having established that carbon monoxide emissions from this boat killed the victim, counsel next focuses on getting an admission that this manufacturer should have warned about the carbon monoxide threat.

TRANSCRIPT

Duty to Warn
***Samba Sports Drowning* Wrongful Death Case**

Q. You have the responsibility to try and get the word out to customers about a potential threat to human life or health?

A. We need to do that.

To establish moral blame during the cross-examination story, plaintiff's counsel tells of defendant's lack of effort to warn product users when the manufacturer had information about the dangers that caused the harm well before the incident. Counsel gets the CEO to admit that his company never bothered to do any research on the carbon monoxide danger.

TRANSCRIPT

Failure to Warn About the Risks to Users
***Samba Sports Drowning* Wrongful Death Case**

Q. You have people at your company who know how to use computer search engines, like Google?

A. Yes.

Q. Have you, as president of this company, ever given an order to any employee to find out all available information on carbon monoxide poisoning?

A. Not in that method, no.

Advertising for Samba Sports boats presents their products in a desirable, highly glamorous light. No information was given to consumers that it may hurt or kill them. This is similar to the arrogant prince, who gives no warning to the public of his carriage's approach. The cross-examination story theme of moral fault in this wrongful death case is reinforced by the absence of any mention of the risks. During trial preparation, counsel went through back issues of consumer boating magazines and pulled the advertisements for defendant's boats over the years. Counsel's goal is to contrast the difference between the idealized brand image of this boat in the ads with the dangerous reality of the product.

TRANSCRIPT

Failure to Warn—Continued
***Samba Sports Drowning* Wrongful Death Case**

Q. *[Plaintiff's counsel has introduced the magazines into evidence as exhibits.]* Nearly every one of the ads in exhibits 45 through 55 made a point that your boats offer more value for the money than the competition right?

A. In general that would be right. I mean, that's kind of one of the themes that follows our product line.

Q. If we look at the people in this ad, once again, they appear to be young people in their 20s or early 30s?

A. Yes, they are.

Q. Nothing is mentioned in these ads about the fact that they could be killed by carbon monoxide poisoning?

A. No, not there.

Q. Did you know of this danger at the time you ran these ads?

A. Yes.

The owner's manual for the Samba ski boat failed to mention the danger that caused Lindsay's death. Counsel confronts the CEO with this failure as well.

TRANSCRIPT

Failure to Warn—Continued
Samba Sports Drowning **Wrongful Death Case**

Q. Prior to the year of Lindsay's death, the owner's manual did not tell the purchasers of your product that carbon monoxide was a silent killer?

A. We didn't state anything regarding carbon monoxide being a silent killer in the manual.

Q. You failed to tell any of your customers in the users manual that carbon monoxide poisoning on a boat could overcome an individual in a matter of seconds?

A. It's not in any of the owner's manuals prior to that.

Counsel then covers the power of this company to have prevented the harm involved in this case and the CEO's personal responsibility for not warning.

TRANSCRIPT

Failure to Warn—Continued and the Buck Stops with the CEO
Samba Sports Drowning **Wrongful Death Case**

Q. Mr. Howell, you've heard a phrase used by President Harry Truman, "The buck stops here"?

A. I've heard that, yes.

Q. What does that phrase mean to you, sir?

A. It means someone is ultimately accountable.

Q. That phrase also applies to the president of a business corporation?

A. In a lot of cases, depending on the situation, but yes.

Q. And at your company, that would be you?

A. I'm the president.

Q. So the buck stops with you?

A. In a lot of cases. In some cases it may be with other people, but yes.

Q. Prior to the time that Lindsay died, you never attempted to send out carbon monoxide warnings to customers, correct?

A. Correct.

Q. You never sent any letters to past customers warning them in any way of carbon monoxide danger?

A. No, sir.

One of the most significant risks for a lawyer is to lose the flow of the cross-examination story by getting too bogged down in details. It is best to select a few things that are most essential to the theme of the story. Counsel did this in his cross-examination of Mr. Howell, taking one photograph from a government safety study showing how easy it would have been for the defendant to test carbon monoxide emissions on ski boats. Counsel confronts Mr. Howell with this photo.

TRANSCRIPT

Failure to Conduct an Easy Test
Samba Sports Drowning **Wrongful Death Case**

Q. Your company never tested any of its boats in the fashion you see in this picture, exhibit 89, for carbon monoxide emissions?

A. No. We have not specifically tested in this environment.

Q. Because you never tested your boat's emissions, you can't tell us what the carbon monoxide readings are around the swim platform of any boat you make?

A. That's correct.

By focusing on key issues of the cross-examination story with the defendant company's CEO, plaintiff's counsel established that the defendant company just did not care. While this cross-examination did not literally use the elements of the arrogant-greedy-prince fairy tale, it did so in a thematic way, taking the same moral high ground. The fairy tale served as a focusing tool for the examination, helping to answer the question, "When I am finished with this witness, how do I want the jury to feel about the defendant?" The whole point of this cross-examination was to establish that, just like the prince, the boat company could have prevented harm by caring about the well-being of others. By not doing so, an innocent person was killed. The defendant emerges every bit as villainous as the arrogant prince.

VII. SCOPE OF CROSS

In constructing the cross-examination, the examiner can only do what evidence law permits, and the Federal Rule of Evidence on scope is a restrictive one.

Rule 611. Mode and Order of Interrogation and Presentation

(b) Scope of cross-examination.
Cross-examination should not go beyond the subject matter of the direct examination and matters affecting the witness's credibility. The court may allow inquiry into additional matters as if on direct examination.

Accordingly, in federal court and in those states that have adopted Rule 611(b), the cross is confined to (1) matter brought out on direct or (2) the credibility of the witness, which includes bias, interest, prior inconsistencies, and so on. Therefore, if the subject was covered on direct, the cross may explore it. *State v. Ferguson*, 100 Wash. 2d 131, 138, 667 P.2d 68, 73-74 (1983). On the other hand under Rule 611(b), if the cross-examiner asks about a subject not covered on direct, such as a concession supporting the examiner's case theory, it is outside the scope and thus inadmissible. The scope of cross-examination is determined within the discretion of the trial judge. *United States v. Smith*, 591 F.3d 974, 981 (8th Cir. 2010); *State v. Lord*, 117 Wash. 2d 829, 870, 822 P.2d 177, 201 (1991).

If opposing counsel objects on the basis that the inquiry is outside the scope of direct and the objection is sustained, counsel may be able to recall the witness and cover the subject then. When the witness is recalled, counsel can ask that the witness be declared hostile and that leading questions be permitted. Fed. R. Evid. 611(c) in part provides:

> Ordinarily, the court should allow leading questions: . . . when a party calls a hostile witness, an adverse party, or a witness identified with an adverse party.

A better strategy for the cross-examiner is to request that the court overrule the objection "in the exercise of discretion" and permit additional questioning rather than causing the inconvenience to the witness and to the court that will result from having to recall the witness. The Advisory Notes' history of the provision allowing the judge to exercise discretion in expanding the scope "is designed for those situations in which the result otherwise would be confusion, complication, or protraction of the case, not as a matter of rule but as demonstrable in the actual development of the particular case."

Your state may not have adopted the restrictive Federal Rule, preferring to adhere to common law that permits wide latitude in cross-examination. For example, Texas Rule of Civil Evidence 611(b) states:

> A witness may be cross-examined on any matter relevant to any issue in the case, including credibility.

The Michigan Rule of Evidence is identical to the Texas Rule but adds this sentence: "The judge may limit cross-examination with respect to matters not testified to on direct examination." Whether your evidence rule is restrictive or wide open will dictate your strategy and how you construct your cross or your cross with a backup plan to recall the witness as your own.

VIII. LENGTH OF THE CROSS

There is no specific time frame that fits all cross-examinations because the extent of cross will vary depending upon the circumstances of the case. However, endless cross is tiresome, and the jurors will not recall much beyond the high points. Therefore, we recommend brevity. By editing down the content, the cross-examiner can better maintain the jury's interest and be more effective.

To make the best allocation of time and to have a powerful cross, adhere to the following guidelines:

- *Limit the total number of topical units* to be covered to less than a handful;
- Concentrate your cross on *only significant points*—avoid minutiae;
- Once you have covered the material in a unit, such as cross on an expert's bias, *move on* to the next unit; and
- Above all, *do not be tempted to conduct an exploratory cross* because something the witness testified to piqued your curiosity.

CHECKLIST: CONSTRUCTING THE CROSS

Your Time to Testify

- ❑ The cross-examiner selects the content, wording, exhibits, pace, duration, and factual sequence for the story told on cross.
- ❑ Cross is the time when the examiner, not the witness, communicates the content to the jury.

Cross Notes

- ❑ Write out the questions to be asked.
- ❑ Utilize the cross-notes format with the argument at the top of the page, factual statements in the left column and references and notes in the right column.
- ❑ Statements in the right column are composed of powerful verbs and nouns in plainspoken English.
- ❑ The left column is filled with statements because that will cause the examiner to ask leading, not interrogatory, questions.
- ❑ Utilize the stacking technique to help the jury retain information.

Types of Questions

- ❑ Avoid interrogatory questions, such as, "How . . .?" and "Why . . .?"
- ❑ Ask only leading questions, except:
  - When you have the witness locked in and the payoff is much greater than any risk;
  - The examiner is on the side of the truth and the witness is honest and nonpartisan;
  - The witness tells an ill-conceived lie and the examiner can lead the liar to self-destruction; and
  - When the examiner does not care what the answer is because it can do no damage to the case.
- ❑ Subcategories of leading questions that can be effective include:
  - The anticipatory question is designed to highlight the answer;

- The accusatory question, which normally should not be asked because the conclusion can be reserved for closing argument; and
- The agreement question that is intended to solicit concessions from the witness.

Organization of Cross

❑ Cross notes are organized into units, which are like scenes in a movie.

❑ Units are then organized into a persuasive story the way scenes are arranged into sequence for a movie.

❑ Utilize the rule of primacy by beginning with a unit that grabs the jury's attention:
  - Normally, it is best to begin by gathering concessions.
  - Only if the cross-examiner is certain should the cross begin with an attempt to destroy the witness or witness's testimony at the outset.
  - It is best to gather concessions first and impeach later or, if the witness concedes enough, abandon the impeachment.

❑ Finish on a high note, which includes finishing not only the total cross with a good line of cross but also plan to finish court sessions and recross with a major point.

❑ Use transitional phrases to help the jury follow the cross.

Scope of Cross

❑ Limit the scope of cross to what the controlling evidence rule (such as Fed. R. Evid. 611(b)) allows.

❑ If the court does not permit the examiner to go outside the scope of direct, the witness may be able to be recalled later as an adverse witness and be subject to leading questions and impeachment.

Length of the Cross

❑ Keep the cross-examination brief because endless cross is boring, and jurors will not retain much beyond the high points.

❑ Guidelines for editing:
  - Limit number of points to a handful.
  - Avoid minutiae and concentrate only on major points.
  - Once you have covered the material in a unit, move on.
  - Do not conduct an exploratory cross.

CHAPTER 5

THE VISUAL CROSS
Seeing Is Believing

"Be sure of it. Give me the ocular proof."
                              Othello, Act 3, Scene 3

I. BRING YOUR STORY ALIVE IN THE COURTROOM AND MAKE IT MEMORABLE

You have developed your narrative story for cross-examination. As we discussed in Chapter 4, cross-examination is your opportunity to testify; an opportunity to tell that story of your case. Now, we focus on how you can bring that story alive in the courtroom and make it memorable for the jury. To accomplish this, visuals are critical. Words are not enough. Jurors expect visual communication. They are visually sophisticated and conditioned by the proliferation of images and videos on the Internet, either owning a computer or having access to one. Many have smart phones and tablets. They also watch television regularly, which presents information in a crisp, visual shorthand style. Over 40 percent of the jury pool nationally belongs to the millennial generation, composed of people who were born after 1982 who grew up with computers in their homes, schools, and businesses. The millennials are accustomed to information being delivered visually and in short order. Consequently, twenty-first-century cross-examinations must track our visual culture, both showing and telling a story. Jurors want to see things for themselves, not just take your word for it.

If you want jurors to retain the narrative you tell on cross, incorporate visuals. Studies have shown that we remember less than 15 percent of what we hear. However, we retain over 80 percent of what we hear and see. Also, adults learn in three different ways. Some are auditory learners. Others are kinetic learners, learning by doing a physical activity. The remainder, approximately 60 percent of the population, are visual learners. Additionally, if you include visuals in your cross-examination, you employ repetition to help jurors retain the cross. This is accomplished by getting the same subject matter before them in verbal and visual form. These two forms of information are processed by the brain differently, so the jurors will not see this as annoying repetition, but rather welcome reinforcement of what they are learning. As an evidentiary matter, visual information is not objectionable as repetitious. For example, on cross you can have the witness describe an intersection while using a diagram. In that words alone are imprecise, the simultaneous use of a visual allows jurors to understand exactly what the witness is saying. If the witness is not describing the scene accurately, the visual will allow the jury to know that immediately. If you do not use a visual at the same time, any mistakes are less likely to be caught by the jury.

Visuals in your storytelling on cross-examination create a consensus among the jurors in a way that words cannot. For example, when the witness verbally describes an intersection, each juror will develop their own mental picture of the intersection, drawing upon their own life experience. Their mental images may not reflect the actual conditions in your case. However, when you display a diagram of the actual intersection, all jurors have an identical understanding of what it looks like.

Finally, visuals can enliven the cross-examination, adding a dynamic multi-media energy to your presentation. Jurors are much more engaged when you give them images to help understand the evidence. You become more interesting and so does your case as you shift from words to visuals.

II. TYPES OF VISUALS AND TECHNOLOGY

Trial visuals range from a simple photograph to a computer-generated animation video. The low-tech photograph may have more of an impact than the high-tech animated video depending upon the circumstances of the case and the content of the visuals. For instance, a photograph of the plaintiff's disfigured face can have more of an impact than an animated video showing an image of her riding her bike, being hit by a passing truck, and being sent to the pavement. The visuals you use at trial must be the result of carefully considered strategic choices. What are the advantages and disadvantages of each visual form? If you show the jury an image that is too graphic and makes them uncomfortable, will this backfire and be held against you? Do you want to use a physical object or model rather than an image? A short list of trial visuals for you to choose from includes: photographs; storyboards; medical illustrations; courtroom demonstrations; scene diagrams; models; timelines; charts; computer animations; and video depositions.

A. Developing Visual Presentations

You or your staff can develop a computer slide show presentation for trial with a software program, such as Windows PowerPoint or Apple Keynote. Resource manuals for creating presentations include William S. Bailey & Robert W. Bailey, *Show the Story: The Power of Visual Advocacy* (Trial Guides, 2011); Ann E. Brenden & John Goodhue, *The Lawyer's Guide to Creating Persuasive Computer Presentations* (2d ed., ABA 2005), which is accompanied by a CD with 12 self-guided tutorials); and Mike Rogers, *Litigation Technology: Becoming a High-Tech Trial Lawyer* (Aspen Publishers 2006). If you work in a prosecutor's or public defender's office, it is quite likely that your staff will consist of you alone. If this is the case, you must be flexible enough teach yourself the necessary skills.

However, for the more high-tech visuals, such as a computer animation, you will need to hire experts to do the science upon which the animation is based and a technology company to program the computer animation. The following are a sampling of companies that can produce trial visual presentations:

- High Impact: http://www.highimpactlit.com
- OnPoint Productions: http://www.onpointpro.biz
- Prolumina: http://www.prolumina.net
- MediVisuals: http://www.medivisuals.com

- Legal Art Works: http://www.legalartworks.com
- Naegeli Trial Technologies: http://www.naegeliusa.com
- Borrowed Ladder Media Services, Inc.: http://www.borrowedladder.com

B. Courtroom Display

How you display your visual in the courtroom depends upon the type of visual, courtroom practice, whether or not you utilize today's technology, and your ingenuity. For example, you could display a blowup of a photo to the jury, project it on a screen with a document camera, or include it in a computer slideshow.

A modern high-tech courtroom would be equipped with the following:

- a document camera;
- wifi;
- television monitors for the judge, jurors, and counsel; and
- a large screen and projector for showing videos, computer slideshows, and other visuals.

If the court does not have the technology you need, you or a company you employ will need to bring it to the court. Naturally, you will need to inform the court in advance and get permission to supply the equipment and as to when to install it. Usually, the court not only determines these matters but also regulates when the jurors will see the visual and what they will see of it.

Documents, photographs, depositions, diagrams, and other exhibits can be digitized for display in an electronic format on a screen or television monitor. Software programs such as TrialDirector by Indata (http://www.indatacorp .com/Support/TrialDirector-Support/) or LexisNexis Sanction (http://www .lexisnexis.com/en-us/litigation/products/sanction.page) store the digitized visuals so that they can be instantly retrieved and shown. Additionally, with this software the visual can be manipulated on the screen. For instance, counsel can retrieve and display a page of a deposition and then call out a sentence on the page and highlight it for the jury. An iPad with the TrialPad app (http://www .litsoftware.com/products/trialpad/) can be utilized in a manner similar to TrialDirector or Sanction. For a further discussion of trial support technology and visual display of a witness's prior statement, see pages 158-159.

III. THE CROSS-EXAMINER AS FILM DIRECTOR

To develop a visual cross, think like a film director. In a film, the story is advanced not only by the words in the script but also by what is seen on the screen. Traditional cross-examinations focus heavily on word play between the lawyer and the witness. Today's cross-examiner, like a film director, must plan out what the jurors see. Film directors plan what the audience will see well in advance of shooting a scene, and so should a cross-examiner.

A. Planning the Visual Cross

The planning of a visual cross-examination is every bit as creative as what a director does prior to shooting a movie. It requires awareness of what both you and your opponent need to prove at trial. How can you visually enhance your witnesses' testimony and weaken that of your opponent? You will need to convince the trial judge that your visual evidence is fair and accurate. Is the evidentiary foundation strong enough to get it in as a part of your case in chief so that it can be used on cross? Or will you have to be satisfied with the lesser status evidence for illustrative purposes, to be used with witness examination and in argument, but not what goes back to the jury room?

The development of a visual cross-examination starts with collecting images that tell the story of your case, why your client deserves to win and your opponent deserves to lose. Whether a civil or criminal matter, visuals fall into the category of either real or demonstrative evidence. Real evidence is something that comes directly out of the underlying action that forms the basis of the legal case. For example, in a criminal matter, police agencies gather physical evidence and take photographs at the scene, later conducting laboratory tests on some of what has been collected. In a civil matter, government agencies often will do an investigation, collecting data and generating reports. Discovery requests later lead to documents and objects that are real evidence, the admissibility of which is determined by relevance and other evidentiary rules.

Real evidence is the starting point for visual cross-examination. Inevitably, there will be holes in what the real evidence covers. Where is the physical evidence and how important is each piece of evidence? You know better than anyone what you need to prove in order for your client to prevail. After you identify what is missing, how can you go about creating images to fill these holes? There are many choices of demonstrative evidence for this purpose, including computer graphics and animations, summary charts, medical illustrations, and timelines. Whether or not demonstrative evidence is admitted for substantive purposes or merely illustrative ones depends on how well you are able to back it up with the evidence. Judges are unlikely to admit the images you develop unless you can come up with a good account of where they came from and the evidentiary foundation for them. With proper foundation, demonstrative evidence may be admitted along with the real evidence in the case. Is there a fact or expert witness who will say that it is fair and accurate? Will it be helpful to the jury in deciding the case? If so, the judge may agree that it is admissible into evidence and not just for illustrative purposes

It often takes months to both gather the real evidence visuals and create the additional demonstrative ones you need to tell your case story. As this process unfolds, there will come a time when you have a sufficient visual critical mass to lay everything down on your conference room table, much like a film director assembles all the story boards showing the action on the screen prior to actually shooting the movie. This is the time to begin thinking of your entire case story in pictures, connecting your proof in a holistic way. The visuals you show in opening, direct, cross, and closing have to work together, reinforcing one another and your advocacy. How do your visuals match up with and support your legal theories? How will your cross-examination build on your visual proof?

The more important the visuals are to your trial story, the more important it will be to bring a pretrial motion to admit them. If they are as good as you think they are, your opponent will be highly motivated to keep them out. You need to know what visuals you will be able to use in your cross-examination as far in advance as possible. Last-minute ambush techniques are inconsistent with modern discovery rules, even for evidence offered for illustrative purposes.

A couple of dramatic differences exist between a director planning to shoot a movie and a lawyer preparing for cross-examination. While a movie director has the luxury of doing multiple takes, you have only one chance to get it right. Further, while directors can use any images or settings they can get away with, you are limited to admissible evidence.

B. Visual in Evidence

If the exhibit has already been admitted into evidence, it may be employed during cross. If the exhibit has yet to be admitted, you must lay the proper evidentiary foundation and get the exhibit into evidence. Also, the new exhibit must fall within the scope of the direct examination's subject matter to be admissible. In some jurisdictions, such as Florida, the acceptable practice is that a foundation for admissibility of an exhibit may be laid during cross, but its actual admission must be delayed until the cross-examiner's case in chief (or until rebuttal in the case of the prosecution). *Walters v. State*, 288 So. 2d 298 (3d D.C.A.), *cert. denied*, 294 So. 2d 661 (Fla. 1974). The rationale for this rule is that a party is permitted to introduce evidence only during its case. Even in such a jurisdiction, opposing counsel should find it expedient to withhold an objection from the standpoint of economy of effort unless a tactical reason exists for the objection.

Prior to trial you can seek a stipulation from opposing counsel that your visual is admissible at trial. If counsel agrees that the visual is admissible, you still need to inform the trial judge of the stipulation so the court can rule on whether or not to admit the exhibit in advance of trial. If opposing counsel will not agree to the visual's admissibility, you can make a pretrial motion to admit the visuals. That motion will give you a good deal of information. How solid is your foundation for the critical visual evidence that will help convince the jury that you should win? Do your experts or fact witnesses have what it takes to convince the judge that the visual is fair and accurate? More importantly, how compelling is your opponent's position that these visuals should not come into evidence? What is of concern to your trial judge? What can you do to assuage these concerns in your foundation? Typically, the judge will allow you to use some of the visuals you have developed as is, while requiring others to be modified, often based on things pointed out by your opponent.

It is essential that you develop your visuals in a timely manner, after discovery has proceeded sufficiently to give you the confidence that you have a foundation for your demonstrative visuals. It is wasteful and frustrating to everyone on your team to attempt to create visuals before the factual record is solid. In civil cases, you will be ready to create the visuals after the key depositions. Thereafter, once your experts and fact witnesses are ready to sign off on your new images as fair and accurate, it is time to show them to opposing counsel. Resist any temptation to try to gain tactical advantage by hiding in the weeds and waiting until the last minute to do this. Not only is this contrary to modern discovery principles, and likely to make the judge think less of your ethics, but this also misses a great opportunity to find out what you may have overlooked.

Your opponent is likely to be every bit as focused on the case as you are, looking for flaws in everything you do. Opposing counsel may find errors and omissions in the foundation for your visuals. If you have shared these well before the trial, this gives you more than enough time to fix the mistakes your opponent has spotted. Then, when you make your motion to pre-admit your demonstrative evidence, you can say to the trial judge, "Your Honor, I shared all of these images with opposing counsel, who spotted some problems with them that I hadn't thought about. I have had changes and corrections made to these images, incorporating the input of opposing counsel." Not only will this undercut your opponent's argument to exclude these visuals, but it will also earn you points with the judge for your adherence to pretrial procedures.

C. Six Visual Categories

The variety and volume of trial visuals can get overwhelming. In planning for trial and in particular a cross-examination, it is helpful to categorize your visuals. This not only aids in keeping track of visuals but also provides guidance in their use in storytelling. Dan Roam, in *The Back of the Napkin: Solving Problems and Selling Ideas with Pictures* (Penguin Group 2008), places visual information in six basic categories with a common example of a visual display that falls into each category:

CATEGORY	DISPLAY
1. Who/What?	Photograph
2. How much?	Chart/Graph
3. Where?	Map
4. When?	Timeline
5. How?	Flowchart/Site Map
6. Why?	Information Graphics

These six visual categories in *The Back of the Napkin,* each paired with a display example, will be very useful for you in conceptualizing a visual cross-examination. Like a movie, every case involves events over time in different places. The How? and Why? of these events are combined with a legal theory to explain why we deserve to win and our opponent deserves to lose. These six visualization categories lend themselves to a checklist approach. Which ones apply to your case and what is the most powerful way to use them? What photographs, illustrations, or drawings exist in reports or other discovery materials? What categories might require you to consult with a graphic artist to develop demonstrative evidence? For example, a video deposition of a witness in a civil case will provide an image of what the deponent looks like, answering the Who? question. Witness photographs can be collected on a chart, giving the jury a visual guide to who will be testifying in the case. Nearly every case, criminal or civil, involves numbers or statistics. The How much? question can be translated into charts and graphs that visualize the background math. Similarly, the events involved in most cases occur in a physical location. Many times, Google Earth and Google Street View allow us to establish what the basic scene looks like without even leaving our office. The process of doing a timeline is a very useful way to do critical thinking about a sequence of events, addressing the When? question. How? often goes to the core issue of whether a pattern of behavior is established in a case. Is there a cause and effect relationship between the actions of a party and an outcome? If so, how do you establish this visually? The question of Why? is closely related to cause and effect.

IV. CIVIL CASE ILLUSTRATION — THE CONCRETE PUMPING WRONGFUL DEATH

To illustrate how to plan a cross-examination with the film-director's methodology, we use the example of a cross-examination of defendant, Mr. Jim Foster, in a wrongful death case. Tom Allen was a 28-year-old construction worker who was killed instantly on a job site when a concrete pumping hose whipped and struck him on the back of the head. Defendant Foster controlled the boom hose that ran from truck-mounted pumping equipment with a radio remote control unit on his belt. Hose whipping is a known hazard of concrete work that can occur when the pump starts and stops or concrete plugs the hose. Both of these things happened in this case, causing the fatal hose whipping of Tom Allen.

Mr. Allen's estate filed a wrongful death lawsuit against the concrete pumping company and its operator. The defense was that this was a freak occurrence that could not be anticipated, a true accident that was nobody's fault. The goal of the cross-examination of defendant Foster was to establish that he was in control of the job site at the time of Mr. Allen's death and that he failed to follow established concrete pumping safety protocol that would have avoided this tragedy.

While Jim Foster was severely shaken at the scene, he had made candid admissions in his statement to the police. Thereafter, he steadily moved to the position that he had no notice of any problem and had done nothing wrong that day. He was a well-respected operator in the industry and made a nice, sincere appearance, genuinely shaken by what had happened. This had the potential to make him a sympathetic witness. And yet, the official investigation revealed that his mistakes had cost another man his life. In order for plaintiff's counsel to make this stick in the wrongful death case, he wanted to give the jury a visual understanding of the procedures and rules of concrete pumping showing that operator error was the sole cause of this tragedy.

A. Gathering the Existing Visuals

Plaintiff had the burden of proving that the death of Mr. Allen was due to the defendant's negligence. The first step for counsel representing Tom Allen's estate was to gather the existing real evidence visuals. The state occupational health and safety agency had investigated the death of Mr. Allen. The agency's team of three people went to the scene, interviewed workers, collected documents, and took photographs. A local police department assisted, taking a statement from the defendant Jim Foster. The state inspectors did a thorough job, but were not concerned with meeting the burden of proof in a wrongful death case. As a result, holes existed in the proof plaintiff's counsel would need to prevail. The official investigation focused heavily on job documents and witness statements, supplying few visuals that would explain what Foster had done wrong. Most jury members would have no frame of reference for evaluating the truth of these verbal statements about this incident. It was critical to the plaintiff's case that the jurors visualize the process and what had gone wrong. Words alone would not make this clear. Plaintiff's counsel wanted to take them to the scene, showing and telling them what happened. This was a challenge as the existing photos did not give a clear idea of who was standing where and what both the concrete pump operator and the equipment were doing every step of the way.

B. The Six Visual Categories

Using the six categories suggested by *The Back of the Napkin* as a reference, plaintiff's counsel identified the holes in the real evidence gathered by the authorities, coming up with a list of the demonstrative evidence that needed to be created. The only category filled to any extent by the official investigation was Where?; the state health and safety agency officers had taken multiple photographs of the construction site, equipment, and the decedent's body. However, from the standpoint of the jury, these photos gave little sense of where the pump operator or decedent were standing prior to the event, the operator's control over the site during the concrete pour, and What? he should have done to avoid the accident. Also, no visual showed where the boom that struck the decedent was before the hose whipped. The official investigation gave no visualization of How?, only a verbal explanation of how the pressure built up in the line. No timeline existed to help sort out the When? factor of all the events that led up to the death.

C. Creating Visuals

Envisioning Cross-Examination Graphics

Given the paucity of visuals in the official report, plaintiff's counsel began to correct this deficit by trying to fill all six *Back of the Napkin* categories. Counsel relied on liability experts, state inspectors, and the investigative reports to develop demonstrative visuals that would convey all elements of the plaintiff's case story to the jury. Given defendant Jim Foster's insistence that he had done nothing wrong, the creation of the illustrations showing his negligence was key to a successful cross-examination. The evidentiary foundation for these illustrations would come from a series of efforts orchestrated by plaintiff's counsel. At the outset, counsel made a CR 34 motion to go to the defendant's equipment yard to take photographs of the truck used on the day of the death and the radio remote control device worn on the defendant's belt. This was a useful supplement to the official report, showing the concrete pumping equipment involved in this event and what the defendant used to control it.

After taking the CR 34 inspection photographs, a series of conferences were held between the attorney, plaintiff's experts, and an illustrator. They wanted to visually illustrate what had happened in a step-by-step manner. Plaintiff's investigator met with the eyewitnesses identified and interviewed in the official state investigation of this fatality to determine what they saw, with the aid of the photographs taken at the scene. Plaintiff's attorney used the same focusing question over and over with the witnesses and the experts: "What happened here that was negligent under the standards of the concrete pumping industry?"

The liability experts used the official investigation as the foundation to develop step-by-step images of how the hose whipping happened, what caused it, and what should have been done to prevent it. The liability experts' reports were provided to the illustrator, along with the background information and photographs of the accident victim, police reports, interviews with the key witnesses, and summations by the investigator. The illustrator's initial step was to look for things about the liability that an average jury member might not understand and that could be explained with a graphic presentation. Working backward from a projection of what the jury would need to understand in order to reach the same conclusion as the state investigation that the defendant was negligent, plaintiff's counsel, the team of experts, and the illustrator came up with the following visualization plan to show the jury:

1. The crew's work procedure, explaining the construction process and the technical terms.
2. What led up to the event.
3. How the pump truck operator bore the responsibility for the safety of the work crew during the concrete pour.
4. How the operator had failed to take the proper precautions.

All of the graphics developed by the plaintiff's attorney for the cross-examination of the defendant would have to be based on the evidence. Even though the state accident investigation report did not have visuals that specifically answered the questions of Who?, When?, Why?, or How much?, the facts in the report when combined with the expert opinions were sufficient for the illustrator to prepare representations of the following:

1. The construction site, buildings, and equipment;
2. An information graphic on how the concrete was pumped;
3. Timeline of the day's key events; and
4. Storyboards of the key events

1. Construction Site Graphics

By definition, a construction site is a work in progress. The accident scene no longer existed as it was on the day Tom Allen was killed. Plaintiff's illustrator had to work with the job photographs and construction plans from the official investigator report. The illustrator took the interior photographs from the accident report, which gave only small portions of the scene, looking for reference points that matched with the floor plan. Placement of windows, doorways, and workers' tools and equipment helped orient the photographs. Next, the illustrator looked for photographs that matched up with each other and keyed the photographs with the floor plan in a working graphic to see how they all fit together.

After assembling the individual investigation photographs into a larger composite, the plaintiff's artist redrew the floor plan in Adobe Illustrator, which has a 3D capability. This allowed him to change the view of the room, coming up with different angles from those seen in the investigation photographs, with great versatility in being able to show why the defendant was negligent. Because these 3D images were based on the real evidence of the official investigation photographs, with no alteration of what was shown, only extension through the computer program, the reliability of this demonstrative evidence could be proven. The illustrator further took the floor plan and extruded sections, and employed them to create the information graphics showing the inside of accident scene. It was also used in the series of illustrations that would storyboard the events and the information graphic of the danger area.

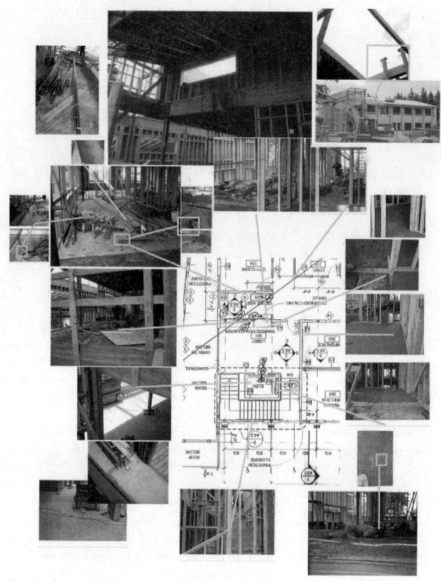

Courtesy of Duane Hoffmann/Hoffmann Legal Design

2. How the Concrete Was Pumped Graphic

[Plaintiff's experts and the illustrator had created an information graphic showing how concrete is pumped to address both the How? and Why? questions.]

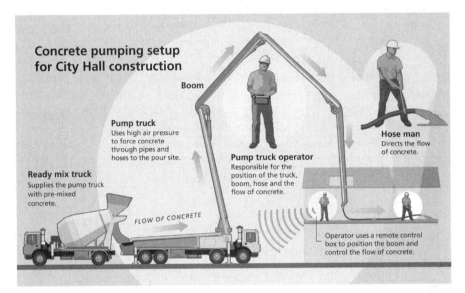

Duane Hoffmann/Hoffmann Legal Design

> *Q.* I'd now like to show you a graphic about concrete pumping. Does exhibit 45 show the basics of what was happening that day?
>
> A. Yes. This is how concrete is pumped. It shows who is doing what.

3. Timeline of the Day's Events

After reading the witness statements and police report, the illustrator found it difficult to understand the order of what had happened. Therefore, the illustrator created a timeline, taking each witness statement to create the sequence of events, layering them so the key events corresponded with each other. This timeline showed which discrepancies existed between the witness accounts, along with the areas of agreement. This identified the uncontested facts that could be utilized as the basis of storyboard illustrations showing what happened that day. Later, the illustrator simplified this timeline into one that could be introduced at trial.

Timeline of events:
Jim Foster uses illegal double-ended hose and doesn't warn workers of danger

		First Plug	Second plug	Third plug	Hose whip
Carl Masters Hose man	•Start with 6-7 hoses. •Sections removed to shorten line. •Single whip hose and double-end hose in use	•Foster removes boom – 2 hose sections still attached •Foster discharges concrete into hopper •Boom & hoses returned to building	•Both hoses are detached •Masters & Mudd take whip hose outside •Boom is removed from building •Plug is cleared •Boom is returned to building •Double-ended hose is attached	•Masters helps guide hose •Hose pops, Masters runs	•Loud booms •Sees Tom Allen is dead •Foster runs down stairs
John Mudd Carpenter	•Start with up to 8 sections •Double-ended hose + single ended whip •Single-ended hose first one removed – never reattached •2 double-ended hoses used	•One double ended hose detached •Boom & hose removed from building •Foster discharges concrete on ground, plug is cleared •Boom & hose returned •Double-ended hose reattached	•One double ended hose is detached •Boom & attached double-end hose removed from building •Plug is cleared •Second hose is not reattached	•Start to remove boom with one double-ended hose	
Conrad Kraft Carpenter	•Whip hose is reattached when a section removed	•Boom removed from building with two hose sections attached	•Whip hose carried outside •Boom removed from building •Plug is cleared, boom returned	•Start to remove boom with one double-ended hose	•Loud bang •Runs for cover •Sees Tom down
James Ryan Carpenter	•Sections of hose removed as pour progressed	•Boom removed from building •Plug cleared •Boom returned	•Boom removed from building •Plug is cleared •Boom returned to building	•Helps hold double-ended hose while boom raises	
Andres Garcia Carpenter		•Whip and a double-ended hose in use	•Whip hose removed and carried outside •One double-ended hose attached		•Loud explosion •Sees Tom on floor

Duane Hoffmann/Hoffmann Legal Design

4. Storyboards of the Day's Events

A persistent gap in the visuals from the state investigation report was that they did not show How? this had happened and Why? it was the defendant's fault. The illustrator used the official report and the liability experts' opinions to develop illustrations of the key events in sequence. When these storyboards were used in the cross-examination of the defendant, they would give the jury an idea of what the work site looked like at the time of the accident and how it happened, making it as if they were witnessing it themselves.

The attorney and illustrator determined the key moments that needed to be shown and the best angle of view to present them. The 3D illustration of the construction site was used along with the photographs to recreate the scenes. Photographs of models were taken for reference and combined with photographs of workers taken the day of the accident to fit into the scenes. Attention was paid to the evidentiary foundations for the visuals throughout this process, knowing that opposing counsel would try to keep these out of evidence as not being fair and accurate.

Duane Hoffmann/Hoffmann Legal Design

D. Motion to Pre-Admit the Illustrations

The process of envisioning and creating these illustrations went on for the better part of a year, filling in all the liability questions of Who?, What?, When?, Why?, and How much? The final versions of the illustrations were approved as fair and accurate by all of plaintiff's experts and the eyewitnesses that had been there that day (other than the defendant). A pretrial motion was brought to establish that all of these illustrations were based solidly on the official investigation report. Though the defendant's counsel argued to the court that these were "cartoons" that should be kept out, the court ruled that the foundation was sufficient and granted plaintiff's motion to admit the illustrations into evidence.

E. Visual Cross-Examination of the Defendant

Cross-examination of defendant, concrete pump operator Jim Foster, was structured around the plaintiff's visuals. Foster had come to trial well prepared, with explanations as to why this event was wholly unanticipated.

The visuals shown to Foster were used to cut off all avenues of escape, one by one, allowing the jury to see and thus know what information had been available to Foster that day. In the early going of the cross-examination, plaintiff's counsel's questions all were designed to elicit a "yes" answer, laying the foundation for the details of the job, and establishing the equipment used, how it worked, and that the pump operator exerted total control. As the cross proceeded, the questions became increasingly accusatorial in nature, with the visuals putting the jurors at the scene, giving them the power to independently verify the truth of the facts asserted in the questions put to the operator.

The following excerpts from the cross-examination show how plaintiff's counsel utilized visuals to communicate the plaintiff's story.

Construction Site and Equipment

[Plaintiff's counsel took advantage of the overhead illustration of the job site to put the jury in the place where the death of Tom Allen occurred. This overhead illustration gave the jury a strong sense of the positioning of the equipment in relation to the building.]

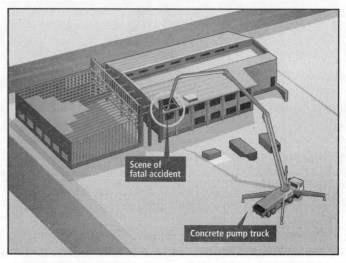

Duane Hoffmann/Hoffmann Legal Design

Q. Mr. Foster, I want to ask you about the events leading to the death of Tom Allen. You recognize this scene as shown in exhibit 12?

A. Yes, it is the concrete pour site where this happened.

[The pump truck was a component of the What? and How? aspects of what occurred; it was the instrumentality that caused the death of Tom Allen. Thus, after counsel examined the defendant about the work site, the cross turned to the truck.]

Q. Showing you exhibit 8, do you recognize this pump truck?

A. Yes, I do, it was the one I was operating.

Q. Can you explain how it works?

A. It pumps concrete through five sections. These unfold. If they are completely flat out, it will reach over 140 feet.

[The back end of the truck was an element of the How? factor because this is where the concrete mix trucks loaded in the product, and where complications occurred that should have put the operator on alert for potential problems with the pour.]

Q. Showing you exhibit 35. Mr. Foster, this shows the back of the pump truck?

A. Yes.

Q. How does the concrete flow?

A. The trucks come and put it in the hopper at the back. One cylinder draws in the mud and another pushes it out into the pipes for placement.

Q. How powerful is the pump?

A. Strong enough to move the concrete through a long system of pipes and hoses.

[Most people on the jury would not be familiar with the remote control box that the operator defendant Foster had on his belt that day. Therefore, plaintiff's counsel used this photograph to familiarize them with Why? the operator is in control during a concrete pumping operation. Foster had the power to determine where the boom was and how much pressure was in the line.]

Q. You control the boom with a remote control box?

A. Yes.

Q. Do you recognize this photograph, exhibit 39?

A. Yes.

Q. What is it?

A. These are the joy sticks that control the boom. This one controls the pump and this toggle switch increases the RPM of the motor.

Q. You've got these controls on your belt, don't you?

A. I do.

Q. They have the power of life and death on a job?

A. Yes.

Q. If you want more concrete, moving this joy stick is similar to stepping on the gas when you want your car to go faster?

A. Yes.

Q. So, you can control how much pressure is on the line by this remote?

A. Correct.

Q. More pressure means more concrete is moving through the line?

A. Yes.

Timeline

[The When? factor was central to determining the fault of the operator. The death of Mr. Allen occurred after the pump truck operator had been on the construction site for several hours. A number of problems had occurred prior to the hose whip. To make the chronology of events clear to the jury and to establish that the defendant had notice of potential danger, plaintiff's counsel employed a timeline summarizing these events.]

Timeline of events

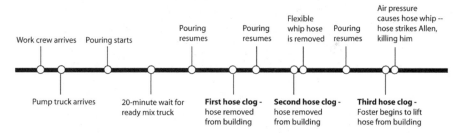

Duane Hoffmann/Hoffmann Legal Design

Q. There were problems with this concrete pour prior to Mr. Allen's death?

A. Yes.

Q. The pump had been stopped and started multiple times?

A. Through the day, yes.

Q. Please look at the timeline, exhibit 10. You see the 20-minute wait after the pouring started. There was a 20-minute wait, correct?

A. Yes.

Q. And here on the timeline, you see where it says "Third hose clog." The hose clogged for a third time?

A. Yes.

Q. You were having trouble with this last load?

A. Yes.

Q. This was a problematic load, wasn't it?

A. It was.

Q. You stopped and started the pump several times on that last batch, didn't you?

A. Yes.

Q. And this always presents the danger of air getting in the line?

A. Yes.

Q. And this is dangerous, isn't it?

A. It is.

Q. It can result in a hose whipping?

A. Yes.

Q. And you knew this on the day Tom Allen was killed?

A. I did.

Foster's Control

[It was crucial to this cross-examination and winning the case to establish that the operator had control over what happened, which addressed the Who?, Where?, When?, How?, and Why? questions simultaneously. The storyboard, constructed based on the construction site plans, photographs, statements, other exhibits, and a photograph of the operator at the scene. With the jury now fully educated as to what was happening on this job, it was time for plaintiff's counsel to focus on the moment, which explained Why? this was the defendant's fault. The illustration shows that he had the means of backing the pressure off the line before he left the scene, and should have, but did not.]

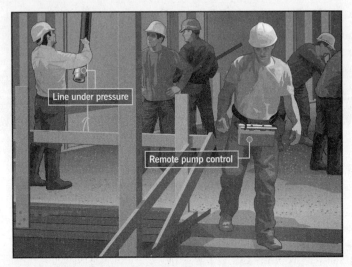

Duane Hoffmann/Hoffmann Legal Design

Q. We know that you were standing there with your control box?
A. Correct.
Q. You can reverse the pressure on the line whenever you want, right?
A. Yes.
Q. Hadn't you actually turned to walk down the stairs when the explosion happened?
A. I did.
Q. So your back was actually to the scene as is shown here in exhibit 45?
A. It was off to my right side.
Q. Before you went down the stairs, you had the capability of reversing the pump and releasing the pressure on the line?
A. Yes.
Q. But you did not, did you?
A. Correct.

Foreseeability — Whip Zone

[Foreseeability was an element in the Why? question. Tom Allen was in the zone of danger at the time the operator turned his back and left the scene. Anyone standing within reach of the hose was at considerable risk. This visual establishes that the operator knew this, and could easily have avoided the danger by backing the crew out of the area before leaving.]

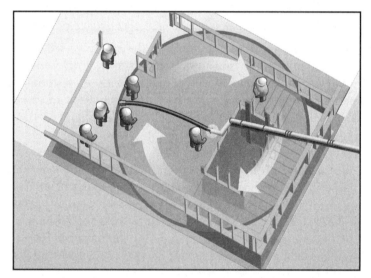

Duane Hoffmann/Hoffmann Legal Design

Q. Showing you exhibit 55. It shows the whip danger zone, correct?

A. Yes.

Q. Are you in any way responsible for what happened that day?

A. No.

Q. Did you tell the construction crew to stand back out of range in this whip zone in the minutes before the explosion?

A. I cannot remember when I said it.

Q. Is there any physical reason why you could not have told the workers to back away before you turned and went down the stairs?

A. No.

Q. You knew that prior to his death Tom Allen was within the whip zone of the hose as shown in exhibit 55?

A. Yes, I did know that.

Q. And as the person in charge of this pour, if you had told them to stand back out of the danger zone, Mr. Allen would still be alive today. Right?

A. (no answer)

Q. You ever think of that?

A. Every day.

Q. Nothing further.

V. CRIMINAL CASE ILLUSTRATIONS

A. Lindbergh Kidnapping Case — Cross-Examination of Bruno Hauptmann

Apart from the O. J. Simpson case, the most publicized trial in the twentieth century was that of Bruno Richard Hauptmann. The jury convicted Hauptmann of murdering 18-month-old Charles Lindbergh Jr., son of world-renowned aviator Charles Lindbergh and Anne Morrow Lindbergh. Expert testimony identified the defendant as the author of the ransom notes sent to Charles Lindbergh Sr. The experts who testified used photographic enlargements of portions of the writing to illustrate the similarities between the handwriting of Hauptmann and the author of the notes, which contained numerous misspelled words. In addition to taking handwriting samples from Hauptmann, the police had also collected numerous documents undeniably written by Hauptmann. The same words were misspelled in the same way as in the ransom note. A side rail of the homemade ladder used to climb up to the window of the nursery on the second floor of the Lindbergh home was tied to a missing floorboard in Hauptmann's attic. Another key exhibit tying Hauptmann to the case was a $10 bill that he spent on which the merchant had written down his license number. This was part of the ransom money that had been paid, proven by the serial number.

Prosecutor Wilentz with photographic enlargements of a ransom note

When Hauptmann took the stand in his own defense, the prosecutor, Attorney General David T. Wilentz, had a wealth of visual evidence to use in his cross-examination. Before Wilentz used the visuals he damaged Hauptmann's credibility, getting him to admit that he had lied repeatedly to the police and in his testimony at the New York extradition hearing. Next, Wilentz walked Hauptmann through the circumstances of each of his prior convictions. Wilentz then prominently displayed a photographic enlargement of a portion of the final ransom note delivered to Lindbergh after the ransom was paid. This final ransom note told Lindbergh he could find his son alive and well on the "boad Nelly." After setting up the photographic enlargement, Wilentz was ready to begin his visual cross-examination. He began with Hauptmann's journal.

Q. Yes. Now I want to show you a little book and ask you if it is yours. Is that your handwriting? Take your time about it. Look at it.

A. Yes, that's my handwriting.

Q. Take a look at this word particularly [indicating the word "boad" on the page of the notebook]. Tell me if that is your handwriting, that one word there.

A. It looks like my handwriting, but I can't remember I ever put it in.

Q. Don't mix it up now. Just stay with that word there for a minute; two dollars and fifty cents. You see that word?

A. Yes.

Q. Alongside of it [the word "boad"]?

A. Yes.

Q. Are they your figures?

A. Yes.

Q. Yes. That [the word "boad"] is your word then, isn't it?

A. I can't remember if I ever put it in.

Q. Why did you spell "boat" b-o-a-d?

A. Well, after you make improvement in your writing.

Q. All right. So that at one time you used to spell "boat" b-o-a-d?

A. Probably eight or ten years ago, and I am not quite sure if I put it in.

Q. Is the whole page in your handwriting?

A. I don't know.

Q. But the word "boad" in there you won't say that is not in your handwriting, will you?

A. I wouldn't say yes either.

Q. You don't say yes or no?

A. I don't say yes or no because I can't remember ever putting it in.

[The prosecutor then referred to the enlargement of the ransom note.]

New Jersey State Police

Q. The reason you don't say yes or no is because you know you wrote "boad" when you got the fifty thousand from Condon, isn't that right [indicating the photographic enlargement of the word "boad" from the ransom note]?

A. No, sir.

Q. Boad Nelly. Look at it. [Wilentz hands the enlargement to Hauptmann.]

A. No.

Q. Do you see the word "boad Nelly"?

A. I see it, certainly.

Q. Look at it again right underneath there, again "boad," do you see that?

A. I see it.

Q. B-o-a-d?

A. I see it.

Q. Let me see this exhibit for identification [referring to S-252 for identification, and handing same to witness]. Do you see that?

A. I see that.

Q. Same spelling?

A. Same spelling.

Trial Transcript, State of New Jersey v. Bruno Richard Hauptmann, pp. 2546-2585. Note that the transcript here is an abridged and edited version of the long and sometimes disjointed examination.

[Wilentz bombarded Hauptmann with visual evidence. No fewer than 40 times Wilentz confronted Hauptmann with a particular piece of evidence and told him to either "take a look" or "just take a look" at it. All of these confrontations proved detrimental to Hauptmann's case, but the most dramatic confrontation came when Wilentz confronted Hauptmann with a board (shown below on the right) on which had been written the name, address, and telephone number of John F.

Condon, the man who acted as a go-between during the ransom negotiations. Investigators had found the board inside Hauptmann's bedroom closet (shown below on the left). Hauptmann had twice previously identified the handwriting as his—once during interrogation by the New York District Attorney, and once when he testified at his extradition hearing.]

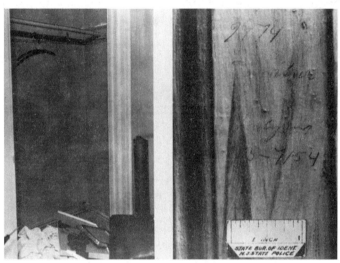

New Jersey State Police

Q. Do you know what this is, Mr. Defendant? [Exhibiting the board, Exhibit S-204, to the witness.] You do, don't you?

A. A piece of board, yes.

Q. From your house?

A. I really don't know if it is from my house. That is a piece of trimming and a piece of trimming from every house looks the same.

Q. That is from your closet, isn't it?

A. I am not quite sure.

Q. That is your handwriting on there, isn't it?

A. No.

Q. That is not your handwriting?

A. [Shaking his head.]

Q. You take a look at that. You have seen it many times before. Take your time about it now. First, tell me, are the numbers your handwriting? [Indicating John Condon's telephone number written on the board.]

A. The numbers look familiar upwards. I can't remember for putting it on.

Q. Just keep looking at those numbers and tell me whether or not they are in your handwriting and that you wrote them, the numbers?

A. I can't remember putting them numbers on.

Q. Did you remember better when you were talking to District Attorney Foley?

A. At that time I was quite excited.

Q. Were you excited when you got before a Supreme Court Justice in the State of New York in your extradition proceedings?

A. I say yes.

Q. You didn't tell the truth there, you mean?

A. Well, I was quite excited then.

Q. Do you remember that you had a hearing before a Supreme Court Justice by the name of Mr. Justice Hammer in the Bronx court house in New York?

A. I remember that, yes.

Q. And you were asked this question with reference to Exhibit 204—

Mr. Reilly [Defense Attorney]: Page, please.

Mr. Wilentz: 83.

Q. Finally you were asked this question: "Finally one day thereafter you were brought in and questioned by District Attorney Foley, were you not?" and your answer was "Yes." "And District Attorney Foley asked you if you recognized a certain piece of wood or lumber, do you remember that?" And your answer was "Yes." Is that correct?

A. I will—let's explain before you read further—

Q. No. Wait a minute. I am going to let you explain when I find out what your answer is. Isn't this the question that was asked of you in the Bronx County Court before a Supreme Court Justice while you were under oath?

A. I can't remember the, what the question was.

Q. And District Attorney Foley asked you if you recognized a certain piece of wood or lumber, do you remember that? And your answer is "Yes." Is that correct?

A. Well, I really can't remember what—all the questions.

Q. Now, the next question, "And you said yes, that was your handwriting, is that so, yes." Is that correct?

A. I really can't remember this question.

Q. You mean to tell me that you don't remember being asked the question about the number on the lumber?

A. There was so many questions that I can't separate it.

Q. And didn't you answer "Yes" to that question? You said the number on there is your handwriting, yes, in the Bronx Court, before Supreme Court Justice Hammer—didn't you say yes?

A. I can't remember this.

State v. Hauptmann Trial Transcript, pp. 2659-2662, edited to remove redundant questions and evasions.

Hauptmann could not possibly have forgotten the very important fact that he had twice admitted writing John Condon's telephone number on a board in his closet. Wilentz's confronting him with the board was damaging, but Hauptmann increased the damage by being evasive. This led to his impeachment by prior inconsistent statement and his even more damaging refusal to admit his prior testimony as it was read to him from the transcript of the extradition hearing. A portion of this cross can be seen in old newsreel footage on YouTube (https://www.youtube.com/watch?v=A1u9Jsqmz_o) beginning approximately six minutes and 21 seconds into the video.

B. "If It Doesn't Fit, You Must Acquit"

This picture—and defense counsel Johnnie Cochran's words, "If it doesn't fit, you must acquit" — prove the power of visuals to accomplish the goals of bringing the case theory and theme alive in the courtroom and making it memorable.

When prosecutor Christopher Darden had defendant Simpson attempt to put on the bloody glove found at the murder scene, he etched the picture in the jurors' minds that the glove seemed too tight (even though this could be explained by the fact that Simpson wore latex gloves and the leather glove may have shrunk because it had been soaked in blood and tested). Although Darden had Simpson demonstrate with the glove during the prosecution's case in chief, he could have done the same thing during cross if Simpson had testified. If the glove had fit, that would have furthered the prosecution's theory and story that Simpson was the killer. But it didn't fit, and this visual refuted the prosecution's theory, told the defense story, and resulted in an unforgettable case theme. This demonstration serves as a historic warning to never gamble with a courtroom demonstration.

C. Courtroom Demonstration — George Zimmerman Trial

A courtroom demonstration in the George Zimmerman murder trial once again illustrates the impact of a visual presentation in the courtroom. But, like the glove demonstration in the Simpson case, it also provides a warning that the use of a visual on cross-examination is risky and may backfire. Former neighborhood watch captain George Zimmerman was on trial for murder in the second degree for shooting 17-year-old Trayvon Martin. Zimmerman claimed he was acting in self-defense and called expert witness Dennis Root to support his claim.

Prosecutor John Guy   Defense Counsel Mark O'Mara

On cross-examination, prosecutor John Guy produced a life-sized foam dummy and utilized it to dramatically elicit concessions from expert Root and show that if Trayvon Martin were straddling Zimmerman, Zimmerman would have had difficulty pulling a gun from a holster at his waist. On redirect examination, O'Mara asked, "May I use your doll?" O'Mara then placed the dummy on the courtroom floor, straddled it, grabbed the dummy by the shoulders, and smashed the dummy's head to the floor, asking: "Would the injuries on Mr. Zimmerman, the back of his head, be consistent with someone doing this on the cement?" Root replied, "I don't think so." Then, putting the dummy's arms against his shoulder, as though the dummy were resisting, and again smashing the dummy against the floor, O'Mara asked, "How about someone resisting the attack? Could that have come from if someone was resisting me pushing down like this?" Root answered, "I believe so." The prosecution's cross-examination demonstration had been transformed by defense counsel into a demonstration of how vulnerable defendant Zimmerman would have been if Martin were straddling and punching him.

VI. OTHER ILLUSTRATIONS

Other parts of this book provide illustrations of how cross-examiners effectively use visuals. In the *Sonics* trial, an expert was cross-examined with the aid of a visual that showed that the expert had essentially copied the same report in another case word for word, just changing it slightly (page 158). Lincoln's production of the almanac was visual evidence refuting the witness's claim that the moon was high overhead at the time of the killing (page 122). At pages 158-159 is a discussion of the value of video in impeaching a witness with a prior inconsistent statement made during a video deposition.

In a discussion of how to control a witness, we cover the technique of writing out the question so the jury can see what the witness is not answering (page 225). If the court permits it, writing down the points made during cross is another way to convey the information visually to the jury. This can be done with a piece of paper displayed by a document camera on a screen or by writing on a board or flip chart.

The types of visuals that you bring into play in a trial to bring your case narrative alive and make it memorable are limited only by the evidence in the case and your ingenuity.

CHECKLIST: VISUAL CROSS-EXAMINATION

Importance of Visuals

- ❏ They tell a story better than words;
- ❏ Enable jurors to better retain information;
- ❏ Create a consensus among the jury about the evidence; and
- ❏ Enliven the cross-examination

Visuals and Technology

- ❏ Use available software, such as PowerPoint, to create trial visual presentations.
- ❏ Consider employing a technology company to develop trial presentations.
- ❏ Employ software to store, retrieve, and display visuals.
- ❏ Utilize today's technology — projecting visuals on a screen or monitor with a document camera or projector.
- ❏ Enliven the cross-examination with visuals.

Plan the Visual Cross-Examination Like a Film Director

- ❏ Plan to tell your case story with pictures during cross.
- ❏ Gather existing visuals.
- ❏ Analyze your case to determine what is missing visually that you need to tell the story using the six visual categories and display examples:

Who/What?	Photograph
How much?	Chart/Graph
Where?	Map
When?	Timeline
How?	Flowchart/Site Map
Why?	Information Graphics

❑ Consider whether the visual could backfire and damage your case.
❑ Create visuals to fix the deficits in visuals for cross-examination.
❑ Have an evidentiary foundation for each visual.
❑ Move to pre-admit the visuals.

CHAPTER 6

IMPEACHMENT CROSS
Reliability

"'And some things you don't forgive, Dr. Gorle? Has your feeling of jealousy and hatred for my client in any way coloured your evidence against him?'

"Of course I expected her to deny this . . . I was surprised, therefore, when . . . [t]here was a prolonged silence.

"'Has it, Dr. Gorle?' I pressed her gently for the answer. . . .

"'I don't think so.' . . . said so unconvincingly that I saw the jury's disapproval. It was the first game to Rumpole, and the witness seemed to have lost her confidence when I moved on to . . . the medical evidence."

        —**John Mortimer**, *The Second Rumpole*
        Omnibus 142 (Penguin Books 1988)

I. IMPEACHMENT CROSS-EXAMINATION IN GENERAL

An impeachment cross-examination aims at discrediting the witness or witness's testimony. Francis L. Wellman observed that it can "separate truth from false-hood," and reduce "exaggerated statements to their true dimension." Francis L. Wellman, *The Art of Cross-Examination* 27 (Simon & Schuster 1997, original ed. 1903). Further, impeachment cross can reveal the truth from an honest but mistaken witness. A winning impeachment cross can spread far beyond the witness, inflicting great harm to the entire case of your opponent. For instance, an exposed perjurer also can reflect poorly on the party that vouched for this witness in the first place.

Impeachment cross-examination is what both courtroom legends and great dramatic scenes are made of. This chapter and the two that follow examine each of the nine areas of impeachment cross with a concentration on three crucial areas: (1) evidentiary law; (2) cross-examination techniques; and (3) how-to illustrations.

First, evidentiary law is critical to a determination of whether the impeachment evidence is admissible and the extent to which counsel can go into it. Second, the cross-examination techniques used must have a powerful impact. Third, the illustrations will give you concrete examples of how to successfully impeach different witnesses.

A. Evidentiary Law

An overriding evidentiary rule is that counsel must have a good-faith basis for any assertion in cross. For example, the defense cannot allege that a government witness cut a deal in exchange for her testimony when the examiner only suspects it. *United States v. Taylor*, 522 F.3d 731 (7th Cir. 2008). *State v. Lowe*, 843 N.E.2d 1243, 1246, 164 Ohio App. 3d 726, 729 (2005), provides the traditional explanation of the good-faith basis requirement:

> It is improper to attempt to prove a case by insinuation or innuendo, rather than with evidence. Questions that are not based on fact or for which there is no good-faith basis are improper.
>
> By its nature, cross-examination often involves a tentative and probing approach to testimony given on direct examination. *State v. Gillard* (1988), 40 Ohio St. 3d 226, 231. Therefore, the examiner need not lay an evidentiary foundation before posing questions upon cross-examination. It is sufficient if there is a good-faith basis to question the witness on the subject.
>
> Where the good-faith basis for a question is not challenged at the trial level, it is presumed that such a basis exists. "Since the prosecutor's good-faith basis for asking these questions was never challenged, we presume she had one." *Gillard, supra,* 40 Ohio St. 3d at 231. . . .

Also as a matter of professional conduct, any assertion made during cross also must be supportable with admissible evidence. ABA Model Rule of Professional Conduct 3.4(e) states:

> A lawyer shall not . . . in trial, allude to any matter that . . . will not be supported by admissible evidence . . . .

The authors freely acknowledge that it is not uncommon for trial lawyers to allude to irrelevant or unsupported evidence during cross-examination. However, the mere fact that it is done does not make it right. Just as a skilled athlete does not need to bend the rules in order to excel, neither does a lawyer.

One of the best, most accurate trial movies ever made — *Anatomy of a Murder* — illustrates the trial tactic of alluding to something that is neither relevant nor provable. Based on the somewhat autobiographical book by the same name, written by Justice John D. Voelker of the Michigan Supreme Court under the pseudonym Robert Travers, the movie involves an Army Lieutenant charged with murdering a man who allegedly raped his wife. Defense counsel Paul Biegler cross-examines the medical examiner, Dr. Raschid. The cross-examination and its aftermath go as follows.

James Stewart as Paul Biegler in "Anatomy of a Murder"
"Anatomy of a Murder" © 1959, renewed 1987 Otto
Preminger Films, Ltd, and Columbia Pictures, Inc. All rights
reserve. Courtesy of Columbia Pictures.

UNETHICAL AND IMPROPER CROSS

Anatomy of a Murder

Paul Biegler: *Q.* In this post-mortem were you also asked to determine whether or not the deceased had had a sexual climax shortly before his death?
Raschid: *A.* No.

---

continued ▶

> *Q.* Could you have made such a determination?
>
> *A.* Yes.
>
> *Q.* Then you were only asked to make such examination as might be useful to the prosecution, but none which might help the defense, although such evidence might have existed?
>
> *A.* Well, yes . . .
>
> Dancer (prosecutor): I object, Your Honor. The question is argumentative. Counsel for the defense is trying to impugn the intent of the representatives of the People.
>
> Judge Weaver: Mr. Biegler, you're aware that the question is highly improper.
>
> Biegler: I'll withdraw the question and apologize, Your Honor.
>
> Judge Weaver: Question and answer will be stricken and jury will disregard.
>
> Biegler: That's all the questions I have.
>
> Mitch (prosecutor): No redirect.
>
> Biegler returns to his table, glances at his co-counsel.
>
> Lieutenant Manion whispering to Biegler: How can a jury disregard something they've already heard?
>
> Biegler: They can't Lieutenant. They can't.

B. Threshold Question

Cross-examination is part of an overall trial plan; it does not exist in a vacuum. Evidentiary law is critical in the formulation of your strategy. Pretrial motions often determine threshold questions regarding the admissibility of impeachment evidence, either keeping the witness off the stand entirely or limiting the scope of the testimony.

The testimonial capacity of a potential witness is for the judge to determine. Fed. R. Evid. 104(a). Is the witness competent? Does he or she have personal knowledge? Is the witness qualified to testify to reputation evidence? If the answer to any of these questions is "No," counsel can move *in limine* pretrial to prohibit the person from testifying.

The party calling the witness may make a preemptive strike, seeking to exclude the impeachment evidence, such as a prior conviction or other misconduct probative of untruthfulness. If the judge denies the motion, the impeachment evidence confidently can be included in the cross. In such a case, opposing counsel may well try to blunt the effect by bringing it out on direct.

If opposing counsel does not move to exclude such evidence pretrial, the cross-examiner must make a strategic decision whether to disclose the evidence to the court beforehand. Any doubts about admissibility should be resolved in favor of disclosure, as the potential consequences of an improper disclosure can be severe, including a mistrial.

C. Nine Impeachment Areas

The classic nine impeachment areas fall into the three broad categories below:

Nine Topics for Impeachment During Cross-Examination

I. Reliability—Chapter 6
1. Lack of Personal Knowledge
2. Mental and Sensory Deficiencies
3. Bias and Interest

II. Report—Chapter 7
4. Improbability
5. Prior Inconsistent Statements
6. Contradiction

III. Reporter—Chapter 8
7. Prior Convictions
8. Prior Misconduct Probative of Untruthfulness
9. Character Witness

We begin the exploration of impeachment cross-examination with the theme of flawed and unreliable observation, where a witness lacks personal knowledge, is inaccurate, has a mental or sensory deficiency, or is tainted by bias and interest.

D. Seven Essential Impeachment Techniques

Seven basic cross-examination techniques may be employed in implementing the nine types of impeachment. The illustrations in this chapter also show how these techniques can enrich the impact, energy, and overall dynamics of impeachment.

Seven Essential Impeachment Cross Techniques

1. Assess and adjust;
2. Lock the witness into the testimony;
3. Establish a motive;
4. Paint a picture for the jury;
5. Close all the exits to prevent the witness from escaping;
6. Surprise the witness; and
7. Use visuals or tangible evidence if possible.

---

1. Assess and Adjust

No matter what type of impeachment the cross-examiner intends to pursue, counsel will want it to fit the witness and the situation. Is the witness honest but mistaken? Is the witness exaggerating? Or, is the witness lying? Over a century and a half ago, David Paul Jones, a British barrister, put it succinctly and well:

> Be mild with the mild; shrewd with the crafty; confiding with the honest; merciful to the young, the frail or the fearful; rough to the ruffian; and a thunderbolt to the liar. But in all this, never be unmindful of your dignity.

Francis L. Wellman, *The Art of Cross-Examination* 401 (2d ed. 1921).

Counsel must adjust the demeanor and presentation of the impeachment to fit the individual witness. This requires not only a firm grip on the facts, including all prior statements by a witness on issues in the case, but also a shrewd, insightful evaluation of the basic character of a witness. Counsel should make every effort to gather this information during the pretrial phase, with sources such as witness interviews or depositions. These pretrial sources of information and impressions are then built upon and modified by counsel's observations during trial. How is the witness coming across? Are there any telltale signs of mistaken, embellished, or false testimony?

Counsel's assessment of each opposing witness will determine what techniques will work best in the cross-examination. The goal of impeachment is discrediting the witness or the testimony. If the witness is honestly mistaken, then the main thrust will be on the testimony, not the witness. If the witness is biased toward a party, causing slanted testimony, then both the witness and the testimony should be discredited. On the other hand, if the witness goes beyond honest mistake into embellishing or falsifying, sterner measures are called for, seeking to discredit both the witness and the testimony. The next three techniques will help counsel achieve this objective.

2. Lock the Witness into the Testimony

Often, in order to successfully impeach a witness, the examiner first will need to lock the witness into the current, inaccurate testimony. The purpose of this is to prevent the witness from wiggling out later. This is particularly true with a prior inconsistent statement or where the testimony conflicts with that of another.

3. Establish a Motive

Strive to establish a motive for the witness to be mistaken or to commit perjury. The jurors will more readily accept the fact that the witness deliberately lied if they understand what would motivate the witness. Is the witness biased in favor of a party? Does the witness have a stake in the case?

4. Paint a Picture for the Jury

The cross-examiner should paint a picture for the jury brushstroke by brushstroke until the picture is complete. This approach allows the jurors to reach their own conclusions as the sketch is gradually filled in. With this technique, the jurors will acquire a proprietary interest in their belief.

5. Close the Exits

Many a carefully planned impeachment cross-examination has failed because the witness found an escape route. Anticipate this possibility by asking yourself, "If I were this witness, where would I try to escape?" Then try to prevent this by closing off all the possible exits to your impeachment.

6. Surprise

The surprise technique goes hand in hand with closing the exits. Any witness who knows where the cross-examiner is going is more likely to think of ways to avoid the destination. Surprise allows the impeachment objective to remain hidden while the exits are closed off. Only if there is no way out for the witness should the destination be revealed in advance to the witness and the jury. Any attempts at evasion will be evident to the jury under those circumstances, discrediting the witness.

7. Visuals and Other Tangible Things

As with any trial activity, cross-examination can be made more persuasive with visuals and other tangible evidence, adding drama and vividness. For example, jurors are much more likely to remember and be persuaded by an impeachment accompanied by a courtroom demonstration, photograph, video deposition, or a 911 tape.

II. LACK OF PERSONAL KNOWLEDGE

A. Evidentiary Law

Threshold Question

Federal Rule of Evidence 104(a) provides that the judge decides the preliminary questions of the qualification of a person to be a witness. The threshold question under Fed. R. Evid. 602 and its state rule counterpart is whether the witness called to testify has "personal knowledge of the matter." The side calling the witness must show "evidence sufficient to support a finding that the witness has personal knowledge of the matter."

Prior to trial, counsel can move the court to prohibit the witness from testifying on the grounds that the witness lacks personal knowledge. Another strategy is to challenge the competency of a witness by getting the court's permission to voir dire at trial. The court may permit counsel to examine the witness on the issue of personal knowledge outside the jury's presence, before the witness testifies. Either way, the goal is to show that the witness lacks the requisite knowledge and should not be permitted to testify as a matter of law.

Weight or Credibility

Federal Rule of Evidence 104(e) states that the rule on preliminary questions "does not limit a party's right to introduce before the jury evidence that is relevant to the weight or credibility of other evidence." Although a judge may find a witness qualified to testify under Fed. R. Evid. 602 because the person has personal knowledge of an act, event, or condition, cross-examination is then proper to reveal any inadequate personal knowledge affecting the credibility of the witness.

B. Illustration: Lincoln's Cross of Charles Allen

Lawyer Abraham Lincoln represented William "Duff" Armstrong, who was charged with murdering James Metzker on August 29, 1857. At the trial in 1858, Lincoln cross-examined witness Charles Allen, who testified on direct examination that he saw Armstrong shoot Metzker. As reported by Francis Wellman in *The Art of Cross-Examination,* Lincoln's cross-examination illustrates not only how to discredit a supposed eyewitness to an event for lack of personal knowledge but also all seven cross-examination techniques previously discussed.

Lincoln the lawyer

IMPEACHMENT WITH LACK OF PERSONAL KNOWLEDGE

**Abraham Lincoln's Cross-Examination
of Charles Allen**

Lawyer Abraham Lincoln represented William "Duff" Armstrong, who was charged with murdering James Metzker on August 29, 1857. At the trial in 1858, Lincoln cross-examined witness Charles Allen, who testified on direct examination that he

---

saw Armstrong kill Metzker by hitting him in the head with a slungshot—a metal weight attached to the end of a cord. As reported by Francis Wellman in *The Art of Cross-Examination*, Lincoln's cross-examination illustrates not only how to discredit a supposed eyewitness to an event for lack of personal knowledge but also all seven cross-examination techniques previously discussed.

[Lincoln paints a picture brushstroke by brushstroke.]

Lincoln: *Q.* . . . And you were with Metzker just before and saw the killing?
Allen: *A.* Yes.
Q. And you stood very near to them?
A. No, about twenty feet away.
Q. May it not have been ten feet?
A. No, it was twenty feet or more.
Q. In the open field?
A. No, in the timber.
Q. What kind of timber?
A. Beech timber.
Q. Leaves on it are rather thick in August?
A. Rather.
Q. And you think this pistol was the one used?
A. It looks like it.
Q. You could see the defendant strike—see clearly that he used a slungshot?
A. Yes.
Q. How near was this to the meeting place?
A. Three-quarters of a mile away.
[Allen could have explained how he saw the shooting by swearing that he did so by lamp light, and Lincoln closes off that exit.]
Q. Where were the lights?
A. Up by the minister's stand.
Q. Three-quarters of a mile away?
A. Yes, I answered ye twiste.
Q. Did you not see a candle there, with Metzker and Armstrong?
A. No! what would we want a candle for?
[Lincoln locks Allen into his testimony that he saw the shooting by moonlight.]
Q. How, then, did you see the shooting?
A. By moonlight! *[Allen claimed that the moon was high overhead.]*
Q. You saw this killing at ten at night—in beech timber, three-quarters of a mile from light—saw the slungshot—saw the man strike with it—saw it twenty feet away—saw it all by moonlight? Saw it nearly a mile from the camp lights?
A. Yes, I told you so before.

Judge J. W. Donovan described what happened next in his work *Tact in Court* as follows:

The interest was now so intense that men leaned forward to catch the smallest syllable. Then the lawyer drew out a blue covered almanac from his side coat pocket—opened it slowly—offered it into evidence—showed it to the jury and court—read from a page with careful deliberation that the moon on that night was unseen and only arose at one the next morning. [Actually, the moon was below the tree line, being just before setting, and not high overhead as Allen had testified.]

Francis L. Wellman, *The Art of Cross-Examination* 74-75 (Simon & Schuster 1997, original ed. 1903), revised here to accurately identify the participants and the weapon.

From Donovan's account, it appears that Lincoln immediately confronted the witness with the almanac. In reality, he first produced the almanac after the state rested. J. Henry Shaw, one of the prosecutors, would later write that the almanac "floored" Allen, who had been allowed to stay in the courtroom after testifying. The almanac not only floored Allen, it threw the prosecution team into such disarray that they were unable to answer Lincoln's evidence. Milton Logan, the jury foreman, recalled that "the prosecuting attorney in [his final argument] never questioned the issue of the almanac, nor did he refer in any way to the moon shining or attempt to answer Mr. Lincoln's undisputed argument on this point."

Surprise

Lincoln kept his objective hidden; the impeachment was a surprise. When he commenced the examination, he had an almanac in his jacket pocket but gave no hint that he could prove that it was too dark for Allen to have seen what he claimed to have seen. Had the witness had any hint that Lincoln would dispute the claim about moonlight, his testimony might have been quite different. And, the impeachment was all the more persuasive because it surprised both the witness and the prosecution team.

Adjust

Lincoln found Allen making a claim that he could prove to be preposterous given the position of the moon. Lincoln, in his cross-examination, aimed at locking Allen into the preposterous claim. He did this by disarming the witness with cordial questioning. John T. Brady, one of the jurors on the case, said that "when Allen lacked words to express himself, Lincoln loaned them to him." Brady recalled that Lincoln had Allen repeat several times that the moon was high overhead. J. Henry Shaw recalled that Allen had been so skillfully set up, when Lincoln eventually produced the almanac, the jury erupted in laughter.

The Tangible Almanac

Also, the examination was more persuasive because Lincoln produced the almanac, a visual piece of evidence that the jurors and judge could see. Because taking judicial notice was rare then, the case was notable because the judge took judicial notice of the information in the almanac even though the witness claimed that the moon was high overhead at the time of the killing. As Juror Brady later wrote, "[T]he almanac evidence led the jury to the idea that if Allen could be so mistaken about the moon, he might have been mistaken about seeing Armstrong hit Metzker with a slungshot."

Contradiction Technique

Lincoln used the contradiction technique to discredit Allen (see pages 120-121). Nail the witness down on an assertion that can be shown to be utterly false, and then produce irrefutable evidence of its falsehood. The questioning must lock the witness down tightly so as to give no opportunity to advance a plausible explanation.

III. PERCEPTION—MENTAL AND SENSORY DEFICIENCIES

A. Evidentiary Law

Threshold Question

The basic competence of a witness is a threshold question for the court. Fed. R. Evid. 601 defers to state law in civil actions and proceedings where the rule of decision is supplied for a claim or defense by state law.

State statutes may govern the determination of competency. For instance, a statute in the state of Washington prohibits persons from testifying "who appear incapable of receiving just impressions of the facts, respecting which they are examined, or of relating them truly." RCWA 5.60.050(2). By statute and case law, the court decides whether a child can testify. A majority of states, including Pennsylvania, permit a competent child to testify to events that occurred years before. *Commonwealth v. McMaster*, 446 Pa. Super. 261, 267, 666 A.2d 724, 727 (Pa. 1995). However, others, like Wyoming, require a showing that the child was competent at the time of the event as a prerequisite to testifying. *Woyak v. State*, 226 P.3d 841, 851 (Wyo. 2010).

Other state statutes may control the question of competency. For example, in Washington a statute declares that "those who are of unsound mind . . . are incompetent to testify." RCWA 5.60.060. Washington case law vests the trial court with wide discretion in determining whether the person understands the oath and can relate accurately what happened. *State v. Mines*, 35 Wis. App. 932, 936, 671 P.2d 273, 276 (1983). Even though a person has suffered from mental illness in the past, that person can still be competent when called as a witness. *State v. Thach*, 5 Wis. App. 194, 199-200, 486 P.2d 1146, 1149 (1971). Alcohol or drug usage also can cause a person to be unable to perceive an event or recount it accurately. A witness's inebriation at the time of trial can render the witness incompetent to testify. The witness's intoxication at the time of the occurrence that is the subject of the testimony may not render the witness incompetent to testify but rather go to the credibility of the witness. *State v. Wood*, 57 Wis. App. 792, 797-98, 790 P.2d 220, 223-24 (1990).

Under Fed. R. Evid. 104(a), the judge determines "any preliminary question about whether a witness is qualified. . . ." Counsel can move to prohibit the witness from testifying on the grounds that the witness is incompetent. If successful, the need to cross-examine disappears. Another alternative is to test witness competency before any testimony is given through voir dire of the witness outside the presence of the jury.

Weight or Credibility

Regardless of whether the judge finds a witness competent under Fed. R. Evid. 601 or state evidentiary law, Rule 104(e) permits the introduction of evidence that is "relevant to the weight or credibility of other evidence." This can include things such as unsound mind or intoxication with drugs or alcohol, only when they reveal mental or sensory deficiencies going to the witness's ability to perceive or recall facts. If the intoxication or mental deficiency existed during the time of the subject matter of the witness's testimony, then it is relevant to the witness's ability to observe and remember. If the witness is impaired on the witness stand, this bears on the witness's ability to remember and recount.

B. TECHNIQUES AND ILLUSTRATIONS

Assess and Adjust

A young child witness poses difficult challenges for the cross-examiner. As we discussed earlier, the cross-examiner should evaluate any witness to determine whether the person is lying, exaggerating, or honestly mistaken, as well as how the witness comes across to the jury. Then, counsel can adjust questions, voice tone, demeanor, and behavior accordingly. This approach takes care not to offend the jurors, who naturally will align with and be protective of a witness until they are convinced that the witness deserves what he gets.

This task of deciding how to adjust is easier with the child witness in one respect: unlike an adult, attacking a child in a voice tone, demeanor, or with accusatory questioning almost never is appropriate. No one likes a bully. When an adult goes after a child, the jury will be inclined to protect the child, even if the child is not telling the truth. The jury will look to explain the child's inaccuracy in the most innocuous manner possible.

Demeanor, Tone, Behavior, and Questions in Cross-Examining Children

Everything about counsel's demeanor, voice tone, position in the courtroom, and phrasing of questions should be suitable for interacting with a young child. Counsel can be solicitous of and show concern for the child, saying for example: "I'd like to ask you some questions. Is that okay with you?" or "Do you want some water?" Counsel can begin in a friendly, conversational way with nonthreatening questions that the child can readily answer. Counsel should stand back, not pressuring the child by invading the physical space around the witness stand, towering over the child.

Any questions to a child should be of an age-appropriate kind. They should be easily understood, short, direct, and worded with simple language. Young children have some trouble with abstract thinking but readily comprehend concrete everyday examples from everyday life. For instance, asking a young child to explain the difference between the truth and a lie is unlikely to elicit a good response. The same subject is best approached in the following manner:

Q. Sarah, what color is my shirt (counsel points to his blue shirt)?

A. Blue.

Q. If I told you that my shirt was white would that be the truth or a lie?

Along the same line, young children generally have not developed clear understandings of concepts such as time, distance, chronology, numbers, and physiognomy. A clearer answer to distance can be obtained by asking the child to tell counsel, who is moving away, to stop when the distance is reached. This is better than asking the child how far apart two things were. Children are susceptible to suggestions, particularly by an adult. Normally, the child wants to satisfy the adult.

Listen to the Child

Counsel should actively listen to children, both during direct and cross-examination, given their susceptibility to suggestion and lack of fully developed conceptions of time and distance. The child's words may well inform the cross-examiner that an adult has influenced the child's testimony.

McMartin Preschool Case Illustration

The *McMartin Preschool* case, the longest and most expensive trial in America at the time, serves as an illustration of how to cross-examine children. In the 1980s, members of the McMartin family, including preschool founder Peggy McMartin Buckey and son Ray Buckey, were charged with hundreds of counts of child abuse upon the children in their care. Trial lasted from 1987 to 1990 and resulted in no convictions. Eventually, all charges were dropped.

The defense theory was that the children were susceptible to suggestions from the employees of the Children's Institute International (CII), a Los Angeles child abuse clinic. CII employed interviewing techniques that combined leading questions with adult approval and support. Videotapes of the children's interview sessions corroborated this.

Defense counsel did not attack the children during cross-examination, instead employing other types of impeachment. The defense ended up not only approaching the children as victims, but also the authorities. Dean Gits, defense counsel for Peggy McMartin Buckey, came right out and said this in his opening statement: "It is the theory of the defense that all these people are victims." This later was modified somewhat:

> Why were the Manhattan Beach Police, and CII victims? Because they believed in what they were doing. They were not entirely victims, because they should have known better.

What follows are samples from defense counsel's cross of a ten-year-old girl at the *McMartin* trial. Counsel attempts to discredit the child's testimony, not the child herself. His questioning is consistent with the defense theory that adults misled her into this testimony.

Counsel asks about a game the children testified they played at the preschool in which they were photographed nude. Counsel had the girl describe when and where the game was played, along with other details. By asking each of the children detailed questions about the game, counsel discredited their testimony. None of them recounted the same details. When counsel asks about prior inconsistent statements, he walks a delicate line, never accusing the child of falsifying.

IMPEACHMENT — CHILD SUSCEPTIBILITY

Dean Gits' Cross-Examination of Ten-Year-Old Child in the *McMartin Preschool* Case

[Defense counsel begins in a solicitous, conversational, and friendly way. Short and simple questions are asked.]

Gits: *Q.* Cathy, I'd like to ask you some questions. If they seem too hard, stop me. Cathy, when you went to McMartin you went for about three years. Is that correct?

Ten year-old girl: *A.* Yes.

Q. And what grade are you in?

A. Sixth grade . . .

Q. As you think about it now, can you remember how long you were in class?

A. About forty-five minutes.

Q. What happened when your mom and dad picked you up?

A. They just came to the gate.

Q. Where would you be?

A. Outside in the yard.

. . .

[Counsel asks about prior inconsistent statement. This is an example of when a cross-examiner's premise is that both the current and prior testimonies are untrue.]

Q. Do you remember telling us at the preliminary hearing that the cat was not cut until about four months after you played the "naked movie star" game?

A. I don't remember.

[Counsel points the finger at the prosecutors, not the child.]

Q. Did Lael Rubin or Gusty (prosecutors) say it's rather strange that the cat was cut four months later?

A. I don't know.

Q. Cathy, if you can, tell us why you're sure now that the cat was cut the first time you played the "naked movie star" game. Do you feel the cat was cut the first time you played the "naked movie star" game?

A. I'm positive.

Q. Was your testimony wrong in the preliminary hearing?

A. I thought about it.

. . .

[Counsel questions about another prior inconsistent statement.]

Q. Going back to your first year at the preschool, was Ray (a defendant) there in Miss Lo's class?

A. I don't remember.

Q. Do you remember testifying in the preliminary hearing that Ray was in Miss Lo's class?

A. I don't remember.

Q. After your testimony in the preliminary hearing did anybody tell you maybe Ray wasn't there at the school when you were in Miss Lo's class?

A. I don't remember.

Paul Eberle & Shirley Eberle, *Abuse of Innocence* 56-61 (Prometheus Books 2003).

IV. BIAS AND INTEREST

A. Evidentiary Law

A Right

In *United States v. Abel*, 469 U.S. 45, 52, 105 S. Ct. 465, 469, 83 L. Ed. 2d 450, 457 (1984), the United States Supreme Court held:

> Bias is a term used in the common law of evidence to describe the relationship between a party and a witness that might lead the witness to slant, unconsciously or otherwise his testimony in favor of or against a party.

Cross-examination of a witness for showing bias, prejudice, or interest is a party's right, with constitutional protection in criminal cases. *Davis v. Alaska*, 415 U.S. 308, 315, 94 S. Ct. 1105, 39 L. Ed. 2d 347 (1974). However, trial courts "retain wide latitude insofar as the Confrontation Clause is concerned to impose reasonable limits on such cross-examination based on concerns about, among other things, harassment, prejudice, confusion of the issues, the witness safety, or interrogation that is repetitive or only marginally relevant." *Delaware v. Arsdall*, 475 U.S. 673, 679, 106 S. Ct. 1431, 1435, 89 L. Ed. 2d 674, 683 (1986).

Examples of Bias

Some examples of witness bias or interest include:

- Investigating officers intimidated a witness into testifying falsely against the defendant. *United States v. Sanabria*, 645 F.3d 505, 513 (1st Cir. 2011).
- Government witness's swastika tattoos probative of racial bias. *United States v. Figueroa*, 548 F.3d 222, 228 (2d Cir. 2008).
- Gang affiliation admissible to show bias and coercion of the witness. *United States v. Takahashi*, 205 F.3d 1161, 1164 (9th Cir. 2000).
- Witness has instituted civil suit against defendant. *State v. Burris*, 131 Ariz. 563, 567, 643 P.2d 8, 12 (Ariz. 1982).
- Hostility toward a party. *United States v. Harvey*, 547 F.2d 720, 722-23 (2d Cir. 1976).
- Witness's status of being on probation as a motive. *Davis v. Alaska*, 415 U.S. 308, 316-17, 94 S. Ct. 1105, 1110, 39 L. Ed. 2d 347 (1974).
- Personal relationship of the witness with a government agent. *United States v. Buchanan*, 891 F.2d 1436, 1442 (10th Cir. 1989).
- Plea bargain including sentencing consideration in exchange for testimony. *People v. Mumford*, 183 Mich. App. 149, 154, 455 N.W.2d 51, 54 (1990).
- Compensation of an expert witness for testifying. *Falik v. Hornage*, 413 Md. 163, 991 A.2d 1234 (2010).

Extrinsic Evidence

The cross-examiner is not required to take the witness's answer; the examiner may offer extrinsic evidence, which is evidence not from the witness's mouth and generally from another witness. While the Federal Rules of Evidence do not establish foundational requirements that must be met before extrinsic evidence of bias is admissible, some appellate courts have required that the witness must first be given an opportunity to admit or deny and explain the facts or statements showing bias. Only then can extrinsic evidence be admitted. *See United States v. Harvey*, 547 F.2d 720, 722 (2d Cir. 1976). If the witness admits the facts of the bias contained in the questions then, under Rule 403, the court may preclude the introduction of extrinsic evidence as cumulative.

B. Techniques and the Leniency Agreement Illustration

The primary technique for impeachment by bias or interest is to elicit factual admissions with the brushstroke-by-brushstroke method. Once the picture is complete, the bias of the witness will be self-evident. This approach allows the facts showing bias to accumulate and the jurors to reach their own conclusions on bias. Because they have arrived at the conclusions on their own, they have an ownership interest in it. For instance, defense counsel's cross-examination of a government witness who has been promised leniency could go as follows.

IMPEACHMENT WITH BIAS OF THE WITNESS

Defense Counsel: *Q.* Mr. Malloy, let's discuss your criminal charges. You are currently charged with a crime, correct?

Witness Malloy: *A.* Yes.

Q. You are charged with robbery in the second degree?

A. Yes.

Q. You are charged with robbing a convenience store?

A. Yes.

Q. In that criminal case, the store's surveillance camera has a picture of you robbing the store?

A. Yes.

Q. And, you confessed to robbing that store?

A. Yes.

Q. You robbed the store?

A. I did.

Q. You have pled guilty to robbery in the second degree, correct?

A. Yes.

Q. You are pending sentencing in that case, and the sentencing date is the 15th of next month?

A. Yes.

Q. Now, before you pled guilty, you contacted the detective in your case about making a deal in exchange for providing testimony against my client?

A. I contacted the detective.

Q. After that you met with deputy prosecutor Ms. Brown about your case?

A. Yes.

Q. Your attorney was with you when you met with Ms. Brown?

A. He was.

Q. The purpose of that meeting was to discuss a plea agreement for you?

A. Yes.

Q. You wanted to meet with Ms. Brown in order to make a deal to get a reduced sentence in exchange for your testimony here against my client?

A. I told the prosecutor that I would tell the truth.

Q. Again, you wanted to meet with Ms. Brown in order to make a deal to get a reduced sentence in exchange for your testimony here against my client?

A. Yes.

Q. And you got a deal?

A. Not what I wanted.

continued ▶

> *Q.* You got a deal that the prosecutor agreed to recommend leniency to the sentencing judge in your case in exchange for your testimony here, true?
> *A.* Yes.
> *Q.* Understanding that deal, you entered a guilty plea to the robbery charge?
> *A.* Yes.
> *Q.* And, you understand that if you testify here today the prosecutor's office will recommend that you get a lesser sentence than you would otherwise have gotten?
> *A.* Yes.

Defense counsel could conclude this line of questioning by accusing the witness of turning on his friend the defendant to get the sentence reduction. Or, counsel could wait until summation to argue the point.

While the brushstroke-by-brushstroke method is effective in most situations, sometimes the jury will get the picture right away. If they get the point, move on. Another circumstance where you will want to limit the number of brushstrokes is when the witness is biased and sympathetic at the same time. An example of this is a mother testifying as an alibi witness for her son, who stands charged with a crime. In that situation, the cross could be reduced to the following:

Q. Mrs. Timson, you love your son, don't you?

Q. You nursed him as a baby?

Q. You tended to him when he was sick?

Q. You helped him with his homework?

Q. You want to help him out here?

Thank you for coming to court, Mrs. Timson.

CHECKLIST: IMPEACHMENT CROSS IN GENERAL

Impeachment Cross

❑ A winning impeachment cross aims to discredit the witness or the witness's testimony.

Evidentiary Law

❑ Counsel must have a good-faith basis for an assertion on cross.

❑ Rules of Professional Conduct require that the examiner not allude to matter that counsel does not reasonably believe to be relevant or that will not be supported by the evidence.

❑ Under Fed. R. Evid. 104(a), the judge decides the threshold questions regarding whether a witness may testify, such as whether the witness has personal knowledge or is competent.

❑ In response to a motion or objection, the judge also makes the threshold determination of whether impeachment evidence is admissible.

Nine Impeachment Areas

Nine areas for impeachment of any witness are as follows:
❑ Reliability
  1. Lack of Personal Knowledge
  2. Mental and Sensory Deficiencies
  3. Bias and Interest
❑ Report
  4 Improbability
  5. Prior Inconsistent Statements
  6. Contradiction
❑ Reporter
  7. Prior Convictions
  8. Prior Misconduct Probative of Untruthfulness
  9. Character Witness

Seven Essential Impeachment Techniques

Seven essential impeachment techniques for implementing the nine types of impeachment are:

  1. Assess the witness and situation and adjust demeanor and presentation.
  2. Lock the witness into the testimony.
  3. Establish a motive for the witness to lie or be mistaken.
  4. Paint a picture brushstroke by brushstroke of the impeachment evidence.
  5. Close all the exits so the witness cannot escape being impeached.
  6. Surprise the witness with impeachment.
  7. Use tangible or visual evidence to enrich the impeachment.

CHECKLIST: IMPEACHMENT CROSS: RELIABILITY

Lack of Personal Knowledge

❑ Under Federal Rule of Evidence 104(a) or the state rule counterpart, the judge decides whether the witness has personal knowledge of the matter as required by Rule 602.
❑ Under Federal Rule of Evidence 104(e) or state equivalent, the cross-examiner can introduce evidence relevant to the weight and credibility of a witness whom the judge has found to have sufficient personal knowledge of the act, event, or condition.

Perception — Mental and Sensory Deficiencies

❑ Under Federal Rule of Evidence 104(a) or the state rule counterpart, the judge decides whether the witness is competent to testify.

❑ Federal Rule of Evidence 601 defers to state law on the question of competency.
❑ Grounds for incompetency: young child; alcohol or drug impairment; mental impairment.
❑ Methods of precluding the witness from testifying: motion in limine or in trial voir dire the witness.
❑ For cross of a young child witness, these techniques normally apply:
  • Adjust demeanor and presentation to be suitable to the child.
  • Use concrete, not abstract, language.
  • Be solicitous of the child.
  • Questions should be short, direct, easily understood, and composed only of simple language.
  • Aim to discredit the testimony, not the child.

Bias and Interest

❑ Under evidentiary law, cross to show bias or interest is a matter of right and constitutionally protected in criminal cases.
❑ According to governing law, extrinsic evidence of bias or interest may be admissible.

CHAPTER 7

IMPEACHMENT CROSS
Report

"The pursuit of truth will set you free; even if you never catch up with it."
— **Clarence Darrow** (1857-1938)

I. THE REPORT

In this chapter we concentrate on exposing the false or exaggerated nature of what the witness reports on the stand. This approach demands that the witness either grant the admission or be impeached with one or more of the following six ways: (1) reduction to the absurd; (2) conflict with common sense; (3) contradictory conduct; (4) prior inconsistent statements; (5) silence or omission; and (6) contradictory evidence.

II. IMPROBABILITY

An improbability cross-examination seeks to show that the substance of the witness's testimony is unlikely.

A. Evidentiary Law

Federal Rules of Evidence 401-403 and 611 or their state counterparts provide the structural framework for impeachment by improbability. Rule 401 defines relevant evidence as that which ". . . has any tendency to make a fact more or less probable than it would be without the evidence; and . . . is of consequence in determining the action." The examiner should be prepared to argue why the examination is relevant and likely to reveal improbable testimony.

Under Rule 403, the judge may exclude relevant evidence if it would cause confusion, waste time, or if unfair prejudice would substantially outweigh the probative value. To meet a Rule 403 objection, the examiner should be prepared to argue that the inquiry is probative of witness credibility by showing improbability, which is at issue and for the fact-finder to decide.

Relevance and Prejudice, Confusion, or Waste of Time

Rule 401. Test for Relevant Evidence
Evidence is relevant if:
(a) it has any tendency to make a fact more or less probable than it would be without the evidence; and
(b) the fact is of consequence in determining the action.

Rule 402. General Admissibility of Relevant Evidence
Relevant evidence is admissible unless any of the following provides otherwise:
- the United States Constitution;
- a federal statute;
- these rules; or
- other rules prescribed by the Supreme Court.

Irrelevant evidence is not admissible.

> **Rule 403. Excluding Relevant Evidence for Prejudice, Confusion, Waste of Time, or Other Reasons**
>
> The court may exclude relevant evidence if its probative value is substantially outweighed by a danger of one or more of the following: unfair prejudice, confusing the issues, misleading the jury, undue delay, wasting time, or needlessly presenting cumulative evidence.

Federal Rule of Evidence 611(a) states that the court may "exercise reasonable control over the mode and order of examining witnesses and presenting evidence so as "to make the procedures effective for determining the truth. . . ." This provision of Rule 611(a) can convince the judge to overrule an objection, allowing an improbability cross-examination to proceed. Rule 611(b) includes cross-examination matters: (1) within the scope of direct; (2) affecting credibility; or (3) that the court decides are pertinent.

> **Ascertainment of the Truth, Scope of Cross, Leading Questions**
>
> **Rule 611. Mode and Order of Examining Witnesses and Presenting Evidence**
>
> (a) **Control by the Court; Purposes.** The court should exercise reasonable control over the mode and order of examining witnesses and presenting evidence so as to:
>
> (1) make those procedures effective for determining the truth;
>
> (2) avoid wasting time; and
>
> (3) protect witnesses from harassment or undue embarrassment.
>
> (b) **Scope of Cross-Examination.** Cross-examination should not go beyond the subject matter of the direct examination and matters affecting the witness's credibility. The court may allow inquiry into additional matters as if on direct examination.
>
> (c) **Leading Questions.** Leading questions should not be used on direct examination except as necessary to develop the witness's testimony. Ordinarily, the court should allow leading questions:
>
> (1) on cross-examination; and
>
> (2) when a party calls a hostile witness, an adverse party, or a witness identified with an adverse party.

B. Reduction-to-the-Absurd Technique and the *Scopes* Trial Illustration

Reduction-to-the-Absurd Technique

One technique for impeaching by showing improbability is to apply the logical form of argument referred to as "reduction to the absurd" or in Latin, "reductio ad absurdum." This technique, also referred to as "proof by contradiction," extends a premise of the witness out to an absurd or ridiculous result, making it implausible. The examiner asks, "If this premise is true, what else must follow?" The original premise and the absurd outcome cannot both be true.

The *Scopes* Trial Illustration

Clarence Darrow's cross-examination of opposing counsel William Jennings Bryan at the famous "Scopes Trial" in 1925 demonstrates the reduction-to-the-absurd approach. Clarence Darrow not only was one of the preeminent trial lawyers of the first half of the twentieth century, but has been a source of inspiration to countless lawyers ever since. Passionate and skilled trial advocacy never goes out of style. Darrow not only was a fearless courtroom advocate in many epic battles, but also a champion of the underdog, a staunch death penalty foe, and a deadly cross-examiner. None of his more than 100 murder clients was ever sentenced to death, including Leopold and Loeb, the young defendants in the highly publicized 1924 "thrill killing" in Chicago.

While most of Darrow's cases have become long-forgotten footnotes in the history of U.S. jurisprudence, his legend lives on due to his performance as defense counsel in 1925 in the "Scopes Trial," or "Dayton Monkey Trial." John Thomas Scopes, a small-town high school teacher, was accused of teaching evolution in violation of a recently enacted Tennessee statute.

This trial was a nationally publicized test case that drew public figures. The Tennessee Attorney General led for the prosecution and Arthur Garfield Hays for Scopes. Clarence Darrow signed on as co-counsel for the defense and William Jennings Bryan, three-time nominee for the U.S. presidency and subsequent fundamentalist anti-evolution activist, as co-counsel for the prosecution. The climax of the trial came when Darrow, a militant atheist, called Bryan to the stand, seeking to subject Bryan's fundamentalist Christian principles to cross-examination.

This was to become one of great moments in courtroom history, dramatized in the play and then the movie *Inherit the Wind*. The real-life cross-examination was even more dramatic than its Hollywood rendition. The courtroom was so packed that the judge moved the cross-examination onto the courthouse lawn for fear that the floor would collapse under the weight of spectators.

Darrow proceeded to demolish Bryan. Some go so far as to say that this public embarrassment contributed to Bryan's death five days after the trial concluded. Even the most ardent Bryan supporters would have to admit that Bryan was handily defeated by Darrow in the encounter.

Clarence Darrow cross-examines William
Jennings Bryan during the Scopes Trial

Clarence Darrow's cross-examination, which lasted a full day, reduced Bryan's fundamentalist beliefs to the absurd.

IMPLAUSIBILITY: REDUCTION-TO-THE-ABSURD TECHNIQUE

Clarence Darrow's Cross-Examination of William Jennings Bryan

[Darrow locks Bryan into the premise.]

Darrow: *Q.* . . . Do you consider the story of Jonah and the whale a miracle?

Bryan: *A.* I think it is.

Q. Do you believe Joshua made the sun stand still?

A. I believe what the Bible says. I suppose you mean that the earth stood still?

Q. I don't know. I am talking about the Bible now.

A. I accept the Bible absolutely.

Q. The Bible says Joshua commanded the sun to stand still for the purpose of lengthening the day, doesn't it; and you believe it?

A. I do.

Q. Do you believe at that time the sun went around the earth?

A. No, I believe that the earth goes around the sun . . .

Q. . . . If the day was lengthened by stopping either the earth or the sun, it must have been the earth?

A. Well, I should say so.

Q. Yes? But it was the language that was understood at the time, and we now know that the sun stood still as it was with the earth.

A. Well, no —

Q. We know also the sun does not stand still?

A. Well, it is relatively so, as Mr. Einstein would say.

Q. I ask you if it does stand still?

A. You know as well as I know.

Q. Better. You have no doubt about it.

A. No. And the earth moves around.

Q. Yes? . . .

Q. Now, Mr. Bryan, have you ever pondered what would have happened to the earth if it had stood still suddenly?

A. No.

Q. Have you not?

A. No; the God I believe in could have taken care of that, Mr. Darrow.

[Darrow extends the premise to the absurd result.]

Q. I see. Have you ever pondered what would naturally happen to the earth if it stood still suddenly?

A. No.

Q. Don't you know it would have been converted into a molten mass of matter?

A. You testify to that when you get on the stand. I will give you a chance.

[The examination continues later with inquiries about Adam, Eve, and the serpent.]

Darrow: *Q.* And you believe that came about because Eve tempted Adam to eat the fruit?

Bryan: *A.* Just as it says (in the Bible).

continued ▶

> Q. And you believe that is the reason that God made the serpent to go on his belly after he tempted Eve?
>
> A. I believe the Bible as it is, and I do not permit you to put your language in the place of the language of the Almighty. You read the Bible and ask me questions, and I will answer them. I will not answer your questions in your language.
>
> Q. I will read it to you from the Bible, in your language. "And the Lord God said unto the serpent, because thou hast done this, thou art cursed above all cattle, and above every beast of the field; upon thy belly shalt thou go and dust shalt thou eat all the days of thy life."
>
> Do you think that is why the serpent is compelled to crawl upon his belly?
>
> A. I believe that.
>
> Q. Have you any idea how the snake went before that time?
>
> A. No, sir.
>
> Q. Do you know whether he walked on his tail or not?
>
> A. No sir. I have no way to know.

Attorney for the Damned: Clarence Darrow in the Courtroom 193-98 (Arthur Weinberg ed., University of Chicago Press 1989).

Of course, the jury must be willing to accept that the principles endorsed by the witness are in fact absurd. It is highly questionable whether the *Scopes* jury, all from the heart of the Bible Belt, would have been favorably impressed by Darrow's cross-examination of Bryan. A seldom-quoted portion of the transcript shows Darrow crossing over the line in a manner in which a modern jury would find reprehensible.

IMPLAUSIBILITY: REDUCTION-TO-THE-ABSURD TECHNIQUE

Clarence Darrow's Cross-Examination of William Jennings Bryan

Darrow: *Q.* You want to make a speech on Buddha, too?

Bryan: *A.* No sir, I want to answer your question on Buddha.

Q. I asked you if you knew anything about him.

A. I do.

Q. Well, that's answered, then.

A. Buddha . . .

Darrow: Well, wait a minute. You answered the question.

Judge Raulston: I will let him tell what he knows.

Darrow: All he knows?

Judge Raulston: Well, I don't know about that.

Bryan: I won't insist on telling all I know. I will tell more than Mr. Darrow wants told.

Q. Well, all right, tell it. I don't care.

A. Buddhism is an agnostic religion.

> *Q.* To what? What do you mean by "agnostic"?
>
> *A.* I don't know.
>
> *Q.* You don't know what you mean?
>
> *A.* That is what "agnosticism" is— "I don't know." When I was in Rangoon, Burma, one of the Buddhists told me that they were going to send a delegation to an agnostic congress that was to be held soon at Rome and I read in an official document . . .
>
> *Q.* Do you remember his name?
>
> *A.* No sir, I don't.
>
> *Q.* What did he look like? How tall was he?
>
> *A.* I think he was about as tall as you, but not so good-looking.
>
> *Q.* Do you know about how old a man he was? Do you know whether he was old enough to know what he was talking about?
>
> *A.* He seemed to be old enough to know what he was talking about. *[Laughter.]*
>
> Darrow: If Your Honor please, instead of answering plain specific questions we are permitting the witness to regale the crowd with what some black man said to him when he was travelling in Rangoon, India.

John Thomas Scopes, *The World's Most Famous Court Trial: Tennessee Evolution Case* 295 (John Scopes & William J. Bryan, National Book Company 1957).

C. Common-Sense Technique and the *Senator Stevens* Trial Illustration

Common Sense

An appeal to common sense is an effective theme in closing argument, particularly when the testimony of a witness does not comport with the jurors' common sense and everyday experiences. The cross-examiner is always on the alert for any witness's assertion that does not ring true. Common sense can be used even when the examiner does not have direct evidence that would refute the witness's claim. The examiner can confront the witness directly with the improbability, save the point for closing, or both.

Senator Stevens Trial Illustration

The cross-examination of Ted Stevens, who served 40 years in the U.S. Senate, exposed testimony that was improbable in light of common sense. In 2008, Stevens was convicted in Federal Court of seven corruption charges for failing to disclose gifts and free labor on his cabin remodel exceeding $250,000. Later, the conviction was vacated and the case was dismissed with prejudice because, ironically and sadly, the prosecutors failed to disclose discoverable material favorable to the defense.

Assistant U.S. Attorney Brenda Morris cross-examines Senator Stevens at right. Illustrated by Dana Verkouteren

Among the gifts that Senator Stevens did not report on Senate disclosure forms was a $2,700 vibrating Shiatsu massage chair given to him by an Alaskan restaurant owner. Stevens claimed on direct examination that the chair had been loaned to him: "It's not my chair, it's not my chair. It's his chair, he put it in the house." On cross-examination, Assistant U.S. Attorney Brenda Morris asked Stevens if he had other furniture on loan. Senator Stevens appeared steadily more ridiculous as the examination proceeded, losing all credibility.

IMPLAUSIBILITY: COMMON SENSE

Brenda Morris's Cross-Examination of Senator Ted Stevens

Morris: *Q.* And the chair is still at your house?

Stevens: *A.* Yes.

Q. How is that not a gift?

A. He bought that chair as a gift, but I refused it as a gift. He put it there and said it was my chair. I told him I would not accept it as a gift.

Q. Where is that chair now?

A. In our house. We have lots of things in our house that don't belong to us, ma'am.

. . .

Q. So, if you say it's not a gift, it's not a gift?

A. I refused it as a gift. I let him put it in our basement at his request. I've had three back operations, ma'am. I do not use that chair.

. . .

[An e-mail from Stevens to the restaurateur was introduced into evidence that read: "The CHAIR arrived and I tried it out last night. It is great: I can't tell you have [sic] much I enjoyed it. Catherine and Beth tried to get me out of it, I just went to sleep in it.

> *Thank you and thanks to Bill. It will be a godsend this year. It is just a loan; but, I really appreciate it being here now."]*
>
> Q. But you kept it?
> A. It's still there.
> . . .
> Q. Isn't it a fact that you're calling it a loan when it's actually your chair?
> A. It's not my chair.

Dana Milbank, The Washington Post, October 21, 2008.

With the implausibility of Senator Stevens's story established, another member of the prosecution team used this to good effect in final argument.

D. Contradictory-Conduct Technique and the *Sonics* Trial Illustration

Contradictory-Conduct Technique

The contradictory-conduct technique is anchored by the maxim: "Action speaks louder than words." The witness testifies to one proposition, but the witness's behavior is quite the contrary. The method requires a thorough fact investigation of not only the witness's expected testimony but also of the witness's conduct. Then, the examiner creatively determines how the conduct undercuts the testimony. As with other impeachment, the examiner has the options of confronting the witness with the inconsistency immediately, waiting until closing, or doing both.

Sonics Trial Illustration

The Seattle SuperSonics lawsuit in federal court for specific performance of a lease agreement against the new Oklahoma City ownership group illustrates this technique. The Oklahoma Group wanted a cash buyout, moving the basketball team before the term of the lease ran out. In the 2009 bench trial, Seattle's first witness, Mayor Greg Nickels, was tripped up by his contradictory conduct.

The mayor testified on direct that the Sonics were an integral part of the city's pride and should be held to their lease. He recalled the championship in 1979: "I remember the celebration after they won the championship. There was a parade down Fifth Avenue and a gathering on the plaza and street area, University Street, in front of the Olympic Hotel. I remember standing up on the roof of what was then the Rainier Bank Tower." The mayor testified that he was a fan and the Sonics were community role models.

On cross-examination, defense counsel Brad Keller explored how avid a Sonics fan the mayor really was.

Sonics attorney Brad Keller cross-examines Seattle City Mayor Greg Nickels. Picture by Julie Notarianni, Seattle Times

---

IMPLAUSIBILITY: CONTRADICTORY CONDUCT

Brad Keller's Cross-Examination of Mayor Greg Nickels

Keller: *Q.* I'm going to switch gears and ask you about something else, Mr. Mayor.

Nickels: *A.* Okay.

Q. You talked about some of the things that you perceive as the value of having the Sonics here. I guess I wanted to ask you, you know that the PBC purchased the team in the fall of '06, right?

A. Right.

Q. So there's been, what, two full basketball seasons since PBC purchased the team?

A. Right.

Q. Tell us how many Sonics games you've been to since PBC purchased the team.

A. I don't think I've been to one yet.

Q. How about prior to that, the last year the Schultz group owned the team, when you were down there in Olympia trying to support their efforts to get funding. Tell us how many Sonics games you showed up at to show your support for the team that year.

A. I don't know if I went to any.

Q. You didn't, did you?

A. I don't think so.

Q. Am I right that the last two games that you can remember attending was the last—one is the last time the team was in the playoffs and the other was when Gus Williams' jersey was retired?

A. Those are the last two that I remember, yes.

Q. You know that Gus Williams' jersey was retired almost seven or eight years?

A. It was—I think I was mayor. But it could have been seven. Six.

Seattle Times transcripts, 102-03, Greg Nickels testimony.

While the mayor's words sought to leave the impression that he was a Sonics fan, his conduct belied the claim. For this and other reasons, the city fared badly as the trial progressed. The case settled for a cash buyout just before Judge Marsha Pechman was to issue her ruling.

III. PRIOR INCONSISTENT STATEMENTS

"That's not what you told me before!" How many times have we heard that angry statement in everyday arguments? We dislike and distrust people who cannot keep their stories straight. If a witness changes a previous statement, then we question his or her credibility. This can be powerful impeachment, particularly when discussed later in closing, where counsel can show the jury a chart documenting the inconsistencies. Hence, it is not surprising that the use of prior inconsistent statements reigns supreme as the most common form of impeachment.

A. Evidentiary Law

Under Federal Rule of Evidence 613, a witness may be examined about prior inconsistent statements, either oral or written, to impeach the credibility of that witness.

Prior Statements

Rule 613. Witness's Prior Statement

(a) **Showing or Disclosing the Statement During Examination.** When examining a witness about the witness's prior statement, a party need not show it or disclose its contents to the witness. But the party must, on request, show it or disclose its contents to an adverse party's attorney.

(b) **Extrinsic Evidence of a Prior Inconsistent Statement.** Extrinsic evidence of a witness's prior inconsistent statement is admissible only if the witness is given an opportunity to explain or deny the statement and an adverse party is given an opportunity to examine the witness about it, or if justice so requires. This subdivision (b) does not apply to an opposing party's statement under Rule 801(d)(2).

The following prerequisites apply for the admissibility of a prior inconsistent statement.

Inconsistency

It is critical to make sure that the prior statements used really are inconsistent. Experienced trial judges report that attorneys often try to impeach witnesses with prior statements that do not meet this description. For this reason, before attempting impeachment by a prior inconsistent statement, the examiner must lock down the witness's current testimony. Literal inconsistency is not required. For instance, *McCormick on Evidence* cites this test: "*. . .* could the jury reasonably find that a witness who believed the truth of the facts testified to would be unlikely to make a prior statement of this tenor?" Charles T. McCormick, *McCormick on Evidence* § 34 at 63 (6th ed., West Group 2006).

Confrontation

At common law, the cross-examiner was required to confront the witness with the circumstances of the prior statement, such as the time, place, and person to whom the statement was made. If the prior statement was written, the cross-examiner was required to show it to the witness. *Queen Caroline's Case,* 2 Brod. & Bing 284, 313, 129 Eng. Rep. 976 (1820).

Under Federal Rule of Evidence 613(a), the foundation no longer requires confronting the witness with the prior statement though, on request, the statement shall be revealed or shown to opposing counsel. It remains a good technique to confront the witness with time, place, and persons present, showing the fairness of the cross-examiner.

Extrinsic Evidence
1. Witness Admits

If the witness admits to having made the prior statement, it can be argued that impeachment has been completed and extrinsic evidence should be inadmissible. Federal Rule of Evidence 403 gives the court discretion to exclude cumulative or other evidence that would cause undue delay or be a waste of time. Accordingly, most jurisdictions hold that extrinsic evidence of an inconsistent statement is inadmissible once the witness acknowledges making it.

2. Witness Denies

If the witness denies making the prior statement, unless it is a collateral matter, extrinsic evidence is admissible to prove it. *United States v. Roulette*, 75 F.3d 418, 423 (8th Cir. 1996), *cert. denied,* 519 U.S. 853, 117 S. Ct. 147, 136 L. Ed. 2d 93 (1996). If a collateral matter, the cross-examiner is stuck with the witness's denial.

But, what constitutes a denial? The witness must admit making the prior statement unequivocally and without qualification. *State v. Blalock*, 357 S.C. 74, 81, 591 S.E.2d 632, 636 (S.C. App. 2003). If so, the witness is impeached and any additional evidence is unnecessary. *See State v. Dixon*, 159 Wis. 2d 65, 76, 147 P.3d 991, 996 (2006). *See also* 98 C.J.S., *Witnesses* § 727 (2010) (stating that the admission must be "unequivocal").

On the other hand, if the witness claims not to be able to recall the prior statement or equivocates about it, the court may admit the extrinsic evidence. *United States v. Dennis*, 625 F.2d 782, 795 (8th Cir. 1980). Otherwise, a witness could elude prior inconsistencies by claiming a lack of memory. Extrinsic evidence of the prior statement can be either the authenticated written statement itself or an oral statement overheard by another witness.

Impeachment by a prior inconsistent statement should never be attempted if the statement cannot be proven. Some lawyers ask about a prior statement without proof of this in the hopes that either the witness will admit it or, if the witness denies it, that the jury will believe the statement was made anyway. Whatever the examiner's motivation, it is unprofessional conduct. Model Rule of Professional Conduct 3.4(e) states "a lawyer shall not in trial, allude to any matter that the lawyer does not reasonably believe is relevant or that will not be supported by admissible evidence, assert personal knowledge of facts in issue except when testifying as a witness . . . ."

The greatest temptation to do this will come when counsel has had a one-on-one interview with the witness, and the witness has said something only counsel's ears have heard. Counsel cannot blurt out "But didn't you tell me . . . ?" A cross-examiner cannot become a witness without running afoul of ethical requirements under Model Rule of Professional Conduct 3.7 prohibiting a lawyer from being a witness except under limited circumstances.

Rule 613(b) Fairness Requirements

Federal Rule of Evidence 613(b) requires that for extrinsic evidence to be admissible, the following must occur:

- At some time the witness must be given an opportunity to deny or explain the statement (it would satisfy Rule 613(b) if the witness could be recalled and the witness need not be confronted with the statement at the time of the examination); and
- Opposing counsel must have an opportunity to question the witness.

The idea behind this aspect of Rule 613(b) is that several witnesses who are colluding could be cross-examined before they are confronted with the prior statement. Rule 613(b) does not apply to party opponent statements qualifying under Rule 801(d)(2).

For Impeachment Purposes or as Substantive Evidence
1. Impeachment Purposes Only

Ordinarily, a prior inconsistent statement is admissible for the limited purpose of impeaching the credibility of the witness by showing the person told different tales. It is not substantive proof of facts encompassed by the prior statement. And, because it is not offered for the truth of the matter stated, the statement is not hearsay. Instead, it is admissible to cast doubt on the credibility of the witness and does not constitute substantive evidence. *State v. Clinkenbeard*, 130 Wash. App. 552, 123 P.3d 872 (Div. 3 2005). If requested, a limiting instruction to the effect that the prior inconsistent statement may be used only for that purpose should be given to the jury. The following Oklahoma pattern instruction is an example of such an instruction:

> ### Oklahoma Uniform Jury Instructions Criminal 9-10
>
> #### Evidence—Impeachment by Prior Inconsistent Statements
>
> Evidence has been presented that on some prior occasion (the defendant)/([Name of Witness]) (made a statement)/(acted in a manner) inconsistent with his/her testimony in this case. This evidence is called impeachment evidence and it is offered to show that the defendant's/witness's testimony is not believable or truthful. If you find that (a statement was made)/(the acts occurred), you may consider this impeachment evidence in determining what weight and credit to give the testimony of (the defendant)/(that witness). You may not consider this impeachment evidence as proof of innocence or guilt. You may consider this impeachment evidence only to the extent that you determine it affects the believability of the defendant/witness, if at all.

2. Substantive Evidence

In five instances, the content of a prior statement is admissible as substantive evidence, not barred by the hearsay rule:

1. **Prior Inconsistent Statement Under Oath:** Under Fed. R. Evid. 801(d)(1)(A), when the prior inconsistent statement was "given under penalty of perjury at a trial, hearing, or other proceeding or in a deposition" it is nonhearsay and is admissible as substantive evidence.
2. **Statement of a Party in a Deposition:** Fed. R. Civ. Proc. 32(a)(3) states that "(a)n adverse party may use for any purpose the deposition of a party or anyone who, when deposed, was the party's officer, director, managing agent, or designee under Rule 30(b)(6) or 31(a)(4)." In other words, the statements in the deposition may be used as substantive evidence.
3. **Statement of Party Opponent:** Under Fed. R. Evid. 801(d)(2), statements of party opponents are nonhearsay and therefore admissible as substantive evidence. This includes not only the party's own statements but also those "made by the party's agent or employee on a matter within the scope of that relationship and while it existed." The same applies to statements "made by the party's coconspirator during and in furtherance of the conspiracy."
4. **Prior Statement of Identification:** Prior statements of identification covered by Fed. R. Evid. 801(d)(1)(C) are nonhearsay and admissible as substantive evidence.
5. **Prior Statement Falling Under a Hearsay Exception:** Other out-of-court statements that qualify as exceptions to the hearsay rule, such as present sense impression, are admissible as substantive evidence.

Impeachment of Defendant with an Inadmissible but Voluntary Confession

A defendant in a criminal case who was not advised of *Miranda* rights may be impeached by a confession inconsistent with the defendant's testimony. *Har-*

ris v. New York, 401 U.S. 222, 226 (1971). However, *Mincey v. Arizona*, 437 U.S. 385, 397-98, 98 S. Ct. 2408, 57 L. Ed. 2d 290 (1978), held it a violation of due process to use an involuntary confession against a defendant. In *Michigan v. Harvey*, 494 U.S. 344, 345-46, 110 S. Ct. 1176, 1177-78 (1990), the U.S. Supreme Court extended the *Harris* doctrine under the Fifth Amendment to custodial statements taken in violation of the Sixth Amendment right to counsel. *Kansas v. Ventris*, 129 S. Ct. 1841, 1845 (2009), held that when a defendant testifies at trial, the defendant's prior inconsistent statement that was obtained in violation of the defendant's Sixth Amendment right to counsel may be used to impeach him. The Supreme Court reasoned as follows:

> . . . Once the defendant testifies in a way that contradicts prior statements, denying the prosecution use of "the traditional truth-testing devices of the adversary process," *Harris*, supra, at 225, is a high price to pay for vindication of the right to counsel at the prior stage.
>
> On the other side of the scale, preventing impeachment use of statements taken in violation of *Massiah* would add little appreciable deterrence. Officers have significant incentive to ensure that they and their informants comply with the Constitution's demands, since statements lawfully obtained can be used for all purposes rather than simply for impeachment . . . .

Id. at 1846-47.

B. Avoid Minor Inconsistencies

The skilled cross-examiner wants more than a legally sufficient impeachment; it must be effective and persuasive. Good judgment is called for when deciding what prior statements to ask about and the techniques to be used to achieve a flowing and forceful presentation. It is critical that the inconsistency itself be significant. Any effort to impeach with minor inconsistencies is tedious, boring, and irritatingly nitpicky.

However, there are two situations where impeachment by minor prior inconsistencies can succeed. First, the cumulative effect of a myriad of inconsistencies can reveal that the witness is not credible. Second, evasive professional witnesses trying to support a position sometimes can be shaken when confronted with minor inconsistencies. The goal of this approach is greater witness compliance. If the witness just shakes off the inconsistencies as trivial, this technique is best dropped.

Opposing counsel may ask about minor inconsistencies for tactical purposes. This may be to try and unsettle or distract an inexperienced opposing counsel, prone to overreacting. Ignoring this hazing ritual will cause it to pass quickly. Alternatively, it may be part of an effort to unsettle a witness. Preparation of the witness is the best way to deal with this tactic. A cross-examiner also may be desperate, asking about minor inconsistencies because he or she has no case. Such lawyers also attempt to select jurors dim enough to fall for such tactics.

C. Context: The Rule of Completeness

Rule of Completeness

Fed. R. Evid. 106 states what is referred to as the "rule of completeness," which guards against counsel plucking a statement out of context and using it to mislead. Federal Rule of Civil Procedure 32(a)(6) restates the rule of completeness, applying it to depositions.

Fed. R. Evid. 106. Remainder of or Related Writings or Recorded Statements
If a party introduces all or part of a writing or recorded statement, an adverse party may require the introduction, at that time, of any other part — or any other writing or recorded statement — that in fairness ought to be considered at the same time.

Fed R. Civ. Proc. 32(a)(6). Using Part of a Deposition
If a party offers in evidence only part of a deposition, an adverse party may require the offeror to introduce other parts that in fairness should be considered with the part introduced, and any party may itself introduce any other parts.

There are three important points about the rule of completeness as codified in the Federal Rules or its state rule counterparts. First, it applies only to writings, recorded statements, and depositions, not to unrecorded or undocumented statements. Second, the remedy is immediate; the opposing party can insist the other evidence be introduced contemporaneously. Third, while Fed. R. Civ. Proc. 32(a)(6) provides that "any other parts" of the deposition are admissible, Fed. R. Evid. 106 is not so restrictive and allows for introduction of either "any other part or any other writing or recorded statement which ought in fairness to be considered contemporaneously with it."

Ironically, the codified rule of completeness is incomplete. It ignores oral statements, which may be explained or rebutted by the balance of the oral statement. *United States v. Prince*, 516 F.3d 597, 604 (7th Cir. 2008); *United States v. Tarantino*, 846 F.2d 1384, 1411 (D.C. Cir. 1988); *State v. West*, 70 Wis. 2d 751, 754, 424 P.2d 1014, 1016 (1967). Opposing counsel may argue that the rest of the unrecorded oral statement should be introduced contemporaneously, relying on Fed. R. Evid. 611(a). Rule 611(a) vests the judge with authority "to exercise reasonable control over the order of . . . presenting evidence so as to (1) make the interrogation and presentation effective for the ascertainment of the truth . . . ."

The rule of completeness has been held to open the door to the introduction of even inadmissible evidence to correct a misimpression. *United States v. Sutton*, 801 F.2d 1346, 1368 (D.C. Cir. 1986), held, "Rule 106 can adequately fulfill its function only by permitting the admission of some otherwise inadmissible evidence when the court finds in fairness that that proffered evidence should be considered contemporaneously." *See also United States v. Bucci*, 525 F.3d 116, 132 (2008).

Avoid Misleading with Partial Prior Statements

Evidentiary law regarding the rule of completeness makes obvious the risks inherent in cross-examining a witness with a prior statement picked out of context and used to present a misleading picture. First, opposing counsel can derail the cross by interrupting it and demanding that the full picture be made known to the jury. Second, when the remainder is admitted into evidence, the other side's case usually will be bolstered. Third, the door may be opened to what would otherwise be inadmissible evidence. Fourth, and worst of all, it may be apparent to the jurors that the cross-examiner attempted to misrepresent the situation to them. The cross-examiner can steer clear of these harmful consequences by working hard to ask only about prior statements that are fair and not out of context.

D. The Refreshing-Recollection Alternative

Rather than embarking on an impeachment cross with a prior inconsistent statement, a better approach may be to refresh the witness's memory with that prior statement. This technique accomplishes the same goal as impeachment with a prior inconsistent statement, which is to establish the prior statement is true and correct. Frequently, the activity of refreshing a witness's memory can be accomplished in a nonconfrontational manner, unlike that used in an impeachment cross. This technique is particularly appropriate when the witness's uncertainty, memory lapse, or testimony contrary to the prior statement is likely the product of forgetfulness or nerves, not deceptiveness.

While the court will require on direct examination that counsel lay a complete evidentiary foundation as set out below before allowing counsel to refresh a witness's memory, the judge is likely to relax the requirements when counsel is cross-examining.

State v. Williams, 137 Wis. App. 736, 750, 154 P.3d 322, 330 (2007), quotes *State v. Little*, 57 Wis. 2d 516, 521, 358 P.2d 120, 122 (1961), regarding the evidentiary foundation for using written material to refresh a witness's memory:

[T]he criteria for the use of notes or other memoranda to refresh a witness'[s] recollection are (1) that the witness'[s] memory needs refreshing, (2) that opposing counsel have the right to examine the writing, and (3) that the trial court be satisfied that the witness is not being coached — that the witness is using the notes to aid, and not to supplant, his own memory.

Fed. R. Evid. 612. Writing Used to Refresh Memory

    (a) **Scope.** This rule gives an adverse party certain options when a witness uses a writing to refresh memory:

---

continued ▶

(1)   while testifying; or

(2)   before testifying, if the court decides that justice requires the party to have those options.

(b)   **Adverse Party's Options; Deleting Unrelated Matter.** Unless 18 U.S.C. § 3500 provides otherwise in a criminal case, an adverse party is entitled to have the writing produced at the hearing, to inspect it, to cross-examine the witness about it, and to introduce in evidence any portion that relates to the witness's testimony. If the producing party claims that the writing includes unrelated matter, the court must examine the writing in camera, delete any unrelated portion, and order that the rest be delivered to the adverse party. Any portion deleted over objection must be preserved for the record.

(c)   **Failure to Produce or Deliver the Writing.** If a writing is not produced or is not delivered as ordered, the court may issue any appropriate order. But if the prosecution does not comply in a criminal case, the court must strike the witness's testimony or — if justice so requires — declare a mistrial.

This is an illustration of the refreshing-recollection technique:

REFRESHING RECOLLECTION

Q. You testified on direct that the last time you spoke to the Director was on your last day with the company and not after that?

A. Yes.

Q. Do you remember coming to my office for a deposition?

Q. At that deposition you were asked about your conversations with the Director?

A. Yes, I did.

Q. Handing you your deposition. Will you please read to yourself line 5 on page 45? (Witness complies)

Does that refresh your recollection?

A. Yes, it does.

Q. You spoke to the Director another time after you left the company — specifically on July 6th?

A. Yes.

E. Techniques: Eight Essentials and the Negligence Illustration

For an impeachment with a prior inconsistent statement to be effective it should dynamically reveal the inconsistency in the witness's statements, damage the witness's credibility, and be conducted smoothly and professionally. These goals can be achieved by applying the following eight essentials of a successful impeachment with a prior inconsistent statement.

> ### Eight Essential Techniques for Successful Cross With a Prior Inconsistent Statement
>
> 1. *Recognize* the inconsistency;
> 2. *Retrieve* the prior statement;
> 3. *Repeat* the testimony;
> 4. *Resonate* with the jury;
> 5. *Reinforce* the truthful statement;
> 6. *Reference* the prior statement;
> 7. *Read or display* the statement; and
> 8. *Refute* the witness's denial.

1. Recognize

The first prerequisite for impeachment with a prior inconsistent statement is to recognize that the witness's testimony differs from a previous statement. To accomplish this, counsel must have a thorough understanding of the facts of the case and the witness's prior statements. The failure of this technique is most often attributable to a lack of knowledge.

For example, suppose that in an automobile collision case, a passenger in defendant Josephine Bollard's car, Beatrice Tharp, testifies on direct that Bollard came to a complete stop before entering the highway. Plaintiff's counsel *recognizes* that this does not match the statement of this witness to the police at the scene and that she was on her cell phone, not paying attention to the driver.

2. Retrieve

The next essential for a successful impeachment is the prompt retrieval of the prior statement, which creates drama and places the inconsistency in sharp contrast. Chapter 11, Preparing the Winning Cross, offers retrieval systems that work.

In the automobile collision case, plaintiff's counsel must be able to *retrieve* the officer's statement, either from a tabbed trial notebook or a case management software program.

3. Repeat

The cross-examiner should have the witness repeat the testimony that is inconsistent with the prior statement, which is the single exception to the usual rule of not repeating the direct on cross. Repetition puts the present testimony right next to the prior statement, highlighting the inconsistency for the jury:

> *Q.* You are telling us that you saw Ms. Bollard come to a complete stop before entering the highway?
>
> *A.* Yes.

Q. Isn't it true that you were on your cell phone and paid no attention to whether Ms. Bollard stopped at the stop sign?

A. That's not correct.

An incredulous tone by the examiner can make the contrast even more stark.

4. Resonate

The cross-examiner can emphasize the inconsistencies by both voice and demeanor, without being flamboyant, achieving the desired effect with the jury. For example, in the automobile collision case illustration, plaintiff's counsel first can express doubt about the truthfulness of the witness's claim in court, shifting to an accusatory tone in referencing the prior statement at the scene to the trooper.

Five Ws

The easy way to reinforce is to remember the five Ws to reinforce the prior statement:

1. *Who* heard: The witness(es) who heard it.
2. *What* said: The substance.
3. *When* said: The date and time.
4. *Where* said: The place where the statement was made.
5. *Whether* said: An opportunity to admit or deny making it.

The concept is that by eliciting the details of each W, the prior statement becomes more concrete and therefore believable. With each of the Ws, the cross-examiner emphasizes those facts that make it more likely that the person making the statement would have been truthful. For example:

1. *Who* heard: The statement was made to a person to whom the normal person would tell the truth, such as a police officer.
2. *What* said: The statement is against the person's interest or it was important that the person tell the truth.
3. *When* said: It was made shortly after the event and therefore more likely an accurate recitation of what happened than one at trial.
4. *Where* said: The formality of the place where the statement was made, such as at the police station, may lend credence to the statement.
5. *Whether* said: The witness is given the opportunity to admit or deny making the statement.

In the automobile collision case, the cross-examiner wants to convince the jury that the witness's original oral statement to the State Trooper was truthful. Reinforcement of that initial statement intensifies the impact of the inconsistent statement by the passenger-witness to the jury.

PRIOR INCONSISTENT ORAL STATEMENT: REINFORCEMENT TECHNIQUE

(Where said)

Plaintiff's counsel: *Q.* You recall speaking to the State Trooper at the scene?

Ms. Tharp: *A.* Yes.

Q. The officer spoke to you in her patrol car?

A. Yes.

(When said)

Q. This was at 9:30 p.m.?

A. I don't know what time it was.

Q. It was within a half hour after the collision, correct?

A. Yes.

(Who heard)

Q. Only you and the officer were in the patrol car?

A. Yes.

(When—establish proximity to the event)

Q. This was right after the collision, so what had just happened was fresh in your mind?

A. I was dazed from the impact.

Q. But you had no difficulty recalling what had just happened?

A. Yes.

(Establish that the officer recorded an accurate account from the witness)

Q. The officer took notes of your conversation, true?

A. Yes.

Q. You just testified that the defendant came to a complete stop before entering the highway?

A. Yes.

(What said and whether said)

Q. Yet, within a half hour of the collision, you told the State Trooper that you had been distracted by your cell phone and did not know when the defendant entered the highway?

A. I said no such thing.

Deposition

If the prior statement is in a deposition, in addition to the 5 Ws counsel can add reinforcement by eliciting testimony that the prior statement was made:

1. *Under oath;*
2. *When the deponent's counsel was present;* and
3. Followed by an *opportunity to review and sign* the deposition, as is illustrated on page 156.

5. Reinforce

Two inconsistent statements cannot be reconciled. Only one can be true, unless both are false. The mere inconsistency between the two statements can discredit the witness's testimony. However, the impeachment can be enhanced by proof of the truthfulness of one of the statements. The goal is to convince the jury that the witness made the statement and that that statement is true. The circumstances under which the statement was made can make it more credible. Usually, the examiner seeks to reinforce the prior statement as truthful, for reasons such as proximity to the event, lack of motive to falsify, or difference in the background circumstances.

6. Reference

The examiner should, when possible, reference the document containing the statement, such as a deposition or written statement, with page and line numbers. For instance, holding the deposition, counsel can say to the witness: "Directing your attention to page 20, line 6." This allows opposing counsel to locate the statement in the document. With opposing counsel following along, the jury will expect an objection if the claimed statement is somehow incorrect. Otherwise, the jury will know that it likely is true.

7. Read or Display

The examiner should read the prior statement rather than the witness. Otherwise the witness will take the initiative in attempting to explain it away. The tone of the witness also may lessen the impact of the statement.

If the prior statement can be shown or displayed to the jury, for instance with a video deposition, it is even more effective. Then counsel can ask the witness, "Have I read this accurately?" The jury will know the answer, having seen it up on the screen.

8. Refute

Counsel must meet the legal requirements for the prior inconsistent statement, getting the witness to admit making it or, failing that, prove it by extrinsic evidence. This can be in the form of a deposition statement or calling a witness to testify to the prior oral statement. In the automobile collision case illustration, after witness Tharp denies making the prior statement, counsel must prove it through the rebuttal testimony of the State Trooper.

Rebuttal testimony by the witness who heard the prior inconsistent statement provides another opportunity to convince the jury that the first statement was true. The examination of the Trooper would cover the five Ws: whether the statement was made; where the statement was made; when it was said; who heard it; and what was said. In this way the initial oral statement is reinforced and the witness's testimony at trial to the contrary is discredited.

F. Deposition — Cross-Examination Strategy

The deposition-cross strategy is aimed at getting the same answers in trial as in the deposition of the witness, extracting the same concessions. Generally, these build and preserve the examiner's case theory, while damaging that of the opposing party.

The cross-examiner must be careful to phrase the question on cross in the same way as it was phrased during the deposition. That way, the inconsistency is manifest. The witness cannot explain it away. The examiner either can refresh the witness's memory with the deposition or openly confront the witness with the prior inconsistency. This strategy also will control a witness who varies from deposition testimony. Even without quoting from the transcript, counsel can make it readily apparent and the witness will be forced to give the desired answer. This technique can train the witness to answer honestly and without equivocation.

G. Impeachment with a Deposition—Illustration

The eight essentials of impeachment with a prior inconsistent statement apply with equal force, if not more, to a prior statement in a deposition.

Step 1: Recognize the Contradiction

First, the cross-examiner must recognize that the witness's answer on direct or cross departs from the one given during the deposition. The inconsistency should be readily apparent.

Step 2: Retrieval

Counsel must be able to promptly identify the prior deposition statement by page and line, so it can be retrieved quickly if necessary. This is easily accomplished if the question asked is in cross-notes format, as shown in the following cross-examination of Mr. Erskine:

CROSS NOTES

TOPIC: Erskine met with Probert

You met with Ms. Probert in the conference room in your office complex	Erskine dep – 31:5

The reference on the right side of the cross notes indicates page 31, line 5. With trial support software, discussed at pages 246-247, counsel can call up the deposition page by page number, label, or a swipe of a bar-code wand and display the excerpt from the transcript for the judge and jury to see. The reference on the right may be to a clip from the video deposition, discussed at pages 158-159.

Step 3: Repeat

Repeat the testimony that is to be contradicted before confronting the witness with the deposition. That way, the witness cannot escape the impeachment.

Step 4: Resonate

Emphasize the inconsistencies for the jury by tone of voice before the line of questions is concluded. Counsel can ask whether the witness ever made a prior conflicting statement. If the witness answers "yes," counsel can then go to the deposition and the inconsistent answer it contains. If the answer is "no" or "I can't recall," counsel has laid the foundation to either impeach or refresh the witness's memory.

PRIOR INCONSISTENT STATEMENT: DEPOSITION

Steps 3 (Repeat) and 4 (Resonate)

Cross-examiner: *Q.* Mr. Erskine, you just told this jury that you never met with Ms. Probert, correct?

Witness Erskine: *A.* That's correct.

Q. In fact, you did meet with Ms. Probert in the conference room in your office complex, isn't that true?

A. I did not.

Q. In the past, did you ever testify differently?

A. No.

Step 5: Reinforce

Reinforce the prior statement to show it was given under circumstances conducive to telling the truth. Since jurors are unfamiliar with the deposition process, it should be described in sufficient detail initially.

PRIOR INCONSISTENT STATEMENT: DEPOSITION

Step 5 (Reinforce)

Q. Do you recall having your deposition taken?

A. Yes.

Q. It was taken in June of last year, you remember that?

A. That seems right.

Q. The deposition was taken in my office conference room?

A. Yes.

Q. Your lawyer was present?

A. Yes, she was.

III. Prior Inconsistent Statements

Q. Do you remember that a court reporter was there taking down the testimony?

A. Yes.

Q. You were sworn under oath, just as you were here, correct?

A. Yes. I recall taking the oath.

Q. At the deposition I asked you whether you understood that the oath you took there had the same effect as one taken in a courtroom?

A. Yes.

Q. I told you then that your deposition could be read in a courtroom?

A.

Q. And, after your deposition, you had an opportunity to review and make corrections to your deposition before you signed it.

A. Yes.

Q. You read it and this is your signature here?

A. Yes, it's mine.

Step 6: Reference

After establishing the scene of the deposition, counsel moves to the page and line of the statement. The witness, opposing counsel, and the judge all have a copy of the deposition before them.

Step 7: Read or Display and Step 8: Refute

Once everyone is on the same page and line, as indicated previously, counsel reads from the deposition, not the witness. Out of fairness, the passage read should include all the pertinent material. Otherwise, opposing counsel will bring it out, which will not reflect well on the cross-examiner. The statement in the deposition proves the prior statement, even if the witness does not admit it.

Another approach is to ask the witness after drawing attention to the deposition statement: "Does that refresh your recollection?" If the witness answers "yes," then reinforce the inconsistency, referring to the original question and answer that launched the impeachment. In the illustration, the original question was: "You met with Ms. Probert in the conference room in your office complex, correct?" After the witness has refreshed his recollection, the answer should be "yes." If counsel can get the desired answers through refreshed memory, impeachment may not be necessary.

PRIOR INCONSISTENT STATEMENT: DEPOSITION

Steps 4 (Resonate), 6 (Reference), 7 (Read or Display), and 8 (Refute)

Q. Your Honor, may I approach the witness?

Judge: You may, counsel.

Q. Your Honor, counsel, and Mr. Erskine, I am going to read from your deposition on page 31, starting at line 5. Please, follow along as I read.

continued ▶

157

> *[Cross-examiner reads from deposition.]*
> "Question: Did you meet with Ms. Probert at any time?
> "Answer: Yes, we met in our office conference room."
> Q. Is that the question that I asked you at your deposition and the answer you gave?
> A. Yes.
> [Step 4: Resonate. Again, in asking this last question in the series, counsel expresses doubt about the statement that he never met with Ms. Probert.]
> Q. You just testified to this jury that you never met with Ms. Probert. However, in your deposition you swore under oath that you had met with her, correct?
> A. Yes.

Video Deposition

Jurors retain more of what they see than what they hear. They retain even more when they both see and hear the evidence. Therefore, the cross-examiner should find a way to show the statement to the jurors. If the witness testified at a video deposition, then the video can be projected on a television or movie screen in the courtroom. For example, in the *Sonics* case mentioned earlier, Seattle Mayor Nickels testified on cross-examination that he wanted the basketball team to be purchased by local people. The cross continued:

Q. Have you been working to try and make a sale of the team to the Ballmer (local) group happen?

A. I support that. But I don't—working toward it, no.

Defense counsel Mr. Keller: Can we please pull up page 87 of Mayor Nickels' deposition?

At this point the video deposition was played, and, in it, the mayor was asked essentially the same question and answered, "Yes." The video can be edited in such a way that the jury not only hears and sees the witness at the deposition but also sees the exhibit and a scrolling transcript.

Techniques

Cross-examination impeachment techniques apply with equal force to a deposition. Don't introduce more of the deposition than necessary as this reduces the impact. Only impeach with major inconsistencies on major points, avoiding minor inconsistencies.

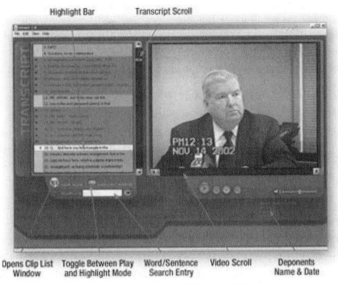

Highlight Bar   Transcript Scroll

Opens Clip List Toggle Between Play Word/Sentence Video Scroll Deponents
   Window   and Highlight Mode   Search Entry   Name & Date

www.gradillas.com 310-859-6677 Beverly Hills, CA 90210

H. Impeachment with Silence or Omission

Contrary to Human Nature

Impeachment with silence or omission is achieved when the cross-examination reveals that the witness failed to act or relate the same information in the past, when it would have been human nature to do so. This form of impeachment shows that the testimony is improbable because it does not comport with common sense.

To be effective, the impeachment by silence must refer to a material omission of a fact that the witness would naturally have been at pains to reveal. Many impeachments by prior silence fail because the examiner forgets this requirement:

Q. You didn't tell me that when I took your deposition, did you?

A. No, you didn't ask.

As often as not such a reply would elicit a chuckle from the jury. Only silence when speech is demanded will cast any doubt on the witness's testimony.

This includes alibi witnesses who do not come forward when the defendant is charged with a crime. But before the prosecution can offer evidence of this, it must be shown that:

> (T)hey were aware of the nature of the charges pending against defendant, had reason to believe that they possessed exculpatory information, had reasonable motives for acting to exonerate defendant, and were familiar with the means of making such information available to law enforcement authorities.

People v. Wilson, 43 A.D.3d 1409, 1411, 843 N.Y.S.2d 899, 901 (2007).

The import of these and other cases is that silence impeaches only when:

1. The audience wants or needs to know the information;
2. The speaker is aware of that need or desire; and
3. There is no good reason to withhold the information.

The following example from a grave-robbery case demonstrates impeachment from silence. The defendant's ex-girlfriend, Mrs. Rose Charland, who lived with him and his mother for nearly a year and a half, testified she helped him rob a grave on Christmas Eve and then attended a Satanic ritual over the stolen body. The defendant's mother contended that Charland had fabricated her testimony as an act of revenge against the mother, who had made a theft complaint against Charland after she broke up with the defendant. The cross-examination began with the theft complaint:

IMPEACHMENT WITH PRIOR SILENCE

Prosecutor: *Q.* Mrs. Charland left during the night time, is that right?

Defendant's mother: *A.* Yes, sir.

Q. What all did she take?

A. She took the dog, the dog food, she took an emerald and diamond ring, she took a 22-inch chain of (son) Vince's that has a gold nugget that looks like this, she took his radio, she took my clothes, gowns, negligees, teddies, shoes, purses, she took all the shampoo, soaps, hair sprays, everything that was in the bathroom cabinet.

Q. Anything else?

A. She took bathing suits, a suit that was checkered, a silk suit, a very expensive silk suit, she took a white suit, that my husband had bought me for my birthday, she took quite a bit of my underwear, slips, gowns, house shoes, purses, and a silk jacket.

Q. Anything else?

A. She took a jean short set, that is made all together, which my husband bought me for my birthday with the matching blouse, two pair of pants, they were bought at Penney's, they are Penney's best brand, and all of my blouses and some of Vince's shirts.

Q. You live in a single-wide trailer, don't you?

A. Yes, sir.

Q. It's a pretty small area?

A. It's a pretty large trailer.

Q. All right, some time during the night, Mrs. Charland took all these things out of the trailer. Is that correct?

A. That's right.

Q. Mrs. Charland was pedestrian at that time, she didn't have any means of transportation other than if somebody gave her a ride, is that right?

A. Yes, she had people coming and picking her up.

Q. She had to have made several trips in and out of the trailer that night?

A. I would assume so.

Q. All that stuff you described. You can't pick that up in one handful and walk out the door with it, can you?

A. No.

Q. You did not immediately report this theft to the Sheriff's Department?

A. No, sir.

Q. And she left the first or second week of May?

A. Yes, sir.

Q. And so, the third or the fourth week of May you had not reported it to the Sheriff's Office?

A. I was trying to find her.

Q. The first and second week of June you had not reported it?

A. No. I was doing everything that I could to find her.

Q. The third week of June you didn't report it to the Sheriff's Department?

A. No, sir.

Q. As a matter of fact, you did not report it to the Sheriff's Department until June the 20th, is that right?

A. That's right.

Q. And your son was arrested on June the 18th?

A. Yes sir.

Q. Two days before you reported the theft?

A. Yes, sir.

Q. Okay, you then immediately reported this theft to your insurance company?

A. No. I didn't.

Q. Did you ever report it to the insurance company?

A. No. I read my policy and my insurance company will not pay for any member of my household and Rose was a member of my household.

Q. Ma'am, back on October 15th, you came to this court to testify, did you not?

A. Yes, I did.

Q. Do you remember at that time being asked this question and giving this answer on page 25, lines 4 through 8:

Question: And you immediately reported it to your homeowner's insurance?

Answer: No, I didn't. I thought if I could find her, I could simply talk her into giving it back to me.

Q. That was the explanation you gave me as to why you had not reported it to your insurance company, was it not?

A. That's right.

Q. You said nothing about, "Well, I checked on the insurance policy and it provided that a member of the household was not covered," you didn't say anything about that?

A. It's the same thing just what you read.

Q. You did not mention having read the insurance policy, did you?

A. No, I didn't mention that I had read the insurance policy.

Q. Okay, referring you to page 26, lines 14 through 16. Do you remember this question and answer:

Question: And you never reported it to your insurance company, did you?

continued ▶

> Answer: No, I haven't.
> Q. Ma'am, you didn't find out that the insurance wouldn't cover the loss until after you testified on October 15th, right?
> A. Yes.
> Q. Okay, so back in May and June, when you were not reporting it to the insurance company, you had no idea that the insurance wouldn't cover the loss, did you?
> A. No, I didn't.

The prosecutor began with a reductio ad absurdum showing the silliness of the theft complaint and moved to three impeachments by silence: (1) the witness's failure to immediately report the purported theft to the police; (2) the witness's failure to file an insurance claim relating to the purported theft; and (3) the witness's failure, on the first occasion she testified in the case, to offer the insurance's non-coverage of the theft as an explanation for her failure to file a claim.

Impeachment of Defendant in Criminal Case with Silence
Rule on Post-Miranda Warning Silence

Use of a criminal defendant's post-*Miranda* warning silence to impeach the defendant's testimony violates the due process clause of the Fourteenth Amendment and is reversible error. *Doyle v. Ohio*, 426 U.S. 610, 617-18, 96 S. Ct. 2240, 2244-45 (1976). For example, when a defendant claims for the first time at trial that he had been framed, it would be reversible error for the prosecutor to cross-examine about why the defendant had not told this to the police right after his arrest and *Miranda* warning.

On the other hand, in *Brecht v. Abahamson*, 507 U.S. 619, 628-29, 113 S. Ct. 1710, 1716-17, 123 L. Ed. 2d 353, 367 (1993), the Supreme Court discussed impeachment with pre-*Miranda* silence and held:

> . . . The first time petitioner claimed that the shooting was an accident was when he took the stand at trial. It was entirely proper — and probative — for the State to impeach his testimony by pointing out that petitioner had failed to tell anyone before the time he received his *Miranda* warnings at his arraignment about the shooting being an accident. Indeed, if the shooting was an accident, petitioner had every reason—including to clear his name and preserve evidence supporting his version of the events—to offer his account immediately following the shooting. On the other hand, the State's references to petitioner's silence after that point in time, or more generally to petitioner's failure to come forward with his version of events at any time before trial, see n. 2, *supra*, crossed the *Doyle* line. For it is conceivable that, once petitioner had been given his *Miranda* warnings, he decided to stand on his right to remain silent because he believed his silence would not be used against him at trial.

Partial Story Distinction

If a defendant waives her right to remain silent in response to *Miranda* warnings and gives an explanation inconsistent with the one raised at trial, she could be cross-examined concerning her failure to relate the trial defense to the police. *State v. Tuzon*, 118 Ariz. 205, 207, 575 P.2d 1231, 1233 (Ariz. 1978). In *State v. Kendrick*, 47 Wash. App. 620, 628, 736 P.2d 1079, 1284 (Wash. Ct. App. 1987), when the defendant introduced evidence of post-arrest cooperation, the door was opened to cross-examination on post-arrest silence to impeach defendant's version.

IV. CONTRADICTION

A. Evidentiary Law

The cross-examiner can contradict the witness through extrinsic evidence that is relevant and substantive. Otherwise, generally contradictory evidence on a collateral matter is inadmissible because it is irrelevant under Fed. R. Evid. 402 or a waste of time under 403. The traditional test for whether matter is collateral matter is this: Is the evidence admissible for some purpose independent from contradicting the witness? In other words, if a witness testifies that he ate cornflakes, before the court is going to let counsel take up the time to put on a witness to testify that the initial witness ate granola, counsel must convince the judge that this inconsistency is somehow of importance ("material") to the case.

Contradiction by Counsel

May the cross-examiner use opposing counsel's statements that contradict the witness against the witness? *State v. Rivers*, 129 Wash. 2d 697, 921 P.2d 495 (1996) illustrates this strategy. The defendant was charged with robbery. The victim testified that he ran an outdoors espresso bar and that he was taking the proceeds from the bar in a bag to the bank when a man threatened that he had a gun and demanded the bag. They struggled over the bag, the man ran off with it, and the victim pursued him but eventually gave up the chase when the robber threatened to shoot him.

Defense counsel gave the following opening statement:

> Back on December 20th, this man here, Paul Rivers, didn't rob anybody — not Joseph Slobodzian or anyone.
>
> . . . .
>
> In identifying Mr. Rivers, you will find that what the officers did was take Mr. Slobodzian (victim) to a house, show him the bank bag which had been taken, said essentially we found the bank bag in the house, bring Mr. Rivers out in handcuffs, the only African American there, the only guy not in a police uniform,

brought him out in front of the house, shined a spotlight on him, said Mr. Slobodzian, do you see anybody who can be a suspect.

Now, every lawyer dreams of getting a case like this, based on a shaky ID. . . .

State v. Rivers, 129 Wash. 2d at 708.

The defendant testified that he had sold marijuana to the defendant and the defendant owed him money. When he saw the victim put the money sack on a table and turn his back, he ran off with the money. The prosecutor's cross-examination was as follows:

> Q. [By Prosecutor] Now, you were sitting through opening statement; is that correct?
> A. [By Defendant Rivers] I was.
> Q. And you heard your attorney make some reference to the jurors that identity was an issue in this case; is that correct?
> [Defense Counsel]: I object to that, Your Honor.
> THE COURT: Overruled.
> Q. [By Prosecutor] That identity was an issue in this case; is that correct?
> A. That's correct.
> Q. But identity is not the issue in this case, is it?
> A. Just as I told you in my statement, the investigation.
> Q. You were the person that took the money?
> A. Yes, from the espresso.

Id. at 708.

The Washington State Supreme Court held that the trial court did not abuse its discretion in allowing the cross where under the facts of the case the defendant was present during the opening statement, cross was permissible because the defendant's testimony contradicted his counsel's statements and "the examination was relevant to the extent that it would assist the jury by clarifying the nature of the defense to the crime charged." *Id.* at 709.

While an attorney's statement may qualify as an admission of the client and therefore by definition be admissible as nonhearsay, "this rule should be applied with caution, in part due to the danger of impairing the right to counsel." *State v. Williams*, 79 Wash. App. 21, 28, 902 P.2d 1258, 1262 (1995). In *Williams*, the prosecutor cross-examined the defendant about defense counsel's statements at a pretrial omnibus hearing concerning the defense theories of the case. The appellate court reversed holding that the statement by counsel did not constitute an admission of a party.

Pitting Witness Against Witness—Who's Lying Here?

Cross-examination designed to compel the defense witness to contradict other witnesses by calling them liars has been held to be improper, even classified as prosecutorial misconduct. The Kansas Supreme Court, in *State v. Manning*, 270 Kan. 674, 698, 19 P.3d 84, 100-01 (2001), listed an array of cases with illustrations from across the country, and condemned pitting, as follows:

Questions, which of another witness, are improper. It is the province of the jury to weigh the credibility of the witnesses. *See People v. Riley*, 63 Ill. App. 3d 176, 184-85, 379 N.E. 746, 19 Ill. 874 (1978) (holding that asking the defendant on cross-examination whether the State's witnesses had told a "bunch of lies" was improper); . . .

The cross-examiner does this with a series of questions similar to this:

Q. Mr. Dorman, you are saying when Officer Green said he saw you go up to Sergeant Hickey on the steps, he was not telling the truth, is that right?

A. Yes, sir.

Q. And when Officer Green said that he saw you take that radio from Sergeant Hickey, he was again not telling you the truth, is that correct?

A. Yes, sir.

Q. And when Officer Green said that he saw you walk away with that radio, he was again not telling the truth?

A. Yes, sir.

Dorman v. United States, 460 A.2d 986, 991 (D.C. 1983) (dissenting opinion).

Some case law, however, allows a carefully controlled form of pitting. These cases draw a distinction between asking a witness whether someone else is lying and asking a witness whether she disagrees with another witness. Although this distinction may at first blush seem disingenuous, many courts have found it proper if the questioner avoids the word "lying." In *United States v. Gaind*, 31 F.3d 73, 76-77 (2d Cir. N.Y. 1994), the court found it proper to ask whether another witness was "mistaken" rather than "lying." Other courts have held it proper to ask whether the other witness was "wrong" or "not accurate," *Joseph v. State*, 868 So. 2d 5, 8 (Fla. Dist. Ct. App. 2004); or whether the witness "disputes" specific points of another witness's testimony, *People v. Ackerman*, 257 Mich. App. 434, 449, 669 N.W.2d 818, 827 (Mich. Ct. App. 2003); or "disagrees" with specific points of another witness's testimony, *State v. Atkins*, 163 W. Va. 502, 519, 261 S.E.2d 55, 65 (1979). And, when one witness's testimony squarely contradicts another, it has even been held proper to ask if the other witness's testimony was "untrue":

Q. I'll ask you again. In October 1981, had Fred Blake already told you he was not going to invest in the corporation? Yes or no.

A. No. No.

Q. No he had not?

A. No.

Q. So his testimony to that effect was untrue. Is that correct?

United States v. Bryant, 770 F.2d 1283, 1291 (5th Cir. 1985), held this line of questioning proper under the circumstances.

Such questioning is most effective when the witness testifying under cross-examination has actually heard the testimony of the contrary witness. Thus, pitting most commonly occurs on the cross-examination of a criminal defendant.

Further, if the witness was not present during the conflicting testimony, the line of questions is objectionable on the grounds that it violates the rule of sequestration, which bars the witness from hearing the testimony of another witness.

Even though you seem to have case law in your jurisdiction on your side that would permit carefully worded questions pitting the witness against another, you run the risk of committing error. The appellate court may distinguish its prior decisions from your situation or depart from precedent and follow the majority of courts that prohibit pitting.

Why take the risk when an equal, if not better way, of accomplishing the same thing—making the contradiction apparent to the jury—is available to you? The technique is to simply and emphatically lock the witness into the position ("You are telling this jury . . .") and then produce the contrary witness. When cross-examining a criminal defendant, the contrary witness has usually already testified. In that case, you may further highlight the discrepancy by framing your questions using the same language as used by the witness. The cross-examination of Mark Fuhrman, discussed in the next section, serves as an excellent example of this technique.

B. Contradiction Technique and the Cross-Examination of Mark Fuhrman

Critical to the contradiction technique is that the witness must be locked into a factual or opinion assertion that can be proven false. No better illustration of this exists than F. Lee Bailey's cross-examination of investigating Los Angeles detective Mark Fuhrman in the prosecution of O. J. Simpson for murdering his wife, Nicole Simpson, and Ronald Goldman. Fuhrman was the investigator who found a bloody black leather glove at Nicole Simpson's condominium where she and Goldman were murdered.

F. Lee Bailey, O. J. Simpson, and Johnnie Cochran hear a "not guilty" verdict

---

IMPEACHMENT BY CONTRADICTION

F. Lee Bailey's Cross-Examination of Detective Mark Fuhrman

Bailey: *Q.* Do you use the word "nigger" in describing people?

Ms. Clark: Same objection.

The Court: Presently?

Bailey: Yes.

The Court: Overruled.

Fuhrman: *A.* No, Sir.

Bailey: *Q.* Have you used that word in the past ten years?

A. Not that I recall. No.

Q. You mean if you called someone a nigger you have forgotten it?

A. I'm not sure I can answer the question the way you phrased it, Sir.

Q. You have difficulty understanding the question?

A. Yes.

Q. I will rephrase it. I want you to assume that perhaps at some time, since 1985 or 6, you addressed a member of the African American race as a nigger. Is it possible that you have forgotten that act on your part?

A. No, it is not possible.

Q. Are you therefore saying that you have not used that word in the past ten years, Detective Fuhrman?

A. Yes, that is what I'm saying.

Q. And you say under oath that you have not addressed any black person as a nigger or spoken about black people as niggers in the past ten years, Detective Fuhrman?

A. That's what I'm saying, Sir.

To contradict Fuhrman, the defense called witnesses who testified he had used the racial slur within the prior ten years. Also the defense produced an audiotape interview in which he said the word. Fuhrman was later convicted of perjury for his false testimony at the *Simpson* trial and sentenced to three years' probation.

The trial transcript excerpt shows how Bailey employed the fundamental cross techniques for cross-examining a perjurer. First, Bailey decided that he was crossing a liar and that he could expose him, adjusted his demeanor to be firm and confrontational. Second, the motive for denying to have used the pejorative term was self-evident; a law enforcement officer who is investigating a crime where the prime suspect is a racial minority would not want to be viewed as racist. Third, he painted a picture for the jury of Fuhrman's denial. Fourth, he locked Fuhrman into the factual assertion. Fifth, he closed off the exits so the witness could not claim faulty memory later. Sixth, Bailey used surprise. He could have confronted Fuhrman with the audiotape of his prior use of the racial epithet, but did not reveal the full extent of the impeachment evidence until the defense case. Seventh, the impeachment was done with tangible evidence—the audiotape.

The Fuhrman cross further illustrates the holistic nature of cross-examination. When Bailey laid the groundwork for the devastating contradiction, the media reported that Fuhrman had withstood Bailey's cross quite well. The media, of course, were evaluating the cross in isolation. It was only after the defense offered their contradictory evidence that the skill of the cross-examination could be fully appreciated.

CHECKLIST: IMPEACHMENT CROSS: REPORT

Improbability

- ❏ Evidence of improbability is relevant and therefore admissible because it makes what the witness claims less probable. Fed. R. Evid. 401402.
- ❏ Under Fed. R. Evid. 611(b) and a similar state rule, cross should be limited to "matters affecting the credibility of a witness," and a cross that reveals that the testimony is improbable goes to the witness's credibility.
- ❏ The *reduction-to-the-absurd technique* exposes improbability by extending the original premise of the witness to an absurd result.
- ❏ The *common-sense technique* highlights the witness's assertion and shows that it is unlikely because it defies common sense.
- ❏ The *contradictory-conduct technique* emphasizes the witness's claim and then contrasts it with the person's actions under the theme that action speaks louder than words.

Prior Inconsistent Statements

- ❏ Federal Rule of Evidence 613 and state equivalent rules provide that a witness may be examined about prior inconsistent statements.
  - • If the witness admits the prior statement, extrinsic evidence of the statement may be excluded as cumulative under Rule 403.
  - • If the witness does not unequivocally admit the prior statement, extrinsic evidence of the statement is admissible.
  - • The witness must be given an opportunity to deny or explain the statement.
  - • The prior statement is admissible only for impeachment, not substantive, purposes unless admissible under another rule of evidence.
- ❏ Avoid impeaching with minor inconsistencies, except:
  1. When the cumulative effect of the minor inconsistencies show the witness is not credible; or
  2. When necessary to force an evasive witness to yield concessions.
- ❏ Don't pluck a prior statement out of context because, under the rule of completeness as stated in Fed. R. Evid 106, opposing counsel can have the rest of the statement introduced contemporaneously, which may open the door to what would otherwise be inadmissible evidence.

❑ Eight essential techniques for impeachment with a prior inconsistent statement are:
1. Recognize the inconsistency;
2. Retrieve the prior statement;
3. Repeat the testimony;
4. Reinforce the truthful statement with where said, when said, who heard, what said, and whether said;
5. Reference the prior statement;
6. Resonate with the jury;
7. Read or display; and
8. Refute the witness's denial.

❑ Utilize the deposition strategy to extract the same answers from the witness that were given at the deposition.
- Apply the eight essential techniques when impeaching with a deposition.
- With video deposition clips the impeachment has a greater impact on the jury than with just the transcript.

❑ Impeach the witness's trial testimony by revealing that the witness previously failed to act or relate the same information when it would have been human nature to do so.

Contradiction

❑ Extrinsic evidence contradicting a witness is admissible if it is relevant and substantive, not collateral.

❑ Having a witness comment on the credibility of another witness — pitting — is improper.

CHAPTER 8

IMPEACHMENT CROSS
Reporter

"No man has a good enough memory to make a successful liar."
   —**Abraham Lincoln** (1809-1865)

I. THE REPORTER

Is the witness a credible reporter of the facts? The jury will be instructed that it is their duty to judge the credibility of the witness:

> You are the sole judges of the credibility of each witness. You are also the sole judges of the value or weight to be given to the testimony of each witness. In considering a witness' testimony, you may consider these things: the opportunity of the witness to observe or know the things he or she testifies about; the ability of the witness to observe accurately; the quality of a witness' memory while testifying; the manner of the witness while testifying; any personal interest that the witness might have in the outcome or the issues; any bias or prejudice that the witness may have shown; the reasonableness of the witness' statements in the context of all of the other evidence; and any other factors that affect your evaluation or belief of a witness or your evaluation of his or her testimony.

Washington Pattern Jury Instruction 1.02.

In this chapter we focus on three forms of impeachment that aim at showing that the witness is not believable: (1) the witness's prior conviction of a crime; (2) prior misconduct of the witness probative of untruthfulness; and (3) character evidence. We have taken the liberty of covering both the cross-examination of a character witness (governed by special rules) and the character witness regarding the reputation for untruthfulness of another.

II. PRIOR CONVICTIONS

Prior convictions serve not only as a reason to distrust the witness but also carry with them compelling reasons to disrespect or dislike the person. However, when a prior conviction is admitted into evidence, the jury will be instructed that it may only be considered in deciding the weight or credibility given to a witness's testimony.

A. Evidentiary Law

Federal Rule of Evidence 609 or its state rule counterpart governs the admissibility of prior convictions to impeach.

Impeachment With Prior Conviction

Fed. R. Evid. 609. Impeachment by Evidence of Conviction of Crime

  (a) **In General.** The following rules apply to attacking a witness's character for truthfulness by evidence of a criminal conviction:

    (1) for a crime that, in the convicting jurisdiction, was punishable by death or by imprisonment for more than one year, the evidence:

(A) must be admitted, subject to Rule 403, in a civil case or in a criminal case in which the witness is not a defendant; and

(B) must be admitted in a criminal case in which the witness is a defendant, if the probative value of the evidence outweighs its prejudicial effect to that defendant; and

(2) for any crime regardless of the punishment, the evidence must be admitted if the court can readily determine that establishing the elements of the crime required proving — or the witness's admitting — a dishonest act or false statement.

(b) Limit on Using the Evidence After 10 Years. This subdivision (b) applies if more than 10 years have passed since the witness's conviction or release from confinement for it, whichever is later. Evidence of the conviction is admissible only if:

(1) its probative value, supported by specific facts and circumstances, substantially outweighs its prejudicial effect; and

(2) the proponent gives an adverse party reasonable written notice of the intent to use it so that the party has a fair opportunity to contest its use.

(c) Effect of a Pardon, Annulment, or Certificate of Rehabilitation. Evidence of a conviction is not admissible if:

(1) the conviction has been the subject of a pardon, annulment, certificate of rehabilitation, or other equivalent procedure based on a finding that the person has been rehabilitated, and the person has not been convicted of a later crime punishable by death or by imprisonment for more than one year; or

(2) the conviction has been the subject of a pardon, annulment, or other equivalent procedure based on a finding of innocence.

(d) Juvenile Adjudications. Evidence of a juvenile adjudication is admissible under this rule only if:

(1) it is offered in a criminal case;

(2) the adjudication was of a witness other than the defendant;

(3) an adult's conviction for that offense would be admissible to attack the adult's credibility; and

(4) admitting the evidence is necessary to fairly determine guilt or innocence.

(e) Pendency of an Appeal. A conviction that satisfies this rule is admissible even if an appeal is pending. Evidence of the pendency is also admissible.

Threshold Questions

Customarily, the admissibility of a prior conviction is determined at a pretrial hearing after counsel, who intends to call the witness, moves *in limine* to exclude it. Prior convictions are admissible under Rules 403 and 609 when attacking the credibility of a witness if they satisfy the following requirements.

Type of Crime and Balancing
1. Balancing and Burden of Proof

The court must perform a Rule 403 balancing test to determine the admissibility of a felony conviction to impeach a *witness*. Rule 403 provides that evidence may be excluded if its probative value is "substantially outweighed" by the "danger of unfair prejudice." In contrast, Rule 609(a)(1) provides that evidence of the *defendant's* conviction shall be admitted if "the court determines that the probative value of admitting the evidence outweighs its prejudicial effect to the accused . . . ."

It is important to note that while the court engages in a balancing test for both the witness and the defendant, the burden is different. For a witness, the usual 403 burden of showing unfair prejudice substantially outweighing probative value applies. However, for impeachment of the defendant, the cross-examiner has the burden of showing that probative value exceeds prejudicial effect. When the witness is not the defendant, the danger of unfair prejudice is slight. The usual 609 concern—that the jury may use the prior crimes to find the defendant guilty of the current offense—does not exist for a non-defendant.

A jurisdiction's case law must be researched to determine what pertinent factors the court will use in the balancing test for admissibility of the prior crime. Some of these include: impeachment value; remoteness; similarity between the prior crime and the current charge; the age and circumstances of defendant; and how central the credibility issue is. 36 Am. Jur. POF2d 747 § 78.

2. Crimes of Dishonesty or False Statement and Any Witness

Any witness, including the accused, may be attacked by evidence of a prior conviction of a felony or misdemeanor crime of dishonesty or false statement. Rule 609(a)(2). Here the court neither engages in a balancing of factors, nor does it have any discretion. The conviction "shall be admitted regardless of the punishment, <u>if it readily can be determined that establishing the elements of the crime required proof or admission of an act of dishonesty or false statement by the witness.</u>"

While crimes of violence generally do not qualify, crimes such as embezzlement, perjury, and the like meet the definition. Again, a jurisdiction's law must be researched to determine whether the prior crime qualifies under this rule. 36 Am. Jur. POF2d 757 § 6.

Time Limit — Less Than Ten Years

For the conviction to be admissible, less than ten years must have elapsed since the conviction or release from confinement, whichever is later. However, a conviction over ten years old is admissible if: (1) the judge finds that the probative value outweighs the prejudicial effect and (2) the adverse party gives advance written notice of intent to offer the conviction into evidence.

Conviction Still Active

For the conviction to be admissible, it must not have been voided by either:

- A pardon, annulment, certificate of rehabilitation, or equivalent (however, the conviction will be admissible if there has been a subsequent conviction of a felony); or
- Any of those actions mentioned above if the basis was the defendant's innocence.

Not a Juvenile Conviction

The prior conviction is inadmissible if it is a juvenile adjudication. However, the court may admit juvenile convictions to impeach a witness, other than the defendant, if the conviction would be admissible if the witness were an adult and if the court decides that the prior conviction is "necessary for a fair determination of the issue of guilt or innocence."

Appeal

The fact that the case is on appeal does not render the prior conviction inadmissible; however, the fact that the case is on appeal is admissible.

Proving the Prior Conviction

Authentication of Conviction

If the witness admits the prior conviction, the cross-examiner may be precluded from offering a prior conviction document as cumulative. Fed. R. Evid. 403. On the other hand, the cross-examiner may offer the prior conviction document as a self-authenticated document (certified or exemplified copy) of the prior conviction document under Fed. R. Evid. 902.

To prove the conviction in the state in which the conviction occurred, the cross-examiner can offer a certified copy of the judgment and sentence of conviction. The court clerk in the certification swears that it is a true copy of everything within the stapled document. If the conviction occurred in another state, the examiner can offer an exemplified copy of the judgment and sentence. An exemplified copy is a triple authentication: the clerk swears the document is authentic; the presiding judge swears that it is authentic; and the clerk swears that the judge is the judge and the judge's signature is authentic. Because the document is self-authenticating, the cross-examiner need only offer the prior conviction documents into evidence.

Proving the Prior Conviction

Fed. R. Evid. 902. Self-authentication

The following items of evidence are self-authenticating; they require no extrinsic evidence of authenticity in order to be admitted:

(1) *Domestic Public Documents That Are Sealed and Signed.* A document that bears:

(A) a seal purporting to be that of the United States; any state, district, commonwealth, territory, or insular possession of the United States; the former Panama Canal Zone; the Trust Territory of the Pacific Islands; a political subdivision of any of these entities; or a department, agency, or officer of any entity named above; and

(B) a signature purporting to be an execution or attestation.

(2) **Domestic Public Documents That Are Not Sealed But Are Signed and Certified.** A document that bears no seal if:

continued ▶

> **(A)** it bears the signature of an officer or employee of an entity named in Rule 902(1)(A); and
>
> **(B)** another public officer who has a seal and official duties within that same entity certifies under seal — or its equivalent — that the signer has the official capacity and that the signature is genuine. . . .
>
> **(4)** *Certified Copies of Public Records.* A copy of an official record — or a copy of a document that was recorded or filed in a public office as authorized by law — if the copy is certified as correct by:
>
> **(A)** the custodian or another person authorized to make the certification; or
>
> **(B)** a certificate that complies with Rule 902(1), (2), or (3), a federal statute, or a rule prescribed by the Supreme Court

Proving the Identification of the Witness as the Convicted Person

What if the witness denies being the person who was convicted? How can the cross-examiner prove it? The judgment and sentence document may bear the fingerprints of the person who was sentenced. If so, counsel can obtain the witness's fingerprints through discovery or court order and have a fingerprint expert compare those on the documents with those of the defendant. Also, case law, such as *State v. Ammons*, 105 Wis. 2d 175, 713 P.2d 719, 718 P.2d 796 (1986), holds that the fact that the witness has the same name as the person named on the judgment and sentence is sufficient in the absence of a sworn oath rebuttal by the witness to the contrary.

Extent of Information About the Conviction

The extent to which the conviction can be gone into varies from one jurisdiction to another. It may be confined to the fact of the conviction, the type of crime, and the punishment. In one jurisdiction, any examination "exceeding these bounds is irrelevant and likely to be unduly prejudicial, hence inadmissible." *State v. Copeland*, 130 Wash. 2d 244, 285, 922 P.2d 1304, 1326-27 (1996). In another jurisdiction, cross may be limited to asking whether the crime was a felony or crime involving dishonesty or false statement. More than that is reversible error.

B. Techniques and Illustrations

Circumstances of the Conviction

Theoretically, if the witness tries to minimize the conviction by giving some of the details, counsel may go into the specifics. The witness has opened the door (see pages 194-196). This rule is a trap for the unwary. Trial judges and appellate courts are hostile to this type of character evidence. This is especially true with impeachment of the defendant in a criminal case by a conviction. The concern is that the jury will misuse the evidence, inferring from the prior conviction that the defendant committed the crime charged. Admitting the prior conviction can result in a reversal on appeal. Trial judges would much rather grant a mistrial. Even if counsel is confident that impeachment with a prior conviction will be upheld on appeal and that the witness has opened the door, it is wise to use caution. Ask to approach the bench and find out if the judge agrees with you before launching into the subject. Find out just how wide the judge thinks the defendant has opened the door.

The Litany

In some jurisdictions, appellate decisions have reduced impeachment by prior conviction to a ritual. The examiner cannot ask about the crimes or their circumstances. In some jurisdictions, the examiner is confined to what is on the face of the judgment and sentence. In other jurisdictions, the examiner can only ask about felony convictions for crimes involving dishonesty or false statement. The litany that follows must be used word for word to avoid reversible error in such a jurisdiction.

IMPEACHMENT WITH PRIOR CONVICTION

Q. Mr. Timson, have you ever been convicted of a felony?

Q. How many times?

Or:

Q. Mr. Timson, have you ever been convicted of a crime involving dishonesty or false statement?

Q. How many times?

Suppose the witness was convicted of one count of felony forgery. Here the examiner must make a strategic decision. Which sounds better, "Convicted of a felony," or "Convicted of a crime involving dishonesty or false statement"? The lawyer cannot have it both ways. The decision can only be based on the dynamics of the case.

Opposing counsel should be told how the question will be asked, allowing for preparation of the witness to answer it. Usually, this will be with a "yes." It is unfair to try and exploit the confusion that could ensue from the witness fumbling for the answer or blurting out inadmissible evidence. For example, on cross-examination, the prosecutor asks the defendant, "Have you been convicted of a crime?" And, the defendant responds, "I did time once for manslaughter, but I didn't kill him. I just stabbed him; he died in the hospital."

Witness's Response

What makes impeachment by prior conviction effective is not how the lawyer asks the question, but how the witness responds. Reasons to distrust, dislike, or disrespect do not necessarily translate into reasons to disbelieve. Many people are sitting in prison today based on the testimony of completely reprehensible, untrustworthy, disreputable villains. Snitches, accomplices, traitors, and other assorted scoundrels regularly convince juries that they are telling the truth and the defendant is convicted. A jury may reject a witness's testimony because the witness is untrustworthy, unlikable, or unrespectable, but they may not. In order to persuade the jury to reject the testimony, counsel must also give them a case-specific reason to disbelieve the witness. This comes in the form of a motive to lie in the case on trial or proof of a lie in the case on trial. Proof of both makes the witness's impeachment likely.

No matter how thoroughly a lawyer tries to prepare her client to answer the questions, sometimes the client will lie about his convictions. Experience has shown that this sort of witness will underestimate the number of convictions by half. When this happens, be prepared to prove them. Then both the lie in the case and the prior convictions combine to discredit the witness.

III. PRIOR MISCONDUCT PROBATIVE OF UNTRUTHFULNESS

A. Evidentiary Law

Under Fed. R. Evid. 608(b), cross-examination, in the judge's discretion, may cover specific acts of conduct probative to show untruthfulness. Such misconduct under Rule 608(b) includes acts of fraud or deceit, but not drug usage or violent acts. Counsel may not ask whether the witness was arrested or convicted of the act. The cross-examiner must have a good-faith basis for the question. *United States v. Zaccaria*, 240 F.3d 75, 81-82 (1st Cir. 2001). Rule 403 may bar the cross if the probative value of the prior bad act evidence "is substantially outweighed by the danger of unfair prejudice."

Impeachment With Prior Misconduct Probative of Truthfulness or Untruthfulness

Fed. R. Evid. 608. Evidence of Character and Conduct of Witness

. . .

(b) Specific Instances of Conduct.

Except for a criminal conviction under Rule 609, extrinsic evidence is not admissible to prove specific instances of a witness's conduct in order to attack or support the witness's character for truthfulness. But the court may, on cross-examination, allow them to be inquired into if they are probative of the character for truthfulness or untruthfulness of:

> **(1)** the witness; or
>
> **(2)** another witness whose character the witness being cross-examined has testified about.
>
> By testifying on another matter, a witness does not waive any privilege against self-incrimination for testimony that relates only to the witness's character for truthfulness.

Examples of Prior Misconduct

- Cross-examination into defendant's lying responses on income tax return and financial disclosure statements was held proper. *United States v. Sullivan*, 803 F.2d 87 (3d Cir. 1986).
- Forgery. *United States v. Waldrip*, 981 F.2d 799, 802-03 (5th Cir. 1993).
- Previous use of a false name, which is also a prior inconsistent statement because the first thing the witness did on direct was to state his name. *United States v. Ojeda*, 23 F.3d 1473, 1476-77 (8th Cir. 1994).

No Extrinsic Evidence

If the witness denies the prior bad act, the cross-examiner must take the answer and may not introduce extrinsic evidence to prove it. The rationale for this rule is that the trial should not get sidetracked with collateral matters. *United States v. Adams*, 799 F.2d 665 (11th Cir. 1986).

B. Techniques and Prior Perjurious Statement Illustration

Many of these techniques apply equally to impeachment of a witness with prior misconduct showing untruthfulness. These include: locking the witness into testimony; eliciting the testimony about the misconduct bit by bit; and using tangible evidence if it exists.

Assume that plaintiff's witness Liz Allways testified on direct examination that she and her husband, Henry, lived together when they rented a duplex from the defendant. Mr. and Mrs. Allways sued for breach of contract claiming that the defendant failed to maintain and repair in accordance with the lease agreement. Mrs. Allways had filled out a Department of Social Services application for public assistance under penalty of perjury that Henry was not a member of her household during the time they lived in the duplex. Cross by defense counsel is as follows:

IMPEACHMENT WITH PRIOR MISCONDUCT PROBATIVE OF UNTRUTHFULNESS

Breach of Contract Case

[Repeating and locking in the witness]

Defense counsel: *Q.* You told us during your direct examination that Henry, your husband, was living with you at all times when you rented the plaintiff's duplex, correct?

Mrs. Allways: *A.* That's correct.

[Counsel begins painting the picture one brushstroke at a time and closing the exits so the witness cannot explain away the prior misconduct.]

Q. You have received financial assistance from the Department of Social Services?

A. Yes.

Q. In order to get financial assistance, you had to complete DSS forms?

A. I filled them out.

Q. You applied for DSS financial assistance while you lived in plaintiff's duplex?

A. Yes.

Q. You filled out the forms while you were residing in that duplex?

A. I believe so.

[Defense counsel has the DSS form marked, shows it to opposing counsel, and goes to the witness.]

Q. Mrs. Allways, showing defense exhibit 21, do you recognize it?

A. It's the DSS application for financial assistance.

Q. This is the application we have been discussing?

A. Yes.

Defense Counsel: Offer exhibit 21.

[Pretrial the judge denied the plaintiff's motion in limine *to exclude any mention of the DSS document. Plaintiff's counsel decided not to mention it on direct because, among other reasons, counsel did not want to risk waiving the issue for appeal. Counsel objects in order to make a record for appeal.]*

Plaintiff's counsel: Objection, violation of Rules 608 and 403.

Judge: Overruled. Defense exhibit 21 is admitted.

[Displaying the document so the jury can see and remember it.]

Defense counsel: May I publish the exhibit to the jury on the document camera?

Judge: Yes.

[Defense counsel places the exhibit opened to page 3 on the document camera.]

Q. Mrs. Allways, on page 3 of the exhibit, it's right here *(pointing to the page)*, you see what it says there, I'll read it: "Does your spouse reside in your household?" And you answered, "No," as it shows here?

A. Yes.

Q. And, here on page 4 the document is dated, and on that date your husband was residing with you?

A. Yes.

Q. At the bottom of the page as we can see is an oath, and it says: "I certify (or declare) under penalty of *perjury* under the laws of this state that the foregoing is true and correct"?

> *A.* Yes.
>
> *Q.* This is your signature right under the oath?
>
> *A.* It is.

IV. CHARACTER WITNESS

A. Evidentiary Law

Threshold Questions

Federal Rule of Evidence 405 provides that admissible character evidence may be proved "by testimony about the person's reputation or by testimony in the form of an opinion." While the Federal Rule allows a character witness to render an opinion on a pertinent trait, such as a defense witness in a theft case testifies that the defendant is an "honest person," some states adhere to the common law rule that only testimony as to reputation is admissible.

If reputation evidence is all that is permitted, an evidentiary foundation must be laid for the testimony. If counsel can strategically keep the witness from testifying, there will be no need to cross-examine. Counsel may move *in limine* to exclude the testimony or, when the witness is called, ask the court for permission to voir dire the witness on qualifications to serve as a character witness. Such questioning is in essence a cross-examination, designed to show that a proper foundation does not exist.

The evidentiary foundation for reputation testimony requires:

- The witness testifies to being acquainted with the person;
- The witness knows the general reputation of the person for the pertinent trait, such as peacefulness; and
- That the reputation exists in a generalized and neutral community.

During voir dire questioning, counsel could attempt to establish that the foundation is inadequate by showing that the acquaintanceship is too remote in time and that the witness has only spoken to the person's friends, never with members of the community.

The litany for a character witness testifying to a person's reputation is strict under common law. Opposing counsel should object to any variance from it. The witness is to answer "yes" or "no" to the question: "Do you know the reputation of (name the person) in the community in which she lives for (pertinent trait)?" If the answer is "no," then the questioning is concluded. If the answer is "yes," the next question is: "Is it good or bad?" And, the witness should answer "good" or "bad."

Another threshold question is whether the character evidence is admissible. This issue also can be resolved by the court's ruling on a pretrial motion *in limine* to exclude improper character evidence. Under Fed. R. Evid. 404(a), "(e)vidence of a person's character or trait of character," "for the purpose of proving action in conformity therewith" is only admissible if the party calling the character witness can establish that it fits under one of the exceptions listed in the Rule as follows:

1. **Criminal Case: Defendant's Character**

   Defendant Offers the Evidence — The defendant may introduce evidence of a pertinent trait of the defendant's character ("peacefulness" when defendant is charged with homicide, "honesty" when charged with theft). Also, under Fed. R. Evid. 412 dealing with sexual offenses, character evidence about the victim is admissible if the victim puts it into controversy.

   Prosecution Offers the Evidence — The prosecution may call a character witness to rebut the defense character evidence. If evidence of the victim's character is admitted under Rule 412 dealing with sexual offenses, evidence of the same trait of the accused is admissible when offered by the prosecution. Rule 404(a)(1).

2. **Criminal Case: Victim's Character**

   Defendant Offers the Evidence — The defendant may introduce evidence of the victim's pertinent trait of character of the victim, such as in an assault case when the defense calls a witness to testify that the victim has a bad reputation for "peacefulness."

   Prosecution Offers the Evidence — The prosecution may call a character witness to rebut character evidence introduced by the defendant, such as a good reputation for "peacefulness" in an assault case. Also, the prosecution may introduce evidence of the victim's peacefulness to rebut evidence that the victim was the first aggressor. Rule 404(a)(2).

3. **Character Evidence Provided for by Rule 607** — Credibility may be attacked by any party. Rule 404(a)(2).

4. **Character Evidence Provided for by Rule 608** — Rule 608 governs the introduction of evidence bearing on truthfulness.

Character Evidence

Fed. R. Evid. 404. Character Evidence Not Admissible To Prove Conduct; Exceptions; Other Crimes

 (a) **Character Evidence.**

  (1) *Prohibited Uses.* Evidence of a person's character or character trait is not admissible to prove that on a particular occasion the person acted in accordance with the character or trait.

  (2) *Exceptions for a Defendant or Victim in a Criminal Case.* The following exceptions apply in a criminal case:

> **(A)** a defendant may offer evidence of the defendant's pertinent trait, and if the evidence is admitted, the prosecutor may offer evidence to rebut it;
>
> **(B)** subject to the limitations in Rule 412, a defendant may offer evidence of an alleged victim's pertinent trait, and if the evidence is admitted, the prosecutor may:
>
> > **(i)** offer evidence to rebut it; and
> >
> > **(ii)** offer evidence of the defendant's same trait; and
>
> **(C)** in a homicide case, the prosecutor may offer evidence of the alleged victim's trait of peacefulness to rebut evidence that the victim was the first aggressor. . . .
>
> **Fed. R. Evid. 405. Methods of Proving Character**
>
> **(a) By Reputation or Opinion.** When evidence of a person's character or character trait is admissible, it may be proved by testimony about the person's reputation or by testimony in the form of an opinion. On cross-examination of the character witness, the court may allow an inquiry into relevant specific instances of the person's conduct.
>
> **Fed. R. Evid. 608. A Witness's Character for Truthfulness or Untruthfulness**
>
> **(a) Reputation or Opinion Evidence.** A witness's credibility may be attacked or supported by testimony about the witness's reputation for having a character for truthfulness or untruthfulness, or by testimony in the form of an opinion about that character. But evidence of truthful character is admissible only after the witness's character for truthfulness has been attacked.

Specific Instances of Misconduct

Rule 405(a) provides that on cross-examination of a character witness, inquiry is allowed into relevant specific instances of misconduct. The form of the cross-examination question on relevant specific conduct is: "Have you heard that the defendant was arrested for (state the specific act relevant to the character trait) when the character witness has testified that defendant's reputation for peacefulness is 'he's a pussycat'?" *United States v. Scholl*, 166 F.3d 964, 974 (9th Cir. 1999), *cert. denied*, 528 U.S. 873, 120 S. Ct. 176, 145 L. Ed. 2d 149 (1999). A good-faith basis for asking the question must exist and it has been held that, upon objection, the cross-examiner should be required to reveal that basis in the absence of the jury. *United States v. Reese*, 568 F.2d 1246, 1249 (6th Cir. 1977).

Extrinsic evidence is inadmissible if the witness denies knowing the specific instances of misconduct. The cross-examiner must take the answer and cannot prove it by extrinsic evidence. The point of allowing the "have you heard" question is to test the character witness's knowledge of the defendant and the standards he or she is using. The cross is aimed at the weight to be given to the witness's testimony on behalf of the defendant, not the truth of the specific instances. After all, just being arrested, although mistakenly, bears upon one's reputation.

Impeaching a Character Witness

Fed. R. Evid 405. A Witness's Character for Truthfulness or Untruthfulness

   (a)   **Reputation or Opinion Evidence.** A witness's credibility may be attacked or supported by testimony about the witness's reputation for having a character for truthfulness or untruthfulness, or by testimony in the form of an opinion about that character. But evidence of truthful character is admissible only after the witness's character for truthfulness has been attacked.

B. Technique and Illustration

` Begin by locking the witness into testifying that the person whose character he or she is vouching for is good. Follow with a question about a specific act of misconduct that refutes the witness's assertion. This question is restricted by case law to the litany set forth in this chapter. The cross-examiner asks the witness: "Have you heard?" or "Did you know that (person whose character has been testified to) was arrested for committing a first degree assault two years ago?"

CHECKLIST: IMPEACHMENT CROSS: REPORTER

Prior Conviction

- ❏ A witness's prior conviction is only to be considered by the fact-finder in determining what weight or credibility to give to the witness, and for no other purpose.
- ❏ To be admissible at trial, the prior conviction must meet the requirements of Federal Rule of Evidence 609 or the state rule equivalent.
- ❏ The conviction can be proven either by the witness's admission or by a self-authenticated prior conviction document.
- ❏ Identification of the witness as the person who was convicted can be established by witness admission, fingerprints of the witness matching the fingerprints on the conviction document, or by the witness having the same name as the convicted person.
- ❏ The law of the jurisdiction where the case is tried may limit the amount of information the witness may testify to.

Prior Misconduct Probative of Untruthfulness

- ❏ Federal Rule of Evidence 608(b) and similar state rules provide that in the judge's discretion the witness's prior specific acts of misconduct may be introduced at trial if they show untruthfulness.

❑ The cross-examiner must have a good-faith basis for asking about the prior conduct.

❑ Under Fed. R. Evid. 403, the prior misconduct may be excluded because its probative value is substantially outweighed by unfair prejudice.

❑ The cross-examiner must take the witness's answer to the inquiry about the misconduct, and if the witness denies it, no extrinsic evidence is admissible to dispute the denial.

Character Witness

❑ Federal Rule of Evidence 405(a) or state equivalent provides that character evidence may be established by testimony as to either reputation or in the form of an opinion.

- Counsel may be able to keep a reputation witness off the stand by voir diring the witness and revealing that a proper foundation cannot be laid for the testimony.
- Under Fed. R. Evid. 404(a) or state counterpart, character evidence is inadmissible except:
  - In a criminal case where the defendant introduces evidence of a pertinent trait of the defendant or the prosecution counters it with character evidence.
  - In a criminal case where the defendant introduces evidence of a pertinent trait of the victim or the prosecution rebuts that or when the defendant contends that the victim was the first aggressor and the prosecution offers the victim's trait of peacefulness.

❑ Federal Rule of Evidence 608 or state equivalent provides that a witness may be attacked or supported by opinion or reputation testimony regarding the witness's truthfulness; evidence of truthful character is admissible only after the witness's truthfulness has been attacked.

❑ A character witness may be cross-examined about specific instances of misconduct by the person about whom the character witness is testifying.

❑ If the witness denies knowing about the existence of the prior misconduct, the examiner must take the answer and may not introduce extrinsic evidence.

CHAPTER 9

CHARACTER & CONDUCT IN TRIAL

". . .The counsel who has a pleasant personality; who speaks with apparent frankness; who appears to be an earnest searcher after truth; who is courteous to those who testify against him; who avoids delaying constantly

the progress of the trial by innumerable objections and exceptions to
perhaps incompetent but harmless evidence; seems to know what he is
about and sits down when he has accomplished it, exhibiting a spirit of fair
play on all occasions—he it is who creates an atmosphere in favor of the
side which he represents, a powerful though unconscious influence with the
jury in arriving at their verdict. . . ."

> — **Francis L. Wellman**, *The Art of Cross-*
> *Examination* 28 (new ed., Book Jungle
> 2007, original ed. 1903)

"It comes to this: civility, collegiality, and adherence to the highest ethics
make you a more effective lawyer. They help you win. In litigation, you
cannot be a first-rate lawyer without them."

> — **William L. Dwyer**, *Ipse Dixit: How*
> *the World Looks to a Federal Judge* 27
> (University of Washington Press 2007)

I. CHARACTER AND ATTRIBUTES

Cross-examination has a mystique about it that other aspects of trial practice
do not, giving legendary status to the advocate who knows how to do it well.
The ideal cross-examiner always scores major points, invariably finding the
Achilles' heel of the witness's testimony. In this chapter, we examine in depth
the personal attributes, character, and conduct necessary for successful cross-
examination, offering ways to integrate these into your own approach.

Attributes of the Perfect Cross-Examiner

1. Fair and respectful;
2. A prodigious memory;
3. A good ear;
4. Excellent powers of analysis; and
5. Persistence and fortitude.

A. Fair and Respectful

The general rule dictates courtesy and professionalism toward a witness.
Outright clashes are minimized by strategy and polished execution. Above all
else, the cross-examiner must be seen by the jury as a sincere seeker of truth,
fair and respectful to all.

Abraham Lincoln was the epitome of how a trial lawyer should approach a
witness on cross. Joseph Benjamin Oakleaf at the 1912 convention of the Illi-
nois State Attorneys Association described Lincoln's demeanor and method as
follows:

One reason why I think he would have been a successful criminal lawyer was his mastery of the art of cross-examination, in which he had no equal. If an obstinate witness appeared and was determined to conceal facts which Lincoln desired brought out, Lincoln would neither show resentment nor attempt to coerce the witness but would go after him in a nice, friendly way, questioning about things which were foreign to the point desired, thus placing him at ease, making him forget his antagonistic ideas, and, before he was aware of the harm he was doing his side, the whole story would be laid bare, and then Lincoln would compliment the witness on his fairness and would consider himself a hero.

Joseph Benjamin Oakleaf, *Abraham Lincoln as a Criminal Lawyer* 6 (Rock Island, IL: Augustana Book Concern, 1923)

However, this is not to suggest that the cross-examiner should never spar with a witness who the jurors believe deserves a comeuppance. But never get ahead of the jurors and take on the witness before they are ready for you to do so, and maintain your professional demeanor throughout. Examples of this include where the witness is clearly lying, refusing to answer the question, or injecting irrelevant information in the answers. In Chapter 10, Witness Control: Strategies & Techniques, we offer techniques for addressing some of these problems.

The best stylistic advice is to be yourself. You may be businesslike or just one of the common folk. You may be bold and loud or firm and soft spoken. Beyond considerations of individual lawyer styles, different witnesses require changes of tone and approach. A young child witness normally will be treated with kindness and understanding. In a criminal case, defense counsel's cross-examination of an informant-turned-state's witness will be firm, bordering on harsh, suggesting that the witness is not worthy of belief.

You may alter your attitude during the cross of the same witness. For example, at the outset, you may display a friendly and nonconfrontational demeanor intended to gain cooperation and concessions. Once that has been accomplished, a change to a more aggressive manner seeking to discredit the witness may be indicated.

A cross cross-examination does not work. Avoid anger and finger pointing. The jury likely will see this as mistreating the witness or a sign of weakness. Any show of righteous indignation must be sparing.

B. A Prodigious Memory

Any competent lawyer can be courteous and professional. A good memory goes beyond manners and training into genetics. You either have it or you don't. Short-term memory is necessary to compare the witness's testimony to the evidence already presented. Long-term memory retrieves similar stories told by witnesses in similar situations.

The 1911 *Triangle Shirtwaist Company* trial in New York, which centered on the city's worst disaster before 9/11, demonstrates the critical role of memory in cross-examination. One lawyer, Max Steuer, emerged from this trial a legend, largely through his use of cross to destroy what was thought to have been an unassailable prosecution case against the owners for manslaughter.

On March 25, 1911, in Manhattan, a fire broke out on the eighth floor of the Triangle Waist Company, New York's largest blouse factory. While the fire lasted only a half hour, 146 garment workers died, either in the fire itself or in jumping from the windows. The District Attorney based his manslaughter case against the owners, who escaped from the roof, on their practice of locking the exit doors to prevent unauthorized breaks by the factory workers.

Bodies placed in coffins on the sidewalk by the Triangle factory

With outraged public sentiment running strongly against them, the owners needed the best legal talent money could buy. They hired Max D. Steuer to defend them. In *Triangle: The Fire That Changed America,* David Von Drehle describes just how effective a move this was:

> His reputation (was) such that a man would pay an enormous retainer simply to ensure that . . . Steuer would not help his heirs challenge his will . . . (one) jurist . . . (called him) the "greatest trial lawyer of our time."

David Von Drehle, *Triangle: The Fire That Changed America* 222-23 (Grove Press 2003).

Max D. Steuer

Steuer's extraordinary memory was a formidable weapon throughout his career:

> . . . Jurors did not take notes so neither did he. This was no sacrifice, because his memory allowed him to file every detail neatly away, available for instant retrieval. He liked to provoke prosecutors into arguing with him over something a witness had said days or even weeks earlier, so that the jury could see and appreciate his total reliability when the transcript was read and he was proved right.

Von Drehle, *Triangle* at 230.

C. A Good Ear

Prior planning of questions is only a start. Sticking to your script will not work if the testimony comes in differently than you thought, as it often does. Your cross will be largely determined by what the witness says and does. This requires you to listen intently to the witness's testimony. Lawyers tend to be good talkers and not-so-good listeners. Your preconceptions about what a witness should say can prevent comprehending what the witness actually says. It is critical to go beneath the surface of statements and appreciate all their nuances. Not listening carefully to the testimony may cause you to miss opportunities for cross.

Distractions often come in the form of thinking about the next question or looking over notes. Look at the witness and actively listen to the witness's full response. Assimilate it before moving to the next question. If the witness gives you an unanticipated gift, jump on it, moving beyond your prepared notes. Practice questioning without having to read from your notes, which only should serve as reminders. Glance down at them briefly, and then look up, ask the question while looking at the witness, listening to the full answer.

Max Steuer's listening skills paid off during his legendary cross-examination of Kate Alterman, the prosecution's final witness in the *Triangle* manslaughter trial. Kate Alterman was a sewing machine operator on the ninth floor of the factory. On direct examination, she recounted in theatrical detail the panic after the alarm and her path of travel to get out of the flame-engulfed building, using literary phrases such as "throwing around like a wildcat," and a "red curtain of fire."

Von Drehle explains Steuer's thought process upon hearing this testimony:

> . . . (He) . . . detected . . . the telltale echoes of stagecraft. There was the careful pacing of Alterman's account, and the dramatic elements—like the way the smoke cleared just as she turned back to see Schwartz in the grip of death. Some of the words piqued his suspicions—"extinguished," for example, sounded more like a lawyer than a teenage immigrant—and also the literary turns . . . . If Steuer could get the jurors to see these things as he saw them—without an ugly confrontation—they might be softly swayed away from Kate Alterman. But it must be attempted with great care.

Von Drehle, *Triangle* at 245.

D. Excellent Powers of Analysis

Listening intently to the witness's testimony is only the beginning. It must be analyzed in the light of the rest of the testimony and evidence to find the flaws. Sometimes these flaws will be internal to the testimony, other times only in comparison to the other evidence. Extraneous detail must be stripped away to simplify the testimony, and expose any flaw through a series of questions.

In the *Triangle* manslaughter case, Max Steuer concluded that Kate Alterman had memorized her testimony like a script, carefully coached by the prosecution. How could he persuade the jury of this? He laid the groundwork by having Alterman testify to her pretrial meetings with the prosecutors. Steuer then had Alterman repeat her story, getting:

> . . . a perfect playback of the original testimony . . . he had primed the jury to listen for echoes (of) the red curtain and the wildcat. He decided to repeat the exercise (and) . . . circled away from the main story for a few minutes (with) a string of inconsequential questions about the layout of the factory. When enough time had elapsed, he struck once more:
> "Now, could you tell us again what you did?"

Von Drehle, *Triangle* at 247-48.

Steuer had Kate Alterman repeat her story four times. While the prosecutor could have objected that the question had been asked and answered, he may have decided against it figuring that Steuer was making the rookie mistake of repeating direct on cross. By getting the witness to utter the same words each time, the point was made, destroying both Kate Alterman's credibility and that of the prosecution's case. The owners were acquitted of all criminal charges. A subsequent civil suit in 1913 won the plaintiffs compensation in the amount of $75 per deceased victim.

E. Persistence and Grit

Cross-examination often is tough business, requiring persistence and grit to corkscrew the truth out of a reluctant witness. Assistant U.S. Attorney Brenda Morris's confrontation with Senator Stevens at pages 139-141 over whether the chair in the Senator's house was a gift or a loan is a prime example of the necessary tenacity.

F. Nobody's Perfect and CPR

No lawyer, however talented, has a uniform, natural grasp of all these attributes. How can you best attempt to up the level of your game? We recommend CPR: *Composure, Preparation,* and *Resolve* as the best way to build upon your natural talent. The CPR approach is a performance enhancer that will lift you up toward the level of the legendary cross-examiners.

Composure

Many attributes of the gifted cross-examiner flow from maintaining both an outward and inner composure. Adhere to the adage, "Never let them see you sweat," maintaining a poker face free of distress. An inner calm enables you to concentrate better, actively listen to the testimony, and analyze and simplify it.

Preparation

Composure is a product of thorough preparation. Complete preparation has three components. The first component involves life experiences. To be successful counsel must be well rounded, well informed, and well read. The larger your life experiences, the greater a frame of reference you will have for taking on a witness. The second component is a logical, orderly system for assimilating and assessing evidence. The third component is witness-specific, rigorously applying our suggested method of preparation.

Meticulous preparation will enable you to hear and better remember the full depth of the witness's testimony, with a context in which to analyze it.

Resolve

Composure and preparation will only get you so far. You also need resolve to carry you to the end. When knowledge, skill, or ability fails, dogged determination can get the job done.

This book will help with the *preparation* in CPR. It will give an approach to cross-examination and a method for preparing and performing cross-examination. It is not the only way, but it is a good way. Once you are thoroughly prepared the *composure* will come much more easily, leading to *resolve* and a successful cross-examination.

II. IT'S ALL IN THE EXECUTION

Having laid your plans and made your preparations for cross-examination, you must now carry them out effectively in trial. When opposing counsel calls a witness to the stand, what do you do?

A. Writing Used to Refresh Memory

Under Federal Rule of Evidence 612 (or a corresponding state evidence rule), you have the right to see any writings that the witness drew on to refresh memory prior to trial or on the stand. Further, you can introduce into evidence any part of that writing that relates to the testimony. If opposing counsel complains that portions of the writing do not pertain to the subject of the testimony, the judge will make an in camera review, excising any parts that do not relate to the subject matter of the testimony. Portions of the writing withheld "over objections" are to be preserved and turned over to the appellate court if there is an appeal. If the writing is not produced, the judge can enter any order that justice requires. In a criminal case, the judge either must strike the testimony or, if justice requires, declare a mistrial.

To have the witness produce writings reviewed prior to trial, ask, "Have you read any written material prior to taking the witness stand here in order to refresh your memory about (the subject of the witness's testimony)?" If the witness responds in the affirmative, ask the witness to produce the writing. If you see a witness using a document on the stand, ask, "What are those papers in your lap that you looked at during your direct testimony. Did they help refresh your memory while you were testifying?" If the witness answers, "Yes," ask to see them. Even if the witness contends not to have refreshed memory with the papers, the witness's conduct of repeatedly looking at the notes should be sufficient to get them. If opposing counsel objects that portions are not related to the testimony, the court can make an in camera review, ruling on what must be turned over.

Once you have the writing in your possession, take the time to read it, requesting a recess if need be. You may now employ it during your cross, introducing favorable portions under Rule 612.

B. Art of Listening

As we have stressed, listening is key to how you will cross. But, what are you listening for?

The Opening Door

Listen carefully for the door to open, which then allows the introduction of otherwise inadmissible evidence to rebut a false impression. *Byrd v. Maricopa County Sheriff's Dept.*, 565 F.3d 1205, 1213 (9th Cir. 2009). Rules of evidence, including the Federal Rules of Evidence, do not codify the open-door doctrine. As a common law principle, basic fairness requires that a party may counter inadmissible evidence introduced by the opposing party. *Bearint v. Dorel Juvenile Group*, 389 F.3d 1339, 1349 (11th Cir. 2004). However, what comes through the open door rests within the court's discretion. It is limited to countering the prejudice caused, subject to exclusion under Federal Rule of Evidence 403, if it causes "undue delay, waste of time, or needless presentation of cumulative evidence." *Manuel v. City of Chicago*, 335 F.3d 592, 597 (7th Cir. 2003).

As an example, let us see how the doctrine works in a sexual harassment case. Assume that the employer had been previously accused twice of sexual harassment, but that the court kept this out of evidence in a pretrial motion. If the employer testifies on direct that he never sexually harassed an employee, this now makes the prior incidents fair game on cross. The court can limit their use on cross to the extent necessary to explain or rebut the impression left by the direct testimony.

Discrepancies

As an example of applying the art of listening to detect conflicts we use a burglary and sexual battery criminal case. The case began when a young lady, whom we here call Valerie, used her CB radio to arrange a sexual rendezvous with a long distance truck driver. The trucker bragged to the defendant about his rendezvous with Valerie, and the defendant decided he, too, should have sex with her. The defendant, however, did not think it was necessary to obtain her consent, and as a result was charged with burglary and sexual battery.

At trial, the defendant took the stand to testify that Valerie had invited him over to her home to have sex. He said he waited until nightfall, crawled through Valerie's bedroom window, and engaged in consensual sex with her. Approximately one hour and 45 minutes into his testimony, he testified that, at the conclusion of the rendezvous, he went home and knocked on the door to have his mother let him into the house. The prosecutor, who was actively listening to defendant's testimony, immediately seized upon the discrepancy. The defendant crawled through Valerie's window but knocked on his own door? Having heard and identified the weakness in the defendant's testimony, the prosecutor then had to make sure the jury heard it too. The prosecutor took these two incidents, placed them side by side, and let the jury draw their own conclusions. The cross-examination went as follows:

> Q. When you got home, what did you do?
> A. Knocked on the door.
> Q. When you got to Valerie's what did you do?
> A. Crawled through her window.
> Q. You knocked on your own door?
> A. Yes.
> Q. But you crawled through Valerie's window?
> A. Yes.
> Q. You knocked on the door of the house where you lived?
> A. Yes.
> Q. But you crawled through the window of the house where you'd been invited?
> A. Yes.

The jury concluded that the defendant was guilty of both burglary and sexual battery.

Active Listening Checklist

While it is impossible to list every contingency, the following short list is a functional way to refine your active listening skills:

CHECKLIST

Active Listening

Listening for the following in a witness whom you will cross-examine:

❑ • *Conflicts and other discrepancies* between the witness's testimony and a prior statement, another witness's testimony, opposing counsel's opening statement,

continued ▶

discovery (responses to interrogatories and requests for admissions), and common sense
- ❏ • *Concessions* supporting your case theory or undermining the other side's case theory
- ❏ • *Clues to coaching,* such as witness Kate Alterman's testimony in the Triangle manslaughter case (pages 191-192)
- ❏ • *Impeachment material,* such as opposing counsel having the witness admit to making a prior inconsistent statement on direct in an attempt to lessen its impact.
- ❏ • *Exaggerations*
- ❏ • *The opening door*

C. Look

Counsel can gain valuable information by actively watching the witness and the jury. First, how is the witness coming across? While jurors tend to be stone-faced, at times they may show interest, boredom, or incredulity.

Second, the witness's manner while testifying may supply material for summation. The jury will be instructed later to consider the witness's manner in determining credibility. If the witness's direct testimony flows smoothly but then the witness stumbles on cross, this contrast can be emphasized in closing argument. Or, if the witness displays anger during questioning, this may be pointed to as evidence of bias.

Try to read the witness. Look for any signs of uncertainty or untruth. Although a well-prepared witness may not reveal these on direct, the pressure of cross may do so. Watch for averted eye contact, perspiration, heavier breathing, shifts in facial expression, and other signs of nervousness. Of course an accomplished liar, like a good bluffing poker player, may display no hints of deception. And, turned-away eyes may be cultural, not a sign of deception. Draw your own conclusions about the witness by careful observation. This will include a sense of how the witness is being perceived by the jury and how best to approach the witness.

Third, watch others in the courtroom for any signs given to witnesses on how to testify. A striking example occurred during Senator Stevens' corruption trial, discussed at pages 139-141. With the jury present, U.S. District Judge Emmet Sullivan accused attorney Robert Bundy, sitting in the spectator section, of giving head-shaking signals to his client Bill Allen during testimony. The judge later conceded that "maybe he (Bundy) was shaking his head in disbelief at something else." Erika Bolstad & Richard Mauer, Anchorage Daily News, October 7, 2008.

Nevertheless, the point is, watch for any inappropriate signaling in the courtroom and take action to stop it. Object if you perceive any form of this: "Objection, counsel just coached the witness by shaking his head." This should deter further misconduct and alert the judge and jury to the behavior. This is a serious accusation of misconduct and must be done cautiously. The judge may take offense, overrule your objection, and reprimand you. A safer approach is to object, request a sidebar, and state your grounds there.

D. Adjust

Attentiveness to both the witness's testimony and the courtroom environment gives you new avenues to explore. Adjust your cross to suit the situation. If the witness is sympathetic or vulnerable, such as a child or a grieving widow, your demeanor and questioning should reflect this. On the other hand, if the witness is an arrogant and callous corporate executive, the jury will grant you greater latitude to be hard-hitting. If the witness contradicts statements in his or her deposition, impeach with a prior inconsistent statement. If the witness makes an unexpected concession on direct, drop the portion of your planned cross targeted toward obtaining this admission. Further probing may permit the witness to explain away or water down the admission.

E. Note Taking

How actively should you take notes of the witness's testimony? Extensive note taking makes it more likely that you will be distracted and miss something important. But train your ear to recognize and write down what your instincts tell you may be important. The amount of writing you do will vary, depending on the type of case and witness. Another negative of note taking during questioning is that it tends to slow down the pace, which may irritate the judge and the jury.

Civil Case

In a civil case, the witness is likely to have been deposed, which gives you great knowledge about what the witness will testify to on direct, necessitating fewer notes during direct. Concentrate on listening to the answers and looking at the witness. Notes here should be confined to quotes for closing, such as concessions and improbable answers.

Capture significant variances from depositions, as well as prior written discovery, answers to interrogatories, and requests for admissions. Look for new information that opens further cross or wording that is favorable to your case. Accuracy and precision is important in the confrontation of the witness: "On direct examination, you said . . . ." Notations in the right column of the prepared cross notes can allow for easy reference.

Criminal Case

Criminal cases are different. Counsel may not have extensive discovery; depositions are not taken in criminal cases except in Florida and a few other jurisdictions. If the defendant has exercised a Fifth Amendment right to remain silent until taking the stand, a prosecutor only can speculate on what the defendant will testify to. Under these circumstances, notes should capture important points and quotes. But do not allow yourself to be distracted by note taking. Your primary attention should be directed toward observing the witness. The cross-notes format will minimize your need to write things down, as you likely can just add to an existing section.

F. Smooth

Being Prepared and Organized

A successful cross is smooth, flowing, and uninterrupted. This is the product of meticulous pretrial preparation, which will largely eliminate the need for distracting searches for legal authority, prior inconsistent statements, or exhibits.

In previous chapters and in Chapter 11, we provide you with the system for being prepared and organized in trial. We now review those pretrial planning and preparation steps, alongside trial conduct.

Topical Units of Cross Notes

A fumbling cross-examination that lacks focus and unduly repeats the direct testimony usually is the product of poor planning and organization. The cross-notes units described in Chapter 4 will help keep you on point in a leading-question format.

Insert any additional notes from the direct examination into the pertinent unit of the cross notes. You may need to reorder your units as a result of the direct testimony. One approach is to take the units out of your trial organizer (notebook or folder) as soon as the witness takes the stand, reshuffling them during the direct. You then can put them back in the order you want and be ready to cross-examine. Another approach is the use of removable label tabs, which can be changed around during direct.

Ready References to Law and Proof

The cross-notes format organizes prior written statements, deposition answers, legal authority, and other sources so they are ready to use on a moment's notice. If a prior video deposition statement becomes important, your cross notes will take you right to it. Using electronic software, such as Trial Director or Sanction, the pertinent video clip can be pulled up quickly and displayed on the screen or television monitors in the courtroom. This meets the fast pace that modern audiences expect.

Listen, Look, Adjust, and Limited Note Taking

Successful cross-examination combines pretrial preparation with effective trial behavior. The previous sections described the following essential elements of in-court conduct:

Essentials of In-Court Conduct

- *Listen to the testimony.* The witness is the primary person to pay attention to, not your cross notes.
- *Look at the people in the courtroom.* Watch the jury and the witness. Is the jury with you? Or are they bored, wanting you move on?
- *Adjust to the situation.* If the witness makes a major concession that you had not expected, it may be time to stop on that high note.
- *Limit your note taking.* This can be a distraction.

G. Staging

When opposing counsel has finished and says, "Your witness," what do you do? Stand? Sit? Stand behind a podium? Move around? The answer to this varies, depending on the forum. In federal and some state courts, you will question the witness from behind a podium. In North Carolina, you will sit at counsel table. Custom may require that you seek the court's permission before approaching the witness by asking, "May I approach the witness, Your Honor?"

In direct examination, the jury focus is on the witness, who is delivering information, not the lawyer asking the questions. On cross, however, the spotlight shifts to the cross-examiner. Remember what we said about this being your opportunity to testify. Position yourself right in front of the jury so that both players in the drama of cross-examination can be seen by the jury. Movement by counsel can draw the jurors' attention away from the witness. Positioning yourself in front of the jury and moving around the courtroom forces the witness to look away from the jury. This reduces the witness's potential for effective communication.

Getting up close to the witness gives you a good view of the witness's demeanor and behavior. If the witness looks to opposing counsel for help, fidgets, or avoids eye contact, you will be in a prime location to spot this. Eye contact with the witness is the best way to gauge the truth of the witness's responses. The combination of a commanding position up front and steady eye contact with the witness also helps you maintain control.

Before you begin questioning, have everything ready to go. First, your cross notes should be organized and in the correct order. If at all possible, organize them during direct. If you need more time, ask the judge for it before commencing cross. Second, any necessary documents, statements, depositions, or exhibits should be arranged in the sequence you want and close at hand. Third, any visual equipment, such as a document camera or a video, should have been set up, tested, and ready to go. Make these arrangements before or after court or during a recess.

Take your position with notes, exhibits, and documents in place. Lock eyes with the witness. Pause for a short time so the jury is with you. If you start by seeking concessions, do so in a conversational, courteous way, avoiding a feigned friendly greeting. Be sincere and fair, but firm.

The further the cross-examiner is away from the witness, the less stress the witness will feel. Use this to your advantage. When seeking concessions in a relaxed, friendly approach, do so at a distance. However, if the witness is evading or fabricating, challenge the witness by moving in closer. As the questions get more confrontational, you can emphasize and enhance them by moving physically closer to the witness. However, you do not want to hover over the witness, as the judge likely will admonish you for invading the witness's space.

III. PLAY TO YOUR AUDIENCES

You need to be aware of the different expectations of each audience you are playing to during a cross-examination. Now, we focus on how to satisfy the expectations and objectives for each type of audience.

A. Witness: The Most Immediate Audience

Your most immediate audience is the witness, for whom your questions are crafted. Focus on the witness, making eye contact. Determine what effect your questions and presence are having. Does the person's body language reveal signs of deception or doubt? If the witness is being evasive or difficult, apply the control techniques discussed in the next chapter.

B. Jury: The Most Important Audience

We already have discussed the ways in which pretrial preparation will help you to sway the jury with your cross, from case theory development through storytelling. The spotlight now moves to your in-court performance.

The Story Teller

The best story, told well, wins a case. Jurors remember and are shaped by it, fitting the evidence into the narrative that makes the most sense to them. Without a story, they cannot process the information in a meaningful way. Your job on cross is to tell a consistent and credible story throughout the case, keeping the jurors on your side. The story appeal of your cross-examination should be continually reassessed: "How is the jury receiving this?"

The Juror's Role and the Seeker of Truth

Be constantly aware of the jurors' role to apply the law to the facts as they find them and reach a verdict. Their job is to determine the truth. Your demeanor and conduct should be designed to help the jurors meet their responsibilities.

However satisfying it may seem to the cross-examiner to beat up on a witness, the real test is what the jury thinks. Jurors may perceive the conduct in a negative light—as abuse of a witness—particularly if they are not convinced that the witness deserves it. If the witness is patently lying, the situation shifts in favor of a rigorous cross.

Adversity and Caesar's Red Cape

How well you deal with adversity during cross-examination can affect the jury profoundly. Julius Caesar was famous for wearing a red cape in battle, seeking to sustain the morale of his soldiers by masking the blood from any wounds he might suffer. Before Caesar, the Spartans wore red capes for a similar reason.

While a devastating answer elicited by a poorly phrased cross-examination question is not a life and death matter, the same need of Caesar and the Spartans to maintain appearances on the field of battle applies to the courtroom. No matter how badly you are damaged by a witness's answer, do not show your distress, thereby magnifying the devastating effect of the answer. Gather your red cape around you, with no hint that you have been grievously injured.

Juror Expectations

Jurors expect a cross-examination to be exciting, pitting the lawyer against an opposing witness. Meet this expectation with a to-the-point cross that is engaging and never boring. Inject life into your cross-examinations, highlighting the testimony with techniques described on pages 203-204 or with visuals, such as those covered in Chapter 5.

Jurors expect the cross-examiner to take on the witness, to test, probe, and challenge, revealing weaknesses and forcing concessions. Firm and fair treatment of the witness is fine. But, there is a difference between lay witnesses and experts. Jurors are protective of any lay witness, who, like them, is not a professional witness. Great care must be taken to avoid having the jury side with the lay witness, discounting points that you may have scored. Unfair attacks or tricks will cause this to happen. On the other hand, with experts, particularly those with extensive courtroom experience, jurors expect, and even want, a scuffle.

The bottom line is that the jury wants to hear a story in the cross-examination. You must tell one that is factually sufficient and convincing. You have put your story together during pretrial preparation, as discussed in Chapters 2–4. Your demeanor in telling the story is as important as the story itself. Only if the storyteller is credible will the story be received as credible. You must believe in the story and project it, making it real. Although Jean Giraudoux, French diplomat and writer, once said, "The secret of success is sincerity. Once you can fake that you've got it made," few are capable of doing this effectively. Use highlighting techniques, such as altering the tone of your voice to show disbelief, or visuals, such as a prior inconsistent statement in a video deposition.

C. Trial Judge: The Exacting Audience

Your primary objectives for a cross-examination will not likely be the same as the judge's. Your goal is to try and get sufficient latitude from the judge on the content of your cross for it to be persuasive to the jury.

The judge has the final word, guided by the twin desires to make efficient use of court time and not be reversed on appeal. Pertinent, pointed, legally sound questions on cross go a long way toward meeting the judge's objectives.

The trial judge may have other expectations which must be heeded. Judges often have preferences on the following: Where counsel stands while questioning; whether permission is requested before approaching the witness; whether a witness is provided with a copy of his or her deposition; time limits for questioning; sidebar conferences; and pre-marking exhibits. Learn the proclivities of your trial judge in advance, through courtroom observation, talking with colleagues and court personnel, and visiting the court's website. Being well prepared and considerate of the judge's approach to courtroom management will go a long way toward getting the latitude you need for a winning cross.

D. Appellate Court: The Supervising Audience

An appellate court is always a floating specter in the background of a trial, capable of turning your victory into a defeat. Appellate courts look at all aspects of a trial, including cross-examinations of witnesses. Adding insult to injury, an appellate court may even immortalize your lapses of judgment in the pages of the Law Reports. The supervising appellate audience makes it crucial to try the case correctly the first time, within the law, rules of evidence, and Rules of Professional Conduct.

E. Courtroom Fans: The Inconsequential Audience

Your client, co-counsel, and spectators in the courtroom may tempt your natural desire to please and impress. A lawyer's cross-examination methodology can be second-guessed by these and other sources. Trust your own judgment on strategy and tactics. It is the judge's and jury's opinions that really count. Never let impressing your client, co-counsel, or the gallery dictate the course of your cross-examination.

IV. HIGHLIGHTING THE TESTIMONY

Even if you get the answer you want on cross, it only counts if the jury understands it. How can you highlight the information, as though with a yellow marker, so the jury will retain it? One way is with visuals, and Chapter 5 is devoted to this. Here, we will discuss other methods of putting the spotlight on the testimony.

A sparing use of repetition can highlight the testimony. One technique is to echo the answer:

Q. There was no warning on the package?
A. No, there wasn't.
Q. No, there wasn't.

Then, ask the next question. Counsel may repeat the answer asking:

"Did we hear you correctly, you said . . .?"

Another way to emphasize the favorable response is to incorporate it in the next question:

"So after you decided that you wouldn't warn potential customers by putting something on the package about the danger, you . . ."

If, as we have suggested, you end the court session on a high note, the last answers you elicit before the break are worth repeating for emphasis. When court resumes, highlight that testimony by asking the judge to have the court reporter read back the last few questions "to remind us of where we left off and so we don't repeat the testimony."

Yet another way to underscore the testimony with repetition is to summarize the favorable testimony. Lincoln's cross-examination question of Charles Allen is a good example: "You saw this killing at ten at night—in beech timber, three-quarters of a mile from light—saw the slungshot—saw the man strike with it—saw it twenty feet away—saw it all by moonlight? Saw it nearly a mile from the camp lights?" When summarizing testimony in this way, be scrupulously careful that your summary is 100 percent correct. The witness will seize upon the smallest variance between his testimony and your summary as an excuse to disagree with it. Instead of underscoring with the summary, you will lose the jury by debating the witness.

You can highlight with your behavior. Make a dramatic pause to accentuate a favorable answer, coupling the moment of silence with your knowing look. Although the best practice is to maintain a poker face during cross, an answer may call for a response that labels the answer as unworthy of belief. With tone of voice, a look of incredulity in facial expression, and a question expressing that doubt ("Are you saying . . ."), counsel can draw attention to the untruth or exaggeration.

V. KNOW WHEN TO STOP

A. Stop

"When you strike oil, stop boring," is the aphorism for cross-examiners to adhere to. If the witness is discredited or has made a major concession, it is probably time to stop on that topic or even sit down. Additional questioning may result turning the win into a loss, allowing the witness to explain or retract the concession. You are far better off using the transcript of the original concession in closing to drive home your point. You also may wish to use one or more of the highlighting techniques we have discussed at pages 203-204.

However, many cross-examiners have difficulty knowing when to stop drilling. An example of this is the criminal defense lawyer defending a man named Johnny Lee Johnson against a charge of armed robbery. The victim testified that he had been accosted, beaten, relieved of his property, and deposited in a ditch. After painting a dramatic picture of the man's abuse, the prosecutor asked the victim if he could see the man who did those things to him. The victim looked into the jury box. He looked at counsel table. He looked out into the audience. Finally, he examined the court reporter, the bailiff, and the deputy clerk. "I can't say as I see him." Before defense counsel could object, the prosecutor pointed at the defendant and said, "What about him, is he the man that robbed you?" The victim quickly said, "No, I can't say that's the man that robbed me." The prosecutor passed the witness and sat down. With fire in his eyes, the public defender rose to his feet. The cross-examination actually went as follows:

WHEN TO STOP

People v. Johnny Lee Johnson

Q. Sir, take a close look at my client and tell the jury if he's the man who robbed you?

A. I can't say that he's the man who robbed me.

Q. Would it help you if you got a closer look?

A. I don't know, it may.

> Q. With the court's permission, get down off the witness stand and take a few steps toward my client and tell the jury if that's the man who robbed you?
> *[The witness complies.]*
> A. I can't say if that's the man that robbed me.
> Q. Get a little closer, sir, and tell us if that's the man that robbed you?
> *[The witness complies.}*
> A. I can't say if that's the man that robbed me.
> Q. Get right in his face, sir, and tell us if that's the man that robbed you?
> *[The witness complies.}*
> Witness: Have I ever seen you before?
> Defendant: Yes, you have.
> Witness: That's the man that robbed me!
> Defense Counsel: You may return to your seat, now.

Once you have proved your point, stop, honoring Irving Younger's ninth commandment of cross-examination, "Don't ask the 'one question too many."

B. Don't Stop

Unlike drilling for oil, when you strike gold, keep digging. A damning admission that cannot be explained, ignored, or minimized is golden. A good example of striking gold is an admission by the witness to having lied. Consider this murder case in which the defendant testified that he saw the victim attack him with a knife. The defendant had made prior inconsistent statements to the effect that he had not seen a knife. On cross, the prosecutor began by locking down the defendant's testimony that he saw a knife. She then employed the Liar-Liar technique of cross:

DON'T STOP: THE LIAR-LIAR TECHNIQUE

Cross of the Defendant in a Murder Case

Q. During that second confrontation, you never saw a knife?
A. I did see a knife.
Q. Do you remember giving your tape-recorded statement to Ms. Julie Hanson?
A. Yes, I do.
[At this point a transcript of the statement was produced and given to the defendant.]
Q. Then if you'll flip it over to the second page, right down toward the bottom when Ms. Hanson asked you about the fatal confrontation, do you remember her asking you this question and you giving this answer:
  Q. Did you see the knife at that point?
  A. I never saw the knife at all.
A. Yes, I did.

---

continued ▶

> Q. That you never saw the knife at all.
>
> A. Yes.
>
> Q. And when you got through giving that statement, Ms. Hanson asked you to raise your right hand and swear that what you are about to say is the truth, didn't she?
>
> A. Yes.
>
> Q. And so you swore under oath that the statement, "I never saw the knife at all," was true?
>
> A. Yes.
>
> Q. And that is the truth, isn't it?
>
> A. No.
>
> Q. It's not?
>
> A. No.
>
> Q. Was that a lie?
>
> A. Yes, it was.
>
> Q. You lied to Ms. Hanson?
>
> A. Yes, I did.
>
> Q. And the reason that you lied to Ms. Hanson and told her that was—
>
> A. Was because I was upset and I was afraid of going to jail. It was the first time I had ever been in trouble.
>
> Q. So you were telling her a lie that you thought might help keep you from going to jail, is that right?
>
> A. Yes.
>
> Q. You were telling her a lie that you thought might help you through this criminal prosecution, isn't that right?
>
> A. Yeah.
>
> Q. And you thought that saying, "I never saw a knife at all," would help you avoid criminal prosecution, is that right?
>
> A. Yeah.
>
> Q. Let's look on the second page of the statement.
>
> A. *[Witness perusing papers]*
>
> Q. And I believe right down toward the bottom of the page, do you recall Ms. Hanson asking you this question and you giving her this answer:
> At that point in time, did you have a knife in your hands? And your answer: No ma'am. I never had a knife in my hands at all. I don't carry knives. I don't carry weapons. I don't need them." Do you remember being asked that question and giving that answer?
>
> A. Yeah.
>
> Q. And you swore under oath that that answer was true?
>
> A. Yeah.
>
> Q. All right, sir. You've lied to the police, is that correct?
>
> A. Yes, I have.
>
> Q. You've lied repeatedly to them?
>
> A. Yes, I have.
>
> Q. Do you have any idea how many separate, individual lies you have told the police?

> *A.* No.
> *Q.* But it's a lot, isn't it?
> *A.* Yeah.
> *Q.* And the reason for telling all of those lies, and some of them under oath, was to try to get yourself out of a tight spot in this case, is that right?
> *A.* Yeah.
> Prosecutor: I don't have any other questions.

Two caveats about the Liar-Liar method. Before counsel can call a witness a liar, especially the defendant in a criminal case, a firm good-faith basis for it must exist. Second, a prosecutor may not make the argument, "Convict him because he's lying." The argument should be: "Disbelieve him because he's lying. Convict him because the prosecution's evidence proves guilt beyond a reasonable doubt."

The Liar-Liar method, when stripped to its barest essentials involves the following progression:

1. The prior inconsistent statement is untrue.
2. The witness knew the statement was untrue when he made it.
3. The witness admits that he lied.
4. The witness admits he lied in order to mislead. (Why else does someone lie?)
5. The witness admits he lied in order to avoid arrest and prosecution for this case.
6. Argue to the jury that they cannot trust the story of a person who has admittedly tried to lie his way out of trouble in this case.

The line of questions should go something like this:

Q. It wasn't true?
Q. You knew it wasn't true when you said it? (The first two questions give us the factual basis for asking the third. If someone said something they knew wasn't true, then they lied, didn't they?)
Q. You lied?
Q. You lied in order to mislead the police officer?
Q. You wanted the officer to believe something that wasn't true?
Q. The reason you wanted to mislead the officer was to keep him from arresting you, wasn't it?
Q. So you lied in order to avoid being prosecuted for this charge, didn't you?

A fertile imagination can devise scores of variations on the Liar-Liar theme.

VI. "NO QUESTIONS OF THIS WITNESS"

Just because you can cross-examine each witness does not mean you should. When the time is right and opposing counsel says, "Your witness," you can underline the fact that the witness either helped you or offered nothing of consequence by rising and announcing, "We would like to thank and excuse the witness. It is unnecessary for us to cross-examine this witness."

When is the time right to waive cross-examination? In that the witness usually will have served the purpose of advancing the other side's case theory or damaging yours, waiver tends to be uncommon. The right time to waive cross is when the witness has helped or at least done no harm to your case. Even if the content was harmful, the witness may have been so ineffective that the jury will disregard the testimony. The only other time to not cross, and it is a rare situation, is when the witness's direct testimony has damaged your case, but the witness cannot be impeached. If you cannot find any concessions that will help your case or undermine your opponent's, stand clear.

When the witness has offered little or nothing, or is blatantly biased, an alternative approach to waiving cross is to conduct a swift cross that underlines why you are not cross-examining the witness:

Defense counsel in a criminal case:

Q. Dr. Blinky, is it fair to summarize your testimony by saying that the victim died of a gunshot wound to the head?

A. Yes.

Q. You cannot tell this jury who shot the victim?

A. Yes.

Thank you for coming today, doctor.

Temptations to cross arise even though the witness has either done little or no harm or even helped your case. First, if the witness has made statements on direct that were either harmful to your opponent or helpful to your case, you may be tempted to give emphasis to them on cross. A cross on those statements is risky because it will give the witness an opportunity to dilute them or explain them away. Second, opposing counsel may lay a trap by not delving into an area on direct examination. The technique is to bait the trap and have the cross-examiner elicit the damaging information.

If you suspect a trap has been laid and if the rest of the witness's direct was harmless, the cross could be waived. Then, your opponent will lose the damaging information. If a cross is called for because it was otherwise harmful, avoid any questions touching on the omitted subject. By not asking questions on the subject, opposing counsel is precluded from going into it on redirect.

CHECKLIST: CHARACTER & CONDUCT IN TRIAL

Character and Attributes of the Persuasive Cross-Examiner

- ❑ A persuasive cross-examiner is one who is seen as courteous and a sincere seeker of truth.
- ❑ Attributes of the persuasive examiner include:
  - Fair and respectful, and avoids challenging the witness unless confident that the jury believes it is right to do so;
  - A solid grasp of and memory of the facts of the case;
  - A good ear that comes with active listening to the witness's direct testimony and answers to cross-examination questions;
  - An ability to analyze the witness's testimony to seek how it comports with the rest of the evidence; and
  - Persistence and grit necessary to elicit the truth from the witness.
- ❑ Most cross-examiners do not come by these listed attributes naturally, but with CPR can make up for the lack of natural talent:
  - *Composure* assists the examiner in the pursuits of listening, analyzing and simplifying the testimony;
  - *Preparation* is the key to composure and to hearing the depth of a witness's testimony and remembering the evidence, which enables the examiner to properly analyze the testimony of the witness; and
  - *Resolve* will enable the cross-examiner to pursue the truth despite obstacles.

Carrying Out the Winning Cross-Examination

- ❑ Federal Rule of Evidence 612 and state equivalent rules give the cross-examiner the right to disclosure of writings that the witness has reviewed prior to trial or while on the stand.
- ❑ Active listening is critical to a winning cross, and counsel should listen for the following:
  - The witness to open the door allowing otherwise inadmissible evidence to be introduced in trial;
  - Conflicts between the witness's testimony and other evidence;
  - Concessions;
  - Clues to coaching;
  - Impeachment material; and
  - Exaggerations.
- ❑ Look for information that will aid counsel's case, including particularly:
  - How the jury is receiving the witness;
  - Behavior by the witness that may reflect on the witness's credibility; and
  - Spectators and others in the courtroom to see if they are coaching the witness.
- ❑ Adjust your behavior and presentation to the witness and situation.
- ❑ Note taking should not interfere with counsel's concentration on listening to and looking at what is going on in the courtroom, but should note at a minimum quotable quotes for cross and closing and key points in the testimony that are in conflict with other witnesses and the witness's prior statements.

- ❑ A smooth-flowing cross is a successful cross; it should be uninterrupted by fumbling for legal authority or exhibits, and this can be accomplished with:
  - Units of cross notes arranged in a trial organizer—notebook or folder;
  - Ready references to law and proof on the right side of the cross notes;
  - Listening actively to the testimony;
  - Looking at the people in the courtroom;
  - Adjusting to the situations that develop; and
  - Limiting note taking in trial.
- ❑ Stage the cross-examination to have impact on the jury by:
  - Remembering that it is the examiner's time to testify and taking center stage;
  - Being organized with cross notes, deposition, technology, and exhibits in place; and
  - Using distance from the witness for effect on the witness.

Play to the Audience

- ❑ The witness is the most immediate audience; the examiner should focus on how the examination is affecting the person.
- ❑ The jury is the most important audience, and the examiner wants:
  - To tell the story well;
  - To have the jurors perceive her as an honest seeker of truth;
  - To not show the jurors any signs of distress; and
  - To meet the jurors' expectations that the cross will be interesting and engaging.
- ❑ The trial judge is the most exacting audience; counsel should meet the court's expectations by making an economical use of court time, asking legally sound questions, and abiding by the customs of the particular judge.
- ❑ The appellate court is the supervising audience; counsel must satisfy both the rules of evidence, applicable case law, as well as the rules of professional conduct.
- ❑ The courtroom fans, witnesses, and so on are inconsequential to whom counsel should be courteous but not compliant unless the request is in accord with the right thing to do.

Highlighting the Testimony

- ❑ The examiner wants the valuable answer elicited on cross to have impact and may employ these methods of highlighting it:
  - Repetition;
  - Summarization;
  - Silence;
  - Tone of voice.

Know When to Stop

- ❑ If counsel has conducted a winning cross, it is probably time to stop.
- ❑ However, if the examiner has uncovered a point that is "golden," such as an admission of lying by the witness, keep going.

No Questions

- ❑ Usually, counsel should cross-examine the witness because the witness has done some harm.

❑ However, when the witness has not harmed the examiner's case or has helped it, counsel may consider no cross-examination. Counsel should beware that if cross-examined the witness may:

- Dilute the direct testimony that was helpful to the cross-examiner; or
- Provide damaging testimony because opposing counsel deliberately omitted the testimony hoping the examiner would take the bait.

CHAPTER 10

WITNESS CONTROL
Strategies & Techniques

"In cross examination, as in fishing, nothing is more ungainly than a fisherman pulled into the water by his catch."
— **Louis Nizer** (1902-1994)

Jessup (Jack Nicholson): You want answers?
Kaffee (Tom Cruise): I want the truth!
Jessup: You can't handle the truth! Son, we live in world that has walls . . . You don't want the truth. Because deep down, in places you don't talk about at parties, you want me on that wall. You need me on that wall. We use words like honor, code, loyalty . . . we use these words as the backbone to a life spent defending something. You use 'em as a punch line . . .
Kaffee: Did you order the code red?
Jessep: (quietly) I did the job you sent me to do.
Kaffee: Did you order the code red?
Jessep: You're goddamn right I did!
— *A Few Good Men* (1992)

I. CONTROLLING THE WITNESS

Inevitably, some witnesses will not respond as you want and expect on cross, replying with either a quick evasion or a self-serving monologue. Others will meet your question with a question. Because these and all other witness stone-walling strategies are troublesome, we devote this chapter to strategies and techniques for controlling the witness.

First, we revisit the concepts, strategies, and techniques that you learned in earlier chapters. They are instrumental in keeping your examination on track. Second, this chapter offers methods to counteract the tactics of witnesses who refuse to answer questions, enabling you to retain control and get the answers you are entitled to.

II. REVISITING THE YOUR-TURN-TO-TESTIFY APPROACH

Reflect back on the concept of cross-examination as your opportunity to tes-tify and tell the persuasive story of your case. If you adopt this approach, you will take control of what the witness says on the stand, gaining concessions that either build and preserve your case theory or demolish the other side.

The strategies and techniques that you learned for constructing the win-ning cross serve also to ensure that the witness does not evade, volunteer non-responsive testimony favorable to the other side, or just talk aimlessly. Your best strategy is to pose questions that the witness must answer as you expect or suffer impeachment because the answer can be proven to be a lie, mistaken, or improb-able. Depositions and documents help you to back this up. For example, if the witness does not give the expected answer, the examiner will produce the wit-ness's deposition and confront the witness with the prior statement containing the expected answer. The witness either answers as you want or is impeached.

You have learned the powerful strategy of crafting the question that is not a question, but rather a short, declarative sentence: "That is your signature." The sentence declares the answer: "Yes, it is my signature." With this technique you can use the witness to tell your story. If compelled to by the judge or out of a desire to vary things, you can style your declarative sentences like questions: "Isn't that right?" "Correct?" "True?" Or, you can raise your tone of voice at the end of the sentence to make it sound like a question.

Leading questions do not open the door for the witness to say just anything in reply, demanding instead the answer that the questioner wants. These short, declarative sentences will allow you to develop a flowing rhythm to your ques-tions, denying the witness the chance to think about questions and come up with evasive or untruthful answers. At the same time, you do not want to go so fast that you lose the judge, jury, or court reporter. To give the appearance of latitude, you can toss in interrogatory questions where the answers will not hurt you.

III. THE TEN COMMANDMENTS

Professor Irving Younger, now deceased, was and still is nationally recognized for his Ten Commandments of cross-examination, teaching them to a generation of lawyers. Irving Younger, author of *Ten Commandments of Cross-Examination,* summarized from *The Art of Cross-Examination* (ABA 1976) (from a speech given by Irving Younger at the ABA Annual Meeting in Montreal, August 1975). These Ten Commandments are still viable and important rules.

Irving Younger's Ten Commandments of Cross-Examination

1. Be brief.
2. Short questions, plain words.
3. Always ask leading questions.
4. Don't ask a question, the answer to which you do not know in advance.
5. Listen to the witness's answers.
6. Don't quarrel with the witness.
7. Don't allow the witness to repeat direct testimony.
8. Don't permit the witness to explain answers.
9. Don't ask the "one question too many."
10. Save the ultimate point of your cross for summation.

Younger's Ten Commandments echo points we made in earlier chapters about controlling even evasive witnesses. Some exceptions to these do exist. For instance, when the witness is lying and the examiner can prove the lie, non-leading questions work just fine. If the question is crafted so that the examiner does not care what the answer is, it is not necessary to know the answer in advance. This is true particularly when common sense dictates the answer: "Doctor, when doing open-heart surgery, the operating room should be sterile?" "Officer, you try to be accurate in writing your reports?" However, Professor Younger's Commandments are presumptive guidelines and counsel should only vary from them for good reason.

IV. COUNSEL'S CHARACTER AND CONDUCT

Preliminarily, it is important to revisit the subject of counsel's character and trial conduct as discussed in Chapter 8. What is the best, most effective way to control a witness and not offend the jury in the process? It is important to realize that the jury's natural sympathy is with the witness, not the lawyer. Never get out in front of the jury in cross-examining a witness. Only go after witnesses who deserve it. Never let the jury know that you are irritated with an evasive witness until they are too. Never resort to a retaliatory measure for witness control until you are confident that the jury will not resent it.

Courtroom command and witness control requires that you be resolute. The witness must be compelled either to give you the concession or be discredited. Stay with it until the job is done. You must actively listen to the witness's answers in order to counteract evasions effectively. Remarkably, many lawyers fail to do this.

V. "OBJECTION, YOUR HONOR: THE ANSWER WAS NONRESPONSIVE"

If the witness is nonresponsive, one countermeasure is to object. The objection to a witness's nonresponsive answer belongs exclusively to counsel who poses the question. You can also move to strike the nonresponsive answer.

If the witness interjects harmful inadmissible evidence in the nonresponsive answer, you must object in order to preserve the issue for appeal and prevent later use by opposing counsel, such as in closing argument. However, just because you can object, doesn't mean that you should. If the testimony is nonresponsive but admissible, you are better off not objecting because opposing counsel can get it in anyway. You will only highlight it by objecting.

Two important considerations will determine your objection strategy. First, will the jurors react favorably? Is it apparent to them that the witness is dodging your question? Do they want you to cut the witness off? Second, is the judge fed up enough to sustain the objection? Ordinarily, the judge is more likely to side with the witness and rule against you. You don't want both the nonresponsive answer of the witness and the judge's adverse ruling allowing it. Therefore, lean toward resorting to the non-judicial countermeasures discussed in the next two sections and avoid going to the judge. However, if you are confident that the judge will sustain your objection and strike the answer, this countermeasure can help you manage the witness.

VI. WITNESS TACTICS AND COUNTERMEASURES

Never underestimate the capacity of some jurors to be taken in by witness's tactics designed to hide or evade concessions to the truth. Jurors may buy into a witness's tactic because they are stupid, gullible, inattentive, or unwilling to exert the mental effort to penetrate the veneer of plausibility. The cross-examiner must educate the stupid, wise up the gullible, wake up the inattentive, and work for the lazy. Also, jurors may fall for the witness's tactic because they perceive the questioner as being unfair. As we stressed earlier, never appear unfair, and the best way to keep from appearing unfair is to always bend over backward to be fair.

Besides adhering to the your-turn-to-testify methodology, strategies, and techniques, you will need specific countermeasures to rein in the out-of-control witness. Some of these are confrontational, and, thus, they may offend jurors if not done properly and at the right time.

Common evasive tactics that witnesses resort to include singly or in combination:

1. Denial;
2. Diversion; and/or
3. Disguise.

A. Denial

Denial can throw the inexperienced cross-examiner into a panic. The witness is supposed to say "yes." The questioner expects a "yes." When the "no" comes instead, then what? Keep calm. No matter what form the denial takes, stand your ground when seeking a concession that the witness must make.

Denial comes in three types:

1. Complete;
2. Virtual; and
3. Selective.

Complete Denial

Witness Tactic

Some witnesses would not admit eating a cat even if the tail was hanging out of their mouth. They steadfastly deny even the most obvious facts. You have anticipated this in your planning by asking yourself, "What must this witness concede or have the answer seen as a lie, mistaken, or preposterous?" Denial of a well-formed question with evidentiary support discredits the witness.

Countermeasure

A complete denial is the easiest tactic to counter because it does not get the witness off the hook at all. The witness just thinks it does. The witness's ego is swollen, in need of first aid. For swelling and inflammation, first aid manuals tell us to apply RICE: Rest, Ice, Compression, and Elevation. In the field of cross-examination, the RICE acronym means something else:

R — Make the witness *Regret* the denial.
I — *Impeach* the witness with a prior inconsistent statement.
C — *Contradict* the witness with other witnesses.
E — *Expose* the implausibility of the denial.

For example, in the *O. J. Simpson* trial, F. Lee Bailey's cross-examination, set out on page 167, so effectively RICEd Mark Fuhrman on his denial of racial epithets that he wound up convicted of perjury.

Look for factual concessions that a witness must make in those that can be proven by other witnesses, the witness's prior statements, or just plain common sense. Testimonial conflict with these sources can reveal that the witness was not truthful. Impeachment by prior inconsistent statement is the most immediate. Contradiction with other witnesses inevitably means some delay, but you can tell the jury in your questions that someone is waiting in the wings to contradict the denial. Implausibility of an answer can be self-evident or the result of the groundwork you lay. Either way, there is a rather immediate payback for the denial.

When the denial is exposed as false, go only far enough to make sure the jury realizes that the witness is a liar, mistaken, or ludicrous. Do not go overboard and try to turn the witness into a total idiot. The first way, the witness loses credibility. The second way, cross-examiner loses credibility. Exposing the witness's lack of candor is the only goal that matters. Leave the rest.

Most witnesses will not be so foolish as to completely deny the obvious, using instead the more subtle virtual or selective methods.

Virtual Denial and Selective Denial
Witness Tactic — Virtual Denial

A virtual denial is merely a clever evasion. If a child cuts a tree down with a saw and his mother asks him, "Did you chop down that tree?" he can truthfully say "No." His mom has asked a bad question, which gives him an easy way to deny it.

Witness Tactic — Selective Denial

Selective denial is like virtual denial except the witness picks out a portion of the question to deny, ignoring the rest.

Q. Did you chop down the tree?
A. I didn't chop.

Logicians call selective denial a negative pregnant. Denying part of a question tacitly admits the rest of the question. Selective denial usually is the result of poorly worded questions.

Countermeasure

A cross-examiner facilitates selective and virtual denial by trying to cover too much ground with a single question. The more information packed into a question, the more opportunity to deny it by disagreeing with some part of it. Deny the witness an opening to exploit this form of evasion by taking baby steps. Make your questions short, simple sentences. Leave out adverbs and adjectives. Many lawyers have difficulty with this, drawn to long-winded, complex questions. When you realize that the witness is resorting to selective or virtual denial, rethink the question. Eliminate the deniable, and feed the undeniable back to the witness.

> *Q.* You ran down the hall after the victim with a knife in your hand?
> *A.* I didn't run.
> *Q.* You followed the victim down the hall?
> *A.* Yes.
> *Q.* With a knife?
> *A.* Yes.
> *Q.* In your hand?
> *A.* Yes.
> *Q.* You followed the victim down the hall with a knife in your hand?
> *A.* Yes.

Honest witnesses utilize selective denials to combat unfair or imprecise questions. Unfair questions are either by intent or accident. Naturally, you do not want to ask intentionally unfair questions, so take corrective action when you do. A good rule of thumb in assessing the denial of a witness: honest witnesses will grant the concession while denying the bad fact. For instance,

> *Q.* Did you cut down the tree with an ax?
> *A.* I cut down the tree, but not with an ax.

B. Diversion

A stage magician diverts the audience's attention while slipping a card up his sleeve. A witness can do the same thing to hide a bad answer by distracting the jury's attention with a diversion. There are three basic types of diversions:

1. Deflection;
2. Avoidance; and
3. Counterattack.

Deflection

Witness Tactic

Sometimes the witness can escape having to make an admission by simply deflecting the question. He can redefine the question and answer one that he wished the cross-examiner had asked. Or, he can springboard off the question into a nonresponsive monologue.

> *Q.* Mr. Rosewald, did you have sexual relations with Betsy Monroe?
> *A.* That allegation was made as out of spite and jealousy.

Countermeasure

Deflection tries to divert the cross-examiner's attention from the target. A clear-headed focus on your objective will help you to resist this tactic.

A. That allegation was made as out of spite and jealousy.

Q. But the question remains, sir, did you do it?

Avoidance

Witness Tactic

In its purest form, avoidance is a nonresponsive answer. The cross-examiner asks the witness what time it is, and gets a weather report. The witness usually provides an answer that only appears responsive, but really is not.

Q. You armed yourself before going to meet the victim?

A. He was a bad man. I knew I was going to have trouble with him and anyone would have been frightened of him.

Countermeasure

The witness refuses to make the admission, but instead gives a seemingly responsive, self-serving answer. Continued pursuit of the concession is the best response.

Q. You armed yourself before going to meet the victim?

A. He was a bad man. I knew I was going to have trouble with him and anyone would have been frightened of him.

Q. So you armed yourself before going to meet the victim?

Counterattack

Witness Tactic

The witness does not like what the cross-examiner is driving at and responds with an attack on the examiner's case theory, another witness, or counsel personally.

Q. You couldn't say your ABCs in the field sobriety test?

A. You wouldn't have been able to say them either, with an officer yelling at you like a jackbooted storm trooper!

Countermeasure

When the witness counterattacks, the cross-examiner should avoid the bait. Isolate the concession and make the witness admit it.

Q. You couldn't say your ABCs in the field sobriety test?

A. You wouldn't have been able to say them either, with an officer yelling at you like a jackbooted storm trooper!

Q. Nevertheless, you couldn't say your ABCs?

Irving Younger's Sixth Commandment of cross-examination says, "Don't quarrel with the witness." Sometimes this is hard, especially when the witness makes personal insults. Avoid trading one-liners with the witness, which will only make you look unprofessional. If the witness answers your question with a question, it is not only bad manners, but also means you are scoring points.

A good method for dealing with a question from a witness is to politely point out that it is the lawyer's job to ask the questions and the witness's to answer them. Then repeat the question.

Q. Mr. Best, do you understand that it is your duty as a witness to answer questions, not ask them?

Q. And do you further understand that as a lawyer, it is my duty to ask questions, and not answer them?

Q. Now, can you answer my question?

This series of questions is often effective in reestablishing control over a witness. Another approach is to not rise to the bait—the witness's question. Ignore the question and repeat your question.

C. Disguise

The disguise tactic seeks to hide an implicit or explicit admission in a forest of words. Strip the camouflage of verbosity off and expose the admission. If the witness uses disguise to try and mask a denial or make it seem more plausible, expose it. Disguise comes in three varieties:

1. Explanation;
2. Qualification; and
3. Obfuscation.

Explanation
Witness Tactic
The explanation not only camouflages the admission by the witness but also tries to soften it in some way.

Q. Did you point the gun at the victim?

A. I was holding the gun and got just a little queasy, and as I raised my hand to my forehead, the gun got pointed at the victim.

Countermeasure
The countermeasure strips away the explanation and isolates the admission for the jury.

Q. Did you point the gun at the victim?

A. I was holding the gun and got just a little queasy, and as I raised my hand to my forehead, the gun got pointed at the victim.

Q. Your answer is yes—you pointed the gun at the victim?

If you attempt to cut off the explanation, the witness may retort, "Can I explain?" Meet that response by telling the witness that opposing counsel can ask for the explanation when you are through. Some questions, however, demand an explanation.

Q. Have you stopped beating your wife?
A. No, I never started.

If the cross-examiner badgers a witness who has offered an honest explanation to an unfair or complex question, that will reflect poorly on the questioner. If the question is ill-phrased and the answer is honest, the explanatory answer should be accepted.

Qualification
Witness Tactic
A qualification response by the witness seeks to redefine either the question or the answer in more congenial terms.

Q. Did you mislead the plaintiff's attorney?
A. Although my answers were legally accurate, they were misleading.

When a witness seeks to qualify a yes-or-no answer, the absolute worst way to try to control him is by cutting him off with another question. First, it is rude. Second, you show fear of his potential answer. Third, you can come across as heavy-handed. Fourth, you can erode your credibility with the jury, especially when—as sometimes happens—the judge sides with the witness.

Before taking any remedial action, you must quickly analyze the problem. Is the witness qualifying because your question is poorly worded? Is it because the witness is naturally talkative? Is it because the witness is being evasive? Your remedial action will be different depending on how you analyze the witness's motive for qualifying.

Countermeasure
If counsel concludes the witness is being evasive, just as with the explanatory response, the cross-examiner's countermeasure is to remove the qualification and isolate the concession for the jury.

Q. Did you mislead the plaintiff's attorney?
A. Although my answers were legally accurate, they were misleading.
Q. So you did mislead the plaintiff's attorney?

Alternatively, if the question calls for a qualified response, the full response should be left untouched. Having concluded you are not dealing with an evasive witness, you need not take aggressive measures to control the witness. Rather, you can shorten the questions. Short questions demand short answers.

Q. Did you point the gun at the victim?
A. Yes, I was holding the gun and raised my hand to my forehead.
Q. So you pointed the gun at the victim?

Obfuscation

Witness Tactic

When the cross-examiner asks for a sip of information, the obfuscating witness turns on a fire hose of data. The witness hopes the avalanche of words will mask the harmful concession.

> Q. You drank two six packs of beer, didn't you?
> A. It had been a hard day, I stopped off at the bar and there were a lot of my friends there, so I drank two six packs, shot some pool, and then I felt much better, and ramble, ramble, ramble . . .

Countermeasure

To counteract the obfuscation, peel away the excess information in your next question.

> Q. You drank two six packs of beer, didn't you?
> A. It had been a hard day, I stopped off at the bar and there were a lot of my friends there, so I drank two six packs, shot some pool, and then I felt much better, and ramble, ramble, ramble. . .
> Q. So you had two six packs of beer?

This question will likely unleash another torrent of words, to which you reply:

> Q. So you had two six packs of beer?

Keep doing this until the witness either answers or winds up looking like a prevaricator. You also can shorten the question each succeeding time. Short questions demand short answers. The shorter the question and the longer the answer, the lesser the credibility of the witness.

> Q. So you had two six packs of beer?
> A. Ramble, ramble, ramble . . .
> Q. You had two six packs?
> A. Ramble, ramble, ramble . . .
> Q. Two six packs?
> A. Ramble, ramble, ramble . . .
> Q. Two?

VII. REPERTOIRE OF CONTROL TECHNIQUES

Now that we have explored evasive tactics by witnesses and responsive countermeasures, we want to offer you a repertoire of six basic control techniques to use. Some of these are reiterations of countermeasures we have discussed. These techniques are listed in increasing confrontational tone, matched to escalating levels of evasiveness by the witness. Bear in mind that once the jury catches on that the witness is dodging a question, the evasion itself will damage the witness's credibility. These techniques help to make the witness's tactics apparent to the jury.

Before discussing the six techniques, we first consider the tactical maneuver designed to get the witness to agree to answer your questions with "yes" or "no" when the question calls for it.

> Q. Dr. Best, I'm going to try to make my questions simple. Most all of them will be able to be answered "yes" or "no." In this way we can save all of us some time. When I'm through, Ms. Erickson's lawyer will be able to ask you questions so that you can elaborate or explain your answers to my questions. Can we agree that you will answer my questions with a "yes" or "no" if that is what the question calls for?

While this approach may prove effective in producing only "yes" or "no" answers, it may also be counterproductive. Inevitably, after the witness has sworn that he will answer only "yes" or "no," the cross-examiner tries to take unfair advantage in some obvious way:

> Q. Has your drug rehabilitation helped you with your problems of kleptomania?

The jury is likely to see this tactic exactly for what it is—an attempt to force the witness to say what the attorney wants him to say regardless of the truth. You stand a much better chance of succeeding with getting yes-or-no answers by asking short, simple questions. No preliminaries, no bogus yes-or-no contracts, just simple questions. This way, you will not look like you are trying to hide something. Witness evasion is obvious when a self-serving monologue is delivered in response to a short question. If somebody's got to look like they are trying to conceal something, let it be the witness.

Technique #1—Repeat the Question

> Q. Dr. Best, did you speak with Dr. Donhow before you reached your opinion in this case?
>
> A. Ramble, ramble, ramble . . .
>
> Q. Now let's try that again. Did you speak with Dr. Donhow before you reached your opinion in this case? [Note: If the witness continues to ramble and evade your question, it should now be clear to the jury.]

Technique #2—More Confrontational Repetition of the Question

> Q. Can you repeat the question that I asked you, Dr. Best?
>
> Q. Are you ready to answer the question now?
>
> Q. Dr. Best, is there something preventing you from answering the question?

Technique #3—Let the Witness Ramble

While this technique is rarely resorted to, it is great fun. If the witness is determined to ramble on, go over, sit down, and look out the window or at the clock on the wall. When finally the witness has finished, rise and ask, "Are you finished?" If the answer is, "Yes," then ask the question again. The point is made that this witness will do anything to avoid answering the question. The cross-examination of the grave robber's mother on pages 159-161 gives a good example of this technique. As the mother enumerated an impossible number of items allegedly stolen from her, the prosecutor heightened the implausibility of her testimony by repeatedly asking the open-ended question, "Anything else?"

Technique #4—Write the Question

It is also quite effective to write out your question, displaying it on a document camera, flip chart, or board. Then, pointing to the question, say, "Dr. Best, could you answer this question (reading the question slowly), "Did you speak with Dr. Donhow before you reached your opinion in this case?" Then, if you get the desired answer, write "No" in bold letters after the question, and thank Dr. Best for her answer. A variation on this is to write the question that the witness answered instead of the one you asked, and say, "This is the question you answered, correct? What is the answer to the one I asked you?"

Technique #5—Get Physical

You can control the runaway witness by resorting to the physical gesture of raising your hand toward the witness, palm forward, in the universally recognized signal to stop. It usually works.

Technique #6—Go to the Judge

We are most reluctant ever to ask the judge for help with an evasive witness. Nothing is more pitiful than a trial lawyer asking the judge to make the witness answer the question unless it is a lawyer who just had a plea for help brushed off by the judge: "Ask your next question, counsel." There are two exceptions, which we discussed earlier, where asking the judge for help makes sense. First is when you are seeking to preserve a point for appeal and preventing the introduction of harmful information. In this case, make the proper objection. Second is when you are thoroughly convinced that the judge is disgusted with the witness's behavior and wants to pull the trigger.

Cross-Examination

Repertoire of Control Techniques

- Technique #1—Repeat the Question
- Technique #2—More Confrontational Repetition of the Question
- Technique #3—Let the Witness Ramble
- Technique #4—Write the Question
- Technique #5—Get Physical
- Technique #6—Go to the Judge

CHECKLIST: CONTROL STRATEGIES & TECHNIQUES

Your-Turn-to-Testify Strategy Revisited

☐ Cross is your turn to testify. To accomplish this you must take control of the unruly witness with the following techniques:
- Not repeating the direct examination;
- Determining the content of the cross;
- Posing questions that the witness must answer as expected or be impeached;
- Framing questions in leading short declarative sentences;
- Deciding the pace of the examination; and
- Most of all telling the story the examiner wants told.

Counsel's Character and Conduct

☐ Control the witness but do not alienate the jury in the process. You must be perceived as the sincere, courteous seeker of truth.

☐ Character traits and courtroom conduct covered in Chapter 9 are vital to controlling the witness without losing the jury.

Nonresponsive Objection

☐ One countermeasure when the witness is not answering the question is to object that the answer was nonresponsive and move to strike it.

☐ This objection should be reserved for the situation where the answer is harmful, inadmissible, and nonresponsive.

☐ Other considerations include whether the examiner is convinced that the objection is likely to be sustained and whether the jurors will be alienated by the objection.

Witness Tactics and Countermeasures

☐ Denial:
- Complete denial:
  - Countermeasure:
    R—Make the witness Regret the denial.
    I—Impeach the witness with a prior inconsistent statement.
    C—Contradict the witness with other witnesses.
    E—Expose the implausibility of the denial.
- Virtual Denial and Selective Denial:
  - Countermeasure: Short, leading, declarative questions.

☐ Diversion:
- Deflection:
  - Countermeasure: Persistence.
- Avoidance:
  - Countermeasure: Persistence.
- Counterattack:
  - Countermeasure: Persistence.

☐ Disguise:
- Explanation:
  - Countermeasure: Strip away the explanation and isolate the concession.

- Qualification:
  - Countermeasure: Remove the qualification and isolate the admission.
- Obfuscation:
  - Countermeasure: Ignore the excess information and repeat the question.

Repertoire of Control Techniques

- ❏ Technique # 1 — Repeat the question;
- ❏ Technique # 2 — Use a more confrontational repetition of the question;
- ❏ Technique # 3 — Let the witness ramble;
- ❏ Technique # 4 — Write the question;
- ❏ Technique # 5 — Get physical; or
- ❏ Technique # 6 — Go to the judge.

CHAPTER 11

PREPARING THE WINNING CROSS

"I don't know that there are any shortcuts to doing a good job."
— **Justice Sandra Day O'Connor**

"A deposition is one of the greatest weapons a trial lawyer has during cross-examination."

— **D. Shane Read**, Winning at Deposition 20
(2013 Westway Publishing)

I. PREPARING THE WINNING CROSS

We have emphasized the importance of careful preparation for cross-examination throughout this book because it is the key to performing a winning cross. Thomas Edison was right; genius is far more a matter of perspiration than inspiration. So far you have learned these elements of preparation for cross: identifying and selecting content; drafting cross notes in topical units; crafting a persuasive story for the jury; and mentally preparing to perform the cross.

This chapter examines pretrial preparation for the cross-examination of any witness — lay or expert. Here, we explore preparation in six parts.

Part one reinforces earlier material.

Part two examines informal case development steps including investigation and witness interviews.

Part three covers formal discovery tools — interrogatories, requests for production, and requests for admissions — and the importance of obtaining full discovery including information in the social media.

Part four discusses the interplay between the deposition and cross-examination.

Part five discusses how to prepare witnesses' prior statements for trial.

Part six opens the discussion of cross-examining expert witnesses. We begin with the evidentiary requirements of expert testimony, such as qualifications and reliability of the expert's field, factual basis, and opinions. Then we will offer guidance on the preparation necessary to effectively cross-examine an expert, showing how this was done in the cross-examination of an economic expert in the *Educator Collision* personal injury case. In Chapter 12, Expert Witnesses, the *Educator Collision* case is further utilized to illustrate how to conduct cross of an expert in trial.

II. PREPARING TO CROSS-EXAMINE ANY WITNESS

A. Recapitulation

The capsule summary below on cross-examination preparation reinforces the lessons of earlier chapters.

Recapitulation of Preparation Steps

To prepare the winning cross, counsel should:

- Develop a case theory, which has a legal and factual component, blended into a persuasive story;
- Analyze the other side's case theory;
- Determine what the purpose(s) of the cross of the witness will be—to build, preserve, or demolish;
- Identify and select concessions that the witness must make by:
  - Asking what the witness must concede or be impeached;
  - Envisioning summation and what concessions will support your case theory or undermine the other side's case theory or the witness;
- Brainstorm to identify and select impeachment material;
- Use cross notes organized into topical units;
- Organize each topical unit so it has a beginning, middle, and end;
- Construct a persuasive cross by:
  - Telling a story with short, declarative sentences and powerful words;
  - Arranging the topical units into a story with a beginning, middle, and end, like the scenes of a movie;
  - Start strong;
  - Finish with a strong, unassailable line of cross; and
  - Edit to keep it interesting.
- Utilize performance elements such as:
  - Sincere, truth-seeking;
  - Maintaining a manner appropriate to the situation and witness;
  - Highlighting important testimony;
  - Avoiding or meeting objections;
  - Visuals;
  - Listening to the witness; and
  - Playing to the various audiences.

B. Additional Steps to Prepare

Your trial preparation must be in synch with the rest of your case. The new steps introduced in this chapter are as follows:

> ### Additional Preparation Steps for Any Witness
>
> 1. Utilize all informal case development tools including full investigation and witness interviews;
> 2. Obtain full formal discovery through discovery devises including interrogatories, requests for production, requests for admissions, and Freedom of Information Act;
> 3. Take the witness's deposition to gain and make a record of concessions and impeachment evidence and to assess the witness; and
> 4. Prepare witness prior statements for trial.

III. COMPLETE INFORMAL CASE DEVELOPMENT

A. Investigation

Investigator

Preparation for cross ordinarily calls for investigation into the backgrounds of all potential witnesses, their testimony, and how the witness relates to the facts of the case. In criminal cases, investigations are conducted by law enforcement agencies—state and local police agencies, or their federal counterparts, such as the Federal Bureau of Investigation. The prosecutor may serve as an advisor or in some instances lead the investigation. Some prosecutors' offices have their own in-house investigators. Hired or in-house investigators perform investigations for defendants in criminal cases.

For civil cases, no set pattern exists. The investigation could be assigned to a hired or in-house investigator or a paralegal or an attorney. However, it always is a concern when lawyers do their own investigation, as this raises the possibility that the lawyer may have to become a witness. For this reason, many civil lawyers prefer to delegate investigations to others. In certain limited circumstances, this may also include the client. However, this ordinarily will be sparing, because when clients do investigation work they are exposed to potential cross-examination and impeachment risks.

The Internet has become an important low-cost or free investigative tool. Here are just a few of the things you can do with it:

> ### Case Investigation Websites
>
> #### For Locating People and Doing Background Investigations
>
> - Telephone directory—www.yellowpages.com and 411—www.411.com
> - Background investigations—www.pipl.com and www.123people.com
> - Social network search of MySpace, LinkedIn, Facebook, and others—www.yoname.com

- Public cyber sleuthing of public records, corporate licenses, criminal record, vital statistics, real and personal property records, and more — www.kcll.org
- Westlaw
- LexisNexis

Investigative Tasks

A short list of investigative tasks critical to preparing for cross-examination includes:

- Do witness interviews—see Step 3 at pages 234-235;
- Obtain all witness statements—see Step 4 at pages 244-245;
- Get impeachment evidence —see Step 5 at page 242;
- Visit the scene of the occurrence; and
- Conduct an Internet search for each witness.

Impeachment Evidence

The investigation and formal discovery can be planned to uncover impeachment evidence that applies to both lay and expert witnesses. Eight areas of impeachment evidence that you are seeking in both the investigation and discovery, along with illustrations, are:

1. *Lack of Personal Knowledge:* This evidence proves that the witness could not have known what he claims to know. In preparing to cross-examine Charles Allen in the murder trial of his client William "Duff" Armstrong, Abraham Lincoln checked the *Farmers' Almanac.* He learned that at the time of night that the witness claimed to have seen the killing by the light of the moon high overhead, the moon was on the horizon below the treeline. See pages 120-121 for more on Lincoln's cross.

2. *Mental and Sensory Deficiencies*: Does any evidence exist that the witness's mental or sensory capacities were deficient? For instance, does your investigation show the witness was drunk or on drugs at the time of the event?

3. *Bias and Interest*: Does the witness have any bias or interest in the case? Pretrial preparation should delve into personal and business relationships that may influence the witness to testify falsely. For example, defense counsel's pretrial investigation may determine that the prosecution's witness is a member of a gang to which the victim belonged.

4. *Improbability*: Is any of the witness's story improbable? Can you commit the witness to an improbable position when taking the witness's deposition? Clarence Darrow in cross-examining William Jennings Bryan extended Bryan's beliefs to an absurd conclusion. See pages 137-138.

5. *Prior Inconsistent Statements*: Did the witness make any prior statements pertinent to the case? If not, what pretrial statements can you generate through taking the witness's deposition? See Step 3 at pages 234-235.

6. *Contradiction*: Does any evidence exist to contradict the witness to be cross-examined? Pretrial preparation involves the search for witnesses and other evidence that will contradict the account of witnesses to be cross-examined.

7. *Prior Conviction*: Has the witness ever been convicted of a crime admissible for impeachment? Defense counsel in a criminal case requests disclosure from the prosecutor of both the defendant's prior convictions and those of the government's witnesses. The prior conviction may be admissible under Fed. R. Evid. 609 or the state's evidence rule.

8. *Specific Instances of Untruthfulness*: Has the witness ever committed specific acts that are probative of untruthfulness, other than a conviction of a crime? For instance, the pretrial investigation could uncover evidence that the witness lied on an income tax return. This prior misconduct may be admissible under Fed. R. Evid. 608(b) or a similar state rule.

B. Interview the Witnesses

Civil versus Criminal

In a civil case, you likely will depose most if not all witnesses whom you will cross-examine at trial. If the witness is a party, you will also have received their responses, interrogatories, and requests for production and admissions. This normally will give you some good information for cross-examination.

With the limited discovery in criminal cases, pretrial witness interviews are your single best source of information. Law enforcement normally conducts the government's initial witness interviews. Once a prosecutor learns of any defense witness who has not been interviewed, a law enforcement investigator should be directed to conduct an interview. Alternatively, the prosecutor can do this. Of course, the defendant is off limits after any exercise of the constitutional rights to silence or counsel. Through formal discovery, defense counsel will normally learn the identity of the government's witnesses and their statements.

A Prover

If the prosecutor or defense counsel conducts the interview of a potential adverse witness, it is critical that a prover be present. A prover is a credible witness who can testify at trial to what the witness said during the interview. Without a prover, counsel will be in an untenable position at trial if the witness changes stories. ABA Model Rule of Professional Conduct 3.7, "Lawyer as Witness," which has a counterpart in most states, provides that "[a] lawyer shall not act as advocate at a trial in which the lawyer is likely to be a necessary witness" except on uncontested issues, when the testimony relates to legal services, or when a disqualification of the lawyer would work a "substantial hardship on the client." By having a prover present, a lawyer interviewer avoids the risk of becoming a witness over a prior inconsistent statement. Ideally, the prover should have some method of recording the interview. Convincing proof of witness's interview statements also is important, memorialized either through video or audio recording or a written statement.

Interview Refuser

If the witness refuses to speak with you, make sure that you can prove the refusal. This can come after either you or your investigator makes in-person contact with the witness. You may decide to contact the person by mail. If so, do use certified mail with a return receipt. The letter should be courteous and invite the witness to meet at a time and place convenient for him or her. At pages 301-304 we explore strategies and skills for laying the foundation for impeaching a witness who refuses to speak with you prior to trial.

IV. FULL FORMAL DISCOVERY

The success of your cross-examination is to a great degree dependent on how well you plan and execute discovery. The more you know, the more effective your cross-examination can be. Take advantage of all available formal discovery devices, such as interrogatories, requests for production, and requests for admissions to gain as much information as possible about the case, particularly the adverse witnesses and their potential testimony. What you can obtain through discovery will vary depending on whether you are in a federal, state, county, or city court and on whether your case is civil or criminal.

A. Civil Case Discovery

Federal Rules of Civil Procedure, or their state rule counterparts, provide counsel with the full panoply of formal discovery devices:

- *Initial Disclosure:* Under Fed. R. Civ. P. 26, a party must provide initial discovery prior to a discovery request from the opposing party. Rule 26 covers: witnesses "likely to have discoverable information" supporting claims or defenses along with contact information; copy or description by category and location of documents, electronically stored information, and tangible things supporting claims or defenses; computation of damages; insurance agreements that may cover a judgment in full or in part; and the names of any expert witnesses who may be called to testify at trial and their reports.
- *Deposition:* A party may depose both party and non-party witnesses. A deposition is the best discovery device for learning details, gaining concessions, locking witnesses into a position, evaluating witnesses, and preserving testimony. Fed. R. Civ. P. 27-32. In Chapter 14 we explore how to depose a witness so the deposition will be a valuable tool for cross-examination and how to apply cross techniques during a deposition.

- *Interrogatories:* While interrogatories are a good way to gain fundamental information, such as names of witnesses and their contact information, they are not the best for getting helpful facts or details. A deposition is far better for this purpose. Fed. R. Civ. P. 33.
- *Requests for Production:* Requests for production are used to get the other side to produce documents, electronically stored information, and tangible items, and to gain entry onto land to inspect. Fed. R. Civ. P. 34.
- *Physical and Mental Exams:* A party may move for the court to order a party to have a physical or mental examination when the party's physical or mental condition is in controversy. Fed. R. Civ. P. 35.
- *Requests for Admissions:* Requests for admissions are used to compel a party to admit or deny "facts, the application of law to fact, or opinions about either; and the genuineness of any described documents." If admitted, the matter is conclusively proved. Fed. R. Civ. P. 36.
- *Subpoena Duces Tecum:* A subpoena duces tecum to a deposition commands the deponent to produce such things as documents, electronically stored information, or other tangible objects. Fed. R. Civ. P. 45.

Despite the philosophy of modern discovery in favor of full disclosure, expect to fight to get any valuable information, keeping a close eye on the responses provided. If necessary, counsel should move to compel compliance.

B. Criminal Case Discovery

In criminal cases, counsel does not have as many discovery tools as in civil cases. Interrogatories, requests for production, and requests for admissions are only authorized for civil cases. A few states permit depositions in criminal cases, including Florida, Indiana, Connecticut, New Hampshire, and Missouri. In other states depositions in criminal cases are ordinarily only allowed to preserve testimony. Of course, the defendant, who has a Fifth Amendment right against self-incrimination, cannot be deposed.

Federal Rule of Criminal Procedure 16 or the corresponding state rule or statute on discovery dictates formal discovery in criminal cases and lists what the prosecution and the defense must exchange. Fed. R. Cr. P. 16 mandates that the government must turn over to the defense: the defendant's oral, written, and recorded statements; the defendant's prior criminal record; evidentiary items for inspection that the government intends to offer in the case in chief and those "material to preparing the defense"; and inspection and copying of reports and tests. Under the U.S. Constitution, the government is required to provide the defense with material exculpatory evidence bearing on guilt or punishment regardless of whether the defense has specifically requested such evidence.

While the government does not have the discovery devices for civil cases that it has in criminal cases, it can obtain information through its powers of search and seizure, arrest, police interrogation, and grand jury investigation. Fed. R. Cr. P. 16 and counterpart state rules or statutes require the defense to provide the prosecution with some formal discovery. For instance, under Federal Rule 16(b)(1), if the defense has requested and received disclosures of evidentiary items that the government intends to offer at trial, the defense is required to make similar disclosures. However, the Fifth Amendment prevents the government from obtaining much information from the defense, except for notice of insanity and alibi defenses. The prosecution can obtain non-testimonial evidence from the defendant, such as a blood sample, fingerprints, and having him or her stand in a lineup because it is not governed by the Fifth Amendment.

C. Freedom of Information Act

Under the Freedom of Information Act (FOIA), 5 U.S.C. § 552, a requestor can obtain reasonably described records from a federal agency if involved in civil or criminal litigation, or even when not. FOIA is a disclosure device intended to open federal agency actions to public scrutiny by enabling public access to such information. FOIA allows access to any federal agency records. In 1996, the law was amended to include records in electronic format, placing more information online and creating electronic reading rooms. Almost any person can make a request for the records. Under § 552(b), nine discretionary exemptions to FOIA are listed: those exempted by Executive Order; matters "related solely to the internal personnel rules and practices of any agency"; trade secrets; and "personnel and medical files and similar files the disclosure of which would constitute a clearly unwarranted invasion of personal privacy."

States have enacted laws similar to FOIA that can be used to obtain disclosure from state and local agencies. FOIA requests can be made in both civil and criminal actions, as well as in states with very restrictive discovery rules.

V. SOCIAL MEDIA AND E-MAIL

A. Vast Storehouses of Unguarded Communication

Facebook. Twitter. Instagram. Blogs. E-mails. Online social networking is generating more and more information. Since 2005 social media usage has risen 800 percent. Steve Olenski, "Social Media Usage Up 800% for U.S. Online Adults in Just 8 Years," Forbes.com (Sept. 6, 2013).

Conceivably because of the easy, informal, and personal nature of online communication, people often post unguarded information on the Internet or put it in their e-mails. This candid communication can be damaging to the person's position in a lawsuit. For instance, in *McMillen v. Hummingbird Speedway, Inc.*, 2010 WL 4403285 (Pa. Ct. Com. Pl. Sept. 9, 2010), plaintiff sued to recover damages for injuries he allegedly got when the defendant rear-ended him in a cool-down lap of a stock car race. Plaintiff alleged substantial injuries, including possible permanent impairment; loss and impairment of general health, strength, and vitality; and inability to enjoy certain pleasures of life. Nevertheless, plaintiff posted comments on the public portion of his Facebook account about his fishing trip and his attendance at the Daytona 500 race in Florida.

Social media can provide powerful evidence for concession-seeking cross-examination explained at page 239 and the contradiction technique discussed at pages 166-167. *Boudwin v. General Ins. Co. of America* is a striking example of the effectiveness of the contradiction technique utilizing social media (2011 WL 4433578, La. App. Ct. 9/14/11 affirmed without published opinion, 90 So. 3d 542 (2011)). At trial, two plaintiffs claimed physical disability and loss of enjoyment of life. The appellate court had no difficulty upholding the jury's decision that plaintiffs were not entitled to any damages because "(the) record clearly shows that neither Jessi nor Lee have experienced any significant limitations or impairments as a result of the injuries they sustained in the May 31, 2008 accident."

Both plaintiffs testified on direct that they were in pain after the accident. On cross, defense counsel cross-examined them with their Facebook pages. The court noted that Jessi conceded when faced with her entries that "she runs, or rather jogs, regularly to stay in shape, and even attempted to do an exercise program called P9OX with a friend, which she described as being 'really tough.' . . ." The court described the cross-examination of Lee in this way: ". . . Lee acknowledged several entries from his Facebook page where he reported frequently 'working out' and also playing sports such as basketball, tennis, 'ultimate Frisbee,' and softball, sometimes engaging in multiple sessions of sporting activities in a single day. He further acknowledged that he wrote on his Facebook page that he had participated in a softball tournament in the month before trial . . . ."

In *Embry v. State*, 923 N.E.2d 1 (Ind. App. 3/8/10), the defendant was convicted of felony domestic battery for beating his ex-wife, and the court affirmed the conviction. The defense, in an effort to establish self-defense, cross-examined the ex-wife about statements about the defendant she had posted on MySpace prior to the alleged battery:

> BY [DEFENSE]: *Q.* . . . Prior to Au—April 22nd, 2008 had you ever expressed or communicated in any way that you wanted your ex to die a slow painful death?
>
> *A.* I believe you're referring to my "My Space" . . .
>
> *Q.* I'm not—I—no, I'm not referring to anything. I'm just asking you a simple question: if you'd ever expressed or communicated in any way that you wanted your ex-husband, Mr. Embry, to die a slow painful death?
>
> *A.* I see it right there on your desk.
>
> *Q.* Okay.
>
> *A.* It's my "My Space" blog.
>
> *Q.* Okay, did you say it?
>
> *A.* I typed it.
>
> *Q.* Okay. But the answer is, did you say it? I mean is that your communication.

A. I typed it.

Q. Okay. And did you ever express um, or communicate in any way that you wanted to be present and dance the cha-cha around his slow painful death?

A. It's all there in the blog.

Q. Okay. The answer's a simple yes or no. You said it; you've communicated it some way, did you?

A. If you want to put that blog there, I . . .

Q. I'm just asking you a simple question.

BY COURT: Ma'am, will ya just answer the question yes or no?

A. Yes, I did. . .

B. Obtaining Social Media Information and E-mails

A Google search may be all you need to obtain the witness's social media page because it is open to the public. Alternatively, the user may have a privacy setting that only allows certain "friends" to access the website page. If that is the situation in a civil case, you can make a discovery request for production of the information to the social media user, and you can make a motion to compel if the user does not comply. While the courts frown upon discovery "fishing expeditions," a limited discovery request can produce results. Pamela W. Carter & Shelley K. Napolitano, "Social Media: An Effective Evidentiary Tool," *Louisiana Bar Journal* Vol. 61, No. 5, Feb./Mar. 2014. For example, when the defendant corporation in a discrimination and harassment case made a request for production of plaintiff's Twitter and Facebook accounts between her date of hire through the date of the request, the court held that because of the broad scope of relevancy in the discovery process, the plaintiff's activity on social media sites could lead to relevant information regarding alleged discrimination and harassment. The court noted that the defendant had limited the scope of the discovery request to a relevant time frame. *Kear v. Kohl's Dep't Stores Inc.*, 2013 WL 3088922 at 17 (D. Kan. 2013).

Besides seeking the social media information from the user, you can seek it from the social media site. However, the federal Stored Communications Act, 18 U.S.C. § 2702, prohibits disclosure of electronically stored information without consent of the user. While the social media site commonly will produce fundamental user information in response to a subpoena, it will not reveal webpage posts.

To obtain e-mails in a civil case, you can use the customary discovery tools directed at a party and issue subpoenas to recipients of the e-mails.

You will want to send a preservation letter early in the litigation in an effort to prevent a nefarious party from trying to destroy electronic evidence and as an essential step toward later establishing bad faith, a disregard of the responsibility to preserve relevant evidence, and thus establish a claim of spoliation.

VI. INTERPLAY BETWEEN DEPOSITION AND CROSS

The success of a cross-examination at trial can depend on how you deposed that witness. Your deposition objectives, strategies, and techniques should be trial-driven. If you are preserving testimony of a friendly witness for trial, approach the deposition as you would a direct examination. You prepare and present the witness so that the transcript or video of the deposition fully and clearly presents the witness's testimony. A discovery deposition is more of a mixed picture. In part, you are trying to gather evidence that will either help you in building your case or in figuring out what your opponent will use, so you can meet it. But there is more to it than just this. If you are deposing an adverse witness, which includes an opposing party, a hostile witness, an adverse party, and a witness allied with the other side, you must think ahead to your potential cross-examination of that witness at trial. Plan how you will depose the witness so that the testimony you elicit lays the foundation for your cross-examination in trial. In other words, use ends-means thinking. We begin by exploring how to take a deposition in preparation for cross-examination of any witness, lay or expert. Later in this chapter, we discuss extra steps for taking an expert's deposition in preparation for cross.

A. Witness Assessment

During the deposition you will be able to assess the credibility and communications skills of the deponent, thus gaining an understanding of how the witness will come across on the stand. What you learn about the witness can help you prepare for the cross. Pay particular attention to the witness's demeanor and manner of responding to questions.

The witness may have attributes that will work to your advantage. For instance, the witness may be arrogant or indifferent, which won't endear the witness to the jury. Or the witness may be quick to anger, which at trial your cross may encourage, providing you with evidence to support your argument in closing that the witness was biased. Or, the deponent may display qualities that will cause you to adjust your cross-examination approach to accommodate the witness's need. For example, a sympathetic and sincere witness may call for a gentle and respectful cross.

The witness's appearance and delivery may also give you insight into person's truthfulness. Maybe you will spot the witness fidgeting or displaying a furtive look in the eye. Knowing the witness's mannerisms that indicate deception, you can watch for the same body language during cross-examination, make note of it, and then argue to the jury in closing that the witness's manner while testifying revealed a lack of candor.

Also, during the deposition, you can learn how the witness is likely to answer questions. This knowledge can be important to your preparation for cross. For example, if the witness is evasive, you can prepare your cross-examination with the need to control the witness as a central focus. Your questions will need to be short and clear. You will need to be prepared to use the control techniques that we recommend at pages 223-227.

B. Concessions and Impeachment

Your objectives for cross-examining a witness at trial are what we have gone over in depth in earlier chapters:

- Gain concessions supporting your case narrative and theme;
- Gain concessions that undercut your opponent's case theory; and/or
- Impeach the witness.

Plan how you will take the deposition of an adverse witness with these cross-examination goals in mind. Your objective is to create a deposition record of concessions that build your case theory and theme and/or demolish the other side's. Also, develop a deposition record that contains impeachment information. This cross-examination-focused approach to taking a deposition aims to lock down the witness's concessions and impeachment deposition testimony so that the witness cannot vary from them at trial. The witness must give the same answers at trial or be impeached with the deposition. The following are some techniques for making the record.

Concessions

While the deposition of an adverse witness to gain concessions should resemble a good concession-seeking cross-examination, this does not eliminate other objectives. Typically, your examination also will probe to see what the deponent knows about the matter in controversy. You may begin taking the deposition with one goal in mind and then change, depending on the answers you receive. For instance, you could begin to depose a witness with a discovery objective in mind. If the witness is revealed to be adverse, then you likely will change your approach, attempting to gain concessions and impeach the witness.

Preparing and carrying out a concession-seeking deposition examination is much like preparing for and conducting a cross-examination with the same objective. You force the witness to make concessions that will serve to preserve and build your case theory or damage your opponent's. You want to lock the deponent down and eliminate potential escape routes, applying the control techniques you have learned.

Using the concession-seeking method during the deposition, you win if the deponent concedes the point that you can prove or that makes common sense. You also win if the deponent does not concede. If the witness refuses to concede, you make a deposition record of that answer. Lock the witness into a lie. At trial you can reveal the lie, mistake, or improbable position.

Impeachment Evidence

What impeachment information are you seeking when you take the opposing party's or adverse witness's deposition? The impeachment evidence you seek falls into the categories previously covered (see pages 233-234). You may be able to get the witness to concede the impeachment evidence: "Yes, I have been convicted of perjury." At trial, the witness must either admit the prior conviction for perjury or be impeached with not only the prior conviction but also the prior inconsistent statement in the deposition.

C. Making a Record of Concessions and Impeachment

Eliciting a Clear Answer

Primary techniques for extracting a clear answer from a witness and locking the witness into that answer are the same as the countermeasure techniques we discuss in Chapter 10 for gaining information from an evasive witness during cross-examination (pages 223-227). The following is a summary of the ways in which witnesses evade and effective countermeasures and techniques to deal with the attempted evasion:

WITNESS EVASION METHOD	COUNTERMEASURE
Complete Denial	R—Make the witness Regret the denial.
	I—Impeach the witness with a prior inconsistent statement.
	C—Contradict the witness with other witnesses.
	E—Expose the implausibility of the denial.
Virtual Denial and Selective Denial	Short, leading, declarative questions.
Diversion by Deflection or Avoidance or Counterattack	Persistence.
Disguise by Explanation	Strip away the explanation and isolate the concession.
Disguise by Qualification	Remove the qualification and isolate the admission.
Disguise by Obfuscation	Ignore the excess information and repeat the question.

Also, you can resort to the repertoire of control techniques to get a direct, clear answer on the record, and those include repeating the question in an increasingly aggressive manner until the desired answer is provided (pages 223-227).

Summary of Testimony

A particularly useful technique for locking down deposition testimony for use at trial is to summarize the witness's responses and then ask whether the summary is correct. Your summary will phrase the testimony of the witness as you would like it read to the jury at trial. For example:

> *Q.* Mr. Williams, it's your testimony that you gathered the information, typed it into a report and presented that report to Ms. McFarland all on the same day, July 2nd?
> *A.* Yes.

If Mr. Williams were to testify differently at trial, saying that he wrote the report in late May, he could be confronted with the summary after preliminary questions about the facts that he was deposed and that he was under oath:

> *Q.* Mr. Williams, you see here on page 45, line 13, please read this silently. At your deposition, is it correct to say that you were asked the following question and gave the following answer: "Question: Mr. Williams, it's your testimony that you gathered the information, typed it into a report and presented that report to Ms. McFarland all on the same day, July 2nd?"
> *A.* Yes.
> *Q.* Mr. Williams, is that the question you were asked and the answer you gave?
> *A.* Yes.

D. Different from Cross

You want your deposition to be different from your cross-examination. You don't want it to be a dress rehearsal and a source of information for your opponent. If your deposition is a precursor of your intended cross, you will lose the considerable advantage of surprise. The witness will know what to expect and may be a better witness at trial, and the other side may prepare to meet what they would not have otherwise known. For these reasons, there should be at least four basic differences between cross and a deposition of an adverse witness.

First and foremost, hold some things back from the deposition to preserve the element of surprise in trial. In the *Sonics* trial discussed earlier, defendant's counsel Brad Keller held back from the deposition a nearly identical report that the City of Seattle's expert economist Andrew Zimbalist used in another sports team valuation case. Mr. Keller's strategy was to save this as a devastating trial surprise that likely would send shockwaves through the media. This proved to be exactly the right choice. All the news media focused on how the City of Seattle's expert was "undressed" on the witness stand. The *Sonics* trial illustrates that the best lines of questioning to reserve for cross are those that cover concessions or impeachment material that have solid proof. The cookie-cutter template report of Dr. Zimbalist in the other case destroyed his credibility in one fell swoop.

Second, do not give the witness a script for your cross. This would be the equivalent of a college football coach giving the team's playbook to the other team prior to a game. Rather, get the answers you want at the deposition, but wait until trial to assemble them into a full cross. It is like shooting scenes (deposition topical units) for a movie, which are not combined into a full movie (trial cross-examination) until the editing room.

Third, the availability of prior statements is limited in a deposition. A principal reason for taking a discovery deposition in the first place is to find out what the witness is going to say, and then hold him to it. Certainly, you likely will have documents, such as reports, letters, memos, and e-mails, to drive your deposition questioning of a fact witness. Special rules exist for the depositions of expert witnesses, which are covered in Chapter 12.

Fourth, when taking a deposition, you can break several of the guidelines for cross. You can ask open-ended "why"-type questions or those to which you don't know the answer. Although it is counterintuitive, you do need to find out what potentially damaging answers a witness may give. This allows you to better anticipate how to minimize the damage to your case from the witness. It may be the foundation for a motion *in limine* to strike this testimony. While the one-too-many question that risks a devastating response is far less damaging in a deposition than before a jury, nevertheless, even in a deposition, some circumspection is called for. An overly aggressive questioning strategy can have the paradoxical effect of dropping a gift into the lap of your opponent, uncovering a testimonial gem that she did not know existed. Additionally, aggressive questioning can turn a noncommittal witness into a highly motivated witness.

VII. PREPARING PRIOR STATEMENTS FOR TRIAL

A. Acquiring Prior Statements

Chapter 8 presented trial strategies and techniques for impeachment by a prior inconsistent statement. This type of impeachment first requires the hard work of acquiring those prior statements through discovery and fact investigation. These prior statements can include documents, letters, memoranda, witness statements, and electronically stored information, such as e-mail. As discussed at page 302-303, these prior statements also can be invaluable when taking a deposition of the witness.

B. Creating Prior Statements

You will also create prior statements for trial through depositions, interrogatories, and requests for admissions. In Chapter 13, we explain how to effectively depose an adverse witness.

At trial, a witness's deposition statement is admissible as nonhearsay during cross under Fed. R. Evid. 801(d)(1), if it is inconsistent with the deponent's trial testimony. In Chapter 14, we go into how to create prior statements in depositions for later use in cross.

Requests for admissions are admissible as an admission by a party-opponent under Fed. R. Evid. 801(d)(2). Under Fed. R. Civ. P. 36, they cannot be contested at trial.

Answers to interrogatories are nonhearsay as admissions by party-opponent under Fed. R. Evid. 801(d)(2), and, if relevant and otherwise admissible, they can be inquired into on cross.

C. Organizing, Storing, and Retrieving

Whether retrieved electronically or by the old-fashioned method of reaching into a file, prior statements must be readily available at trial. Study all prior statements and be thoroughly familiar with them, ready to plug them into your cross-examinations for two basic types of concessions: (1) those that build upon or preserve your case theory and (2) those that diminish the other side's case theory or the witness. You must know the statements well enough to instantly recognize any departures by the witness in trial.

The following apocryphal tale demonstrates what happens too often in attempted impeachments with a prior statement, a case study in what not to do:

Counsel tried to get an opposing expert to give the testimony he wanted, telling her it was in one of her reports. She denied this. He indignantly demanded that she retract her statement and testify in conformity with his recollection of the report. She refused. He then began diligently looking for the statement in the several pages he had carried to the lectern with him. Upon failing to find it, he went back to counsel table and began to root through the papers scattered about. After an interminable period, he decided that the statement was not there. He refocused his search to a banker's box full of documents on the floor. The entire courtroom waited silently, watching his every move. At last he found the document, turning to the pertinent page. It was not as he had remembered, instead perfectly consistent with the expert's live testimony. He apologized to the expert and moved on to another subject.

This kind of courtroom fiasco can be avoided with preparation. All reports should be indexed and organized for easy retrieval. If an expert gives testimony that seems inconsistent, retrieve the report, confirm this and then impeach. Preparation saves both time and embarrassment. It also goes directly to your credibility as a lawyer. Post-verdict interviews with jurors have confirmed that lawyers who are well-organized and able to lay their hands on the right documents at the right time are viewed as highly professional and worthy of belief.

No-Technology System
Lacking any technological support, keep all prior witness statements in a tabbed file or notebook, indexed both chronologically and topically for quick retrieval. The witness's deposition can be indexed with page and line numbers, with a reference in your cross notes. See page 155 for an example.

Trial Support Technology

Trial support software enables a trial lawyer to effectively and efficiently store, organize, and quickly retrieve prior statements in the forms of documents, e-mail, depositions, and video depositions. Commonly used forms of litigation support software include:

- West LiveNote®—www.livenote.com
- LexisNexis Concordance®—www.law.lexisnexis.com/concordance
- inData TrialDirector®—www.indatacorp.com

Even as generic a program as Adobe Acrobat Professional® can assist you with evidence management by allowing you to reduce statements, reports, and depositions to the portable document format. These documents are then searchable with the program's optical character recognition feature. Data that you initially assessed as inconsequential can sometimes assume major importance in a trial. You can quickly find this using the multi-document search function.

The software you rely on may be dictated by your firm or organization or by the trial support service provider that your firm or you employ. If you select the software, pick the one you find the most comfortable and effective. Software vendors typically provide free trials of the software as well as tutorials. Here, we discuss TrialDirector® by inData as an example of what the software can do. If you are going to be operating the software during trial, practice enough to build the necessary confidence and proficiency needed to operate it smoothly and effortlessly. Always have a backup plan if the software fails. For instance, go with the deposition transcript if you cannot pull up the video deposition clip you want.

With TrialDirector®, documents, photographs, exhibits, deposition transcripts, and video depositions are electronically stored for retrieval with an identification label or number or bar code. In TrialDirector®, you can organize the materials into labeled workbooks, moving them around as needed. An individual workbook can be created for a witness whom you plan to cross-examine, and pertinent documents, deposition transcripts, deposition video clips, and exhibits can be placed in it and indexed.

You can request that videographers and court reporters produce a video deposition on inData's DepoView DVD. With the DepoView DVD in a laptop, counsel can review the deposition transcript, perform word searches for words in the transcript, and create video clips of the deposition that can be shown at trial. What counsel creates with DepoView can then be imported into TrialDirector® or other trial support software.

Rather than utilizing trial support and/or a computer program such as TrialDirector®, you could decide to use a tablet, for instance, an iPad, with the TrialPad application (www.litsoftware.com/products/trialpad/). TrialPad enables counsel to store exhibits that have been converted to PDFs. With TrialPad, the exhibits can be projected onto a screen in the courtroom. TrialPad enables counsel to annotate the enlarged image. For instance, counsel can call out a sentence in a displayed document and annotate it. TrialPad is less expensive than software programs such as TrialDirector®.

In preparation for trial, counsel or a trial support service provider can edit the video deposition into clips for display during cross. The video clip may be synchronized with the transcript so that it scrolls as the witness testifies. Also, when a witness discusses an exhibit, that exhibit can also be displayed along with the video of the deposition and the scrolling transcript. In trial, counsel may call up the video clip of witness's prior statement with either an identification number or label or bar code, and it will be projected on a courtroom screen or television monitors. Another feature of the software is that it allows counsel to annotate the deposition transcript or exhibit during trial. For example, counsel can circle a part of a photographic exhibit or can use a call-out to pull out and magnify a portion of a deposition transcript.

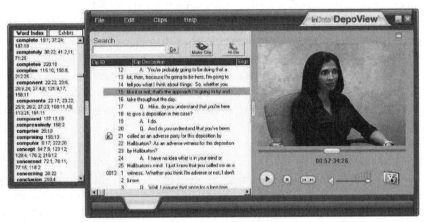

Video deposition with scrolling transcript and exhibit with inData TrialDirector®

The impact of a deposition video clip on the jury in the impeachment of a witness is significantly greater than merely reading the transcript. Jurors can directly compare for themselves what the witness just said in court with a prior inconsistent statement during a video deposition, evaluating the demeanor of the witness. Finally, the video clip prevents witnesses from using the common ploy of blaming the court reporter for a mistake in the transcript.

VIII. ESSENTIAL EVIDENCE RULES: EXPERTS

Now we turn to one of the most formidable challenges in trial—cross-examining an expert witness. In order to properly prepare to cross-examine an expert and to conduct the cross, it is important to understand the law of evidence concerning expert witnesses, when and on what grounds you either can disqualify an opposing expert or attack his or her credibility.

Even if testimony meets the specific evidentiary requirements for experts, the trial court will apply all the general evidence rules to the testimony. For instance, the court will make a relevancy inquiry (Fed. R. Evid. 401) and a determination of whether the expert testimony's probative value is substantially outweighed by danger of unfair prejudice (Fed. R. Evid. 403).

The Federal Rules of Evidence that apply to expert witnesses are critical because they apply not only in federal courts, but, with some variations, in most state courts.

A. Qualifications and Ultimate Opinion

Under Federal Rules of Evidence 702 and 704, an expert witness may testify factually or in an opinion, including an opinion on an ultimate issue to be decided by the jury, if:

- Scientific, technical, or other specialized knowledge will assist the trier of fact (for example, expert testimony in a criminal case would assist the jury by explaining how a pipe recovered from the defendant was used to smoke crystal methamphetamine); and
- The expert is qualified by knowledge, skill, experience, training, or education.

Federal Rule of Evidence 104(a) provides that the judge decides the preliminary questions of the witness's qualifications and admissibility of evidence. Counsel can make a pretrial motion to prohibit an expert from testifying as an expert on the grounds of insufficient qualifications. This is the most effective way to accomplish this goal. Even if the expert is not stricken, the court may limit the subjects on which the expert can testify, or the opinions that may be offered. The witness's competency to testify also can be challenged by asking the court's permission to voir dire the witness at trial, through questions showing a lack of qualifications to testify as an expert. Counsel should request to voir dire the witness outside the jury's presence before the witness testifies. If counsel prevails, the court prohibits the witness from testifying as a matter of law. This is not the preferred method of challenging an expert's testimony, as it interrupts the flow of the trial and often irritates the judge for this reason.

Opinion testimony may embrace the ultimate issue to be decided by the fact-finder. However, experts are not permitted to tell the fact-finder what result to reach or to render an opinion on the law except in those rare cases involving a standard of care in the interpretation of the law, such as in a case involving a claim of legal malpractice. Under Fed. R. Evid. 702, moreover, an expert does not need to provide an opinion. In the proper case, an expert can provide the jury with background information that counsel will use in arguing the case.

B. Reliability of the Expert's Field

Before an expert can render an opinion, the lawyer who calls the expert may have to prove to the court that the expert's field is reliable. Often enough, this is not a major issue, as many scientific fields are so widely accepted. Under most circumstances, a court will acknowledge the scientific reliability of disciplines such as ballistics, DNA analysis, or medicine.

However, other fields are not so widely accepted and require proof of reliability. Issues concerning the reliability of the area of the expert witness's testimony generally are raised through motions *in limine* to exclude the expert testimony. Made outside the presence of the jury in the months prior to trial, these motions usually require briefing and argument or written briefs, with reference to written discovery, depositions, affidavits, learned treatises, and expert witness testimony.

Frye Test

For over half a century, *Frye v. United States*, 293 F. 1013 (D.C. Cir. 1923), enunciated the classic test for a novel science. Under *Frye*, expert testimony was required to conform to the standard generally accepted in the scientific community. Thus, on direct examination, the trial lawyer would lay the foundation for the *Frye* standard as follows:

> Q. Has the technology of brain-imaging been generally accepted by the scientific community in the scientific field of forensic psychology?

Daubert Test

The U.S. Supreme Court, in *Daubert v. Merrell Dow Pharmaceuticals Inc.*, 509 U.S. 579 (1993), set aside *Frye* in our federal courts, holding that Federal Rule of Evidence 702 replaced it. Under *Daubert*, the trial court acts as a gatekeeper and makes a Fed. R. Evid. 104(a) preliminary inquiry into whether the proffered expertise is reliable. In subsequent cases, the Supreme Court held that *Daubert* applies not just to science, but to all forms of expertise under Fed. R. Evid. 702. Judicially relevant factors under *Daubert* include:

- Whether the theory or technique can be and has been tested;
- Whether the theory or technique has been subjected to peer review and publication;
- The known or potential rate of error and the existence and maintenance of standards controlling the technique's operation; and
- The level of acceptance in the scientific community.

Daubert controls in the federal system. On the state level, some states adhere to the *Frye* test and others adopted *Daubert* or crafted their own test. Even if expert testimony passes *Daubert* muster, the trial court will still make Federal Rules of Evidence 401 and 702 inquiries into whether the expert has scientific knowledge that will help the fact-finder decide or understand a fact in issue.

Finally, Fed. R. Evid. 403 comes into play to exclude scientific evidence when its probative value is substantially outweighed by danger of unfair prejudice. See pages 276-278 for an illustration of how to structure lines of questions concerning the Rule 702 qualifications.

C. Basis for Opinion

Federal Rule of Evidence 703 governs the types of data or facts on which an expert may base an opinion. The categories of data or facts include the following:

- Those perceived by the expert or made known to the expert at or before the hearing:
  - *Perceived by the expert:* for example, a doctor performs a physical examination of a patient;
  - *Made known at trial:* for example, at trial, a hypothetical question is posed containing a description of a person's physical condition or the expert is made aware of other testimony presented to the finder of fact.
- Otherwise inadmissible evidence, if reasonably relied on by experts in a particular field in forming opinions or inferences. For example, a doctor may render an opinion in part based on a discussion with a radiologist, which is inadmissible hearsay. As long as other experts in the doctor's field would reasonably rely on such a conversation, it may form the basis for the doctor's expert opinion. Federal Rule of Evidence 703, however, bars the expert from revealing the otherwise inadmissible evidence unless its "probative value substantially outweighs its prejudicial effect." Of course, cross-examination can open the door to allowing the introduction of otherwise inadmissible hearsay.

D. Hypothetical Questions

Traditionally, based on the common law of evidence, an expert who lacked personal knowledge had to learn the facts by either listening to the testimony or hearing a hypothetical question that fairly summarized the trial evidence. Federal Rule of Evidence 705 permits the expert to testify in terms of inferences and opinions without first testifying to underlying facts and data. Consequently, Rule 705 provides the party presenting the expert with the strategic option to present the expert's opinion before presenting the underlying reasons and analysis. The advantage of proceeding in this manner is that the jury is given context within which to appreciate the series of questions about the basis for the opinion.

Q. Doctor, have you formed an opinion to a reasonable degree of medical certainty as to the cause of Mr. Sim's illness?

A. Yes.

Q. What is that opinion?

A. Exposure to substance Z.

Q. Now, let's talk about how you arrived at that conclusion . . .

However, Rule 705 also grants the judge the discretion to require that the expert testify to the underlying facts and data before rendering an opinion. Under Rule 705, hypothetical questions are not required. A hypothetical question asks the expert to assume certain facts that are admissible in evidence or will be introduced into evidence and then to base an opinion on those facts. Failure to include a material piece of evidence or misstating or including inadmissible evidence can render the hypothetical flawed and objectionable.

IX. PREPARING TO CROSS AN EXPERT

To illustrate how to prepare to cross-examine an expert witness, imagine the *Educator Collision* case and that you represent the plaintiff Claire Butterfield.

Educator Collision Personal Injury Case

Plaintiff Claire Butterfield is a 49-year-old Ruston School District Program Director. On her way home from work, the defendant Alfred Purcell rear-ended Ms. Butterfield's car. While liability is not an issue, the economic effects of Ms. Butterfield's chronic back pain on her economic future are contested. The spread between the plaintiff and defense economic experts is significant, with plaintiff's at $950,000 and the defendant's at $11,551.

Your economist points to the following facts about Ms. Butterfield in determining her loss:

- Ms. Butterfield has a Master's degree, is a charismatic figure, and has had stellar job evaluations;
- She was making $110,000 per year at the time of the collision;
- Because of continuing medical problems she had to take a lesser-paying principal's job at $90,000 per year;
- After the accident she frequently missed work over a four-year period because of pain and medical appointments;
- She had to take a medical retirement at age 55; and
- She had not planned to retire until age 65.

You must prepare to cross-examine the defense forensic expert, certified public accountant, W. Thomas Booster. Mr. Booster took a minimalist view of plaintiff's economic losses in his expert's report relying on the following assumptions and reasoning to reach his opinions in the case:

- Plaintiff's change to a lesser paying job after the accident was a lifestyle choice—shorter hours, shorter commute, and less stress;
- Internet research shows a number of job openings she is qualified for, or she could become self-employed as a consultant;
- Plaintiff has good transferable job skills and could be hired elsewhere at the same pay;
- Her job change is just part of her overall career pattern;
- No difference in level of retirement benefits between age 60 and 65, and plaintiff is fully vested at age 60;
- Plaintiff's total damages should be reduced to present value, using a 5.7% mid-term T-bill rate as a discount;
- The amount she would have paid for taxes should be reduced;
- If not full-time, the plaintiff certainly could work part-time, substantially reducing her economic loss; and
- Plaintiff's economist substantially overstated future wage increases.

You may well spend over 100 hours preparing for this cross-examination of Mr. Booster. This is necessary as the entire damages case rides on which economic expert was perceived as the most believable. The following is a checklist of tasks you can perform to thoroughly prepare to cross Mr. Booster:

Preparation for Cross of an Expert

A checklist of tasks to perform when preparing to cross-examine the expert includes these essentials:

- Conduct *legal research* regarding a motion to exclude;
- Consult with *your expert* about cross-examination;
- Do a *background investigation* of the expert;
- Obtain *full discovery;* and
- *Consult with others* about the cross.

A. Legal Research and a Motion to Exclude

Preparing for an effective cross-examination of an expert begins with a solid understanding of the applicable evidentiary law. While most of this chapter assumes the admissibility of expert testimony, the first line of defense against expert testimony is a motion *in limine* to exclude all or part of it because of non-compliance with the evidence rules and case law. The exclusion of the expert's testimony usually is a favorable alternative to having to cross-examine the expert. However, there are rare occasions when you may conclude that the opposing party's expert will do more good for your case than harm. This can occur when the expert is vulnerable to impeachment or gives support to your position.

The following is a checklist of grounds for moving to exclude the expert's testimony:

CHECKLIST

Grounds for Excluding Expert Testimony

Counsel can consider making a motion *in limine* to exclude expert testimony on the following grounds with references to the Federal Rules of Evidence:

❏ The witness lacks sufficient qualifications to be an expert—Rule 702.

❏ The subject is not beyond the common understanding of the fact-finder and therefore will not assist the fact-finder—Rule 702.

❏ The field is not sufficiently reliable—Rule 702; *Frye, Daubert*.

❏ The opinion would render an opinion on the law or on a witness's credibility, or dictate to the jury what decision to reach—Rule 704.

❏ The testimony's probative value is substantially outweighed by unfair prejudice—Rule 403.

❏ The testimony would be a waste of time or presentation of cumulative evidence—Rule 403.

❏ The testimony is irrelevant to any issue at trial—Rule 401.

❏ The expert lacks a basis in fact or data on which to render any opinion—Rule 703.

❏ The opinion is too speculative ("could have," failing to be expressed in certain terms)—Rules 401, 403.

You must also be alert to the opposing party's expert straying too far from his or her particular field. This is common. An expert qualified to testify in one area will slip in an opinion on a related but distinctly different area of expertise. For instance, in the *Educator Collision* case, a collision reconstruction expert who has been qualified to reconstruct the speed of a vehicle at impact might slip in the opinion that the plaintiff could not have been hurt at such a low speed. Such medical testimony is clearly beyond the scope of the collision reconstructionist's expertise.

Another example of a more subtle but equally inappropriate attempt to wander outside of an expert's qualifications is when a collision reconstruction expert qualified to estimate the speed of a vehicle involved in a collision based on skid marks attempts to make a speed estimate based on impact damage to the vehicle and complicated mathematical calculations. Should this occur, you can object on the grounds that the witness is not qualified to provide such an opinion.

B. Your Expert

When it comes to planning a cross-examination of the other side's expert, your own expert on the same subject is your best initial resource. After you have identified the other side's potential expert and have obtained discovery (opposing party's expert report), you should consult with your expert about potential areas for cross-examination. You may want to have your expert present when you take the deposition of your opponent's expert. Your expert can point out areas of potential vulnerability in the other expert's qualifications, opinions, or methodology. Also, your expert may be able to suggest ideas and insights for cross-examination.

In the *Educator Collision* case, you, as the plaintiff's lawyer, will go over opposing expert Booster's report, identifying all vulnerabilities and getting any resource materials to assist in impeachment. This consultation will reveal a certain lack of adherence to accepted standards by the defense economist. Your economist critiqued Mr. Booster's report in the following e-mail to you:

From: Soojin Park
To: You
Subject: Booster's Report

I am highly critical of the defense economic expert making conclusions such as:

> No evidence has been produced to substantiate any relationship between change of employment and the accident. Our calculations assume that she left her job for reasons unrelated to the accident. If it is determined that consideration for future losses is appropriate, any losses would be significantly offset by the increased quality of life in her new position.

I have never seen this kind of lifestyle analysis in an economist's report before. There may be research done on lifestyles and quality of life, but to be quite frank, unless he has an expertise that I'm unaware exists, I would consider it inappropriate to be including that.

Economists are asked to calculate wage and benefit losses. We can't make judgments as economists or as accountants as to an individual's "quality of life". . . . I think the discussions of quality of life or even such things as less commuting time or more commuting time are not things that we can calculate accurately.

C. Background Investigation

When you first learn about your opponent's expert, you begin an investigation into that expert's background. Your informal investigation into the expert's background can be done by an investigator, a legal assistant, co-counsel, and/or you. At little or no expense, these investigative steps can produce valuable information.

Investigative Steps

- *Internet search:* Search for any information about the expert, such as an expert website or articles and print them out for review.
- *Jury verdicts:* Run the expert's name through the jury verdicts and settlements in the region, noting all costs, cause numbers, and courts, as well as the names of all counsel.
- *Public records check:* Run a public records check to determine if the witness had been personally involved in any prior lawsuits.
- *List serve:* Send out an e-mail request for information on the expert over the lawyer listserv to which he belonged.
- *Request to opposing counsel:* Request a complete copy of the expert's file from opposing counsel, including all correspondence and e-mail. Also, request a list of all cases in which the expert testified over the past five years, including case name and number, jurisdiction, and names of all counsel involved.
- *Contact counsel:* Contact all counsel whom your research efforts identified as having been opposite to the expert. Get copies of their complete files on this expert, as well as any depositions. Also, debrief counsel who deposed or cross-examined the expert previously to determine what worked and what did not.
- *Scholarly publications:* Identify any articles written by the expert that pertain to the subject matter of his or her testimony, obtain and read copies of those articles, and carefully note discrepancies between the expert's present opinion and his or her prior writings.

D. Collecting and Reading

As an essential part of your preparation, you want to research and read everything that the opposing expert has written or testified to that is pertinent to the subject that the expert will testify to at trial. As a result of both formal and informal discovery and investigation you may be able to locate a great deal of information pertinent to the expert that either supports your case theory or undercuts the other side's or even impeaches the expert.

Reading Material

The reading material you gather through investigation and discovery can include, among other things:

- Formal discovery in the current case, including: responses to interrogatories, requests for production, requests for admissions, and depositions;
- Books;
- Articles;
- Reports in other cases;

continued ▶

> - Transcripts from prior trials;
> - Depositions in other cases (indexed transcripts of trial and deposition testimony of thousands of experts are now available through online services for a fee);
> - Papers presented at conferences; and
> - Blogs and Internet postings of papers, articles, and videos.

An example of the benefits of reading everything carefully is the *Sonics* case we first discussed at pages 141-142. The City of Seattle sued in federal court to require the new Oklahoma ownership of the Sonics basketball team to play out the last two years of its lease in Seattle. To support its case, Seattle hired sports economist Andrew Zimbalist, a professor at Smith College. On direct, Zimbalist testified to the effect that the basketball team created intangible benefits for Seattle, such as civic pride that were impossible to quantify and could not be replaced by a cash payment.

Sonics lawyer Paul Taylor crossed Zimbalist with the aid of a 2005 report that this same expert wrote on the effect of a baseball team leaving Anaheim, California. In the 2005 report, Zimbalist put a value on the team to the city. Taylor questioned Zimbalist about the wholesale copying of sections of the 2005 expert report for Anaheim into the Seattle report at issue in the trial.

The first use of contingent valuation analysis to quantify the quality of life benefits of a sports facility was published in 2000.[11] Johnson and Whitehead applied the method to estimate the value of a minor league ballpark and a new basketball arena for the University of Kentucky. In each case the authors found that the quality of life value to the community was between $3.6 million and $7.3 million. In 2001, Johnson, Groothuis and Whitehead applied the method to estimate the quality of life value of the Pittsburgh Penguins hockey team to the residents of Pittsburgh. Their estimate was between $17.2 million and $48.3 million.[12] Notably, this estimate was well below the expected $200 million that it would cost to build the Penguins a new arena.

Expert Report of Andrew Zimbalist, 5/2/08, pp. 15-16
The City of Seattle v. PBC, W.D. Wash. C07-1620MJP

The first use of contingent valuation analysis to quantify the quality of life benefits of a sports facility was published in 1970.[13] Johnson and Whitehead applied the method to estimate the value of a minor league ballpark and a new basketball arena for the University of Kentucky. In each case the authors found that the quality of life value to the community was between $3.6 million and $7.3 million. In 2001, Johnson, Groothuis and Whitehead applied the method to estimate the quality of life value of the Pittsburgh Penguins hockey team to the residents of Pittsburgh. Their estimate was between $17.2 million and $48.3 million.[14] Notably, this estimate was well below the expected $200 million that it would cost to build the Penguins a new arena.

Expert Report of Andrew Zimbalist, 11/21/05, p. 17
City of Anaheim v. Angels Baseball, L.P., Sup. Ct. of Cal.

Projecting sections of the Seattle and Anaheim reports on a screen side by side, Taylor made his point:

Taylor: *Q.* If you find the change, tell us.

Zimbalist: *A.* I don't see any changes, looking at it quickly.

Q. Well, don't rush. If you think there is a change, we're entitled to know about it.

A. I don't see any changes.

In the *Educator Collision* case, one of the most important things you need to do is get your hands on every report or deposition that defense economist W. Thomas Booster has given in other cases. What you are looking for is a testimonial pattern, in the same way that counsel did in the *Sonics* case with Professor Zimbalist. After getting this information, you read the defense expert's deposition in another case and come across this exchange about his income:

DEPOSITION TRANSCRIPT

W. Thomas Booster

Q. Can you tell me what percentage of your business involves injury and wrongful death cases?

A. No, I couldn't tell you.

Q. You've never looked at that?

A. No.

Q. Are you able to estimate at all?

A. Not with any degree of precision, no. We just don't keep track of that kind of information. It's not important to us.

Q. You have no idea; is that what you're telling me?

A. No idea regarding personal injury and wrongful death versus all of the others.

Q. How much of your business is it; do you know?

A. I couldn't tell you from year to year. It could change dramatically.

Q. I appreciate that. Can you tell me how much it was this last year?

A. I guess I can say that a significant portion of our practice is personal injury and wrongful death. I can't tell you what percentage. I just don't know.

The deposition went on in this vein with Mr. Booster giving evasive and noncommittal answers when questioned about how much he made as a professional witness. As we will see later, this reluctance to disclose income will become part of the cross of Mr. Booster.

E. Discovery

Automatic Discovery

The more discoveries you have of your opponent's expert, the better. Under Federal Rule of Civil Procedure 26(a)(2)(A)-(D) and similar state rules, a party planning on calling an expert must provide the opposing party with the identity of any expert witness it may call in the trial to present evidence under Federal Rules of Evidence 702, 703, and 705. A written report that includes the expert's opinion, data or information used to form an opinion, exhibits, qualifications (including a list of publications authored in the last ten years), a list of cases during the last four years, and a statement about compensation must also be provided to the opposing party.

Other Traditional Discovery Devices

You can utilize all of the traditional discovery devices to obtain information from the expert witness you will later cross-examine at trial. In the civil *Educator Collision* case, you can serve Mr. Booster with a set of interrogatories, make requests for production and admissions, and depose him.

Subpoena Duces Tecum

Consistent with Mr. Booster's behavior in prior cases that you have identified through collecting other reports and depositions of this witness, he refused to provide you with the requested information on his forensic income voluntarily. Now, as plaintiff's counsel, you can use a subpoena duces tecum to compel him to bring financial information to his deposition. The following document is the subpoena.

HONORABLE JUSTICE T. WISDOM

Claire Butterfield	)	SUBPOENA DUCES TECUM
Plaintiff	)	FOR DEPOSITION
	)	DIRECTED TO
v.	)	W. THOMAS BOOSTER, CPA
	)	
Alfred Purcell	)	
Defendant	)	
_____)		

TO: W. THOMAS BOOSTER, CPA

Greetings:

You are commanded to appear at the offices of Fury Bailey, 710 Tenth Avenue East, Ruston, Major 98102 on July 9, 20XX + 1, at 10:30 a.m. to testify as the custodian of the records for W. THOMAS BOOSTER, CPA, concerning the documents that are being requested below. Your deposition is being sought at the request of the plaintiff in the above-entitled cause, and you are to remain in attendance at the deposition until discharged by the undersigned attorney.

You are further commanded to bring with you to the deposition at the above stated time and place the following documents:

1. A list of all cases in which you have provided forensic consultation during the last five years, including the name of each case, the jurisdiction, the case number, whether you consulted for the plaintiff or defendant, the nature of the case, and the name and address of the attorney who retained you.
2. Any and all billings concerning any charges for all cases listed above.
3. All record of the payments made to you, either individually or through your firm, for any forensic economic evaluations and/or expert testimony in which you participated from 20XX-5 to the present.

> 4. All 1099 forms issued to you, either individually or through your firm, for any forensic economic evaluations and/or expert testimony from 20XX-10 to the present.
>
> DATED this 6th day of April 20XX+1
>
> *R. J. You*
> _____
> Attorney for Plaintiff

When Mr. Booster refused to respond to the subpoena, you, as plaintiff's counsel, filed a motion to compel production with the trial judge. Opposing counsel and Mr. Booster submitted sworn declarations arguing that such disclosure was improper, citing relevance, privacy, and undue burden. The judge ordered Mr. Booster to produce his 1099 forms produced for a two-year period, despite Mr. Booster's and opposing counsel's objections. The declaration filed by the expert could come back to haunt him later, during the cross-examination.

HONORABLE JUSTICE T. WISDOM

Claire Butterfield	)	DECLARATION OF
Plaintiff	)	W. THOMAS BOOSTER, CPA
	)	IN SUPPORT OF MOTION TO
v.	)	QUASH SUBPOENA
	)	
Alfred Purcell	)	
Defendant	)	
_____	)	

W. Thomas Booster makes the following declaration based on personal knowledge.

1. I am a certified public accountant, fully licensed to practice in this jurisdiction.
2. The legal community frequently requests me to do forensic economic evaluations. It is a major part of my CPA practice.
3. The defendant's lawyer asked me to do an assessment of the plaintiff's lost earnings and earning capacity following her automobile accident. I issued my findings and conclusions in a report, which has been made available to the plaintiff's counsel.
4. Recently I was served with a subpoena duces tecum by plaintiff's counsel, seeking records of all payments to my firm for forensic consultations over the last five years, including 1099s.
5. My firm does not routinely compile what is being sought in this subpoena. This information is not in a form that can be easily completed, requiring a significant

continued ▶

amount of staff time. I also consider it an unfair invasion of my privacy. My income is nobody's business but mine.

I DECLARE UNDER THE PENALTY OF PERJURY THAT THE FOREGOING IS TRUE AND CORRECT.

DATED this 5th day of May 20XX.

W. Thomas Booster
_____
W. Thomas Booster, CPA

F. Consult with Others

Others, particularly colleagues and other lawyers, may be able to assist you in preparing and planning for your cross-examination of Mr. Booster. You e-mail a trusted lawyer friend for her input about the cross of Booster:

To: Robin Kroger
From: R. J. You
Subject: Ideas for Cross of Booster

I would like your thoughts on how to better cross Mr. Booster. It seems to me that his "economic value of leisure lifestyle" analysis is a fertile ground for cross examination, but I don't want to get too cute either. I am tempted to get a bit personal with him. How about asking him whether he has any hobbies or outside interests? Then go into how much money these add to his net worth. How would he feel if he was injured and had to retire years before he'd planned? How much value would you put on those hobbies if it was your own income that was being diminished?

Another approach is to just attack his basic mathematics. My client had not planned to retire until at least age 65. If you multiply what she was making by 10 years, you get x, just as shown on this page of your report. Yet, you end up trying to perform some economic magician's trick for the insurance company and make all this income loss disappear. People have retirement plans, don't they? Do you have any special talent to get inside my client's head and say that she is not correct in saying that she did not want to retire until age 65?

Did you bother to read her personnel evaluations? Let me share a few paragraphs with you. Does this sound like somebody who was good at their job and loved doing it?

The economic bias piece itself is a no-brainer. I expect that the witness will have some pretty large insurance company payments to admit to.

I have to keep in mind that the jury will probably have a limited tolerance for an extended harangue on my part, so your input will be appreciated.

Robin Kroger e-mails her reply to you:

From: Robin Kroger
To: R. J. You
Subject: Thoughts on Booster Cross-Examination

I think it is an unnecessary risk to get sarcastic with him. You risk the jury not liking you, rather than the reverse. Also, this witness is no dummy. He may well find a way to send the shots right back to you.

I would do a straight-ahead cross-examination, establishing economic bias on his part, doing recalculations with other assumptions, and discussion of what is (economics and calculation), and what is not (lifestyle evaluation) within his expertise.

One other area to perhaps talk about is the personal value of work, i.e., that a person gets a sense of accomplishment, self-worth, etc. Why else do Bill Gates, Sumner Redstone, George Soros not just lead a life like Paris Hilton?

G. Deposing the Expert

Your Objectives and Deportment

Approach the taking of an expert's deposition with the goal of conducting a successful cross-examination firmly in mind. This will inform your objectives in taking the deposition.

First, the expert should not be forearmed. Do not turn your playbook over to a person being called to dismantle your case. The more you can do to conceal your case theory and theme the better. If a defect exists in the expert's qualifications, basis for opinion, or the opinion itself, the flaw may be best saved for your cross at trial. If you expose the defect during the deposition, you may only provide your opponent with an opportunity to fix it.

Second, just as you don't want to reveal your case analysis and strategies, you are better off not showing your assertive cross-examination demeanor unless absolutely necessary. If you are aggressive during the deposition, this may only serve to prepare the expert for your cross-examination at trial.

Third, you are more likely to elicit favorable concessions and impeachment evidence if you are restrained and even cordial toward the expert.

The following is a nonexclusive list of areas to cover when taking the deposition of an expert witness. In the next chapter on expert witnesses, you will learn how the gathering of this information during the deposition plays out during cross-examination. Again, it is best to consult with your expert about subjects to cover during your deposition of the adverse expert.

Concessions

To the extent possible, you want to make the other side's expert your own, conceding facts favorable to your case. This will prepare you for a concession-seeking cross-examination at trial. Be respectful and inquisitive in this effort, not confrontational. Will the expert concede that your expert is qualified? More qualified? Will the expert concede that your expert followed correct procedures and used sufficient data in the analysis? Concede that experts' opinions in the field may differ?

You will find an illustration of cross-examination producing favorable concessions at pages 269-270.

Qualifications

Is any part of the expert's qualifications less than those of your expert? Is there any exaggeration or falsification? Are the expert's memberships in professional organizations invitational or do they only require dues payments? Does the expert take an active role in the organization? Is the expert board certified (having gone through peer evaluation and rigorous testing) or board qualified (the applicant has met the requirements to take the boards)?

Examine the deponent's background and expertise closely. Does the expert lack practical experience in the field about which the expert will testify? If the expert has published, were the publications on the subject in question? If the expert teaches, is it in the field?

At pages 277-278 you will find an illustration of cross-examination of an expert on qualifications.

Procedures and Factual Data

Are any of the procedures and data relied upon by the expert deficient, making the findings and opinions unreliable? How much time did the expert devote to reaching conclusions? How much time did the expert take to investigate? Who did the expert speak to during that investigation? How much time did the expert spend examining the patient? How much time did it take to prepare the expert's report? Was the expert supplied with all the pertinent information? Did it come from an impartial source? What did the expert decide not to investigate?

You will find an illustration of cross-examination of an expert about inadequate procedures and data at pages 291-293.

Financial Bias

Is there a relationship between the expert and the party or attorney? Does the expert testify exclusively for one side? Has the expert worked with opposing counsel before? How many times? Because Fed. R. Civ. Proc. 26(a)(2)(B)(vi) requires disclosure of the expert's compensation, you may not go into that during the deposition.

At pages 273-284 you will find a discussion of cross-examination to show financial bias, forcing disclosure of details of financial bias and an illustration of cross-examination impeachment with financial bias.

Learned Treatise

What sources does the expert consider authoritative in field? If the expert acknowledges a learned treatise as reliable, you can cross-examine about its content. Be alert for departures between what the learned treatise says and what the expert did or says in your case. What professional publications does the expert subscribe to? What publications does the expert consider authoritative in the area of expertise?

At pages 294-296 you will find an illustration of cross-examination of an expert with a learned treatise.

Your Expert

What sources does your expert consider authoritative? Your experts are a critical resource in deconstructing the ones called by your opponent. Spend time with them, asking for guidance in identifying the weak spots in the opposing expert's testimony.

Opinion

What are all the opinions the expert will offer at trial? Sometimes these go beyond what is contained in a written report. Methodically seeking out all the opposing expert's opinions on the record will eliminate the chance of surprise at trial. A deposition will allow you to study carefully the opinions being offered, exposing any faulty assumptions. What is the expert's degree of certainty behind each opinion? What is it based on? An expert's assumptions often are the weak link that you can expose on cross-examination as garbage in, garbage out.

CHECKLIST: PREPARING THE WINNING CROSS

Recapitulation of Already Covered Preparation Steps

❑ Develop a case theory, which is composed of a legal theory and a persuasive story.

❑ Analyze the other side's case theory.

❑ Determine what the purpose(s) of the cross of the witness will be—build or preserve counsel's case theory or demolish the other side's theory and/or witness.

❑ Identify and select concessions that the witness must make by:
  • Asking what the witness must concede or be impeached;
  • Envisioning summation and, with that closing in mind, brainstorm for concessions that will support counsel's case theory or undermine the other side's case theory or the witness.

❑ Identify and select impeachment material by brainstorming.

❑ Write the cross with the cross-notes format in topical units, each unit having a beginning, middle, and end.

❑ Construct a persuasive cross by:
  • Telling a story with short, declarative sentences and the right words;
  • Arranging the topical units into a story with a beginning, middle, and end, like organizing scenes into a movie;
  • Starting strong;

- Finishing strong with a surefire line of questions;
- Editing your cross to keep it interesting.

❑ Perform cross by:
- Being a sincere, seeker of truth;
- Adjusting your manner to the situation and witness;
- Highlighting testimony;
- Avoiding and meeting objections;
- Employing visuals;
- Listening to the witness's responses; and
- Having broad audience appeal.

Additional Preparation Steps

❑ Obtain full discovery about the witness and what the witness might testify to utilizing:
- Formal civil or criminal discovery tools and
- The Freedom of Information Act.

❑ Obtain all helpful social media information and e-mails

❑ Conduct a thorough fact investigation of the witness and the facts relating to that witness.

❑ Interview the witness

❑ Depose adverse witnesses
- Assess the deponent's credibility and communication skills;
- Seek concessions;
- Seek impeachment evidence;
- Make a record of concessions, refusals to concede, and impeachment evidence;
- Hold back things for cross; and
- Learn what the witness can testify that will hurt your case.

❑ Regarding prior witness statements:
- Obtain all existing statements;
- Create statements through discovery devices;
- Organize all statements for prompt in-trial retrieval.

❑ Obtain all impeachment evidence, including evidence that the witness:
- Lacks personal knowledge;
- Suffers from mental or sensory deficiencies;
- Harbors a bias or interest;
- Made an improbable statement;
- Made a prior inconsistent statement;
- May be contradicted by other evidence;
- Has a criminal history; and/or
- Committed prior acts probative of untruthfulness.

Essential Evidence Rules Regarding Expert Witnesses

❑ Under Fed. R. Evid. 702 and 704 or state equivalent, the person may testify in the form of fact or opinion if the person is qualified in accordance with the Rules.

❑ While under Rule 104(a) the judge decides whether the witness is qualified as a matter of law and the jury decides what weight to give to the testimony.

- ❏ The expert's field of expertise must be reliable under the jurisdiction's legal test for reliability.
- ❏ Federal Rule of Evidence 703 outlines what facts and data the expert may rely upon in rendering expert testimony.
- ❏ Under Fed. R. Evid. 705, an expert may render an opinion without first testifying to the facts and data upon which it is based.
- ❏ The left column of your cross notes is filled with statements because that will prompt leading questions.
- ❏ Utilize the stacking technique to help the jury retain information.

Preparation to Cross-Examine an Expert

- ❏ All the preparation steps previously discussed apply equally to expert witnesses.
- ❏ Additional tasks to perform when preparing to cross-examine an expert include:
  - Conduct legal research regarding a motion to exclude;
  - Consult with your expert about cross-examination;
  - Do a background investigation of the expert, which may include the following:
    - Internet search;
    - Verdicts of cases in which the expert was involved;
    - Public records;
    - Lawyer listserv;
    - Request full file on the expert from opposing counsel;
    - Contact counsel who have had experience with the expert;
  - Obtain full discovery;
  - Collect and read these among other things:
    - Books;
    - Articles;
    - Transcripts from other trials;
    - Depositions in other cases;
    - Papers presented at conferences; and
    - Blogs and other Internet postings of papers, articles, and videos; and
    - Consult with colleagues.
- ❏ Depose the expert on the following:
  - Concessions supporting your case;
  - Expert's qualifications;
  - Procedures and factual data;
  - Financial bias;
  - Learned treatises; and
  - Opinion.

EXPERT WITNESSES

"The atomic bomb will never go off, and I speak as an expert in explosives."
      —**Admiral William Leahy**, on the U.S.
      Atomic Bomb Project, to President
      Truman (1945)

"Challenging an expert and questioning his expertise is the lifeblood of our legal system—whether it is a psychiatrist discussing mental disturbances, a physicist testifying on the environmental impact of a nuclear power

plant . . . It is the only way a judge or jury can decide whom to trust."
— **David L. Bazelon**, Chief Judge, U.S. Court
of Appeals, Dallas Times Herald, May 13,
1973

I. CROSSING THE EXPERT

In this chapter, we discuss the challenges presented in cross-examining expert witnesses. We also examine how to conduct an effective cross-examination of an expert witness. This discussion centers on both how to gain favorable concessions from the other side's expert and how to impeach expert testimony with both the standard means of impeachment and in ways that are only available for expert witnesses. The *Educator Collision* case is carried forward here from the previous chapter to demonstrate how to conduct the cross of an expert.

II. EXPERT CHALLENGES

Expert witnesses present the cross-examiner with challenges that lay witnesses normally do not. Experts know their subject well; unlike most lay witnesses, they have considerable experience in testifying. By a process similar to Darwinian natural selection, only the strongest experts survive. Many of those are employed again and again by lawyers because they are reliable and tend to hold up on cross-examination.

At the outset, it is best for a lawyer to soberly appraise just what she is up against in cross-examining experts. Although not all-inclusive, the following list explores the depth of the challenges when crossing experts:

Top Ten Reasons Why Cross-Examination of Expert Witnesses Is Demanding

1. Experts have superior knowledge in their fields of expertise.
2. They have been hired to advance your opponent's case theory; that is, experts have agendas.
3. They may not be intellectually honest.
4. They are competitive, rising to meet any challenges by lawyers.
5. Experts are elusive. It is difficult to pin them to "yes" or "no" answers. They will strive to explain their answers.
6. Many experts have at least a surface charm, making overt verbal aggression by the lawyer seem rude.
7. Expert testimony can be complex in nature. Getting bogged down in a technical cross-examination will bore and then irritate the jury.

---

8. They are usually experienced and streetwise. Most top experts have been cross-examined multiple times. They often know what is coming and how to get around it.
9. Experts are quick to seize on any opening or ambiguity in a question, making the lawyer look bad. Questions have to be tightly framed.
10. They are unshakable on major points. Lawyers often cannot resist the temptation to do too much, such as seeking admissions to mistakes on major points. Rather than swinging for home runs, it is usually better to settle for an infield hit.

III. SELECTING CONTENT OF CROSS

The content of your cross of an expert, like that for any witness, flows from your objectives for that witness. And, the objectives for an expert witness's cross-examination are the same as they are for any other witness. You want to:

- Obtain concessions that build or preserve your case theory or your expert's testimony;
- Obtain concessions that damage the other side's case theory or the expert's credibility; or
- Demolish the adverse expert witness or the witness's opinions or versions of the facts.

A. Concession-Seeking Cross

Expert witnesses are especially susceptible to the concession-seeking cross-examination approach covered in Chapter 3. Because most forensic experts usually want to continue being retained by the legal community, they want to maintain their credibility and will not exceed the bounds of reasonableness in their field of expertise. They want to avoid becoming readily impeachable. Therefore, assuming that your case theory is reasonable and your experts are correct in their conclusions, and further assuming that the other party's experts are honest and qualified, you should be able to obtain some favorable concessions. Under the right circumstances, you may even be able to turn an opposing expert to your advantage.

For example, in the involuntary manslaughter trial of Conrad Murray, Michael Jackson's doctor, the defense called Dr. Paul White to testify, among other things, that Jackson self-medicated with his own stash of propofol, thereby causing his own death.

Dr. Paul White (left) is cross-examined by prosecutor David Walgren

Prosecutor David Walgren relied on concession-seeking cross-examination to build his case against Dr. Conrad. Walgren asked questions which he knew the defense expert had to answer in a manner favorable to the prosecution, as follows:

Q. Doctor White, if you were asked to provide inappropriate medical care that you thought was harmful to the patient and the patient insisted upon it, would you walk away?

A. I would never administer what I consider inappropriate medical care to a patient.

Q. So, is that an answer "Yes, you would walk away if the patient insisted upon it."?

A. Yes.

Prosecutor. Thank you.

Q. Do you agree that there are instances where Dr. Murray deviated from the standards of care in his treatment of Michael Jackson on June 25, 2009?

A. Yes, I would.

Q. And would you agree that there were instances where Dr. Murray deviated from the standards of care in the preceding two months of treatment, as relayed by Dr. Murray in his statement to police?

A. Yes, I would.

Q. And I assume — Have you ever administered propofol in someone's bedroom?

A. No, I have not.

Q. Have you ever heard of anyone doing that prior to this case?

A. No, I have not.

Where the other party's expert has an emotional attachment to your opponent's case or to a specific issue, do not necessarily expect the same degree of logical concessions from the expert. However, the expert's failure to make logical concessions may form the basis of an effective impeachment.

B. Impeachment Cross

While in this chapter we emphasize five areas of impeachment that are applicable only to experts, the nine areas of impeachment we covered in Chapters 6 through 8 have equal force with experts. In addition, because experts must be qualified and are allowed to render opinions and discuss inferences, cross-examination can be used to attack witnesses' credentials as well as to impeach them. For instance, learned treatises can reveal deficiencies both in the experts' opinions and their bases for them.

CHECKLIST
Areas for Impeachment During Cross-Examination

All Witnesses
  I. Reliability—Chapter 6
      1. Lack of Personal Knowledge
      2. Mental and Sensory Deficiencies
      3. Bias and Interest
  II. Report—Chapter 7
      4. Improbability
      5. Prior Inconsistent Statement
      6. Contradiction
  III. Reporter—Chapter 8
      7. Prior Convictions
      8. Prior Misconduct Probative of Untruthfulness
      9. Character Witness

Expert Witnesses
All of the above and Expert Witness — Chapter 12
      10. Qualifications
      11. Reliability of the Field
      12. Basis for Opinion
      13. Opinion
      14. Learned Treatises

C. The Four-Step Methodology

The four-step process for identifying the content of your cross, which is discussed in detail in Chapter 3 at pages 24-35, can be used to develop the content for your cross of an expert witness. Those four steps are:

- Step 1: *Formulate your case theory* because you will be seeking concessions that build or protect that theory.
- Step 2: *Analyze the opposing party's case theory* because (1) it may afford you concessions that support your case theory and (2) you must have a firm grasp of it in order to seek concessions that undercut it.
- Step 3: *Brainstorm for concessions* that build your case theory or undercut the other side's case theory. Ask yourself, "*What must the witness concede* or face having the answer labeled a lie, mistaken, or preposterous?"
- Step 4: *Brainstorm* the law and facts of the case to come up with a list of the points you want to make with the witness that involve *impeachment* of the witness.

Later, you will assemble the content of your cross into a persuasive presentation for the jury.

To illustrate how to determine the content of your cross examination of an expert, let's continue to assume that you represent plaintiff Claire Butterfield in the *Educator Collision* case.

Step 1—Plaintiff's Case Theory

The first step in trial work is to formulate a case theory which, as you learned in Chapter 2, is composed of a legal and factual theory. Regarding damages in the *Educator Collision* case, your legal theory is that if liability is established, plaintiff is entitled to compensation for her economic loss. Plaintiff's expert can testify to facts sufficient to establish this. But, you want to do more than that. You look for ways to construct a persuasive factual story that will compel the jury to want to render a favorable verdict in Claire Butterfield's behalf. For her economic loss to be credible, your forensic economist has to be both qualified and credible. The testimony of your client, other witnesses, and your experts combine to tell a story of Claire and how the defendant's conduct deprived her of health and happiness. It will be a human story about Claire, focused on values in her life that a jury can relate to, such as hard work and dedication to excellence on the job. Before the collision, she was a 49-year-old, charismatic, School District Program Director who wanted to work until she was 65 years old. After the collision, she was constantly in pain, had numerous medical appointments, missed work, and was forced to take a lower-paying job. Ultimately, she had to take a medical retirement at 55 years of age. Your goals on cross are to preserve and build on this story.

Step 2—Analyze the Defense Case Theory and Expert

The defense case theory is designed to chip away at the plaintiff's case theory. For example, the defense economist asserts that plaintiff's expert overstated Claire's wage increase and that Claire made a job change for career reasons, not because of her medical problems. The defense story about Claire is that she changed jobs and retired early in pursuit of an easier lifestyle.

When you analyze the defense case theory, you recognize three significant areas of vulnerability for cross. First, the defense story about Claire is unsupported by evidence; the expert does not know Claire. Second, when the defense economist renders opinions about Claire's lifestyle, he ventures outside his area of expertise. Third, this expert's credentials are less impressive than your own economist.

Step 3—Brainstorm for Concession Points

Having constructed your case theory, analyzed the other side's, and studied the expert's background and opinions in the case, you can plan your tentative closing. Consider how the opposing expert's testimony can build or at least preserve your case theory. Think about how you will attack the opposing expert's credibility in summation. Later in this chapter, we offer several illustrations of tentative closing arguments that serve as guides for identifying the content of cross.

With the tentative closing argument in mind, the next step is to ask yourself: "What factual concession(s) must this expert witness concede or face having his answer labeled a lie, mistaken, or preposterous?" The answer to your question will be those factual points that the witness must provide on cross-examination because you can either prove the fact or draw the inference from the proven facts or common sense.

With the tentative closing in mind, planning shifts back to cross. Ask yourself, "What can I gain during cross to support these points in closing?" As this process evolves, you will discover more ideas for closing and more factual points to cover on cross. Create a list of concessions that you reasonably can expect to win.

Step 4—Brainstorming for Impeachment Material

Equally important as concession points to seek are the potential impeachment areas that may be covered during cross-examination. Consider the list of nine areas of impeachment applicable to all witnesses and the five additional ones that apply exclusively to experts. Discrediting or exposing weaknesses in an adverse expert witness is a challenge. Realistically, you will seldom demolish the adverse expert witness. Rather, while you may be able to diminish the expert's credibility or persuasiveness with the jury, you are unlikely to destroy it.

In the *Educator Collision* case, the initial brainstorming was based on the information gathered through investigation and through pretrial formal and informal discovery. Later, we will cover the concessions that the defense economist must make in depth, as well as areas where he or she is vulnerable, but here is a short list:

> ### Expert Witness
>
> ## Initial Brainstorming
>
> #### The *Educator Collision* Personal Injury Case
> - Although numbers are seemingly objective, they can be manipulated dishonestly. Examples of this include accounting fraud that the general public is aware of, such as the Arthur Andersen firm's complicity in the Enron scandal, as well as fraud by the former telecommunications company WorldCom.
> - Mr. Booster, the defense economist, only consults for the insurance industry in legal cases.
> - He makes considerable income from the insurance industry, which sets up his financial bias and motive to stretch his opinions in defendant's favor.
> - He is going beyond the recognized limits of economic analysis, opining on psychosocial issues.
> - He changed opinions from his first report after receiving the critique of this report by the plaintiff's expert.
> - There are deficiencies in his qualifications, which were swept under the rug in his resume.
> - Your economic expert is better qualified.
> - He exaggerated in his depositions when he claimed that marketing seminars to insurance companies are "public service" and "giving back."
> - He makes far more doing forensic work than he would in straight-out consulting in a normal business context.
> - He resisted turning over information on how much he makes from forensic consults. What is he trying to hide?
> - He lacks personal knowledge of the plaintiff and the demands of her profession.
> - The plaintiff was outstanding in her job and had no plans to retire.
> - He submitted a declaration in an effort to quash the subpoena seeking his 1099 forms from forensic consultations.
> - The judge granted plaintiff's counsel's pretrial motion to compel production of the 1099 forms.
> - Pretrial motion practice resulted in some of the expert's opinions being struck on hearsay and speculation grounds.

In the following sections, we apply the four-step methodology and provide examples of how to plan and conduct a cross-examination to gain concessions and to impeach the expert.

D. Danger Zone

Here is one last principle before we turn to illustrations of how to plan and conduct cross-examination. Beware of the temptation to challenge the expert in their area of expertise. The expert is trained and experienced in the field, and ordinarily the trial lawyer has only a surface knowledge of the subject. Consequently, cross-examinations that match wits with the other side's expert are rarely fruitful and commonly lead to disastrous results. Such a cross-examination should be entered into only with the greatest caution.

Generally, the less you let the expert talk, the better. Ask short, crisp leading questions, make your points, and stop. Sprinkle in a few non-leading questions where you are certain you cannot be hurt by the answer so the examination will not be tedious and completely controlling. Before venturing to cross-examine within the opposing expert's field, it is advisable to have had a prior consultation with your own expert.

You can keep your distance from the adverse expert by concentrating on the areas where it will be easier to expose vulnerabilities, points that are outside the expert's technical expertise. This can be some of your most effective cross-examination. For a list of examples of this type of attack, see page 285. Or, you can just concentrate on gaining admissions to accepted common principles in the area of expertise.

IV. CONCESSION-SEEKING CROSS—THE *EDUCATOR COLLISION* ILLUSTRATION

In this section on obtaining concessions from the expert witness and in the following sections on discrediting the expert, you will find illustrations from the *Educator Collision* case of both how to identify the content of cross and then the final products—excerpts from transcripts. The transcripts enable you to see how the cross-examination would work in court. For each illustration, the information is presented in this order:

- *Tentative closing*—This is a brief snippet of the envisioned closing regarding the expert, which can be drawn on during the brainstorming session to identify factual points for closing;
- *List of factual statements*—These are the factual points that are identified during brainstorming for concessions and impeachment, and
- *Transcript*—The transcript of the cross, which is the result of planning the particular cross-examination.

We present the closing first for clarity even though brainstorming for facts may produce more ideas for closing. Also, we omit examples of the cross-notes format for cross-examination that were discussed on pages 51-52 because you have already learned how to create them.

Now, we turn to the first example of how to cross-examine an expert. A lawyer needs to be alert for an argument that his or her expert's credentials are better than the opponent's. Always check the opposing expert's resume carefully, verifying all claims made, alert for credential inflation and exaggeration issues. In the *Educator Collision* case, such an inquiry bears fruit. Mr. Booster's certified public accountant credential is arguably inferior to the PhD in economics held by your university professor expert. If all other things are equal, this difference may not matter to the jury. However, not all things are equal in your case as we shall see. Also, Mr. Booster's resume states that he took coursework in pursuit of a master's in business administration, but no mention is made that he was ever awarded a degree. Reading between the lines, it is apparent that Mr. Booster dropped out prior to completion of his course requirements. This makes him somewhat susceptible to an unfavorable contrast to qualifications to the plaintiff's economist.

Probing this dropout subject with Mr. Booster may stimulate defensiveness on his part. Lay jurors expect true experts to be above the fray, secure in their credentials. If an expert is forced to make excuses and rationalize deficiencies, their presumed credibility can dissipate.

The area of the expert's qualifications is ripe for a concession-seeking cross because Mr. Booster must concede that plaintiff's expert has superior academic credentials. And, his concession to this point not only builds plaintiff's expert's credibility but also undercuts that of Mr. Booster. Attacking an expert's qualifications is also on the list of the five areas of impeachment that apply exclusively to experts. A tentative closing that focuses on a comparison of the two experts' qualifications is as follows:

Tentative Closing Argument

Expert Witness Concession-Seeking Cross: Lesser Qualifications

The *Educator Collision* Personal Injury Case

Judge Martinez has read jury instruction number 9 to you, and it states: "In determining the weight to be given expert opinion, you should consider the qualifications and credibility of the witness and the reasons given for the expert's opinion." You have heard from two economic experts in this case and their opinions as to the loss suffered by Claire are at odds. They differ on this as much as their qualifications differ. You'll recall that the defense insurance expert, Mr. Booster, admitted that our expert has a Ph.D. in economics, while Mr. Booster does not. In fact, the defense expert tried for a while to get a Master's in Business Administration but dropped out of school without completing the program. When during your deliberations you consider the opinions of the experts, recall that jury instruction 9 directs you to consider the expert's qualifications when you decide what weight to give to the expert's opinion.

This list of factual points for cross of Mr. Booster stems from ends-means brainstorming with the tentative closing argument in mind:

List of Factual Points

Facts Pertinent to Lesser Qualifications

The *Educator Collision* Personal Injury Case

- Plaintiff's expert has a Ph.D.;
- Defense expert has a bachelor's degree;
- Defense expert dropped out of an MBA program;
- Plaintiff's expert is widely published in both peer-reviewed journals and authoritative books on economics; and
- Defense expert has neither published peer-reviewed articles nor authored books.

Now that you understand how these factual points can be crafted into a concession-seeking cross, we provide a transcript. Assume that Mr. Booster on direct examination, in an effort to minimize his own educational shortcomings, put down plaintiff's expert's Ph.D. by implying that all academics are ivory-tower know-it-alls lacking in real-world experience. On cross, plaintiff's counsel examines Mr. Booster's qualifications as contrasted with plaintiff's expert's credentials. To highlight the differences, counsel displays a chart with the credentials of the two experts side by side.

TRANSCRIPT

Expert Witness Concession-Seeking Cross: Lesser Qualifications

The *Educator Collision* Personal Injury Case

Q. Mr. Booster, counsel for the defense used the phrase "apples to apples" earlier in comparing your report to that of our economist. Do you remember that?

A. Yes.

Q. What I would like to do is extend that apples-to-apples analysis and compare your qualifications to our expert. You'll see behind you on the board I've written certain things. Are you aware that our expert has his Ph.D. in economics?

A. I'm aware that he has a Ph.D. I don't know what it's in.

Q. Now, let's look in this apples-to-apples analysis at your educational credentials. I'm going off your resume that has been marked as Exhibit No. 45. It appears you have a bachelor's degree in finance?

A. Well, actually the major is in economics and the minor in finance, yes. I also completed all the coursework required for graduation with an MBA.

Q. But, it's fair to say you dropped out of college before you got your MBA?

A. I was just hired by a national accounting firm and was instructed to get my CPA certificate. I focused my direction toward where my career was taking me.

continued ▶

Q. You dropped out and didn't get an MBA?

A. I didn't write the required paper and therefore didn't receive the MBA degree.

Q. And that's why on your resume, it just says "general business administration" with no degree after it?

A. That's correct.

Q. So rather than get the MBA, you went where you thought you would make the most money the fastest?

A. I went where I wanted my career to be. My background wasn't in accounting. It was in finance and economics. So I began studying accounting diligently to come up to speed so I could advance as quickly as possible. I advanced very rapidly there.

Q. Apparently the studying wasn't diligent enough, because you flunked the CPA exam the first time through, didn't you?

A. I passed two parts, failed two parts. That's a usual experience for most people.

Q. You are aware that our expert is a professor of economics at the university you once attended?

A. Yes, I was aware of that.

Q. And you're aware that for someone to be a tenured faculty member at a university level, generally they have to have a doctor's degree in their field?

A. Generally.

Q. You are not qualified to be a university professor?

A. I had exceptional opportunities, which I took full advantage of. Somebody sitting studying for a Ph.D. is still looking at books trying to learn how to do it.

Q. I'll ask you again, you are not qualified to be a university professor, correct?

A. That's correct.

Q. The only things you have published have been in insurance adjustor magazines?

A. No, that's not right.

Q. Is this your resume here, Exhibit No. 45?

A. Sure.

Q. Do you have a section in here that talks about your publications?

A. Sure.

Q. Could you please read for the jury the three publications that you contribute frequently to from your resume?

A. *Insurance Adjustor Magazine, Claims Adjustors Newsletter,* and *Insurance Defense Journal.*

V. STANDARD IMPEACHMENT AREAS — FINANCIAL BIAS ILLUSTRATION

Here, we discuss and provide an example of one of the standard nine areas available to cross-examine any witness, expert or not. Later, we will explore the five other categories applicable only to experts.

As an illustration, let's focus on discrediting an expert by exposing the witness's financial bias. Forensics can be big business, with experts earning substantial yearly incomes. Fees from forensic services often are far more remunerative to the expert than any kind of work within their own field. How much compensation is the expert receiving in the case? If the expert witness's fee is unreasonable based on the work done, the witness may be biased. Or, instead of monetary compensation, there may be an exchange of services. But, keep in mind that jurors do not expect experts to work for free. If an expert did work for free, she could be labeled as biased, as someone promoting some cause.

More significant is whether the expert is a professional expert who either testifies just for plaintiffs or for defendants. The expert may be a professional expert for a particular client—a law firm, government, or industry. If so, the expert may have testified in many cases, providing an identical or a similar opinion. The more his business, or at least a significant percentage of his income, involves expert testimony, the greater the particular expert's motive to win for this client with an eye toward getting the next client.

Some experts limit their vulnerability to financial bias questions by balancing their work between plaintiffs and defendants. With such experts, financial bias questions will not be effective under most circumstances. The mere fact that an expert has made a large sum of money from testifying, without more, is not enough to convince a judge or a jury of bias. In such circumstances, where the expert has testified for both sides equally, the cross-examining lawyer is well advised to touch briefly on the financial bias, such as high returns from legal consultations, and then move on. Establishing any big payouts to the expert is effective only if the expert's testimonial pattern cuts heavily to one side or the other.

For example, in the *Educator Collision* case, your background investigation of Mr. Booster determined that he consistently has been retained by the defense to render opinions regarding damages in personal injury, medical malpractice, wrongful death, wrongful termination, and unfair competition, among other types of cases.

It is essential for lawyers to utilize the pretrial phase of a case to document the financial bias of an expert, first using subpoenas and, then, if resisted, motion practice. Even with the more stringent pretrial disclosure requirements for expert witnesses in federal court, the actual income earned from past cases is not given, often requiring the lawyer to take active steps in order to get it. The one caveat to be applied here is that the same tactics can be turned around and used on your experts by your opponent. If your own expert has a similar financial bias vulnerability, it is usually best to leave this area alone. Trading one black eye for another does not advance your client's case.

Bringing a motion to force an opposing expert to disclose the details of financial bias often operates as follows:

1. Financial bias is a recognized and legitimate area for cross-examination of an expert.
2. The philosophy behind modern pretrial discovery is that information should be disclosed, unless it is privileged or attorney work product.

3. Experts who have something to hide resist turning over financial bias information.

4. While judges are sensitive to the financial privacy concerns of experts, they are likely to grant motions that are carefully crafted requests limited to litigation related income.

5. Jurors look to judges to tell them what the rules are. If an expert resists turning over financial bias information and then is ordered to do so by the judge, that expert is likely to be discredited with a jury when this comes out on cross. Reluctant disclosure makes the financial bias information seem even more dramatic.

In this *Educator Collision* case, the successful motion to force Mr. Booster to turn over two years of litigation-related income from the insurance industry can make him look even more biased during cross. His sworn declaration that the disclosure sought was too burdensome was untrue. Once the jury knows this, it will damage his credibility.

With all this information at hand, you prepare a tentative closing argument that you, as plaintiff's counsel, would like to deliver. From this tentative closing, you will be able to brainstorm and identify the factual points you wish to obtain in cross-examination.

Tentative Closing Argument

Standard Impeachment Financial Bias

The *Educator Collision* Personal Injury Case

Mr. Booster is what you might call a professional defense witness—a hired gun. You heard him testify that he only testifies as a defense expert witness. He has more than 25 insurance companies as clients. Over the last two years, insurance companies have paid him over $1 million. In this case alone, he had made up to $20,000 when he took that witness chair, and he wasn't done billing the insurance company yet. Does Mr. Booster have a financial interest in this case? How much is his opinion worth?

This list of factual points that may be used in cross of Mr. Booster stems from ends-means brainstorming using the tentative closing argument:

List of Factual Points

Facts Pertinent to Financial Bias

The *Educator Collision* Personal Injury Case

- Expert witness refused to turn over financial information;
- Declaration states that the financial information "is not in a form that can be easily compiled";

> - The judge ordered the expert to turn over the information;
> - Expert has 25 insurance company clients;
> - Expert collected fees for two years of over $1 million;
> - Over $20,000 has been billed in this case; and
> - Expert markets his business to insurance companies.

Now, for a sense of how this content would be elicited in cross, the following is the transcript of the cross of Mr. Booster on financial bias.

TRANSCRIPT

Standard Impeachment Area: Financial Bias

The *Educator Collision* Personal Injury Case

Q. You remember I served you with a subpoena to get certain financial information from you?

A. Yes.

Q. And you refused to turn over that information, didn't you?

A. I believe some of it was irrelevant, yes.

Q. And you submitted a declaration in this matter to the judge?

A. Yes.

Q. And that is your declaration there?

A. Yes, it is.

Q. You see there where you say, "This information is not in a form that can be easily compiled."

A. Yes.

Q. The judge ordered you to turn over 1099 forms, didn't she?

A. Yes.

Q. It wasn't hard for your staff to just go to your files and make copies of the 1099 forms, was it?

A. For the 1099 forms, it was not.

Once the attorney gets the expert's financial bias information, the challenge is to present it in an interesting and compelling fashion. The almost irresistible temptation is to engage in a prolonged interrogation on the money issue, particularly when armed with the documentary backup to make it stick. Also, in that it does not deal with an area of the expert's special knowledge, the lawyer has greater comfort with the subject of financial bias and tends to overemphasize it. Resist this temptation. Get in, tell the story of financial bias (the large amount the expert has made testifying for one side in legal cases), and get out. Then, go on to billings in the immediate case as this cross-examination of Mr. Booster does.

TRANSCRIPT (CONTINUED)

Standard Impeachment Area: Financial Bias

The *Educator Collision* Personal Injury Case

Q. Do you recognize the names of the companies on this list as your clients?

A. Some.

Q. Do you see that you received over a half a million dollars two years ago, as reflected in the 1099s from insurance companies?

A. Yes.

Q. And there are more than 25 companies on this list?

A. Appears to be, yes. I haven't counted them.

Q. Well, go ahead and count them.

A. *[Witness complies.]* Yes, there are in excess of 25 here.

Q. Thank you. Now, showing you Exhibit 18, the judge also ordered you to turn over insurance company 1099s for last year, didn't she?

A. Yes.

Q. And could you please read the total for last year from insurance companies to your firm?

A. $612,482.

Q. You have a number of employees working for you at this point?

A. I do.

Q. And any time you bill one of their hours, you make money on what you're billing the clients?

A. I hope so, yes.

Q. And you've had a number of employees working on this case?

A. I believe so, yes.

Q. I want to show you copies of the partial billings you've submitted to the insurance company. Do you recognize those invoices?

A. Yes.

Q. And as of that time you had just shy of $10,000 billed in this case? You can add them up with your calculator if you like.

A. Well, I'll trust your math.

Q. And your billings in this matter are considerably more than are reflected in those invoices?

A. That's correct. The time that I have today, the time that I spent yesterday, and my preparation time isn't included on these invoices.

Q. And how much time did you spend preparing for this?

A. I would say at least six hours just reviewing my files.

Q. Not included in those billings in front of you is the amount of time that you spent on preparing this latest report marked as Exhibit 2, correct?

A. That's correct.

Q. And you're probably up to $20,000 on this case by now?

A. I don't know.

Q. You still haven't sent your last bill to counsel have you?

A. No, I haven't.

Plaintiff's counsel continues with the financial bias subject but with a brand-new theme: "Don't bite the hand that feeds you." Counsel envisions a closing argument that insurance companies have been feeding business to Mr. Booster and that he, in turn, is biased in their favor and would not "bite the hand that feeds him." Just as a good jazz musician must improvise off a basic musical idea in a solo, making it seem new and interesting through creative exploration, so must a lawyer with a cross-examination theme. The plaintiff's lawyer now does a roll call of some of the different insurance companies that have been feeding this expert.

TRANSCRIPT (CONTINUED)

Standard Impeachment Area: Financial Bias

The *Educator Collision* Personal Injury Case

Q. Insurance companies pay a portion of your fees?

A. Yes.

Q. And by what we just went over earlier, they have paid your firm more than a million dollars over a two-year period, correct?

A. That's correct.

Q. That's a significant share of your business revenue?

A. That represents probably a quarter of our total revenue, so it's a significant portion, but it's certainly not all.

Q. And your firm's insurance business is growing steadily?

A. I can't tell you if the insurance work is growing at the same rate as it did in the past.

Q. Well, let's go with the known world, then. Remember I just had you calculate the increase in your insurance business as recorded in the 1099 forms? Remember that?

A. Yes.

Q. And what answer did you give me?

A. It was a little over 14 percent.

Q. 14.9, wasn't it?

A. Yes.

Q. All right, I'm just going to write that up here on the board. "Expert's insurance referral business up 14.9 percent." The growth in your firm's insurance business isn't a random occurrence. You've done some marketing over the years?

A. Actually we do very little marketing. A good-quality job is generally what sells our work.

Q. How about the seminars you give to insurance companies?

A. I have given insurance seminars in the past, yes.

Q. You've been out to State Farm?

A. Yes.

Q. Farmers?

continued ▶

> *A.* Yes.
>
> *Q.* Allstate?
>
> *A.* Yes. I think you're mischaracterizing the seminars. They're not marketing seminars. The purpose I perform them is for educational purposes so that insurance companies understand how to calculate claims, how to understand accounting data.
>
> *Q.* And, once an insurance company uses your firm, you hope they'll use you again in the future, don't you?
>
> *A.* What we try to do is do our work as fairly and accurately as possible, and the chips kind of fall from there.
>
> *Q.* Let's try that again. Once an insurance company uses your firm, you hope they'll use you again in the future?
>
> *A.* Yes.

Notice how the example above ties bias with the type of self-interest when being a professional witness is the expert's business.

VI. FIVE EXPERT IMPEACHMENT AREAS

Now we turn to these five areas of impeachment cross that apply only to experts:

1. Lack of qualifications to testify as an expert witness;
2. Unreliability of the scientific area;
3. Deficiencies in the procedure and factual data used;
4. Limits and problems with the opinion; and
5. Learned treatises.

When you plan the content of cross-examination, think about all five potential areas that apply only to experts that you might explore, but be mindful that a successful cross-examination can be based on any one of these categories. Also, throughout this section there is a continuum between admissibility and weight. For example, the same attack on qualifications by which you seek to exclude the expert's testimony will, if your objection to admissibility is overruled, serve as the basis for an attack in cross-examination geared to diminishing the weight the jury should give the expert's opinion.

A. Qualifications

Your purpose in attacking the expert's qualifications in cross-examination is not to disqualify the expert from testifying because efforts at keeping the expert off the stand will already have taken place during an *in limine* motion or in voir dire during direct examination. Rather, any attack you make on the expert's qualifications during cross-examination will be designed to persuade the jury to give little weight to the expert's testimony.

An Area of Vulnerability for an Expert

The following are some areas where the expert may be vulnerable to a cross-examination designed to discredit the expert based on lack of qualifications:

- The expert is *less qualified* or lacks credentials that your expert has. For example, the witness lacks practical experience in laboratory work while your expert works in a lab. This approach sets up closing argument that contrasts the two expert's qualifications.
- The expert is *deficient* in education, experience, or other area normally associated with qualifying the particular type of expert.
- There are *inaccuracies* in credentials. For instance, a law enforcement officer claims to have a master's degree in biology but has only a bachelor's degree.
- The credentials are *exaggerated or hollow.* The expert belongs to professional organizations that require only the payment of dues to belong.
- The expert is testifying *outside the witness's area of expertise.* The expert is knowledgeable about respiratory physiology but has little experience in neurophysiology.

An illustration of how to cross-examine on qualifications can be found at pages 277-278.

Another subject for cross arises when the expert ventures outside his or her field of expertise. It is typical for lawyers to cross-examine experts on the limits of their expertise, in turn attacking the foundation for, and scope of, their opinions. This can get very tedious quickly for the judge or jury. If the expert has overreached the limits of his or her qualifications in rendering opinions, the better approach is to go directly to that, establishing why this is so.

In the *Educator Collision* case, plaintiff's counsel consulted with their expert economist, who said that the defense forensic accountant went beyond his expertise in rendering opinions on Claire's medical condition and on the supposed lifestyle benefits to her from a disability retirement. To plan cross on this subject, plaintiff's counsel thinks ahead and formulates a tentative closing on these subjects.

Expert Witness Impeachment Area: Outside Area of Expertise in the *Educator Collision* Personal Injury Case

And then Mr. Booster rendered opinions on subjects for which he has absolutely no qualifications whatsoever. He gave his medical opinion that Claire didn't leave her job because of the day-in, day-out pain she suffered as a result of the collision. He gave his medical opinion that it had nothing to do with her health. He's no doctor;

continued ▶

> he told you he has no medical training. And, then, he told you that Claire left her job as the School District Program Director because she wanted a better lifestyle. This time he gave his opinion as a mind reader — a mentalist. A mind reader who has never even met Claire. You heard her testify. She loved her job. She left because she had no choice.

This list of factual points that may be elicited during cross of Mr. Booster is the product of ends-means brainstorming using the tentative closing argument:

List of Factual Points

Facts Pertinent to Qualifications

The *Educator Collision* Personal Injury Case
- Expert has no medical training;
- Expert has no training in quality-of-life issues; and
- Expert ignored Claire's statements in her deposition that she loved her job and that she had to quit for medical reasons.

In the *Educator Collision* case, if the defense expert stated during direct examination that he had read all the depositions in the case prior to giving his opinions, plaintiff's counsel is then entitled to bring up inconsistencies between the deposition and the expert's report. The transcript of the cross of Mr. Booster on his lack of qualifications is as follows:

TRANSCRIPT

Expert Witness Impeachment Area: Outside Area of Expertise

The *Educator Collision* Personal Injury Case

Q. Let's discuss your qualifications to evaluate Claire Butterfield's health and lifestyle. You're not a doctor?

A. No.

Q. You don't have any medical training?

A. No.

Q. Have you heard the term CRC before, Certified Rehabilitation Counselor?

A. Yes, I have.

Q. You aren't a CRC?

A. No. I'm not.

Q. You don't make medical judgments about whether or not a person is disabled?

A. No.

Q. In your report, you talk about increased quality-of-life issues that may be of benefit to my client?

A. Yes.

Q. You don't have any specific training in how the length of workweeks affects the emotions of human beings?

A. Correct.

Q. Yet you offered an opinion on that subject in this report?

A. I did.

Q. You also state on page 6 of your report, "No evidence has been produced to substantiate any relationship between the change of employment and the accident."

A. Yes.

Q. Now, I want you to go back to her deposition.

A. Sure.

Q. Do you see where my client said in her deposition, "So it's a job emotionally that has been very, very difficult to leave because it's so rewarding."

A. Yes.

B. Reliability of the Expert's Field

An assault on the reliability of the expert's field is available to you even if you do not present your own expert in the same field. Or, you may use this area of cross if you intend to offer an expert in the field who will testify that those in that field should not venture the type of opinion the other side's expert intends to render.

Expert Witness Unreliability

Area of Vulnerability for an Expert

Some components of a discipline that may provide fruitful topics to explore on cross-examination are as follows:

- The field of expertise is *subject to manipulation* to achieve the expert's goals;
- The *lack of training* that a person has in the field ("There is no particular training required to do what you do?" "No degree required?" "And there's no certification or licensing?");
- The *imprecise nature of the tests and procedures* used ("So, you consider ten factors, none of which has more weight than any other?" "Then you decide if there's a match?" "But your field has no set standards for how to assess those factors?" "And you do not need all ten factors to find a match?" "You just know it's a match?");
- The *unreliability of instruments;* and
- The field's *failure to gain acceptance* by other professional disciplines.

Cross-examination regarding the unreliable nature of the field can convince the jury to adopt a skeptical frame of mind about the expert's results and opinion, thus giving the opinion little or no weight.

When counsel cross-examines about the unreliability of the expert's field, she moves into the expert's territory, and the going gets potentially much rougher. Judges and jurors hate an extended course of trivial pursuit questions propounded by the lawyer to the expert. And, often enough, the expert is likely to be able to have a reasonable sounding explanation for nearly any substantive questions the lawyer poses.

Muhammad Ali's boxing strategy of "float like a butterfly, sting like a bee" best outlines the technique for successfully cross-examining an expert in substantive areas. The lawyer should not get bogged down in any one area, turning the cross-examination into a debate. The goal is to keep it moving, winning the fight of impression by a series of jabs, all of which appeal to the jury's common sense and experience.

In the *Educator Collision* case, plaintiff's counsel can focus cross on the unreliability of the field because numbers can be manipulated. Given general public knowledge of accounting fraud scandals in the corporate world, the expert has to concede that accounting fraud has happened. People do manipulate numbers improperly for financial gain. Note carefully that Mr. Booster is never asked directly if he manipulated the numbers in this case in this fashion, as he would have given a self-serving speech in response. The question is raised and either answered in summation or not mentioned at all and left hanging in the air for the jury to answer on their own. In this tentative closing, which is a guide to brainstorming for the content of cross, the answer is suggested.

Tentative Closing Argument

Expert Witness Impeachment Area: Unreliability

The *Educator Collision* Personal Injury Case

Accounting is not a hard science. In fact, it's really soft. Why? Because numbers can be manipulated. The defense expert conceded this. He told you that Arthur Andersen manipulated numbers for Enron. There is a quip attributed sometimes to Mark Twain that goes this way: "There are lies, damn lies and statistics." Looking at defense accountant's calculations of Claire's loss, you may conclude during your deliberations that the quotation should be reworded to say: "There are lies, damn lies and accounting." It's up to you to decide if the dollar amount that Mr. Booster gave you is accurate and fair.

This list of factual points for the cross of Mr. Booster comes from brainstorming with the use of the tentative closing argument:

List of Factual Points

Facts Pertinent to Unreliability

The *Educator Collision* Personal Injury Case
- Numbers can be manipulated
- Arthur Andersen manipulated the books for Enron Corporation

---

TRANSCRIPT

Expert Witness Impeachment Area: Unreliability

The *Educator Collision* Personal Injury Case

Q. Now, why don't we discuss accounting? Numbers are capable of being manipulated in dishonest ways?

A. Well, I guess you would have to give me some context.

Q. All right, let's give you some context here. You are familiar with the story of the Arthur Andersen firm's complicity in preparing fraudulent statements for Enron?

A. Yes, I am.

Q. Have you ever heard the vernacular phrase "cook the books" before?

A. Yes.

Q. What does that mean when an accountant cooks the books?

A. That would mean that they would enter transactions on the books and records of a company that are not consistent with generally accepted accounting principles.

Q. That would be fraud?

A. Well, there are two issues that are involved there. It depends on how the information and the application of those principles were used.

Q. We can agree that certain Arthur Andersen partners manipulated numbers in dishonest ways for Enron, correct?

A. Yes, I think we could agree with that.

Q. And that ended up having rather disastrous consequences for the Arthur Andersen firm?

A. It did.

Q. And led to criminal convictions?

A. It did.

Q. So the integrity of numbers all depends on the integrity of the person that is working with them?

A. That's true.

Q. And we can agree that at least some of the Arthur Andersen partners with Enron did not have the requisite integrity?

A. That's correct.

C. Procedures and Factual Data

Cross-examination assailing the data or procedures used by the expert challenges the reliability and trustworthiness of that expert's opinion. In this regard, urging the jury to discount your opposing party's expert opinion because of deficiencies in the underlying basis for the expert's opinion is often the strongest point you can make. It also allows you to attack the expert's opinion without actually taking on the expert. Experts rely on three kinds of data: data created by the expert through experiments and investigation; information that is given to the expert about the case; and data prepared by others and relied on by experts in the field.

Expert Witness — Procedures and Data

Areas of Vulnerability for an Expert

The expert's opinion may be vulnerable in the following areas:

- The *time* the expert had or used in analyzing the data. For instance, the doctor examined the patient for ten minutes; psychiatrist did not examine criminal defendant until ten weeks after the crime.
- *Information was incomplete.* The engineer did not receive all the blueprints.
- Expert is making an *incorrect assumption about the data.* For example, the expert assumes that the core soil sample he was given was from "quadrant 4"; you will present evidence that the sample was from "quadrant 3," which invalidates the expert's calculation.
- Expert received *faulty or biased data.* Much of the data is from an interested party.
- Expert's procedures or experiments for analyzing the data were *faulty, unreliable, left undone, or wrong.* For example, a metallurgist failed to heat the metal to the appropriate temperature.

Another impeachment technique involves asking the expert witness either to assume additional facts or to substitute different facts that you know will be presented at trial. You can then ask the adverse expert whether the different or additional facts might change the expert's opinion. If the expert answers in the affirmative, the expert's opinion is significantly weakened. If, however, the witness is reluctant to change or modify her testimony no matter how you change the facts, it may become apparent to the jury that the witness is biased, inflexible, and really advocates an unrealistic position.

In this piece of a tentative summation, which is used to plan cross, the argument points were derived from brainstorming with a focus on portions of Claire's deposition testimony that this Booster had read but ignored.

Expert Witness Impeachment Area:
Inadequate Procedures and Data

The *Educator Collision* Personal Injury Case

The opinions that the defense economist gave you are not just unsupported by the evidence, those opinions are in direct conflict with the evidence. Contrast what Mr. Booster testified to with what you have learned during this trial. The defense expert said Claire's "choice to retire does provide her with an increased quality of life including the following benefits," and then Mr. Booster went on to list those benefits. The evidence clearly proves that the quality of Claire's life has not gotten better. It's gotten worse. Claire took that chair of truth over there and told you that her physical well-being has gotten worse and worse. She loved working, even at a lower-paying job. She was forced into retirement by her medical condition caused by the defendant's negligence.

The following list of factual points for cross-examination of Mr. Booster is the product of ends-means brainstorming using the tentative closing argument:

Facts Pertinent to Inadequate Procedures and Data

The *Educator Collision* Personal Injury Case

- Booster listed benefits of retirement for Claire;
- Claire's physical health has gotten worse since the collision;
- Claire loved her work;
- Expert never spoke to Claire; and
- Expert never spoke to Claire's colleagues.

The transcript of this line of questioning reads as follows:

TRANSCRIPT

Expert Witness Impeachment Area: Inadequate Procedures and Data

The *Educator Collision* Personal Injury Case

Q. You read my client's deposition?
A. Yes.
Q. Do you have that with you now?

continued ▶

A. Yes.

Q. Could you please turn to page 56?

A. *[Witness complies.]*

Q. Are you there?

A. Yes.

Q. When you read this deposition, did you note on page 56, line 5, where my client says, "I would say the day-to-day living is difficult. Everything that I do is related to how much pain I am feeling. I am in constant pain, even with all the medication. It reduces the level of pain, but I'm rarely without." Did you see that there?

A. Yes.

Q. I read that accurately?

A. Yes, you did.

Q. All right, please turn to page 57.

A. *[Witness complies.]*

Q. Do you see on line 11 where my client says, "For the last several years I've had days where I would say to my secretary, I wish I could climb out of my skin, it hurts so bad."

A. Yes.

Q. And now if you can turn to page 85.

A. *[Witness complies.]*

Q. At line 8 do you see where she says, "I have not improved, and I believe that I am doing right now the maximum exercise program that I can do." Do you see that?

A. Yes.

Q. And there at the bottom where she says, "I don't see a dramatic increase in my physical well-being. It concerns me that as I get older it will get worse. The women in my family tend to live into their 90s. They all have, in fact." I read that correctly?

A. Yes.

Q. When you read my client's deposition, you saw these sworn answers she gave that she experiences significant physical pain?

A. Yes.

Q. Thank you. Now, I want to ask you about the narrative in your report. You purport to analyze benefits to my client from no longer being in the workforce on a regular basis, don't you?

A. I am saying that there are factors that the insurance company lawyer may wish to consider.

Q. Do you see where you said on page 87, line 10, leaving her position "may not be related to the accident"?

A. Yes.

Q. "Her choice to retire does provide her with an increased quality of life including the following benefits." Did I read that correctly?

A. Yes, you did.

Q. And your first bullet is, "Her new job involves shorter working hours," right?

A. Yes.

Q. And then you discuss that they own a vacation home where they eventually plan to retire, concluding, "She can spend more time there." Did you say that there?

A. Yes.

Q. And then going, following your bullets here, "She reduced her emotional stress." Is that one of your bullet points?

A. Yes.

Q. And then your next bullet, "Her new position has a shorter job commute."

A. Yes.

Q. And now, I want you to tell us what your conclusion was in this report as to my client's economic loss. What did you conclude here?

A. That at this point she had documented a loss of less than $12,000.

Q. Have you ever met my client?

A. No.

Q. Have you ever talked to any of her colleagues?

A. No.

D. The Expert's Opinion

The most difficult area to explore in cross-examination of an adverse expert witness is the expert's opinion. Getting an expert to concede that his opinion is wrong is improbable. When the cross-examiner ventures into the expert's field, as will happen when the examiner challenges the expert's opinion, the cross-examiner enters into perilous territory.

Expert Witness—Expert Opinion

An Area of Vulnerability for an Expert

Despite the danger of going into the expert's field, it is possible for a well-planned cross-examination to be effective if it follows one of the following four lines of inquiry.

- First, you may be able to expose *inconsistencies* in the expert's opinion by showing the expert's opinion is at odds with the expert's prior opinion (as expressed in interrogatories, deposition testimony, published articles, and so on), the factual data in the case or in similar cases, the literature in the field, or the expert's own notes and records in the case.
- The second cross-examination technique is to make the expert *go to an extreme* in defending her opinion.
- A third line of inquiry is to show that the expert's opinion is a *matter of judgment* based on many factors and not a matter of immutable doctrine. This will be particularly useful if you call an expert who has come to a different conclusion.
- The fourth line of inquiry tries to establish that the *opinion is limited.* After all the dust has settled from extensive qualifications and detailed tests, the expert is not really saying very much concerning the case.

E. Learned Treatise

Unique to the examination of expert witnesses is that counsel can bring learned treatises into play. Federal Rule of Evidence 803(18) provides that a statement in a learned treatise, periodical, or pamphlet is not excluded under the hearsay rule. Under this Rule, an expert may be cross-examined concerning the content of learned treatises if:

- It is called to the attention of the witness on cross or it was relied on by the witness on direct; and
- It is reliable authority established by (a) admission on cross, (b) judicial notice, or (c) testimony by another expert.

Once the treatise is admitted into evidence, it may be read to the jury, but it is not admitted as an exhibit. The information read is substantive evidence. This allows a trial lawyer to draw on learned treatises in dynamic ways. In cross-examination, the trial lawyer can employ an opinion in an authoritative publication to contradict the opinion of the witness under examination.

F. Challenging the Expert's Opinion and Learned Treatise Illustration

One of the prime goals of cross-examining an opposing expert who has done some form of mathematical calculations is to attack both the expert's assumptions and the formulas the expert utilized to reach opinions, and to reveal how the expert's opinion conflicts with authoritative literature in the field. Almost always, some other accepted method of calculation in the expert's field will produce different results than the expert has testified to.

An important pretrial preparation goal of the cross-examining lawyer is to get comfortable with these other formulas and approaches. Then, at trial, counsel can force the expert to do the math in front of the jury, getting a different result.

This do-the-math approach to cross-examination of an expert is a winning approach for the lawyer if it has been carefully thought through in advance. If the expert argues with the approach and resists, a cool, even-keel response from the cross-examining lawyer makes the expert look evasive. If the questions are properly framed, any long speeches by the expert about why the suggested approach is wrong will tend to reflect poorly on his credibility.

The biggest challenge for the lawyer is to get in with these calculation questions and then get out, building drama, not turning the exercise into a tedious mathematics lesson.

Let's return again to the *Educator Collision* case. Forensic accountant Mr. Booster is already on record in prior cases endorsing a particular learned treatise on work-life expectancies as authoritative. Plaintiff's counsel went through this book with care, crafting cross-examination questions based on information in it, which, if used, would give a different result, making the plaintiff's damages greater than in the expert's report.

To plan your cross-examination of Mr. Booster, you draft the following tentative closing argument to assist you in brainstorming.

Tentative Closing Argument

Expert Witness Impeachment Area: Expert Opinion and Learned Treatise

The *Educator Collision* Personal Injury Case

In this courtroom you watched Mr. Booster calculate the economic loss to Claire and arrive at a figure that is close to the amount that we have asked you to award her in your verdict. Their expert did this using work-life expectancy tables from a book he was well aware of. In fact he told you that it is 'a book we refer to regularly in my office.

Brainstorming back from the tentative closing to the concessions the witness must make and back to the closing again, you compile the following list:

List of Factual Points

Facts Pertinent to Expert Opinion and Learned Treatise

The *Educator Collision* Personal Injury Case

- Defense expert will concede that *Work Life Expectancies* is a reliable authority in the field; and
- Using the tables in the book leads to a dollar figure close to what plaintiff is seeking.

With these initial facts, you develop your cross-notes unit on the Work Life Experiences learned treatise. The transcript of the cross on the subject reads as follows:

TRANSCRIPT

Expert Witness Impeachment Area: Opinion and Learned Treatise

The *Educator Collision* Personal Injury Case

Q. Mr. Booster, you are familiar with the book entitled *Work Life Expectancies*?
A. Sure, it's a book that we refer to regularly in my office.

---

continued ▶

> *Q.* And you consider that it is an authoritative source?
> *A.* For the purposes intended, yes.
> *Q.* I want to show you page 173 from this book.
> *A.* Okay.
> *Q.* What is the title of the table on that page?
> *A.* "Work Life Expectancies — White Females."
> *Q.* And do you see the last column where it says "Graduate Degree"?
> *A.* Sure.
> *Q.* Are you aware that my client has her master's degree?
> *A.* Yes.
> *Q.* That's a graduate degree?
> *A.* That's correct.
> *Q.* Could you please step up to the board and write the figure for work-life expectancy from that book for a white female with a graduate degree under the column "All"? Before you do that, you're aware that my client is 55 years old?
> *A.* I think she's older than that at present, isn't she? No, you're right.
> *Q.* And what is her work-life expectancy?
> *A.* Ten years.
> *Q.* And we can agree that my client was making $100,864 on an annual basis at the time she left the public school system, right?
> *A.* Yes.
> *Q.* And now, let's go to page 186 in the book. Could you please read what this table represents?
> *A.* It's titled "Work Life Expectancies by Educational Attainment."
> *Q.* For white females?
> *A.* Yes.
> *Q.* And under a graduate degree, do you see there is a specific column "Master's Degree"?
> *A.* Yes.
> *Q.* And for a 55-year-old female, what number of years is listed in this work-life expectancy?
> *A.* 9.3.
> *Q.* Could you please multiply out 9.3 times the $100,864 that my client was making at the time she left the public school system?
> *A.* $938,035.20.

VII. STRUCTURING CROSS

As we discussed in Chapter 4, sequencing in cross-examination is always an issue. What is the best order in which to proceed in cross-examining the expert? As we have stated, the laws of primacy and recency are useful in making these decisions. People generally remember best what comes first and last, tending to forget the middle. Because you have the jury's attention when you commence cross, you want to start with some of your best material. If you are absolutely sure that you can discredit the expert or the expert's testimony at the outset, that is a fine time to do it.

However, as we have repeatedly warned, experts are challenging professional witnesses and usually you will not demolish the witness or get the witness on the run. Therefore, the best approach generally is to begin with a concession-seeking cross-examination. Another reason to begin in this manner is that, typically, at the outset of cross the witness will be more obliging. To foster the expert's cooperativeness, trial counsel can be courteous and non-confrontational. Once challenged, the expert may well become combative and less likely to grant concessions. A concession-seeking cross is most likely to be fruitful, and, if it succeeds, perhaps even turn the witness to your advantage, allowing you to forgo discrediting the witness.

As an illustration, consider the order of cross in the *Educator Collision* case. You have the written out your questions in topical units in the cross-notes format. Each unit normally is self-contained with a beginning, middle, and an end, much like a scene in a movie. You then organize the units (scenes) into an overarching narrative story (movie). The story should start strong, finish strong, and put lesser material in the middle. Here are the units of the Booster cross organized into the story of a less qualified expert, who with insufficient information reached an ill-informed and erroneous conclusion as to Claire's loss:

- Defense expert is less qualified;
- He has a financial bias;
- He testified outside his field of expertise;
- Accounting is only as reliable as the person who works the numbers;
- He ignored information about plaintiff's medical condition and that information was essential to his opinions as to plaintiff's loss; and
- Using an authoritative book's tables, the defense expert must calculate plaintiff's loss at an amount sought by the plaintiff.

No perfect formula exists that will tell you what to select, and lawyers will differ over the best order. You might conclude that Mr. Booster's financial bias is so strong that you should begin with it and that his bias will cast a shadow over everything else he testifies to on cross. On the other hand, he must concede that your expert is more academically qualified then he is, and this subject could be addressed in a non-confrontational manner. From there you could move on in the concession-seeking approach by having the expert concede that *Work Life Expectancies* is an authoritative book and, using the table in the book, ask the witness to calculate plaintiff's loss.

Then, you could move to an impeachment cross, which is likely to prove more contentious. The order here could be to cross on the unreliability of the field, his testimony outside his field, and the fact that he ignored Claire's complaints about her health and life as reflected in her deposition.

Then again, this planned order may be altered based on Booster's direct examination. For example, although you had planned to begin with the witness's financial bias, you could change your mind. If defense counsel made a sufficiently big deal of the "apples-to-apples" comparison of the report of his accountant with that of your economist, you could feel there would be even more drama and interest by usurping the phrase and a comparison by analogy in cross, while it was still fresh in the jury's mind.

Cross-examination is both drama and a spectator sport. A strong, memorable finish casts an afterglow back through the entire cross, under the principle of recency. How you conclude cross should be not only on a high note but also solid—an irrefutable point.

In the *Educator Collision* case, you finish with your strong irrefutable point: the expert's concession to a dollar figure close to what you are seeking for your client.

TRANSCRIPT

Expert Witness Impeachment Area: Inadequate Procedures and Data

The *Educator Collision* Personal Injury Case

Q. Hypothetically, if a person is 55 years old and becomes disabled, if they had planned to work to age 65 that's ten years of loss, isn't it?

A. Yes. If they're 100 percent disabled.

Q. And let's say their salary when they're 55 is $100,000. Are you with me so far?

A. Yes.

Q. What's ten times $100,000?

A. One million dollars.

Q. Thank you, that's all I have.

VIII. CONDUCTING CROSS

The techniques for conducting cross-examination of lay witnesses discussed in Chapter 9 also apply to expert witnesses. Techniques for controlling the witness, covered in Chapter 10, can be even more problematic when dealing with an adverse expert witness.

The expert has a point of view and opinions to express. The skilled expert will advocate for those views and opinions if given any chance. The problem is compounded by the fact that many experts have extensive experience in the witness chair. Some of them have more courtroom time than the attorneys trying the case. The witness may evade your questions or jump from quick answers to your questions to lecturing you. Remain courteous and calm. Keep your ego out of your cross-examination. Do not try to show everyone that you know as much as, if not more, than the expert. Just focus on obtaining information and you will be fine. Choose a few points to establish in your cross-examination of the adverse expert witness, and then know when to stop, particularly if the cross-examination has produced a favorable concession.

As you prepare to conduct the cross, keep asking yourself: "Will my choice of words communicate with the jury?" The expert is well-versed in her arcane area of expertise, and you have educated yourself to a certain level of understanding of that expertise. The jury, however, knows nothing about the subject. Work to word your questions as simply as possible. If you have performed a cross that only another lawyer or expert can appreciate, you have failed no matter how brilliant you may have been.

CHECKLIST: CROSS-EXAMINING THE EXPERT

The Expert Challenges

❑ The expert witness presents the cross-examiner with challenges that lay witnesses do not, including, among others, trial experience and superior knowledge of the subject matter.

Selecting the Content of Cross

❑ Concession-seeking cross can be very effective with an honest and qualified expert.

❑ Impeachment cross areas include the following areas applicable to all witnesses:
1. Lack of personal knowledge;
2. Mental and sensory deficiencies;
3. Bias and interest;
4. Improbability;
5. Prior inconsistent statements;
6. Contradiction;
7. Prior convictions;
8. Prior misconduct probative of untruthfulness; and
9. Character witness.

❑ Additional impeachment-cross areas applicable only to expert witnesses include:
1. Qualifications;
2. Reliability of the field of expertise;
3. Basis for the expert's opinion;
4. Opinion; and
5. Learned treatises.

Four-Step Methodology

❑ The four steps for identifying the content of cross for an expert witness are:
1. Formulate the case theory;
2. Analyze the opposing party's case theory for concessions;
3. Brainstorm for concessions by asking what the witness must concede or face impeachment; and
4. Brainstorm the law and facts for concessions and impeachment areas.

❑ Avoid challenging the expert in the field of expertise because of the expert's superior knowledge.

Five Expert Impeachment Areas

1. Qualifications of the expert may be attacked as vulnerable because:
   • By comparison, the opponent's expert is less qualified;
   • The expert's qualifications are deficient;
   • There are inaccuracies in the credentials;
   • Credentials are exaggerated or hollow; and/or
   • The subject is outside the expert's area of expertise.
2. The expert's field of expertise is unreliable because:
   • The field of expertise is subject to manipulation;
   • People in the field lack training;
   • The tests and procedures are imprecise;
   • Instruments used are unreliable; and
   • The field has failed to gain acceptance.
3. Procedures and factual data relied on by the expert were deficient because:
   • Insufficient time was used analyzing the data;
   • The expert had incomplete information;
   • Assumptions that the expert made were incorrect;
   • Data was faulty or biased; and/or
   • The procedures or experiments employed to analyze the data were faulty, unreliable, left undone, or wrong.
4. The expert's opinion is vulnerable to attack because:
   • It is inconsistent with a previously expressed opinion, published articles, factual data in similar cases, and so on;
   • Defending it is a stretch;
   • It is a matter of judgment in a soft science field of expertise; and/or
   • The opinion is limited and says little about the issue.
5. Under Fed. R. Evid. 803(18) learned treatises may be used in the cross-examination of an expert if the treatise is called to the attention of the witness on cross or was relied on by the witness on direct and is reliable.

Structuring and Conducting Cross of an Expert

❑ The principles, strategies, and techniques for structuring and conducting cross as explained in Chapters 4, 9, and 13 apply with more force to the cross of experts.
❑ Because it is rare that an expert witness is demolished, a concession-seeking cross is a preferable approach.
❑ Control strategies and techniques are particularly important for cross of an expert because the expert is employed to communicate the other side's case theory and may seek to wrench control away in order to do that.

CHAPTER 13

FORGETTERS, PERJURERS, ADVERSE WITNESSES & MORE

". . . (T)he classic Anglo-Saxon method of cross-examination is still the best means of coping with deception, dragging the truth out of a reluctant witness, and of assuring the triumph of justice over venality. This process is as successful as the lawyer's thorough preparation and skill make it . . ."
— **Louis Nizer**, *My Life in Court*
366 (Doubleday and Company 1961)

"A pessimist sees the difficulty in every opportunity; an optimist sees the opportunity in every difficulty."
— **Winston Spencer Churchill** (1874-1965)

I. PROBLEMATIC WITNESSES

Difficult witnesses present definite challenges to cross-examiners. For instance, how do you successfully cross-examine a witness who claims to be unable to recall? On the other hand, the problems posed by these witnesses fall into predictable categories and that is a blessing. Effective strategies and techniques for handling difficult witnesses have been developed. This chapter presents some of these, helping you to turn challenges into opportunities.

II. FEIGNING FORGETFULNESS AND/OR IGNORANCE

The witness who feigns forgetfulness ("I can't recall," "I don't remember") or pretends to be ignorant ("I really don't know") is raising a shield to guard against the examiner.

A. Strategies and Techniques

Six techniques can be applied to expose the faking forgetter or ignorant witness:

Forgetfulness or Ignorance

Six Cross-Examination Techniques

1. Establish that the person is neither ignorant nor forgetful.
2. Ask about significant and unforgettable matters.
3. Elicit as many "I don't remember" or "I don't know" answers as possible.
4. Show that the witness remembers things less significant than that which the witness claims not to know.
5. Confront the witness with a prior statement proving that which the witness claims either to have forgotten or not to know.
6. Lock the witness into not recalling a favorable fact that the examiner can prove through another witness.

When the witness dodges questions by claiming not to recall or not to know, establish the facts that this assertion is improbable. Then, argue this improbability in your summation.

First, seek to establish that despite claims to the contrary, the witness has a good memory, or is knowledgeable.

Second, because the witness normally will falsely claim forgetfulness or lack of knowledge on subjects that he or she does not wish to be explored, create the contrast by asking about nonsensitive matters. A pattern of selective recall will emerge and counsel can point out this contrast to the jury in summation:

Closing Argument

Mr. Howell had no trouble whatsoever remembering the details of day-to-day business operations when his attorney questioned him on direct examination. He had no problem answering my questions about opening the new shipyard in Ruston. However, his mind conveniently went blank when I asked about warning users and customers of product hazards.

Third, make the witness profess forgetfulness or ignorance a number of times. The more a witness evades a question that the witness should be able to answer, the worse he or she looks. Count the number of times the witness says, "I can't recall" or "I don't know," giving the jury the total in your summation, "You heard Mr. Howell hide behind his claim that he didn't remember 42 times when asked about his failure to warn product users."

Fourth, ask the witness a question about something of equal or greater importance in a nonsensitive area that occurred in the past and that he or she is likely to answer. If the witness does answer, it sets up this attack in final argument based on selective recall: "For most of us, our memories fade with time. However, Mr. Howell's is different. Like fine wine, his seems to get better with age."

A fifth technique designed to counter the feigned forgetful or ignorant witness is through confrontation with a prior statement preserved in a document or e-mail. Cross-examiner: "Maybe this will help you. I'm going to read your e-mail to Ms. Locker dated February 14, two years ago. Follow along to make sure I read this correctly . . . ." See pages 315-316 for other examples of how to get a witness to concede the contents of a prior statement.

A sixth and final technique for handling a forgetter is to ask a line of questions capitalizing on the witness's claimed lack of memory and that the cross-examiner has a witness who can establish the fact that the witness claims not to be able to remember. The questioning goes like this:

Q. Because you can't remember, you don't really know whether X (favorable fact) occurred?

Q. Because you can't remember, you're in no position to say that X didn't occur?

Q. To find out whether X occurred, should we ask someone who can remember?

Q. And if that someone said X occurred, you couldn't dispute it?

This last technique should be used sparingly, and only with a fact for which you have testimony from another witness.

B. Illustration: The Cross-Examination of Jeffrey Skilling

Assistant U.S. Attorney Sean Berkowitz's cross-examination of Jeffrey Skilling in the *Enron* case turned this witness's "I can't recall" responses to advantage. In 2006, Kenneth Lay and Jeffrey Skilling, respectively former chairman and former president of Enron Corporation, were charged, tried, and convicted of securities fraud and other charges related to the collapse of Enron. Skilling was sentenced to 24 years in prison and Lay died while awaiting sentencing.

Courtroom observer Bethany McLean, editor-at-large for *Fortune* magazine, reported:

> On direct, he (Skilling) was very confident, very smooth, walking through details of the business with precise recollection. And on cross-examination, you heard "I don't recall" out of his mouth almost every other sentence. And he was very almost meek, very subdued.

The Newshour with Jim Lehrer, April 17, 2006.

Enron Prosecutors Kathryn Ruemmler and Sean Berkowitz

On cross, Skilling's sketchy recall of events was in sharp contrast to his detailed direct examination responses. Prosecutor Berkowitz pressed Skilling about his investments in an ex-girlfriend's photo-sharing business, which did business with Enron. When asked if he reported the potential conflict of interest, as required by Enron's Code of Ethics, Skilling replied, "It was a small investment, I don't really recall." He testified that he may have informed Ken Lay but didn't recall writing to the board about this ethical issue. Berkowitz asked if Skilling was aware that the photo-sharing business received most of its income from Enron. The witness responded vaguely, "I may have, I just don't remember." When quizzed about incriminating conversations with previous colleagues turned government witnesses, Skilling repeatedly professed not to remember. Houston Chronicle, Mary Flood, April 17, 2006.

Prosecutor Berkowitz turned the forgetfulness of witness Skilling into an opportunity, asking about subjects that a normal person would be unlikely to forget, such as an $180,000 investment in his ex-girlfriend's business. His repeated probing of this subject caused Skilling to claim lapse of memory multiple times.

III. PERJURER

A. Recapitulation

Chapters 6 through 8 explain strategies and techniques for a winning impeachment cross to expose falsehoods. You have seen how this worked in a number of illustrative cases, such as F. Lee Bailey's cross of Mark Fuhrman that led to Fuhrman's perjury conviction (pages 166-168) and Abraham Lincoln's cross of Charles Allen, which exposed Allen's mistake (pages 120-122). The successful unmasking of a perjurer not only discredits the witness, but also the opponent who called the perjurer. This section focuses exclusively on examining perjurers, applying techniques covered earlier, while adding new ones to the mix. Before we begin, here is a recapitulation of the impeachment techniques covered in earlier material and modified to specifically fit the demonstrable liar:

Perjurer

Cross-Examination Techniques

1. *Assess* to be certain that the witness is lying and you have the evidence to prove it. Adjust your demeanor and presentation to be firm and confrontational.
2. Establish a *motive*.
3. *Paint a picture* for the jury.
4. *Lock the witness into the factual claim* that you can disprove.
5. *Close all the exits* to prevent evasion or explanation.
6. Do not signal the witness where you are going, maintaining the element of *surprise*.
7. Use *visual or tangible evidence* to enhance the impeachment.

B. Avoid It

The first strategy is to avoid accusing a witness of being a liar unless you are sure of two things: (1) it is patently obvious that the witness is lying and (2) the jury has come to dislike the witness. Exposing a perjurer is a risky endeavor, pitting you against the witness. You must be able to deliver the goods to the jury, proving that the witness is a deliberate liar. While you can damage opposing counsel by proving the witness is a perjurer, it is equally true that your failure to fulfill this promise can severely damage you and your case, particularly when combined with an abusive manner toward the witness. As mentioned earlier, jurors are protective of lay witnesses, understanding the mismatch of skill and courtroom savvy between lawyer and witness. Jurors can take sides in this battle, and you usually begin with a handicap.

Rather than accusing the witness of lying, you ordinarily can take the easier route of suggesting a simple mistake. Jurors are much more inclined to find this than outright perjury. Your manner and framing of questions for a mistaken witness are quite different from how you confront a perjurer. They can be noncombative and even understanding.

C. Strategies and Techniques

While all seven impeachment-cross techniques on pages 117-119 are essential to cross-examining a mendacious witness, four need special emphasis: (1) be ready to prove the lie; (2) lock the witness into the lie; (3) show the motive to lie; and (4) project your sincere distaste.

1. Provable

First and foremost, before you set out to expose a perjurer, make sure you can fulfill your promise and prove a deliberate lie, and that you have all the ammunition you need. When F. Lee Bailey conducted the cross of Fuhrman, he had a letter from a witness in which she claimed Fuhrman had used racial slurs. Later in the trial he found out about audio tapes of Detective Mark Fuhrman uttering racial slurs. Abraham Lincoln had an almanac in his pocket that stated the moon was not where Charles Allen said it was.

2. Lock in the Witness's Testimony and Counter Leading

Before you can expose the liar, you want to lock in the lie. You can use a concession-seeking cross to lock the witness into the testimony. You may be able to accomplish this by merely getting the witness to repeat the important portion of the witness's direct examination ("On direct you testified . . ."?) The witness may be contrary because the witness is engaged in concocting a story and is fearful that conceding what you want will lead to exposure. To take advantage of this situation, you can use what has been referred to as "counter leading," which involves asking a leading question that asserts a fact when the examiner wants the witness to provide the opposite fact. Lincoln's cross-examination of Charles Allen, discussed at pages 120-122, illustrates the method. Lincoln wanted to lock Allen into facts that would make it difficult for Allen to see what he claimed. The exchange was:

Q. And you stood very near to them?

A. No, about twenty feet away.

Q. May it not have been ten feet?

A. No, it was twenty feet or more.

Q. In the open field?

A. No, in the timber.

3. Motive to Lie

Trial lawyers take for granted that some witnesses lie, believing it to be a common occurrence. Jurors are much slower to conclude this. Why would they? Unless the motive to lie is self-evident, it is the cross-examiner's job to reveal it. Your questions must show that the witness has an interest in the case, such as a party with something to lose, or bias, such as a relationship to a party. The necessary foundation for a jury to conclude that a witness is lying is a reason to fabricate. Once that foundation has been laid, you are ready to cross about the provable lie.

4. Demeanor

David Paul Brown's oft-quoted advice that the cross-examiner's demeanor must be adjusted to the witness includes the recommendation to be "a thunderbolt to the liar." Francis Wellman, *The Art of Cross-Examination* 401 (2d ed. 1921). When you can prove perjury and you are sincere in your belief that the witness is deliberately lying, project that sincerity to the jury. Be firm, fair, and tough with the witness and display some emotion. The tone of restrained righteous indignation when driving home that the witness is lying is fine: "So you are telling this jury . . . ." However, a cross cross-examination, replete with anger and yelling, is not effective. The proven fact of perjury by the witness will make the jury mad enough, with no histrionics by counsel needed.

IV. SURPRISE WITNESS

What do you do about a surprise witness at trial? In many jurisdictions in criminal cases, it is not unusual that the defense will call a witness to the stand whom the prosecutor has never heard of before. If the other side was required to disclose the witness in discovery and failed to do so, you can ask the court to prohibit the witness from testifying. If the other side has a reasonable explanation, the judge may well decide not to exclude the testimony. You then can make a record of the lack of notice of the witness and ask for a recess to do an interview. Even a brief interview will give you a preview of the testimony and what to expect. Delegating a quick Internet check is also a must. If the person refuses to speak to you, that is a plus, as we discuss at pages 317-319.

Even if the court gives you no time to interview the surprise witness, you can use your case theory to help you, as well as what you know about your opponent's theory. As you listen to the witness's direct, you should be able to identify where the witness's testimony fits in. You can conduct a concession-seeking cross, attempting to make the witness your own. It the witness's testimony contradicts the other evidence in the case, you can elicit testimony that conflicts with the true state of the facts and argue in summation that the witness's testimony should be disregarded because it does not comport with the rest of the evidence in the case.

V. MULTIPLE-WITNESS SITUATION

When your opponent produces multiple witnesses to testify about the same event, you have a potential problem. However, if these witnesses all are mistaken or lying, this situation definitely can work for you. If these witnesses are wrong, the following strategies and techniques will help you turn this situation to your advantage.

A. Sequestration of Witnesses

The Sequestration Order and Sanctions for Violations

An essential strategy for winning cross-examinations in the multiple-witness situation is witness sequestration. In *Geders v. United States*, 425 U.S. 80, 86 (1976), the U.S. Supreme Court explained the importance of sequestration to obtaining the truth by preventing influenced and less-than-candid testimony.

Therefore, it is critical in a multiple-witness situation, and, in fact in any case, that you move to exclude witnesses from the courtroom and from reading transcripts of trial testimony and talking to witnesses who have testified. Federal Rule of Evidence 615 and similar state rules authorize sequestration. State rules of evidence, such as the Washington's Rule of Evidence 615, make sequestration discretionary rather than mandatory, substituting "may" for "shall."

Sequestration Rule

Fed. R. Evid. 615. Excluding Witnesses
At a party's request, the court must order witnesses excluded so that they cannot hear other witnesses' testimony. Or the court may do so on its own. But this rule does not authorize excluding:

(a) a party who is a natural person;
(b) an officer or employee of a party that is not a natural person, after being designated as the party's representative by its attorney;
(c) a person whose presence a party shows to be essential to presenting the party's claim or defense; or
(d) a person authorized by statute to be present.

Many courts permit an oral motion before testimony to invoke the sequestration rule so that witnesses are not allowed in court except to testify. Other courts enter sequestration orders. Sequestration orders are not all the same. The following example was entered in the death penalty sentencing trial of Zacarias Moussaoui, a confessed al-Qaeda conspirator in the 9/11 terrorist attacks.

SEQUESTRATION ORDER

FOR THE EASTERN DISTRICT OF VIRGINIA
Alexandria Division

UNITED STATES OF AMERICA	)	
	)	
v.	)	1:01cr455
	)	
ZACARIAS MOUSSAOUI,	)	ORDER
a/k/a "Shaqil,"	)	
a/k/a "Abu Khalid	)	
al Sahrawi,"	)	
Defendant.	)	

For the reasons stated in open court, it is hereby ORDERED that Fed. R. Evid. 615 (Exclusion of Witnesses) be and is in effect for non-victim witnesses who may be called to testify in this proceeding. Such witnesses may not attend or otherwise follow trial proceedings (e.g., may not read transcripts) before being called to testify. This restriction does not apply to government summary witnesses Aaron Zebley and Jim Fitzgerald. Consistent with 18 U.S.C. § 3593(c), this restriction also does not apply to victim-witnesses, who may attend or follow any portion of the trial before testifying; and it is further

ORDERED that although daily transcripts of the trial proceedings will be available through Exemplaris (www.exemplaris.com), to avoid potential taint of the jury and witnesses, the transcripts of any bench conferences will not be publicly available until after the trial is concluded; and it is further

. . .

Entered this 22 day of February, 2006.
/s/

_____

Leonie M. Brinkema
United States District Judge
Alexandria, Virginia

The *Moussaoui* trial, discussed at pages 33-35, was about to commence when the prosecution informed the court and defense counsel of a possible violation of this order. Carla Martin, a Transportation Security Administration attorney, had, among other things, provided transcripts of the first day of trial to potential aviation witnesses. Ms. Martin sent e-mails and transcripts, including one of opening statements, to seven potential witnesses, six of whom the court determined were tainted by the communication. The ramifications of Martin's conduct were severe. The judge rebuked Martin, saying that she had "never seen such an egregious violation of a court's rule on witnesses . . . ." Transcript, *United States v. Zacarias Moussaoui*, No. 011-455, E.D. Va. 1002, 1025 (Mar. 13, 2006). Federal prosecutors considered filing charges against Martin, but eventually declined to prosecute her.

The judge's sanctions included excluding some of the aviation testimony and exhibits contaminated by Martin's communications. If a sequestration order is breached, with the likelihood of influencing the witness, the need to cross that witness may be obviated. Under these circumstances, the judge may exclude that witness's testimony, as preclusion from testifying is one of the three sanctions that are available. The other two are holding the witness in contempt and permitting cross about the violation. *Holder v. United States*, 150 U.S. 91, 92; *United States v. Hobbs*, 31 F.3d 918, 921 (9th Cir. 1994). However, courts are reluctant to preclude a witness from testifying because this "penalizes the litigant rather than the disobedient witness himself." *Taylor v. United States*, 388 F.2d 786, 788 (9th Cir. 1967).

Exceptions and Strategies to Meet Them
Party Witness in a Civil Case
Under Fed. R. Evid. 615 and its state rule counterparts, a party is not subject to sequestration. Even so, are there any safeguards against a party colluding and tailoring testimony? In *Barber v. Barber*, 257 Ga. 488, 360 S.E.2d 574 (Ga. 1987), the trial court required the party either to testify prior to calling witnesses or be excluded from the courtroom until their testimony was concluded.

Defendant in a Criminal Case
In *Geders v. United States*, 425 U.S. 80, 86 (1976), the Supreme Court reversed Geder's federal criminal conviction on Sixth Amendment right to counsel grounds when the trial court had forbidden the defendant from consulting his counsel "about anything" during the 17-hour overnight recess between his direct and cross-examination:

> . . . The defendant has the right to be present for all testimony, and may discuss his testimony with his attorney up to the time he takes the witness stand, so sequestration accomplishes less when applied to a defendant during a recess. A defendant is ordinarily ill-equipped to comprehend the trial process without a lawyer's guidance; he often must consult with counsel during the trial, and during overnight recesses often discusses the events of the day's trial and their significance.

Geders v. United States, 425 U.S. at 87-89.

Even so, the prosecution is not without strategies to combat coaching and improper collaboration prior to the defendant taking the stand. The Supreme Court laid out a couple of them in *Geders*:

> The problem of possible improper influence on testimony or "coaching" can be dealt with in other ways, such as by a prosecutor's skillful cross-examination to discover whether "coaching" occurred during a recess, or by the trial judge's directing that the examination of witnesses continue without interruption until completed, or otherwise arranging the sequence of testimony so that direct- and cross-examination of a witness will be completed without interruption.

Geders v. United States, 425 U.S. at 89-91.

On the stand, the defendant in a criminal case is treated like any other witness. The court can prohibit the defendant from consulting with others during cross, including his lawyer. *Perry v. Leeke*, 488 U.S. 272, 281-82 (1989). In addition to a sequestration order, the prosecutor may comment on the defendant's unique opportunity to listen to other testimony and adapt it. In *Portuondo v. Agard*, 529 U.S. 61, 73 (1999), the U.S. Supreme Court approved of the prosecutor doing just that:

> In sum, we see no reason to depart from the practice of treating testifying defendants the same as other witnesses. A witness's ability to hear prior testimony and to tailor his account accordingly, and the threat that ability presents to the integrity of the trial, are no different when it is the defendant doing the listening. Allowing comment upon the fact that a defendant's presence in the courtroom provides him a unique opportunity to tailor his testimony is appropriate—and indeed, given the inability to sequester the defendant, sometimes essential—to the central function of the trial, which is to discover the truth.

When the defendant has tailored testimony to other witnesses, the prosecutor's strategy is clear. On cross, the foundation for closing argument is laid by drawing attention to the fact that the defendant listened to other witnesses testify: "You sat over there at counsel table when your witnesses testified?" "You paid attention to what they said?" The prosecutor then can make the tailored-testimony argument.

Victim in a Criminal Case

The victim is not a party in a criminal case and would seem to be subject to sequestration under Fed. R. Evid. 615 and similar state rules. However, like the defendant in a criminal case, the victim may have a constitutionally protected right to attend the trial. For example, Washington State Constitution Article 1, Section 35 provides: "Upon notifying the prosecuting attorney, a victim of a crime charged as a felony shall have the right . . . subject to the discretion of the individual presiding over the trial or court proceedings, [to] attend trial and all other court proceedings the defendant has the right to attend . . . ."

If the victim attends trial, defense counsel can utilize the same strategies to argue tailored testimony as the prosecutor does against a defendant. When the prosecution's case involves the victim and other witnesses testifying to the same event, a prosecutor would be wise to advise the victim not to attend trial. This effectively deprives the defense of this trial tactic.

Person Essential to a Party's Cause

Federal Rule of Evidence 615 excludes from sequestration "a person whose presence a party shows to be essential to presenting the party's claim or defense." Customarily, this provision allows the prosecutor to have an investigator at trial, sitting at counsel table. In that experts may base opinions on facts revealed in the testimony, the same rationale can apply. As the advisory note to Rule 615 states, the Rule "contemplates such persons . . . as experts needed to advise counsel in the management of litigation."

B. Strategies and Techniques

Motive

Like all others, your cross-examinations of multiple witnesses should be planned with summation in mind. The fundamental argument you want to be able to make to the jury is that the witnesses were influenced. Your cross should be designed to make the connection between the witnesses' bias or interest and the testimony apparent to the jury. This can take many different forms. What influence did the outcome of the case, a party, or other witness have over the witness? Does the witness stand to lose or gain money depending on the outcome? Is the witness a friend, business associate, or relative of the party? Does the expert have an expectation that favorable testimony will result in more business?

Collusion or Influence

Besides establishing a motive, the cross-examiner facing the multiple-witness situation should seek to prove that the witnesses have exchanged information. The circumstances and nature of this exchange is important, determining how it can be portrayed to the jury. Meeting with a party to whom the witness is related creates the arguable inference of testimonial influence. So does pretrial preparation by a party. Recall how Max Steuer used witness Kate Alterman's pretrial meetings with prosecutors in the *Triangle* manslaughter trial (pages 189-191). He exposed the coached nature of her testimony and delivered a closing argument attacking the prosecutors for this.

However, a situation like that in the *Moussaoui* case, where the court had entered a sequestration order and the person deliberately delivered transcripts to witnesses in violation of this, can be portrayed as more sinister. Under these circumstances, counsel may suggest in cross or closing argument that the witnesses were colluding to deceive or manufacture testimony.

The preferred approach for a lawyer or an investigator is to interview witnesses separately. A "getting-our-stories-straight meeting," if proven, can be devastating to not only the witnesses involved, but also the instigating party. Witnesses getting together to discuss what happened, comparing mental and sometimes actual notes, inevitably results in a working out of differences and changing testimony.

How do you prove that the witnesses met, as well as the circumstances? In civil cases, you can seek this information through the multiple discovery devices available to you, including interrogatories, requests for admissions, and depositions. In criminal cases, formal discovery is not likely to produce such proof that the defense witnesses communicated.

In both criminal and civil cases, fact investigation may uncover interchanges between witnesses. For example, in a criminal case, the prosecution can examine the visitor's log at the jail where the defendant is being held. At trial, the prosecutor can ask any defense witness whose name appeared on the log: "Have you met with the defendant since his arrest?" If the witness answers, "Yes," that confirms what the prosecutor already knew. If the witness denies it, the prosecutor can produce the visitors' log to prove the contact, impeaching the witness by contradiction.

Cross-examination is another means of determining the nature, extent, and method of witness collaboration. You may inquire about meetings, materials reviewed, and discussions with opposing counsel. If the cross uncovers any element of this, the winning cross goes into all the circumstances of the meeting and what was discussed, and closing can concentrate on how the witnesses met to tailor their testimony.

Unprepared witnesses are inclined reflexively to deny they talked with opposing counsel, thinking that it is not permitted. More often, opposing counsel will explain during the preparation session that there is nothing wrong with this. If asked on cross whether opposing counsel told them what to say, the well-prepared witness is likely to respond, "Yes, she told me to tell the truth." The follow-up question to this is: "That's what she told you to say if I asked you, correct?"

Conflicts

Why would counsel call multiple witnesses to prove something when one credible witness will do? The concern is what quantity of testimony will be enough to convince the jury. Lawyers want the insurance that comes with witness corroboration. The flaw in this reasoning is that each person tends to see things a little differently. The more witnesses called, the more inconsistencies in their accounts. Indeed, a powerful closing argument is that the minor inconsistencies between the witness's testimonies indicate that they have not concocted a story together; it is the truth.

The strategy for revealing collusion between multiple witnesses is to create multiple conflicts in their testimonies, effectively demolishing each other. This strategy is predicated on a good-faith belief that the witnesses are lying. A sequestration order is vital to the effectiveness of this stratagem; the witnesses cannot know what each other is testifying to. In that witnesses ordinarily collude only on broad and chronological facts, they are vulnerable on the fine details of the story.

For example, assume that all the witnesses are falsely testifying to a meeting that never took place. Cross of a succession of lying witnesses could focus on details: "Where were you sitting?" "Where was McArthur sitting?" "How was McArthur dressed?" "Who else was present?" This technique can be both productive and an enjoyable creative process. For instance, if the first witness were to testify that McArthur was sitting at the head of the table, you could ask the next witness: "McArthur didn't sit at the head of the table, did he?" If the witness proves to be combative, answering opposite to what your leading question suggests, you can then counter-lead the witness, suggest an answer opposite to what you want: "McArthur sat the head of the table, right?" Provoke the witness to say that McArthur definitely was not at the head of the table. You could ask the witnesses to diagram the room and place the people in the room, causing the witnesses to produce dramatically different portrayals of the room and placement of people. You may ask the witness questions you don't know the answers to because there are no right or wrong answers, only conflicting ones. Your closing can feature the conflicting room diagrams and a chart with columns pointing out all the discrepancies between the witnesses.

Commonality

If the witnesses have conspired to contrive a story, their trial testimony may use the same words and phrases to describe events. On cross, questioning might include the common wording. Closing can focus on the fact that it is more than mere coincidence all the witnesses make use of the same wording.

VI. ADVERSE WITNESS

We use the phrase "adverse witness" to encompass a "hostile witness, an adverse party, or a witness identified with an adverse party." Fed. R. Evid. 611(c). Adverse witnesses always are problematic; however, although risky to call, adverse witnesses can benefit your case, leading us to discuss them here.

Typically, a plaintiff's attorney calls an adverse witness to prove one or more elements of the case. Another reason is uncertainty whether opposing counsel will call the witness coupled with the fear of losing the evidence the witness could provide.

A. Risk Assessment

Do a risk assessment before deciding to call an adverse witness. What is your upside and what is your downside? First, the witness may be characteristically unfriendly, predisposed to inject information favorable to your opponent. Second, the witness may gain control of the examination and inflict serious damage. The same two risks exist when you cross-examine a witness.

Third, if you call the witness and not your opponent, you likely will not be allowed to do a full cross. Make a record at the start of your examination that you reserve the right to cross-examine if the other side calls the same witness. Even so, the judge may sustain an objection to your cross on the grounds that you already had your chance when you called the witness.

Fourth, opposing counsel may be able to convince the judge to allow a direct examination of the witness, rather than having to recall the witness later. Under Federal Rule of Evidence 611(c) and similar state rules, opposing counsel's cross "should not go beyond the subject matter of the direct examination and matters affecting the witness's credibility. . . ." Limiting the scope of opposing counsel's examination is important because counsel who called the adverse witness wants to be able to limit the testimony only to that which is helpful. However, Rule 611(c) also provides that the judge has the discretion to "allow inquiry into additional matters as if on direct examination." The judge may well grant the request to allow direct in the interests of judicial economy and not inconveniencing the witness. If the direct is permitted, control of what information goes to the jury shifts to opposing counsel. This may derail the strategy of the lawyer that called the adverse witness.

B. Same Evidence Rules as Cross

Announce to the court whenever you call an adverse witness so that the same evidentiary rules govern the examination of both adverse witnesses and cross-examination. The most important Federal Rules of Evidence are (1) Rule 607, authorizing a party who called a witness to impeach that witness, and (2) Rule 611, providing that leading questions may be asked of an adverse witness. The practice of most state trial courts is in accord on this.

Rules of Evidence

Fed. R. Evid. 607. Who May Impeach a Witness
Any party, including the party that called the witness, may attack the witness's credibility.

Fed. R. Evid. 611.
(c) **Leading Questions.** Leading questions should not be used on direct examination except as necessary to develop the witness's testimony. Ordinarily, the court should allow leading questions:
  (1) on cross-examination; and
  (2) when a party calls a hostile witness, an adverse party, or a witness identified with an adverse party.

C. Strategies and Techniques

The best way to think about the examination of an adverse witness is to view it just the same as a concession-seeking cross, formulating the content in the same way. Your purpose is to build and preserve your case theory. And, your examination of an adverse witness applies some of the same concepts, strategies, and techniques as a winning cross-examination.

Concession-Seeking Examination

Constructing the content of the direct of an adverse witness into a persuasive story is identical to the way we described for a concession-seeking cross. Tell your case story by compelling the witness to give you the concessions that you can prove. Commonly, in civil cases, deposition testimony will prove what the witness must concede.

Controlling with the Witness's Deposition

With deposition testimony as a foundation, you should feel confident that you can compel the witness to say what you want. The witness is locked in by the statements made at their deposition, with each question and answer asked and answered before. With questions taken right out of a deposition, inconsistent answers by the witness lead to (1) refreshing the witness's recollection with the deposition or, if not admitted, (2) impeaching with the prior inconsistent statement. The deposition keeps the witness on track. See page 155 for an illustration of how this works.

Adverse Witness Control

To achieve an effective direct examination of an adverse witness, keep control of the witness by restricting its scope. If you have a narrow direct, Rule 611(c) limits the scope of cross to subjects covered. Unfortunately, the Rule also authorizes the judge to exercise discretion and allow opposing counsel to go into matters as if on direct. You can counter this by arguing that counsel will have ample opportunity to call the witness in their case in chief.

The greatest risk here is that the adverse witness will gain control of the examination and damage your case. Besides selecting the subjects to be discussed, the next best tool for maintaining control on cross is the short declaratory sentence posing as a question. Remember this is your chance to testify, eliciting the information that the witness must deliver to the jury. Utilize the same cross-notes format and organizational units described in Chapters 3 and 4.

D. Illustration: The Examination of Adverse Witness Barbara Hedges

Athletic Director Barbara Hedges fired University of Washington football coach Ric Neuheisel for dishonesty. Neuheisel had made high-stakes bets on the March Madness basketball tournament, but denied this when the National Collegiate Athletic Association (NCAA) investigated. Also, he had earlier lied, both publicly and in private to Hedges and other University officials, about interviewing for a head coach job with the San Francisco 49ers.

Neuheisel sued both the University and the NCAA for wrongful termination. As Neuheisel's first witness, his attorney, Bob Sulkin, called the person who fired him.

Sulkin conducted a winning concession-seeking examination with the aid of Hedges' deposition. He forced the witness to confirm points of the plaintiff's case, including that: (1) Hedges was unprepared "to answer any questions about gambling" with the NCAA investigators; (2) the NCAA did not inform Hedges or the University about the gambling allegations; (3) she was responsible for firing Neuheisel; (4) the University compliance officer had issued a memorandum indicating that certain gambling was permitted (". . . if you have friends outside of [the athletic department] that have pools on any of the basketball tournaments, you can participate. You cannot place bets with a bookie or organize your own pool"); and (5) she initially did not disclose the memo to the NCAA or Neuheisel. Seattle Post Intelligencer, Feb. 1 and 2, 2005.

Barbara Hedges questioned by Neuheisel's attorney Bob Sulkin

Ultimately, both the University and the NCAA settled with Neuheisel on the eve of closing argument. The NCAA agreed to pay $2.5 million including legal fees and the University forgave a $1.5 million loan plus interest of $230,000. Seattle Post Intelligencer, Mar. 8, 2005.

VII. INTERVIEW REFUSER

Previously, we recommended that thorough preparation in civil cases requires you or your investigator to interview witnesses that cannot be deposed. Witness interviews are the common practice in criminal cases. But, what if the witness refuses to be interviewed? While the absence of a pretrial interview puts the examiner at a disadvantage, it can be turned to the examiner's benefit.

The fact that the witness declined to be interviewed must be conceded by the witness because you can prove the refusal by calling either the investigator who attempted to conduct the interview or your prover if you were the one who tried to interview the witness. You also may produce the signed receipt from the certified letter that you sent the witness. Should the witness deny refusing to being interviewed, you can impeach her. During trial preparation you must think ahead to your tentative summation; you recognize that the witness's refusal supports an argument that the witness is biased in favor of the other party.

Tentative Closing Argument

Witness Bias — Refusal to Be Interviewed

Her Honor has instructed you that you may consider bias or interest in determining a witness's credibility. Ms. Habersham was the defendant's business partner. Prior to trial, she was more than willing to talk to the defendant, his investigator, or his lawyer. Ms. Habersham had no trouble sitting in that witness chair over there and answering questions posed by the defendant's lawyer. But, when detective Holman went to talk with her about the case, did she speak to him? No. She declined to answer the detective's questions. What did Habersham have to hide? She must have thought that she was helping the defendant by refusing to speak to the detective.

With this summation in mind, you can brainstorm and fashion a list of factual statements into the cross-notes format:

CROSS-NOTES FORMAT

TOPIC: Witness bias and interest

• You own a business—Far Sighted Incorporated—that does Lasik eye surgery	
• The defendant, Mr. Specks, is your business partner in Far Sighted	
• You have been business partners for the last ten years	
• On September 8 of last year, Mr. Specks was arrested	
• You became aware of his arrest the next day	
• You knew at the time that he had been arrested for shooting another man	Jail log shows witness visit
• You've talked to the defendant about the shooting	

• You've talked to the defense investigator about the shooting • Two days after Mr. Specks's arrest, detective Holman of the Ruston Police Department came to your business and contacted you • He identified himself to you • He told you he was a police detective • He told you he was investigating the shooting and that Mr. Specks, your partner, had been involved in it • Detective Holman told you that it was your opportunity to tell what you knew about the shooting • But, you didn't help him with the investigation • You told the detective you wouldn't discuss the case with him • You have spoken to defense counsel sitting over there about this case • This is the first time that we have been able to talk with you about what happened	Det. Holman's follow-up Report # 33

CHECKLIST: PROBLEMATIC WITNESSES

Feigning Forgetfulness or Ignorance

❑ Strategies and techniques for exposing the faking forgetter or ignorant witness include:
- Establish that the person is neither ignorant nor forgetful;
- Ask about significant and unforgettable matters;
- Elicit as many "I don't remember" and/or "I don't know" answers as possible;
- Show that the witness remembers things less significant and more remote than what the witness claims not to know;
- Confront the witness with a prior statement proving the fact the witness claims either to have forgotten or not to know; and
- Lock the witness into not recalling a favorable fact that the examiner can prove through another witness.

Perjurer

❑ If possible, avoid accusing the witness of being a perjurer; it is easier for the jury to find that the witness was mistaken.

❑ Apply the seven essential impeachment techniques as follows:
- *Assess* the witness and evidence—be certain that the witness is lying and you can prove it, *adjusting* your tone and demeanor to be firm and confrontational;
- Establish a *motive*;
- *Paint a picture* for the jury;

- *Lock the witness into the factual claim* that you can disprove;
- *Close all the exits* to prevent evasions or explanations;
- Do not signal the witness where you are going, maintaining the element of *surprise*; and
- Utilize *visual or tangible evidence* to impeach.

Surprise Witness

❑ Object and move to exclude the witness's testimony on the grounds that the witness was not disclosed in required discovery (unless you are a prosecutor and the exclusion could deny the defendant a fair trial).

❑ Ask for a recess to interview the witness on the grounds that you had no notice the person would be called.

❑ Listen to the witness's direct testimony to determine where the witness fits into the case.
- Seek concessions on cross that build and preserve your case theory or undermine the other side's, or
- Elicit testimony that conflicts with other testimony in the case.

Multiple-Witness Situation

❑ A critical strategy for a multiple-witness situation is sequestration. Federal Rule of Evidence 615 mandates it. Some state rules are the same and others make it discretionary with the judge. Exceptions to the sequestration rule are:
- The court has alternative measures to isolate the party from other witnesses;
- The defendant in a criminal case has a constitutional right to be present until the defendant takes the stand;
- The victim of a crime has the right to be present (proved by some state constitutions); and
- A person shown to be essential to the presentation of the cause may be present (provided by Rule 615).

❑ Other strategies and techniques include:
- Establishing witness bias or interest motive to lie or be mistaken;
- Revealing that multiple witnesses met prior to trial;
- Creating conflicts between the details of witnesses' testimonies; and
- Eliciting testimony showing common wording of the different witnesses' testimonies, suggesting coaching.

Adverse Witness

❑ Before calling an adverse witness, conduct a risk assessment, considering whether:
- The witness is likely to inject damaging information;
- The witness is likely to take control of the examination;
- If the other side calls the witness, the cross will be limited to the scope of the direct and credibility; and
- If you call the witness, opposing counsel may be able to convince the court to allow a full cross of the witness, beyond the scope of your direct.

- ❏ The evidence rules governing the examination of an adverse witness are identical to those available on cross, such as leading questions and the ability to impeach. Fed. R. Evid. 607.
- ❏ Strategies and techniques include:
  - Using a concession-seeking cross approach to identify the content, constructing it into an examination at trial; and
  - Witness control by asking the same questions as during the witness's deposition.

Interview Refuser

- ❏ Reveal the witness's bias by contrasting the witness's cooperation with your opponent to the refusal to speak to you or your investigator.
- ❏ Make a record of the effort to interview the witness that can be proven at trial.

ETHICAL & LEGAL BOUNDARIES OF CROSS

"These rules should be construed so as to administer every proceeding fairly, eliminate unjustifiable expense and delay, and promote the development of evidence law, to the end of ascertaining the truth and securing a just determination."

— Federal Rule of Evidence 102. Purpose and Construction

"A team should never practice on a field that is not lined. Your players have to become aware of the field's boundaries."

— **John Madden**, U.S. football coach and sportscaster, in *The Book of Football Wisdom* (Criswell Freeman ed., 1996)

I. ETHICAL AND LEGAL BOUNDARIES OF CROSS

In this chapter, we will pull together all the evidentiary and ethical rules of cross-examination that have been discussed throughout the book and add a few more. We refer to the ABA Model Rules of Professional Conduct because all of the states, except for California, have adopted the format of those rules (http://www.abanet.org/cpr/mrpc/model_rules.html). We rely mainly on the Federal Rules of Evidence because they are authoritative in 42 states. 6 Jack B. Weinstein & Margaret A. Berger, *Weinstein's Federal Evidence,* 2d ed. Table 1 (Joseph M. McLaughlin ed., Matthew Bender 1997).

This chapter also discusses how to handle objection tactics by opposing counsel during your cross.

II. AVOIDING AND MEETING OBJECTIONS

The nature of the adversary process makes it likely that opposing counsel will object even to legitimate cross-examination questions if you are scoring points with their witness. You need to anticipate objections and be ready with a quick, informed response, whether this is on the spot in open court, at a sidebar conference, or when the jury is excused to allow counsel to argue over the objection. Having the supporting legal authority and factual arguments ready for the court will give you the winning edge, providing a solid basis for the judge's ruling.

A. Rules of Evidence and Professional Responsibility

A working knowledge of the rules of evidence is the foundation of any effective objection containment strategy. Criminal trial lawyers—prosecutors and public defenders—have a better grasp of these rules because they are constantly using them in trial. Due to far less frequent court appearances, many civil lawyers lack the equivalent working knowledge of the rules of evidence.

B. Pretrial Work

Anticipating objections is a function of thorough pretrial preparation. It starts with challenging the basis of each piece of evidence you plan to introduce in your own case, asking yourself: "What is my legal authority for getting this in?" After that, step into opposing counsel's shoes and ask, "How can I keep it out?"

Once you have anticipated the possible objections to your evidence in this manner, do the research necessary to convince the judge that it is admissible. Your jurisdiction's rules of evidence will be your primary resource in this effort, along with research into your jurisdiction's case law. Many states have evidence law handbooks to help you out, providing model predicate foundation questions for admissibility tailored to the state's law. Another excellent resource on this same subject is Professor Edward Imwinkelried's *Evidentiary Foundations* (7th ed., Lexis-Nexis 2008).

Assuming that the legal authority supports your right to ask a question, consider making a first strike with a pretrial motion to get the evidence admitted. Many jurisdictions and judges prefer the pretrial resolution of evidentiary issues because it avoids delays and extended argument during trial. Pretrial rulings on evidence also eliminate uncertainty in your trial plan, allowing you to proceed with confidence with your cross.

The more doubts you have about admissibility, the more advisable it is to bring the issue up with the judge in a pretrial motion. If you wait until the trial is underway and the court sustains the objection, you will have to scramble to develop a fallback position on the spot. Worse yet, if the witness answers the question and then the judge sustains the objection, you may be looking at the drastic remedy of a mistrial.

There are strategic reasons why you might hold back on a pretrial motion to admit evidence. First, opposing counsel may not spot the issue and object. Second, the law may unequivocally support your position, making a pretrial motion unnecessary.

We previously mentioned that pretrial preparation includes putting the legal authority supporting admissibility in your cross notes, as well as briefing the issue in enough depth for persuasive argument. A pocket brief can be held in reserve and used as needed for nonroutine evidentiary issues. The brief will assist the judge in ruling on the objection and show your thorough preparation. Naturally, if the court reviews your pocket brief, this will involve some delay of your cross.

C. Trial Work

All of the pretrial steps we just have discussed will enable you to rapidly and effectively respond to an anticipated objection. However, not every contingency can be planned for. In trial, the unexpected happens. Preparation puts you in a better place to respond to it.

One of the worst side-effects of an extended evidentiary argument is the interruption of your flow in cross-examination. When an objection is made, look at the judge or jury, coolly dismissive of opposing counsel. Wait to see if the judge will overrule the objection without a response from you. If the judge solicits a response, make it short and sweet, based on legal authority. For instance, if the objection is "hearsay," cite why it is not hearsay, or what exception exists to the rule, such as business record or excited utterance. Avoid sidebar conferences and excusing the jury if at all possible.

What will you do if the judge sustains the objection? Never show your disappointment or displeasure with the ruling. If the objection is to form, such as "compound" or "calls for speculation," then tell the judge that you will rephrase the question. If the objection is more substantive and you continue to believe that you are entitled to get the information, figure out another way to ask the question.

III. COMMON OBJECTIONS TO CROSS-EXAMINATION

A. List of Common Objections to Cross

A checklist of common objections during cross follows.

CROSS-EXAMINATION OBJECTIONS

Good-Faith Basis
Objection. Counsel lacks a good-faith basis for the question.

Relevance
Objection. Irrelevant. Evidence Rule 402.

Unfair Prejudice
Objection. Unfair prejudice outweighs probative value. Evidence Rule 403.

Not Supported By Admissible Evidence
Objection. The assertion is not supported by admissible evidence. Rule of Professional Conduct 3.4(e).

Conduct Not Probative of Untruthfulness
Objection. The alleged conduct is not probative of untruthfulness. Evidence Rule 608.

Prior Conviction
Objection. Inadmissible under Evidence Rule 609.

Mistreating the Witness
Objection. Argumentative. Harassing the witness. Evidence Rule 611(a).

Personal Knowledge or Opinion
Objection. Counsel is testifying.
Objection. Counsel is expressing a personal opinion.

Scope
Objection. Beyond the scope of direct.

Prior Inconsistent Statement
Objection.

- Counsel has not disclosed the statement. Evidence Rule 613(a).
- The prior statement is not inconsistent.
- The prior statement is not material.

Pitting
Objection. Counsel is pitting one witness against another.

Learned Treatise
Objection.

- No showing that the treatise is reliable.
- To the admission of the treatise as an exhibit. Evidence Rule 803(18).

Form of the Question
Objection. The question:

- Is ambiguous/vague.
- Is not a question but a comment on the evidence.
- Is a jury speech.
- Assumes a fact not in evidence. No witness has said that.
- Is compound.
- Is confusing.
- Is cumulative.
- Misquotes the witness, who said (testimony).
- Misstates the evidence.
- Beyond the scope.
- Is unduly repetitive.
- Has been asked and answered.
- Calls for speculation. Evidence Rule 602.

B. The Rules

Good-Faith Basis

ABA Model Rule of Professional Conduct 3.4(e). Fairness to Opposing Party and Counsel

> A lawyer shall not . . . in trial, allude to any matter . . . that will not be supported by admissible evidence. . . .

State v. Lowe, 843 N.E.2d 1243, 1246, 164 Ohio App. 3d 726, 729 (2005).
It is improper to attempt to prove a case by insinuation or innuendo, rather than with evidence. Questions that are not based on fact or for which there is no good-faith basis are improper.

An in-depth discussion of good-faith basis requirement is at pages 114-115.

Relevant

> ## ABA Model Rule of Professional Conduct 3.4(e). Fairness to Opposing Party and Counsel
>
> A lawyer shall not . . . in trial, allude to any matter that the lawyer does not reasonably believe is relevant . . .
>
> **Fed. R. Evid. 401. Test for Relevant Evidence**
> Evidence is relevant if:
>
> (a) it has any tendency to make a fact more or less probable than it would be without the evidence; and
> (b) the fact is of consequence in determining the action.
>
> **Fed. R. Evid. 402. General Admissibility of Relevant Evidence**
> Relevant evidence is admissible unless any of the following provides otherwise:
>
> - the United States Constitution;
> - a federal statute;
> - these rules; or
> - other rules prescribed by the Supreme Court.
>
> Irrelevant evidence is not admissible.

Unfair Prejudice—Fed. R. Evid. 403

Even when the evidence would be admissible under another evidence rule, it may be inadmissible under Fed. R. Evid. 403. For instance, a specific prior act of the witness may be probative of untruthfulness and therefore admissible under Fed. R. Evid. 608(b), but the unfair prejudice of the conduct may substantially outweigh its probative value and be inadmissible under Fed. R. Evid. 403.

The Assertion Is Not Supported by Admissible Evidence

> ## ABA Model Rule of Professional Conduct 3.4(e). Fairness to Opposing Party and Counsel
>
> A lawyer shall not . . . in trial, allude to any matter . . . that will not be supported by admissible evidence . . .

The Conduct Is Not Probative of Untruthfulness

> ## Fed. R. Evid. 608. A Witness's Character for Truthfulness or Untruthfulness
>
> (b) Specific Instances of Conduct.
> Except for a criminal conviction under Rule 609, extrinsic evidence is not admissible to prove specific instances of a witness's conduct in order to attack or support the

witness's character for truthfulness. But the court may, on cross-examination, allow them to be inquired into if they are probative of the character for truthfulness or untruthfulness of:

(1) the witness; or
(2) another witness whose character the witness being cross-examined has testified about.

By testifying on another matter, a witness does not waive any privilege against self-incrimination for testimony that relates only to the witness's character for truthfulness.

Inadmissible Under Federal Rule of Evidence 609

Fed. R. Evid. 609. Impeachment by Evidence of a Criminal Conviction

(a) In General. The following rules apply to attacking a witness's character for truthfulness by evidence of a criminal conviction:

(1) for a crime that, in the convicting jurisdiction, was punishable by death or by imprisonment for more than one year, the evidence:

(A) must be admitted, subject to Rule 403, in a civil case or in a criminal case in which the witness is not a defendant; and

(B) must be admitted in a criminal case in which the witness is a defendant, if the probative value of the evidence outweighs its prejudicial effect to that defendant; and

(2) for any crime regardless of the punishment, the evidence must be admitted if the court can readily determine that establishing the elements of the crime required proving — or the witness's admitting — a dishonest act or false statement.

(b) Limit on Using the Evidence After 10 Years. This subdivision (b) applies if more than 10 years have passed since the witness's conviction or release from confinement for it, whichever is later. Evidence of the conviction is admissible only if:

(1) its probative value, supported by specific facts and circumstances, substantially outweighs its prejudicial effect; and

(2) the proponent gives an adverse party reasonable written notice of the intent to use it so that the party has a fair opportunity to contest its use.

(c) Effect of a Pardon, Annulment, or Certificate of Rehabilitation. Evidence of a conviction is not admissible if:

(1) the conviction has been the subject of a pardon, annulment, certificate of rehabilitation, or other equivalent procedure based on a finding that the person has been rehabilitated, and the person has not been convicted of a later crime punishable by death or by imprisonment for more than one year; or

(2) the conviction has been the subject of a pardon, annulment, or other equivalent procedure based on a finding of innocence.

continued ▶

(d) Juvenile Adjudications.

Evidence of a juvenile adjudication is admissible under this rule only if:

(1) it is offered in a criminal case;

(2) the adjudication was of a witness other than the defendant;

(3) an adult's conviction for that offense would be admissible to attack the adult's credibility; and

(4) admitting the evidence is necessary to fairly determine guilt or innocence.

(e) Pendency of an Appeal. A conviction that satisfies this rule is admissible even if an appeal is pending. Evidence of the pendency is also admissible.

Normally, any issues regarding the admissibility of a prior conviction to impeach a witness will be resolved pretrial by a motion, avoiding the risk that the jury will become aware of the conviction.

Arguing with, Harassing, or Embarrassing the Witness

ABA Model Rule of Professional Conduct 4.4. Respect for Rights of Third Persons

(a) In representing a client, a lawyer shall not use means that have no substantial purpose other than to embarrass, . . . or burden a third person . . . .

Fed. R. Evid. 611. Mode and Order of Examining Witnesses and Presenting Evidence

(a) Control by the Court; Purposes. The court should exercise reasonable control over the mode and order of examining witnesses and presenting evidence so as to:

(1) make those procedures effective for determining the truth;

(2) avoid wasting time; and

(3) protect witnesses from harassment or undue embarrassment.

Counsel is not permitted to pose argumentative questions on cross. A leading question that asks the witness to agree with a factual statement is normally not argumentative. The phrasing of your question can determine whether they will draw an objection that it is argumentative. Questions that are neither accusatory (see page 69) nor contain a conclusion ("Your advertisement was fraudulent, wasn't it?") avoid the common objection of "argumentative." The manner in which you ask the question also can determine whether the judge will sustain an objection that it is argumentative.

Counsel is also prohibited from harassing or unduly embarrassing a witness. Maintaining a professional but firm demeanor that is nonthreatening to the witness will avoid the objection that you are badgering or harassing the witness.

Asserting Personal Knowledge or Opinion

> **ABA Model Rule of Professional Conduct 3.4(e). Fairness to Opposing Party and Counsel**
>
> A lawyer shall not . . . in trial, allude to any matter . . . that will not be supported by admissible evidence. . . .
>
> **ABA Model Rule of Professional Conduct 3.4(e). Fairness to Opposing Party and Counsel**
>
> A lawyer shall not in trial, . . . assert personal knowledge of facts in issue except when testifying as a witness, or state a personal opinion as to the justness of a cause, the credibility of a witness, the culpability of a civil litigant or the guilt or innocence of an accused; . . .
>
> **ABA Model Rule of Professional Conduct 3.7. Lawyer as Witness**
>
> (a)   A lawyer shall not act as advocate at a trial in which the lawyer is likely to be a necessary witness unless:
>
>   (1)   the testimony relates to an uncontested issue;
>
>   (2)   the testimony relates to the nature and value of legal services rendered in the case; or
>
>   (3)   Disqualification of the lawyer would work substantial hardship on the client.

On cross, a lawyer cannot state a fact as though it comes from the lawyer's personal knowledge. For instance, the cross-examination question, "Remember when I called you and you said . . . ?" is the lawyer's assertion that the phone call occurred. The other problem raised by this example is that, under Rule of Professional Conduct 3.7, the cross-examiner cannot testify that the phone call happened if the witness denies it took place because counsel cannot be a witness. Consequently, under Model Rule of Professional Conduce 3.4(e), counsel has unethically alluded to a fact that cannot be proved by admissible evidence.

The way to avoid this dilemma is for the lawyer to have a prover, which is a person who can testify to what was said between counsel and the witness, present whenever counsel talks to anyone whom counsel may ever have to impeach with a prior inconsistent statement.

Gratuitous Comment

> **ABA Model Rule of Professional Conduct 3.4(e). Fairness to Opposing Party and Counsel**
>
> A lawyer shall not . . . in trial, allude to any matter . . . that will not be supported by admissible evidence. . . .

continued ▶

> **ABA Model Rule of Professional Conduct 3.4(c). Fairness to Opposing Party and Counsel**
> A lawyer shall not knowingly disobey an obligation under the rules of the tribunal . . . .
>
> **ABA Model Rule of Professional Conduct 3.4(e). Fairness to Opposing Party and Counsel**
> A lawyer shall not in trial, . . . assert personal knowledge of facts in issue except when testifying as a witness, or state a personal opinion as to the justness of a cause, the credibility of a witness, the culpability of a civil litigant or the guilt or innocence of an accused; . . .

It is usually improper to make a gratuitous comment ("So you say,") during cross. The remark may be objectionable because it expresses the lawyer's personal opinion about the witness's credibility, asserts personal knowledge of facts in issue, is argumentative, or alludes to something that is either irrelevant or inadmissible.

Beyond the Scope of Direct

> **Fed. R. Evid. 611. Mode and Order of Examining Witnesses and Presenting Evidence**
>
> **(b) Scope of Cross-Examination.** Cross-examination should not go beyond the subject matter of the direct examination and matters affecting the witness's credibility. The court may allow inquiry into additional matters as if on direct examination.

For further discussion of the scope of cross and strategies for meeting the beyond-the-scope-of-direct objection, see pages 79-81.

The Prior Statement Is Not Inconsistent; It's Not Material

> *McCormick on Evidence* on the test for inconsistency: ". . . could the jury reasonably find that a witness who believed the truth of the facts testified to would have been unlikely to make a prior statement of this tenor?"
>
> Charles T. McCormick, *McCormick on Evidence* 63 (Kenneth S. Brown & George E. Dix eds., West Group 2006).

> **Fed. R. Evid. 613. Witness's Prior Statement**
>
> **(a) Showing or Disclosing the Statement During Examination.** When examining a witness about the witness's prior statement, a party need not show it or disclose

its contents to the witness. But the party must, on request, show it or disclose its contents to an adverse party's attorney.

(b) Extrinsic Evidence of a Prior Inconsistent Statement. Extrinsic evidence of a witness's prior inconsistent statement is admissible only if the witness is given an opportunity to explain or deny the statement and an adverse party is given an opportunity to examine the witness about it, or if justice so requires. This subdivision (b) does not apply to an opposing party's statement under Rule 801(d)(2).

Pitting

State v. Manning, 19 P.3d 84, 100-01, 270 Kan. 674 (2001) held:

> Questions, which compel a defendant or witness to comment on the credibility of another witness, are improper. It is the province of the jury to weigh the credibility of the witnesses. *See People v. Riley*, 63 Ill. App. 3d 176, 184-85, 379 N.E. 746, 19 Ill. 874 (1978) (holding that asking the defendant on cross-examination whether the State's witnesses had told a "bunch of lies" was improper); . . .

For a further discussion of pitting and how to make the point that the witness's testimony conflicts with the testimony of another witness without engaging in pitting, see pages 164-166.

No Showing That the Treatise Is Reliable; The Treatise Is Not Admissible as an Exhibit

Fed. R. Evid. 803. Exceptions to the Rule Against Hearsay — Regardless of Whether the Declarant Is Available as a Witness

The following are not excluded by the rule against hearsay, regardless of whether the declarant is available as a witness:

(18) *Statements in Learned Treatises, Periodicals, or Pamphlets.* A statement contained in a treatise, periodical, or pamphlet if:

(A) the statement is called to the attention of an expert witness on cross-examination or relied on by the expert on direct examination; and

(B) the publication is established as a reliable authority by the expert's admission or testimony, by another expert's testimony, or by judicial notice.

If admitted, the statement may be read into evidence but not received as an exhibit.

IV. MEETING OBJECTIONS TACTICS

A. Interruption for the Witness's Sake

When you are scoring points in your cross-examination of a witness, opposing counsel can try to break your momentum by asking for a sidebar. Though counsel's objection invariably will be overruled under these circumstances, the real goal of interrupting the cross to give the witness time to regroup is achieved.

How can you defeat this trial tactic? One approach is to change course, saying, "Your Honor, I will withdraw the question and move on." The judge should permit you to do so. You can maintain your forward motion with the unnerved witness. Later, you can return to the area you asked about originally.

B. Coaching from Counsel's Table

When a witness is struggling for an answer to your question, opposing counsel can try to throw the witness a lifeline in the form of a coaching objection like, "The witness couldn't possibly know that." While the judge will overrule this, it is typical for the witness to echo the objection with, "I don't know," when the question is repeated. Federal Rule of Civil Procedure 30(c)(2) on deposition objections states, ". . . An objection must be stated concisely in a non-argumentative and non-suggestive manner . . . ." In the absence of an explicit evidence rule pertaining to trial objections, the best way to stop coaching objections is to call opposing counsel on it: "Objection. Counsel is coaching the witness." To the extent that it is not already obvious, this will alert the judge and the jury to what is going on, discouraging further efforts of this nature.

C. Speaking Objection

Plaintiff's attorney: "Objection, Your Honor. The question contains an innuendo about my client that is totally unjustified. Plaintiff's counsel cannot support the statement with any real evidence—and counsel knows it. Ever since this trial began, counsel has . . ."

Speaking objections are improper, introducing harmful inadmissible evidence and comments into the case. They also can turn an effective cross into a quarrel between counsel. In the face of improper conduct of this nature by your opponent, you must be careful not to lower yourself to the same level by responding in kind. Judges and jurors have short tolerance for squabbles between counsel, believing it unprofessional.

If the judge does not stop such speeches unilaterally, one effective technique is to call attention to counsel's tactic by responding, "Your Honor, counsel is making a jury speech," coupled with a request that any improper comment be stricken and the jury be instructed to disregard counsel's remarks. The point is made.

CHECKLIST: ETHICAL & LEGAL BOUNDARIES

Cross-Examination Objections

☐ Objection.
- Counsel *lacks a good-faith* basis for the question.
- *Irrelevant.* Fed. R. Evid. 402.
- *Unfair prejudice* outweighs probative value. Fed. R. Evid. 403.
- The assertion is *not supported by admissible evidence.* Fed. R. Prof. C. 3.4(e).
- The alleged conduct is *not probative of untruthfulness.* Fed. R. Evid. 608.
- Inadmissible under Fed. R. Evid. 609.
- *Counsel is testifying.*
- Counsel is expressing a *personal opinion.*
- *Argumentative.* Harassing the witness. Fed. R. Evid. 611(a).
- *Beyond the scope* of direct.

Prior Inconsistent Statement

☐ Objection.
- Counsel has *not disclosed* the statement to me. Fed. R. Evid. 613(a).
- The prior statement is *not inconsistent.*
- The prior statement is *not material.*
☐ Objection. Counsel is pitting one witness against another.

Learned Treatise

☐ Objection.
- No showing that the treatise is reliable.
- To the admission of the treatise as an exhibit. Fed. R. Evid. 803(18).

Form of the Question

☐ Objection. The question:
- Is *ambiguous*/vague.
- Is not a question but a *comment* on the evidence.
- Is a jury *speech.*
- *Assumes a fact not in evidence.*
- Is *compound.*
- Is *confusing.*
- Is *cumulative.*
- *Misquotes* the witness, who said (testimony).
- *Misstates* the evidence.
- Beyond the scope of proper *lay opinion.*
- Is *repetitive.*
- Has been *asked and answered.*
- Calls for *speculation.* Fed. R. Evid. 602.
☐ Avoid and meet objections by:
- Knowing the rules of evidence;
- Anticipating objections prior to trial, having an effective strategy to meet them and crafting questions to avoid objections; and

- In trial, responding to objections with a concise, informed, and summarizing response. If the objection is sustained, rephrase the question.
- Meet the other side's objections tactics by:
  - Avoiding requests for sidebars that are designed to rescue the witness by creating delay;
  - Withdrawing the question and proceeding on, returning to the subject later;
  - Exposing opposing counsel's witness coaching objections for what they are; and
  - Stopping speaking objections by labeling them as a "jury speech."

CASES & ASSIGNMENTS

"I hear and I forget. I see and I remember. I do and I understand."
              — Confucius

"We learn by example and by direct experience because there are real limits to the adequacy of verbal instruction."
              — **Malcolm Gladwell,** *Blink: The Power of Thinking Without Thinking* (2005)

I. EXPERIENTIAL LEARNING

You can learn how to conduct a winning cross-examination through experience using the assignments and the case files contained on the companion website, www.aspenlawschool.com/books/clark_crossexam2e, to this book. This chapter describes the assignments and provides a sample of the assignments. In addition, this chapter provides factual summaries of the two civil and two criminal cases that provide the opportunities for cross-examinations. In law school as in professional development workshops or on your own, you can experience cross in one or more cases.

II. FACTUAL SUMMARIES

Factual summaries for the four cases are provided in this chapter to give you overviews of what happened in each of the four cases. The summaries cover the highlights of what some of the witnesses claim occurred. For specifics and greater detail, refer to the lengthier summaries and documents in the case files, which are contained on the companion website to this book.

III. ASSIGNMENTS ON THE WEBSITE

A. Role-Play Assignments

Role-play assignments for each of the four cases are contained on the companion website, www.aspenlawschool.com/books/clark_crossexam2e, to this book. By performing these assignments, you will learn by experience. Specifically, you will learn how to develop a case theory and theme, identify the content of your cross (including both concessions and impeachment), organize and prepare your cross, and conduct the cross. These assignments parallel the chapters in this book. For instance, Assignment 1 for the *Goodman* case involves case analysis and theory and theme development, which corresponds to the material in Chapter 2. Also, each performance assignment comes with a reading assignment of case file entries and portions of the book. Finally, each assignment includes what we refer to as "Thoughts for This Assignment," which will help you to prepare.

B. Rules for Assignments

Jurisdiction

These fictitious cases take place in the jurisdiction of the state of Major. The city of Georgetown is the state capital, and it is the largest city in Lincoln County. Camden County and Jamner County are adjacent to Lincoln. Camden's largest town is Camden City. The jurisdiction of the state of Major was chosen for a number of reasons but primarily because its laws reflect—although they are probably not identical with—current law on the various issues raised in the cases.

The Procedural and Professional Responsibility Rules

The State of Major Court Rules and Rules of Criminal and Civil Procedure are in most instances identical to the Federal Rules of Civil Procedure and the Federal Rules of Criminal Procedure. The Major Evidence Code is identical to the Federal Rules of Evidence. The standards of professional responsibility in the state of Major are based on the ABA Model Rules of Professional Conduct. These rules are intended to provide a legal structure against which you can analyze the particular ethical situations in the assignments. Of course, your instructor may instead ask you to deal with the ethical situations under the current rules in your jurisdiction.

Dates

The fictitious incidents take place in the following years:

20XX: This year
20XX-1: Last year

To give the cases a feeling of reality, the dates in the Case Files should be converted into actual dates, so that "20XX+4" is changed to four years after this year's date.

Civil Case

Whenever you deal with a civil case, you should assume that any related criminal case has been disposed of in such a manner that the witness cannot legitimately resist answering in the civil case by claiming that he will incriminate himself.

Your Responsibilities

As a class member or as an attorney assigned to conduct a particular performance, your own good sense and the directions of your instructor will make your responsibilities clear. Your responsibilities when role-playing a witness, however, are a different matter. The quality of your effort in preparation, and in the subsequent performance of your role, can make or break the class. Effort put into your role-playing can make a cross-examination come alive by challenging the planning and performance skills of the person who is playing the cross examiner. Lack of effort and enthusiasm can result in an unrealistic, fragmented, boring shambles.

As a witness, you have two responsibilities:

1. *Preparation.* You should prepare for your witness performance by reviewing the Assignment and readings, the confidential witness information from the Actors' Guide, the pretrial Case File documents listed for the assignment for which you are playing the role of a witness, special documents provided by your instructor, and any specific witness

instructions for the assignment. Be certain to bring to class all your witness information.

2. *Innovation.* Although we have tried to make the materials as complete as possible, there may be circumstances in which the factual materials furnished to you are insufficient. Therefore, you will have to be somewhat innovative at times. If you are asked questions on matters not covered by the facts you have been furnished, you may add any facts that are consistent with the supplied facts. You may also add details that provide color and realism to your character. You should not, however, add a fact so important that it would determine the outcome of the lawsuit. If in doubt, ask your instructor.

Depending on the actual selection, sequence, and performance of the assignment in your class, you may encounter gaps in information or may fail to make the acquaintance of some of the witnesses who figure in the principal cases. It has been our experience that such potential gaps in information should not seriously impair your case preparation. If the gaps do present any difficulties, however, consult your instructor.

IV. CASE FILES ON THE WEBSITE

On the website, www.aspenlawschool.com/books/clark_crossexam2e, you will find Case Files for each of the four cases. The Case Files include everything needed to perform the assignments: witness statements, depositions, expert reports, jury instructions, pleadings, research memoranda, statutes, exhibits, and witness statements. The research memoranda are composed of fictional appellate decisions in a fictional jurisdiction, the state of Major. The memoranda provide all the research you need to deal with the legal issues in the assignments. Of course, your instructor may prefer that you instead research and use appropriate, real cases from your jurisdiction. You can print out portions of the Case Files from the website to use during an exercise. For instance, you can print out exhibits, such as photographs, to use during the cross.

V. SAMPLES OF ROLE-PLAY ASSIGNMENTS AND TABLE OF CONTENTS FOR CASE FILES

In this chapter, we have included the role-play assignments for the *Goodman* case as well as a table of contents for the *Goodman* case file so that you can see samples of the assignments and what is contained in a Case File. The assignments and Case Files for the *Goodman* case and three other cases are on the companion website to this book.

VI. TEACHER'S MANUAL

A. Actors' Guide

Your instructor has a Teacher's Manual with an Actors' Guide, found in the instructor pages on the website www.aspenlawschool.com/books/clark_cross-sexam2e, containing acting instructions for the role-players who will perform as witnesses. The witness instructions include: information that the witness knows about the case; the witness's background; and guidance on how to perform the role in the most realistic way.

B. Syllabi

The assignments and Case File materials are intended for not only law school classes and clinics but also for continuing legal education workshops. In the Teacher's Manual for this book, which is provided to the instructor, are syllabi and schedules for a training seminar on cross-examination for both the law school and the workshop situations.

VII. CRIMINAL CASE: *STATE V. GARY GOODMAN*

A. Summary of State v. Gary Goodman

Smith and Wesson Chief Special with Hammer Shroud Seized by Fred Durkin

Gary Goodman and his brother Barry went to the Infernal Club on the evening of May 1, 20XX-1, for an evening of dancing. Gary Goodman had a .38-caliber revolver in his coat pocket. While they were inside the Infernal Club, Barry Goodman became engaged in a "staring" contest with Moe Helton, a local drug dealer who had a history of bad blood with Barry. The staring contest escalated into a confrontation, and the confrontation escalated into a fistfight. Barry came off second in the fistfight and Helton began to get the best of him.

Gary Goodman, who had been dancing on the dance floor, noticed the altercation and went over to intervene. Goodman drew the revolver from his pocket and began shooting. John Elder, a business associate of Helton in the drug trade, attempted to intervene in the fight, trying to disarm Gary. Gary shot Elder in the stomach. When Gary shot Elder, Shemp Campbell, another drug associate of Helton, also intervened and was able to disarm Gary Goodman. When Goodman was disarmed, he and his brother fled the Club. Moe Helton was pronounced dead on arrival at the Lincoln County Hospital, and John Elder underwent emergency surgery to repair the damage done to his stomach by the bullet. Barry Goodman was treated at Riverton Hospital for trauma suffered in the fight with Helton.

B. Assignments for the *Goodman* Case

TABLE OF CONTENTS

ASSIGNMENT 1: Prosecutor's Case Analysis, Case Theory, and Theme Development

You are employed as a deputy prosecutor in the Criminal Division of the Camden County Prosecutor's Office. You have been assigned to the *State v. Gary Goodman* case. Gary Goodman is charged with murder in the second degree, attempted murder in the second degree, and carrying a concealed firearm. The charges result from an altercation between the Goodman brothers—Gary and Barry—on one side and a notorious gang of local hoodlums led by Moe Helton on the other. Gary Goodman is a star athlete at the local high school and is very well known in the community. The local media has taken an interest in the case and has touted Gary Goodman as an innocent victim of circumstance who simply did what he had to do in order to protect his brother. Judging from the letters to the editor printed in the local paper, this characterization has gained some traction in the community.

Plea negotiations have gone nowhere, and you need to get ready for trial. Your first order of business in preparing for trial is to develop a case theory and theme.

PREPARATION
READ: Case Files Entries 1-23; Chapter 2.

THOUGHTS for this Assignment
1. What facts do you need to prove a prima facie case for each of the crimes charged? Are the testimonies of Shemp Campbell and John Elder sufficient to support the charges? Are there any other witnesses who can provide testimony supporting the charges?
2. What is the prosecution's persuasive narrative story? What are the human values, which the jurors will care about, that underpin the story? How can you negate the positive image of the defendant? How can you mitigate the negative image of the victims? What is the plot? Who is the protagonist? Are both the story and the witnesses credible?
3. What are the strengths and weaknesses of your case?
4. What are your plans for addressing the mental health defense?

ASSIGNMENT FOR CLASS
In class, be prepared to discuss your case theory including factual sufficiency and persuasive story, as well as the strengths and weaknesses of your case. Be prepared to discuss your tentative trial plan. Also, be ready to discuss who the witnesses are that you are planning to call and how you will address the mental health defense.

ASSIGNMENT 2: Defense Counsel's Case Analysis and Case Theory Development

You represent Gary Goodman, who has been charged with murder in the second degree, attempted murder in the second degree, and carrying a concealed firearm. Your client has professed innocence to you and pled not guilty to the charges. You have had him examined and developed a mental health defense. This case is going to trial. It is time to build your case theory and plan your trial strategy.

PREPARATION

READ: Case Files Entries 1-23; Chapter 2.

THOUGHTS for this Assignment

1. How do you intend to attack the sufficiency of the state's case? Is the prosecution's legal theory defective in any way? Can the prosecution produce sufficient evidence to support the charges? How is the prosecution's narrative story vulnerable? At this point, how do you plan on attacking the witnesses who are likely to testify for the state?

2. What is the defense's narrative? What are the human values in that story that the jury can relate to? How can you establish a human-interest theme? What is the plot? Who is the protagonist? Are both the story and the witnesses credible?

3. What are the strengths and weaknesses of your case?

ASSIGNMENT FOR CLASS

In class, be prepared to discuss your case theory, including factual sufficiency and persuasive story, as well as the strengths and weaknesses of your case. Also be prepared to discuss your current trial plan including the witnesses that you plan on calling. What are your tentative plans for demolishing the state's case and witnesses?

ASSIGNMENT 3: Prosecutor: Content of the Cross-Examination of Barry Goodman

When Barry Goodman became embroiled in a fistfight with Moe Helton, his brother Gary came to his aid. Barry Goodman has given a sworn statement exculpatory of Gary Goodman, but in conflict with the accounts of both Gary Goodman and the witnesses for the prosecution. You must design a cross-examination that highlights these discrepancies and otherwise discredits Gary Goodman's claim that he was defending his brother.

PREPARATION

READ: Case Files Entries 1-23; Chapter 3.

THOUGHTS for this Assignment

1. What do you plan to say about Barry Goodman in your closing argument? Is he credible? Is he biased? Is he lying or telling the truth? Could he be mistaken? Is he embellishing his testimony?

2. Brainstorm for concessions that will help build your case theory or undercut the defense case theory. What concessions can you seek? Ask yourself: What helpful facts must this witness admit or stamp his answer as a lie, mistaken, or ludicrous?

3. With the aid of the list of nine areas of impeachment found at page 116, identify those areas that are applicable to the witness.

ASSIGNMENT FOR CLASS

Outside of class, prepare a one-page statement summarizing what you intend to argue in closing about Barry Goodman. In class, be prepared to deliver your closing argument and to discuss the content of your cross-examination.

ASSIGNMENT 4: Prosecutor: Content of the Cross-Examination of Gary Goodman

Defendant Gary Goodman gave a full and complete exculpatory statement claiming that he was acting in defense of his brother.

You anticipate that the defendant will take the stand and testify. The defendant's testimony contains inherent improbabilities and is in conflict with the testimony of the defendant's brother, Barry Goodman. Gary Goodman's statement also conflicts with the account of the incident he gave to Dr. Arden Conger.

PREPARATION
READ: Case Files Entries 1-23; Chapter 3.

THOUGHTS for this Assignment
1. What story do you envision that the defendant will tell on the witness stand? What do you plan to say about the defendant's story in your closing argument?
2. Brainstorm for concessions that will help build your case theory or undercut the defense's case theory. What concessions can you obtain from the defendant? Ask yourself: What must the defendant admit or stamp his answer as a lie, mistaken, or ludicrous?
3. With the aid of the list of nine areas of impeachment found at page 116, identify those areas that are applicable to the defendant.

ASSIGNMENT FOR CLASS
Outside of class, prepare a one-page statement summarizing what you intend to argue in closing regarding the defendant and his testimony. In class, be prepared to deliver your closing argument and to discuss the content of your cross-examination of the defendant.

ASSIGNMENT 5: Defense Counsel: Content of the Cross-Examination of Shemp Campbell

Shemp Campbell is the prosecution's chief eyewitness to the shooting. You have yet to interview him, but you do have his sworn statement and certified copies of his prior convictions. His testimony conflicts with that of John Elder and also with the testimony of the Goodmans.

PREPARATION
READ: Case Files Entries 1-23; Chapter 3.

THOUGHTS for this Assignment

1. In your closing argument, what do you plan to say about Shemp Campbell's credibility and his testimony?
2. Brainstorm for concessions that will help to build your case theory or undercut the prosecution's case theory. What concessions can you obtain from Campbell? Ask yourself: What must Campbell admit or stamp his answer as a lie, mistaken, or ludicrous?
3. With the aid of the list of nine areas of impeachment found at page 116, identify those areas that are applicable to Shemp Campbell.

ASSIGNMENT FOR CLASS

Outside of class, prepare a one-page statement summarizing what you intend to argue in closing regarding Shemp Campbell and his testimony. In class, be prepared to deliver your closing argument and to discuss the content of your cross-examination of Shemp Campbell.

ASSIGNMENT 6: Defense Counsel: Content of the Cross-Examination of John Elder

John Elder is a victim of the shooting and an eyewitness to the shooting of Moe Helton. You have yet to interview him, but you do have his sworn statement and certified copies of his prior convictions. His testimony conflicts with that of Shemp Campbell and also with the testimony of the Goodmans.

PREPARATION

READ: Case Files Entries 1-23; Chapter 3.

THOUGHTS for this Assignment

1. In your closing argument, what do you plan to say about John Elder's credibility and his testimony?
2. Brainstorm for concessions that will help to build your case theory or undercut the prosecution's case theory. What concessions can you obtain from Elder? Ask yourself: What must Elder admit or stamp his answer as either a lie, mistaken, or ludicrous?
3. With the aid of the list of nine areas of impeachment found at page 116, identify those areas that are applicable to John Elder.

ASSIGNMENT FOR CLASS

Outside of class, prepare a one-page statement summarizing what you intend to argue in closing regarding John Elder and his testimony. In class, be prepared to deliver your closing argument and to discuss the content of your cross-examination of John Elder.

ASSIGNMENT 7: Prosecutor: Scripting the Cross-Examination of Barry Goodman

Now that your brainstorming sessions have helped you identify the content of your cross-examination, it is time to write out your cross-examination of Barry Goodman.

PREPARATION
READ: Case Files Entries 1-23; Chapter 4.

THOUGHTS for this Assignment
1. What are the topical units that will make up your cross-examination of Barry Goodman?
2. Does each topical unit have a beginning, middle, and end?
3. Does the left column of the cross notes in each topical unit contain short, clear statements, rather than questions? Are the statements well phrased and crafted to control the witness? Are they free of adverbs and adjectives?
4. In the right column of the cross notes (opposite any assertion in the left column), are there references to where the sources for the assertions can be found? Is there legal authority in the right column that can be cited if there is an objection made to the question?
5. Are the topical units organized into a story that has a beginning, middle, and end? Does the cross-examination begin and end in powerful ways?
6. Have you edited your cross-examination to eliminate minutiae, too many topics, why questions, and questions to which you do not know the answer?

ASSIGNMENT FOR CLASS
Outside of class, prepare two topical units of cross notes for the cross-examination of Barry Goodman. In class, turn in your cross notes for the two topical units. Also, be prepared to discuss your lines of cross for the witness.

ASSIGNMENT 8: Prosecutor: Scripting the Cross-Examination of Gary Goodman

Now that your brainstorming sessions have helped you identify the content of your cross-examination, it is time to write out your cross-examination of defendant Gary Goodman.

PREPARATION
READ: Case Files Entries 1-23; Chapter 4.

THOUGHTS for this Assignment
1. What are the topical units that will make up your cross-examination of the defendant?

2. Does each topical unit have a beginning, middle, and end?
3. Does the left column of the cross notes in each topical unit contain short, clear statements, rather than questions? Are the statements well phrased and crafted to control the witness? Are they free of adverbs and adjectives?
4. In the right column of the cross notes (opposite any assertion in the left column) are there references to where the sources for the assertions can be found? Is there legal authority in the right column that can be cited if there is an objection made to the question?
5. Are the topical units organized into a story that has a beginning, middle, and end? Does the cross-examination begin and end in powerful ways?
6. Have you edited your cross-examination to eliminate minutiae, too many topics, why questions, and questions to which you do not know the answer?

ASSIGNMENT FOR CLASS

Outside of class, prepare two topical units of cross notes for the cross-examination of Gary Goodman. In class, turn in your cross notes for the two topical units. Also, be prepared to discuss your lines of cross for the defendant.

ASSIGNMENT 9: Defense Counsel: Scripting the Cross-Examination of Shemp Campbell

Now that your brainstorming sessions have helped you identify the content of your cross-examination, it is time to write out your cross-examination of Shemp Campbell.

PREPARATION
READ: Case Files Entries 1-23; Chapter 4.

THOUGHTS for this Assignment
1. What are the topical units that will make up your cross-examination of Shemp Campbell?
2. Does each topical unit have a beginning, middle, and end?
3. Does the left column of the cross notes in each topical unit contain short, clear statements, rather than questions? Are the statements well phrased and crafted to control the witness? Are they free of adverbs and adjectives?
4. In the right column of the cross notes (opposite any assertion in the left column), are there references to where the sources for the assertions can be found? Is there legal authority in the right column that can be cited if there is an objection made to the question?
5. Are the topical units organized into a story that has a beginning, middle, and end? Does the cross-examination begin and end in powerful ways?

6. Have you edited your cross-examination to eliminate minutiae, too many topics, why questions, and questions to which you do not know the answer?

ASSIGNMENT FOR CLASS

Outside of class, prepare two topical units of cross notes for the cross-examination of Shemp Campbell. In class, turn in your cross notes for the two topical units. Also, be prepared to discuss your lines of cross for Campbell.

ASSIGNMENT 10: Defense Counsel: Scripting the Cross-Examination of John Elder

Now that your brainstorming sessions have helped you identify the content of your cross-examination, it is time to write out your cross-examination of John Elder.

PREPARATION
READ: Case Files Entries 1-23; Chapter 4.

THOUGHTS for this Assignment
1. What are the topical units that will make up your cross-examination of John Elder?
2. Does each topical unit have a beginning, middle, and end?
3. Does the left column of the cross notes in each topical unit contain short, clear statements, rather than questions? Are the statements well phrased and crafted to control the witness? Are they free of adverbs and adjectives?
4. In the right column of the cross notes (opposite any assertion in the left column), are there references to where the sources for the assertions can be found? Is there legal authority in the right column that can be cited if there is an objection made to the question?
5. Are the topical units organized into a story that has a beginning, middle, and end? Does the cross-examination begin and end in powerful ways?
6. Have you edited your cross-examination to eliminate minutiae, too many topics, "why" questions, and questions to which you do not know the answer?

ASSIGNMENT FOR CLASS

Outside of class, prepare two topical units of cross notes for the cross-examination of John Elder. In class, turn in your cross notes for the two topical units. Also, be prepared to discuss your lines of cross for Elder.

ASSIGNMENT 11: Defense Counsel: Cross-Examination of Shemp Campbell

The prosecutor has called Shemp Campbell to testify. Unless your instructor informs you otherwise, you can assume that Campbell has testified consistent with his recorded statement in Case File Entry 7.

Defense counsel has finished direct examination and stated "No further questions." The judge looks in your direction and says, "Counsel, your cross-examination?"

PREPARATION
READ: Case Files Entries 1-23; Chapters 6, 9, and 13.

THOUGHTS for this Assignment
1. What concessions must Shemp Campbell make that will support your case theory?
2. What techniques can you apply if the witness proves to be difficult to control during your examination?
3. Does Shemp Campbell have a motive to fabricate? What could it be? How will you expose the motive, if at all?
4. Are you prepared to respond to objections?
5. How will you highlight the favorable responses that you get from the witness?

ASSIGNMENT FOR CLASS
In class, conduct the cross-examination of Shemp Campbell.

ASSIGNMENT 12: Defense Counsel: Cross-Examination of John Elder

The prosecutor has called John Elder to testify. Unless your instructor informs you otherwise, you can assume that he has testified consistent with his written statement in Case File Entry 6.

Defense counsel has finished direct examination and stated "No further questions." The judge looks in your direction and says, "Counsel, your cross-examination?"

PREPARATION
READ: Case Files Entries 1-23; Chapters 6, 9, and 13.

THOUGHTS for this Assignment
1. What concessions must John Elder make that will support your case theory?
2. What techniques can you apply if the witness proves to be difficult to control during your examination?
3. Does John Elder have a motive to fabricate? What could it be? How will you expose the motive, if at all?

4. Are you prepared to respond to objections?
5. How will you highlight the favorable responses that you get from the witness?

ASSIGNMENT FOR CLASS
In class, conduct the cross-examination of John Elder.

ASSIGNMENT 13: Prosecutor: Cross-Examination of Barry Goodman

Barry Goodman testifies that he was the victim of an unprovoked attack by Moe Helton and that his brother, Gary Goodman, came to his rescue.

Unless your instructor informs you otherwise, you can assume that Barry Goodman has testified consistent with his recorded statement in Case File Entry 8.

Defense counsel: "Your witness, counsel."

PREPARATION
READ: Case Files Entries 1-23; Chapters 6, 9, and 13.

THOUGHTS for this Assignment
1. What concessions must Barry Goodman make that will support your case theory?
2. What techniques can you apply if the witness proves to be difficult to control during your examination?
3. Does Barry Goodman have a motive to fabricate? What could it be? How will you expose the motive, if at all?
4. Are you prepared to respond to objections?
5. How will you highlight the favorable responses that you get from the witness?

ASSIGNMENT FOR CLASS
In class, conduct the cross-examination of Barry Goodman.

ASSIGNMENT 14: Prosecutor: Cross-Examination of Gary Goodman

Defendant Gary Goodman testifies that he came to the rescue of his brother, who was the victim of an unprovoked attack by Moe Helton.

Unless your instructor informs you otherwise, you can assume that Gary Goodman has testified consistent with his recorded statement in Case File Entry 9.

Defense counsel: "Your witness, counsel."

PREPARATION
READ: Case Files Entries 1-23; Chapters 6, 9, and 13.

THOUGHTS for this Assignment

1. What concessions must Gary Goodman make that will support your case theory?
2. What techniques can you apply if the witness proves to be difficult to control during your examination?
3. How will you expose Gary Goodman's motive to fabricate, if at all?
4. Are you prepared to respond to objections?
5. How will you highlight the favorable responses that you get from the witness?

ASSIGNMENT FOR CLASS

In class, conduct the cross-examination of Gary Goodman.

C. Table of Contents for the *Goodman* Case Files

Entry

1. Indictment
2. Durkin Investigative Report
3. Autopsy Report
4. Firearms Report
5. CV—Armor
6. Statement—Elder
7. Statement—Campbell
8. Statement—Barry Goodman
9. Statement—Gary Goodman
10. Psychiatric Report
11. CV—Conger
12. Diagnostic and Statistical Manual
13. Diagram
14. Photo—Firearm
15. Photo—Firearm
16. Judgment and Sentence—Elder
17. Judgment and Sentence—Elder
18. Judgment and Sentence—Campbell
19. Judgment and Sentence—Campbell
20. Judgment and Sentence—Campbell
21. Omnibus Order
22. Statutes
23. Jury Instructions

VIII. CRIMINAL CASE: SUMMARY OF *STATE V. BYRON WARD HOWLAND*

Georgetown, capital of the state of Major

State v. Byron Ward Howland is a high-profile criminal case. The Lincoln County Prosecutor's Office has charged state legislator Byron Howland with rape in the second degree, communicating with a minor for immoral purposes through electronic means, and three counts of child rape in the third degree. The prosecution contends that Howland is an Internet predator who lured in 15-year-old Jenny Sells first through talks in a chat room and later by inviting her to his condominium where he resided when he attended legislative sessions in the state capital of Georgetown. Allegedly, Howland raped her in his condo in December two years ago. Afterward he expressed remorse, and their relationship continued until June of last year, when Jenny's mother took printouts of their Internet exchanges to the Georgetown Police Department's Detective Bill Hutchinson. Jenny told the Detective about her relationship with Howland. Howland has made no pretrial comments about the case except that it is "patently false."

IX. CIVIL CASE: SUMMARY OF *RUFUS T. JONES V. BRAHMIN PREPARATORY SCHOOL*

Brahmin Preparatory School

Rufus T. Jones, an African-American teacher, sues Brahmin Preparatory School, an elite private high school, claiming racially disparate treatment and retaliation against him for engaging in the protected activity of opposing what he believes to be incidents showing discrimination against faculty of color. The discrimination claim is based on allegations that Jones was treated materially different in his employment at Brahmin Prep compared to similarly situated white faculty.

Plaintiff's retaliation claim is based upon the school's Head Master placing him on probation because Jones spoke out at a faculty meeting on October 12, 20XX-2, publicly opposing and criticizing the invitation extended by the school to Walther von Stroheim, a controversial figure who has written extensively on the interpretation of race relations in this country.

Jones claims that Brahmin Prep punished Jones for making what it deemed inflammatory statements at this meeting and refusing to apologize when ordered to do so by school administrators.

Although other white faculty members had made statements of a similar nature in the past, either orally or by e-mail, none were punished. Specifically, the previous year, a white faculty member, Robin Peterson, had sent out an all-faculty-and-staff e-mail criticizing the administration for failure to retain faculty of color and accusing the school of harboring both subtle and overt racism. Brahmin Principal Francis J. Winslow felt that this e-mail was not accurate and used unnecessary language. He and other staff members were stung by the tone and content of Robin Peterson's e-mail. They did not want the meeting called for by Peterson to occur. Discussions were held by the administration on how to deal with Peterson outside of the formal disciplinary system at the school. Vice-Head Master Lynn Polonious met with Peterson and persuaded her to call off the meeting. When she reluctantly agreed, Francis Winslow sent out an all-faculty-and-staff e-mail calling off the meeting. Robin Peterson was not put on probation or otherwise punished in any way for sending the e-mail.

X. CIVIL CASE: SUMMARY OF *TERRY O'BRIEN V. JAMNER COUNTY*

OnPoint Productions, Seattle, Washington

Rollover of Terry O'Brien's Car

This case involves a single car rollover accident that resulted in the death of the driver, 33-year-old Terry O'Brien. O'Brien was driving a 20XX-6 Suzuki SUV southbound on Pioneer Road when the vehicle had drifted off the west edge of new asphalt, which had recently been applied to the surface of the road. Jamner County had received funding from the Major Department of Transportation for this road upgrade. The pavement was 24 feet and 4 inches wide. In that the road surface was newly laid asphalt, there were no fog lines or centerlines painted on yet; only a few temporary markers denoting the centerline. The right shoulder was dirt and gravel sloping downward away from the road. There was a drop of about 3 to 4 inches from the asphalt surface to the gravel surface on the right side. The left shoulder consisted of broken rock of varying size and had a drop of 4 to 5 inches from the paved surface to the broken rock.

Tire marks on the road surface indicate that the vehicle drifted off the west edge of the new asphalt, then swerved to the left, and went off the roadway to the east side of the asphalt. The vehicle rolled several times, ultimately ejecting Terry O'Brien. It was not possible to determine whether or not O'Brien was wearing a seat belt.

The vehicle was a 20XX-8 Suzuki SUV with two doors, a four-cylinder engine, and a canvas top. The vehicle had a 55-inch average track width and its wheelbase was 86.6 inches. The weight of the vehicle was approximately 2,400 pounds, with a standard tire size P205/75R15. The driver, Terry O'Brien, was 33 years old, 5'8" tall, and weighed 155 pounds. There were no witnesses to the accident.

The accident occurred on June 16, 20XX-2 at approximately 12:08 p.m. It was a sunny, dry day and the temperature was 80 degrees Fahrenheit. The posted speed limit along this road was 50 mph.

Terry O'Brien's home was two miles away. This was the road O'Brien regularly traveled between home and the closest shopping area, the Gas City strip mall. O'Brien had traveled this road during the construction, although the conditions changed on a daily basis as the work progressed.

There were no road construction workers present on the date of the accident. The crew worked a 10-hour shift Monday through Thursday and had Friday off, which is the day of the week on which the accident occurred. There were no channeling devices or traffic control signs on Pioneer Road in the construction area.

XI. CHALLENGING AND REWARDING

Trial practice is a rewarding endeavor, but it presents the lawyer with many challenges. Some of the greatest of those challenges can be posed by either taking the deposition of an adverse witness or conducting a cross-examination at trial. With the skills and tools provided in this Cross-Examination Handbook, you will be equipped to meet those challenges with a winning cross.

Index